高等院校特色课程英语系列教材

新编英美国家社会与文化

英国篇

主　编：范建华　毛启红
副主编：何　兖　张厚振　陈　欣
编　者：(按姓氏笔画排列)
毛启红　吴雪峰　刘长城　何　兖
何　玲　张子通　张明权　张厚振
陆巧玲　陈　欣　徐　畅

苏州大学出版社

图书在版编目(CIP)数据

新编英美国家社会与文化.英国篇/范建华,毛启红主编.—苏州:苏州大学出版社,2010.8(2013.1 重印)
ISBN 978-7-81137-567-1

Ⅰ.①新… Ⅱ.①范…②毛… Ⅲ.①英语-阅读教学-高等学校-教材②英国-概况 Ⅳ.①H319.4:K

中国版本图书馆 CIP 数据核字(2010)第 163333 号

新编英美国家社会与文化
英国篇
范建华 毛启红 主编
责任编辑 谢永明

苏州大学出版社出版发行
(地址:苏州市十梓街 1 号 邮编:215006)
丹阳市兴华印刷厂印装
(地址:丹阳市胡桥镇 邮编:212313)

开本 787mm×1 092mm 1/16 印张 22.25(共两册) 字数 555 千
2010 年 8 月第 1 版 2013 年 1 月第 2 次印刷
ISBN 978-7-81137-567-1 定价:48.00 元
(共两册)

苏州大学出版社营销部 电话:0512-65225020
苏州大学出版社网址 http://www.sudapress.com

前 言

“英美国家概况”课程是为高等学校英语专业学生开设的专业知识必修课。按照教育部21世纪我国高等学校英语专业人才的培养目标和要求，在打好扎实的英语语言基本功和牢固掌握英语专业知识的前提下，要拓宽学生的人文学科知识，扩大知识面，对西方不同的政治、经济、文化、历史和科技教育等有较全面的了解，其中重点是对英国和美国国情的梳理和掌握。同时，注重培养学生独立思考、分析问题、解决问题的能力和创新能力，培养学生跨文化交际意识和能力，提高思想道德素质、文化素养，并对今后从事英美问题的研究打下坚实的基础。

一直以来，在这样一门重要课程的教材选择方面，存在着诸多难点：

1. 由于“英美国家概况”课程的知识覆盖面广，涉及历史、政治、经济、文化等方方面面，所选教材在内容上应做到有详有略，既全面翔实，又重点突出。

2. 英美两国在政治、地域、风俗等方面与中国有很大差异，这种差异会对学生的认知和理解造成一定的困难。教材编写者应充分考虑到这种客观存在的文化差异，并在编排上加以妥善考虑。

3. 英文版的教材中存在大量历史事件、地理位置等专有名词和术语，这对于学生的英文水平是一个很大的挑战。教材的语言在地道通畅外还应做到难易适中。

4. 网络时代，学习方式呈多样化，教材的内容不应显得过于陈旧，应能满足网络时代的学习需求。

为此，我们组织国内诸多高校的一线“英美国家概况”课程教师，从实际授课需求出发，在他们多年教学经验的基础上，编写了《新编英美国家社会与文化》(英文版)一书。本书充分考虑了以上提及的问题，综合考量了教师的教学需要和学生的学习需求，对于应该让中国学生掌握的英美国家社会文化知识作了详尽介绍，而对一些只需要了解的知识简要介绍，使教材在有限的篇幅里较为全面地向中国学生展示“尽可能真实的英国和美国”。本教材既可作为大中专院校相关课程的教材，满足人才培养需求，也可以作为英语爱好者的普及性读物。

希望读者通过本套教材的学习，了解英美国家简史，以及英美两国的政治、经济、文化发展状况，了解中国与英美两国国际关系演变的基本情况与信息，进一步认识借鉴外国经验对我国经济社会发展的重要意义，从而增强自己的跨文化交际能力，丰富自己的知识结构，为今后的工作打下良好的文化知识基础。

本书由泰州师范高等专科学校范建华老师和南京人口管理干部学院毛启红老师担任主编。分为英国篇和美国篇两册，共20章。其中英国篇第1章由南京林业大学吴雪峰老师编写，第2章和第3章由南京信息工程大学张厚振老师编写，第4章由南京人口管理干部学院毛启红、刘长城老师编写，第5章由江苏大学张明权老师编写，第6章由广西师范大学陆巧玲、何玲老师编写，第7章由常熟理工学院何究老师编写，第8章由浙江传媒学院陈欣老师编写，第9章由宿迁学院张子通老师编写，第10章由南京医科大学徐畅老师编写。美国篇第1章由淮北师范大学唐永辉老师编写，第2章和第3章由泰州师范高等专科学校范建华、徐小丽和徐佳老师编写，第4章由南京人口管理干部学院毛启红、刘长城老师编写，第5章由江苏大学张明权老师编写，第6章由广西师范大学陆巧玲、何玲老师编写，第7章由常熟理工学院何究老师编写，第8章由海南师范大学关世民老师编写，第9章由桂林电子科技大学邝增乾老师编写，第10章由南京医科大学秦志红老师编写。泰州师范高等专科学校李萍、石莉莉、朱婧、李飒等老师协助收集材料，并审读了全部书稿，提出了许多建设性意见。

成书之际，我们衷心感谢苏州大学外国语学院衡仁权博士帮助审校书稿，感谢苏州大学出版社对此书的大力支持，感谢编辑为此书付出的大量辛劳！

由于编者水平有限，书中一定存在不少瑕疵和谬误，敬请读者和同行批评、指正！

编　者

2010 年 8 月

目　录

Chapter One

General Introduction

Situated in Northern Europe, lying to the north of France and the west of the Netherlands and Denmark, the United Kingdom of Great Britain and Northern Ireland (the UK for short) is made up of four parts known as England, Scotland, Wales and Northern Ireland, whose capital cites respectively are London, Edinburgh, Cardiff and Belfast.

Each of the four parts demonstrates its own geographical characteristics in terms of land forms, of which the most famous ones are the Pennines, Lake District, Grampian Range, etc. The UK is also one country possessing many rivers, some of which provide irrigation, and few navigation. It is well worth mentioning that the Thames River and the Clyde River are respectively the most important rivers in England and Scotland. As an island country, Britain has a long but irregular coastline. The gentler eastern coastline consists mainly of limestone and chalk cliffs, among which the most famous are the White Cliffs of Dover. As for the British climate, 3 characteristics can be summarized. The first is uncertainty and changeability; the second is much precipitation, and the last one is mildness. Small as its territory is, the UK is relatively rich in such natural resources as coal, oil, natural gas, limestone, iron, tin and water resources as well.

The population of the United Kingdom is 60,209,500 (2005 estimates), England being the part with the largest population compared with the other 3 parts of the UK. English is the most widely spoken language in this country, but Gaelic and Welsh are also popular languages respectively in Scotland and Wales. In their daily lives and work, British people show the world four features of their personalities: arrogance, conservativeness, sense of humor and politeness.

Marriage is one of the most important issues for all British people. All children above the age of 18 have the freedom to get married regardless of their parents' consent. The wedding ceremony is usually held in the church, after which relatives and friends are invited to dinner. For British meals, besides the generally accepted breakfast, lunch and supper, British people have a unique and additional course called afternoon tea. There are a large number of holidays and festivals celebrated by British people all through the year and they can be divided into such 3 types as religious holidays, bank holidays and public holidays.

1.1 Topography

1.1.1 England

As the largest and most southerly portion of Britain, England shares land borders with Scotland to the north and Wales to the west; the Irish Sea is to the northwest, the Celtic Sea to the southwest and the North Sea to the east, with the English Channel to the south separating it from Continental Europe.

With a total area of over 130,000 square kilometers, England may be divided into three different regions, each of which bears its specific characteristics.

Rolling downs and low-lying plains are the major landforms of one of the three regions—the east and the southeast. What follows is the second region—middle England, a region of mountains. The most significant mountain range in this region is the Pennines, which, since the 19th century, has been called the "back bone of England". It runs from the Scottish border as far south as Debyshire with the highest point Cross Fell which is 893 meters high. On the west side of the northern Pennines lies the Lake District (also called The Lakes or Lakeland), which is well known for its beautiful lakes and mountains as well. The Lake District National Park formed in 1951 is to protect the landscape by restricting unwelcome change from industry or commerce. It is in the central and most-visited part of the Lake District. Lake Poets, among whom the most famous are William Wordsworth, Samuel

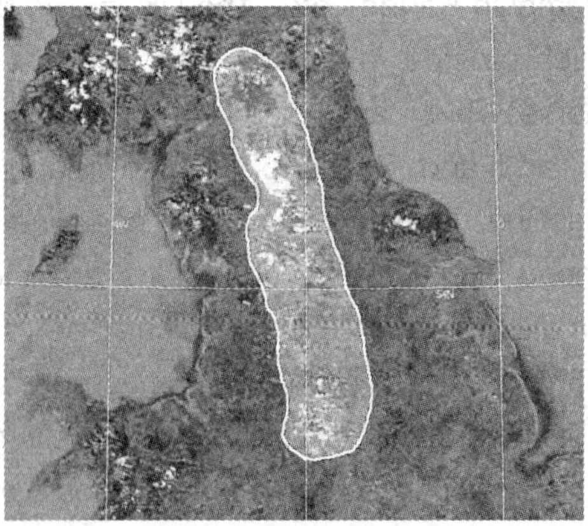

The Pennines

Taylor Coleridge and Robert Southey derive their title from the fact that they used to live in the Lake District in the 19th century and depicted the beautiful sceneries of the district in their literature works. The third region is the north and west of England, most of which is hilly, partly formed by the Cumbrian Mountain Range[1].

1.1.2 Scotland

Occupying the northern third of the island of Great Britain, Scotland shares a border with England to the south and is bounded by the North Sea to the east, the Atlantic Ocean to the north and west, and the North Channel and Irish Sea to the southwest.

Geographically, Scotland can also be divided into 3 natural regions, namely, the northern Highlands, the central Lowlands (also called Midland Valley) and the southern Uplands.

The northern highlands, just as the name implies, is a mountainous, rugged and bare region with a sparse population. The Grampian Ranges lies peacefully in the highlands and the western part of the Range includes Ben Nevis, the highest peak in Britain with an altitude of 1,343 meters. Since the western highlands are close to the Atlantic Ocean, long and narrow sea lochs or fjords are formed in this area, attracting numerous tourists from across the world for sightseeing. South of the Highland boundary, the central Lowlands, which is recognized as the most important area in Scotland and contains most of the industry and population, is a region of hills and rolling country, with Edinburgh and Glasgow serving respectively as the capital city and the biggest city of Scotland. Still farther to the south bordering with England lies the southern Uplands, a region of rolling moorlands cut by some small fertile river valleys. The highest peak of this region is Cheviot Hills of about 816 meters.

1.1.3 Wales

Wales is bordered by England to the east and by sea in the other three directions: Bristol Channel[2] to the south, Celtic Sea to the west, and the Irish Sea to the north, thus possessing a coastline as long as over 1,200 km.

With Cardiff as its capital city, Wales covers an area of approximately 20,700 square kilometers, which is less than 9% of the total territory of Britain. It is about 274 km north south and 97 km east west. Geographically speaking, Wales consists of 3 major parts called respectively the industrial south, the central plateaus and lakes, and mountainous north of farmers and tourists. Most of Wales is mountainous mainly formed by the Cambrian Range, whose highest peak is Snowdon in the northwest (1,085 m), the second highest in Britain, second only to Ben Nevis. The 14 (or possibly 15) Welsh mountains over 3,000 feet (914 m) high are known collectively as the Welsh 3,000s, and are located in a small area in the northwest.

1.1.4 Northern Ireland

This part of the UK, covering an area of 14,147 square kilometers, is situated in the northeast of the island of Ireland and shares a border with the Republic of Ireland to the south, and west. The land of Northern Ireland is in the shape of basin with mountains in the north and south, and plains in the center with Lough Neagh as the largest lake in the whole country. Agriculture is dominant in Northern Ireland while industry concentrates only in the two ports of Belfast and Londonderry.

1.2 Rivers and Coast

1.2.1 Rivers

Due to the topographic relief of Britain and the sufficient annual precipitation, a large number of rivers cover the whole country. Being short and swift, however, few rivers in Britain are navigable.

The longest river is the Severn River (354 km in length), which rises in the mountains of Wales and then discharges into the Bristol Channel which in turn discharges into the Celtic Sea and the wider Atlantic Ocean.

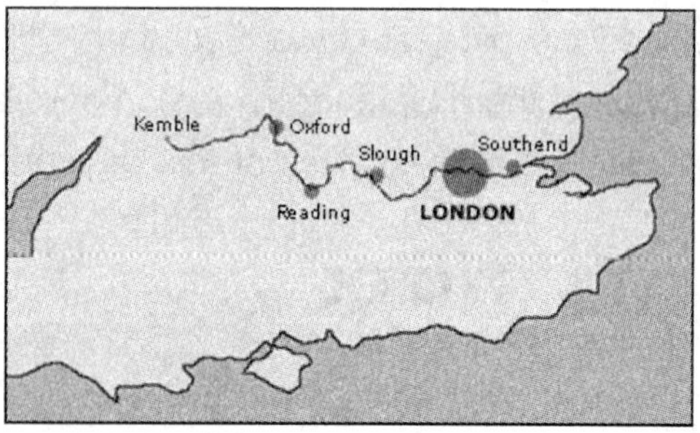

The Flow of the Thames River

The second longest and most important river in Britain is the Thames River (338 km in length). It rises in southwest England and flows through such cities as London, Oxford, Reading and Windsor and out into the North Sea. It has a special significance in flowing through London, the capital of the United Kingdom, although London only includes a short part of its course. Flowing very slowly, the Thames River has always been quite favorable for water transportation. The water under the Tower Bridge in London is one of the most important and busiest commercial routes in the world. Other important rivers in England are the Mersey River, which enters the Irish Sea at Liverpool; the River Humber on the east coast, into which the Trent River and several other rivers flow; and the Tynein River in northern England, which flows past Newcastle upon Tyne to the North Sea.

The Clyde River (170 km in length), which is the most important river in Scotland, rises in Dumfries, flows northwest and empties into the Atlantic at the Firth of Clyde. It is the ninth longest river in the United Kingdom, and the third longest in Scotland. Flowing through the major city of Glasgow, it was an important river for shipbuilding and trade in Britain. In addition to the Clyde River, the Forth River is also one of great importance. It flows eastward into the Firth of Forth, where Edinburgh rises on its south bank.

1.2.2 Coast

Great Britain's coastline is highly irregular, with many bays and inlets that provide harbors and shelters for ships and boats. As a matter of fact, coastal trade has long been carried on ever since ancient times.

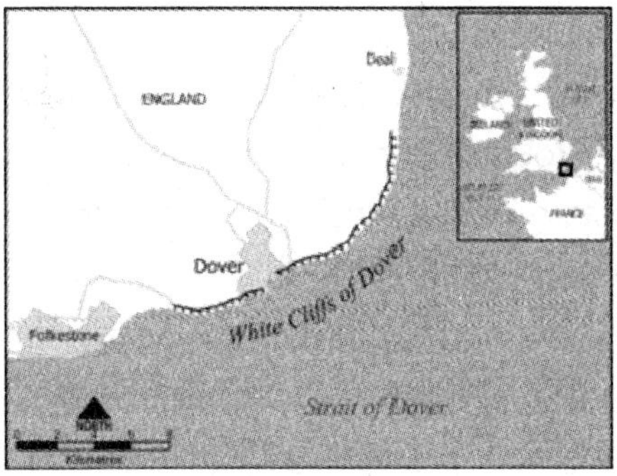

White Cliffs of Dover

The coastline is about 8,000 km long and affords some of the best scenery in Britain. The western coast is characterized by cliffs and rocky headlands, especially where the Highlands meet the sea in northwestern Scotland. On the more gentle southern and eastern coasts, there are many sand or pebble beaches as well as tall limestone or chalk cliffs, the most famous of which are the White Cliffs of Dover in the southeast. These cliffs form part of the British coastline facing France. They have great symbolic value for Britain because they face towards Continental Europe across the narrowest part of the English Channel, where invasions have historically threatened and against which the cliffs form a symbolic guard. Because crossing at Dover was the primary route to the Continent before air travel, the white line of cliffs also formed the first (or last) sight of the UK for travelers.

When referring to the British coast, we can never avoid the discussion of the narrow sea—the English Channel, which separates the UK from France, or to be exact, the whole European Continent. It is about 560 km long and varies in width from 240 km at its widest, to only 34 km in the Strait of Dover. It is the smallest of the shallow seas around the Continental shelf of Europe, covering an area of some

75,000 km^2. With the Channel Tunnel (Chunnel for short), both passenger and freight trains can travel freely through the English Channel, therefore, tourists can enjoy more convenient transportation and Britain is no longer an island after it has been connected with the European continent.

1.3 Climate

Generally speaking, the climate in Britain has three features.

The first one is uncertainty and changeability. There exist such two popular statements as "Other countries have a climate; in England we have weather" and "In no country other than England can one experience four seasons in a single day", which, to a certain extent, vividly show us the peculiar meteorological conditions of British climate. Day may break as a sunny and nice spring morning; an hour later or so black clouds may appear from nowhere and the rain may be pouring down. This explains why English gentlemen tend to go out with umbrellas in their hands even on shiny days.

The second feature is more rainy days but fewer sunny days. The rain drizzles all year round without any marked dry seasons. Annual rainfall ranges from 67 cm in the eastern and southeastern districts to over 254 cm in some northeastern mountainous areas.

The final feature of the British climate is its mildness. The climate of the United Kingdom is classified as an oceanic climate, with warm summers, cool winters and plentiful precipitation throughout the year. The principal factors that influence the country's climate include its northerly latitude (which ranges from 50° to 60° N), the close proximity to the Atlantic Ocean, and the warming of the surrounding waters by the Gulf Stream[3], which make the climate there much milder than that of many places in the same latitude.

1.4 Natural Resources

Despite the fact that the United Kingdom is a country with a relatively small territory, yet it is rich in such natural resources as coal, oil, natural gas, limestone, iron, tin, etc., among which the most important are coal, oil and natural gas. Apart from these, water resources is also a fundamental constituent of all natural resources in this country.

1.4.1 Coal

Britain has large deposits of coal, mined for more than 300 years. For most of the 19th and 20th centuries, coal was Britain's richest natural resource, meeting most of the nation's requirement for energy. The Ayrshire[4] field in Scotland and deposits of the lowlands continue to supply the Scottish industry. The coal mining area of central England, including York, Birmingham and Nottingham, Leicester and Derby, is regarded as the largest one of the country, constituting approximately 2/5 of the total output. Durham, Northumberland and Canterbury in the northeast and southeast of England are also important coalmines.

However, coal production has declined rapidly since the 1970s. In 2000, only 35 million tons of coal was produced compared to 145 million in 1970.

1.4.2 Oil and Natural Gas

In the past, Britain had to totally depend on importing oil supplies so as to meet the needs of the industrial development. This kind of situation had never changed until some big oil fields were discovered under the North Sea, east of the British Isles, generally along the British-Norwegian boundary in 1965. Since that time on, Britain has gradually become self-sufficient in oil. The oil deposit is estimated as 3,000 to 4,500 million tons. Britain began to put oil into production in the 1970s and by 1980 the annual output of oil had reached 100 million tons.

Gas was also discovered under the North Sea during the 1960s and new supplies are still being found today. Gas has been particularly important in replacing coal as a fuel for generating electricity.

Oil and Gas Exploration in the North Sea

Oil and gas were formed from the remains of animals and plants that lived millions of years ago in a marine (water) environment before the dinosaurs. Over the years the remains of the plants and animals were covered by layers of mud and soil which eventually turned to rock, trapping the remains beneath the rock. Pressure and heat changed some of this organic material into coal, some into oil (petroleum), and some into natural gas—tiny bubbles of odorless gas.

1.4.3 Limestone, Iron, and Tin

Limestone is quite widespread in Britain, especially in northern and southern Pennines and north Wales as well. It is acknowledged that northern Derbyshire is the place where limestone of the highest quality comes from. The iron deposits in Britain used to be very rich before. Unfortunately, some have already been exhausted out and Britain is no longer one that can be self-sufficient in iron ore. More than half of its domestic consumption must be imported from abroad each year. Lincolnshire and Northamptonshire are the two districts where the present major iron deposits lie. Tin ore has been worked in Cornwall and Devon for more than 3,000 years and tin mining in this area has reached a depth of 3,300 feet (1,000 meters), providing about 40% of Britain's requirements of the metal.

1.4.4 Water Resources

Judging from the climate of Britain with a heavy precipitation and many existing short and rapid rivers, we may naturally come to the conclusion that Britain is quite rich in water resources. The free-flowing rivers of Britain provide abundant surface water, even though people there have to conserve with much care the supply of water especially in the face of a large population. In addition, large reservoirs provide a water supply in the Welsh mountains and some of the lakes in the Lake District. It is a surprising fact that about 38% of the country's water requirements are obtained from underground sources. In recent years, however, there has been an increasing degree of water pollution that are doing much harm to many English and Scottish rivers, and these are the environmental problems still to be conquered.

1.5 Population and Language

1.5.1 Population

The population of the United Kingdom is 60,209,500 (2005 estimates), which on the whole consists of the English (50 million, 83.8%), Scottish (5 million, 8.4%), Welsh (2.96 million, 4.9%) and Irish (1.7 million, 2.9%) and immigrants as well.

Since the 19th century, however, the population growth has been increasingly slow due to the limitations of immigration, the fall of the birth rate and death rate as well.

(1) The English. With over 51 million inhabitants, England is the most populous country of the United Kingdom, accounting for 84% of the combined total. England taken as a unit and measured against international states has the fourth largest population in the European Union and would be the 25th largest country by population in the world. With a density of 395 people per square kilometer, it would be the second most densely populated country in the European Union after Malta. The English people are decedents of a mixture of different people in the history: the Anglo-Saxons with blond hair and blue eyes, the three Germanic tribes from Europe that invaded England between the 5th century and the 7th century; the earlier Britons and the later Vikings and Normans. Due to such a mixed population in England, local customs and accents vary a great deal and local pride is still quite strong in some parts of the country.

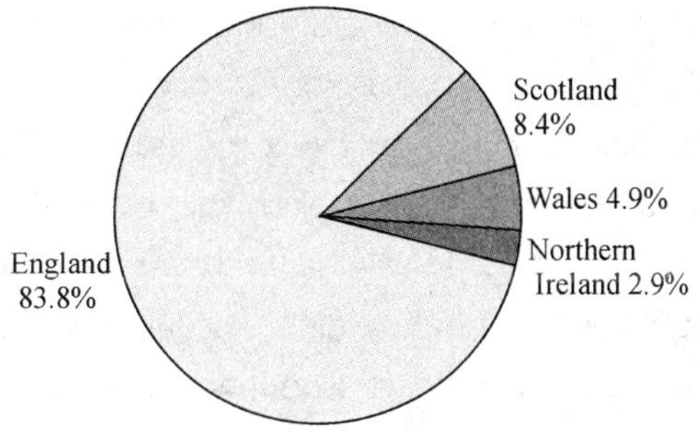

The Constitution of the Population of the UK

(2) The Welsh. Wales has a population of less than 3 million, which accounted for 4.9% of the UK population in 2005, down from 5% in the period from the mid 1970s to the late 1990s. The Welsh are a Celtic people. Different Welsh tribes had been continually fighting against one another for land and wealth until they were conquered by the English in the 13th century.

(3) The Scottish. Scotland has a population of 5,168,000, with a density of 65.6 inhabitants per square kilometer. Around 70% of the country's population live in the Central Lowlands—a broad, fertile valley stretching in a northeast-southwest orientation between the cities of Edinburgh and Glasgow. Other concentrations of population include the northeast coast of Scotland. The Highlands of Scotland have the lowest population density at 8 inhabitants per square kilometer. The City of Glasgow has the highest population density at 3, 292 inhabitants per square kilometer.

(4) The Irish. Compared to other countries of the UK, Northern Ireland has the smallest population of only 1.7 million, which accounts for merely 2.9% of the whole population of the UK.

1.5.2 Language

A Bilingual Sign in English and Welsh

There is no denying that English serves as the dominant language in the UK, and is spoken by most of the population. However, it is by no means the only language spoken all over the whole country. In Wales there are many people who speak Welsh, about one in four, to be exact. In Scotland, Gaelic is adopted by about 80,000 people living on the Highlands. In a word, currently there exist 3 major languages being adopted as a tool for communication in all walks of life of the UK. Dialects that were once heard in different parts of the country are heard less and less in movies, radios, television and other public media so as to promote the use of standard English. With the three co-existing major languages, many road signs, or signs that appear in such public places as train stations, restaurants and so on are bilingual ones. The above picture is taken of a country road in Wales, on which there are words written in both English and Welsh to remind the drivers to slow down their driving speed due to the turning ahead.

1.6 British Characters

Different people have different qualities or characters and the British people are no exceptional to this rule. What's more, their characters are fairly vivid and unique as typically their own. Generally speaking, there are four characters that we can observe among the British people, namely, arrogance, conservativeness, sense of humor and politeness.

1.6.1 Arrogance

Most of the British people, the English people in particular, have a sense of superiority. They regard their ways of behavior are the best, the most reasonable compared to those from any other country of the world. Take the local newspapers for example. They probably tend to have more interest in covering domestic news rather than foreign because British populace is relatively less concerned about what's happening all around the globe. If there is any coverage about the outside of Britain, it is quite likely to be about Europe and America, etc., which has much to do with their national interests. This attitude shows that they are not interested in all those countries "inferior" to Britain. There are two reasons that can explain the arrogance of the British people, one of which is the special geographic location, while the other is its glorious history.

Britain is an island country which is cut off, separated and isolated from the rest of the world by the English Channel and the Atlantic Ocean. It is because of this special geographical location that British people tend to, when staying in Britain, refuse to regard their country as one part of Europe and in their mind, all the Europeans are foreigners. However, this attitude has changed dramatically since the opening of the Channel Tunnel in 1994.

British people have every reason to be proud of the history of their country, because there existed such a large number of well-known people and events in the history as King James Bible, Shakespeare's plays and sonnets (which have been exerting great influence on Western and global culture), the British Parliament (the oldest in Europe), the Industrial Revolution as early as the 18th century and so on and so forth.

1.6.2 Conservativeness

This character means that the British people have an acceptance of things that are familiar, and inclination to be suspicious of anything that is strange or foreign.

Whenever there is a new idea or invention coming from other countries like America, the British people might say, "Be careful. It can be quite dangerous!" One of the examples to illustrate this can be found in adopting rational reforms like the metric system. In spite of the inconvenience that they have always been suffering from sticking to the old ways, yet they refuse to be involved in the trouble of trying the new ones. It was after a long period that metrication of weights and measurements become relatively widely adopted in Britain, although in some shops measurements are still given in inches, feet and yards.

Another example is about British people's choice between traditional fireplaces and central heating. It is a fact that in the past all houses of Britain, including those in such big cities as London, Liverpool, Manchester and Birmingham, had fireplaces in living rooms to keep the family members warm especially in winter. However, when central heating was developed in the USA, British people still regarded fireplaces superior to the new invention, regardless of its effectiveness and convenience. They thought a room without a fireplace lacked the basic character of coziness. After the construction of fireplaces had been forbidden by law in 1960, the British people still installed electric stoves, looking very much like fireplaces.

1.6.3 Sense of Humor

Almost all British people have a strong sense of humor, which is generally self-deprecating. They tend to laugh at the mistakes made by themselves or their own weak points, failures and embarrassments. For instance, they usually complain about some awful aspects of British life. Their complaints may be as follows, trains never arriving on time, bureaucratic bungling that has driven citizens to commit suicide or food so disgusting that even a dog refuses to eat. However, the attitudes shown in the British humor are never cruel or disrespectful or even malicious for it is only an attitude towards life. As a result, you seldom see British people laughing at a cripple or a madman for their misfortune or tragedy.

1.6.4 Politeness

British people are also well known for their politeness which is based on the basic rule of showing consideration for others. An example good enough as proof is what usually happens in public, where everything is in order, making society a highly civilized one. In shops, bus or train stations, or the banks, people have been used to waiting in queues, with certain space kept between individuals. What's more, no matter how long the queue is or how long they have to wait, you can rarely hear any complaints; on the contrary, all people wait in the queue with great patience.

If British people do need some help from others, they prefer to start their request by saying "I know the trouble I am causing you, but would you mind?" After having been helped by others, immediately and spontaneously they express their sincere gratitude and thanks with all words possible.

1.7 British Family Life

1.7.1 Marriage

In terms of marriage, it is against the law for children under the age of 16 to get married even though they have got their parents' approval. Between the age of 16 and 18, getting married is legal but in the meantime it is still necessary for children to get their parents' consent first. However, when children are above the age of 18, parents' consent becomes no longer necessary. Despite the above fact, the majority of boys and girls tend to get married after they have reached the age of 18.

Marriage is considered to be one of the most significant events in British people's whole lives in that it marks the beginning of a new and independent family, which means leaving one's parents and starting one's own life for both the man and the woman. After having got married, new couples face a situation that their parents, brothers or sisters and other close relations have no hand in their personal affairs and new couples are the masters of themselves.

A British Wedding Ceremony

Young people in Britain do not like to have control placed upon them and their love affairs. That a girl at the age of 16 goes out with a boyfriend is considered quite normal and acceptable. Kisses and embraces between them are natural behavior to show their love to each other. If they have been together for a long time and have known each other very well, the girl would bring her boyfriend home to meet her parents, and so would the boy. The purpose of doing this is not merely making themselves familiar with the parents of one another, but more importantly, to ask their permission and hope for their congratulations and encouragement as well. It is, in fact, usually the young couple themselves who made privately the promise to marry. In that case, it has been a tradition that the boy should carry out the first step towards marriage—to buy an engagement ring and place it on the third finger of the girl's left hand, which is a formal declaration of love to the public, discouraging the possible attempts from other men. During the period between engagement and marriage, if the girl changes her mind, she tends to return that ring to the boy; on the contrary, if they continue getting along very well with each other, the engagement ring will be replaced by a wedding ring of plain gold.

For the wedding, many British couples, no matter whether they are religious or not, would choose going to church to hold the ceremony together with some friends and relations who come over for celebration activities. On the marriage day, the bride is usually dressed in a long white dress. The first step of the whole ceremony is that the vicar will ask them whether they are willing to marry the other. The answer, undoubtedly, is usually affirmative. They then have to make promises of loyalty to each other until they die. The bride is usually given away by a close relative to her husband, in most cases, by her father. This is an indication of the concept that marriage bond is stronger than any previous family bonds, stronger even than the bond between the bride and her mother. For the bride's mother, a daughter's wedding is both sad and joyful in that she shares her daughter's happiness, but she feels that she has lost her since the moment. What follows the ceremony is a reception of light meal to which all the relatives and friends are invited. This is paid by the bride's parents.

1.7.2 Meals

Meals are regarded as an important element of family life because this is a perfect time for all the family members to sit together around the table at relatively fixed time. A special attitude British people hold towards meals is that having meals is really private and formal, which means they don't really like to share with outsiders unless they make invitations in advance. As a result, it is impolite to visit a British family at meal time and if you happen to have done so, making an apology for your interruption is quite necessary. Generally speaking, British daily meals consist of such 4 specific steps as breakfast, lunch, afternoon tea and supper.

(1) Breakfast. The traditional English breakfast consists of eggs, bacon, sausages, fried bread, baked beans and mushrooms. Even though not many people will eat this for breakfast today, it is always served in hotels and guest houses around Britain. British people tend to choose a less substantial dish, such as kippers or boiled eggs, which is usually preceded by porridge, fruit juice, or some variety of commercially produced breakfast cereal, an early 20th-century innovation of US origin. However, recently, with the life pace getting faster, many British people have less breakfast and some even have no breakfast at all or only a hot drink.

A Traditional English Breakfast

(2) Lunch. Lunch time is from about 12:30 to 2: 00 p. m. British lunch means different things to different people. For those men who work fairly far away from their homes and students studying in remote schools prefer a packed lunch. This typically consists of a sandwich, a packet of crisps, a piece of fruit and a drink. The "packed

lunch" is kept in a plastic container. However, for those who don't have the above trouble, they would rather stay together with their family members around the dinner table for a formal lunch. The first course is usually a small quantity of soup. The main course consists of meat, potatoes, and other vegetables. The meat, more often than not, is beef or lamb cut into slices; potatoes are boiled or roasted in the oven, while vegetables are commonly cabbages, carrots, peas, beans, onions and cauliflowers. What follows the main course is a light course called the dessert.

(3) Afternoon tea and supper. Tea-time is a small meal eaten in the late afternoon (usually between about 3:30 and 5:00). People may drink tea, and often eat biscuits, cakes or savory foods such as sandwiches, crumpets or tea-cakes.

High tea is a light meal eaten in the early evening served with a pot of tea. Supper is the most common name for the meal eaten in the evening (usually between 7:00 and 8:30). A dinner party is a formal evening meal to which guests have been invited. A common type of cooked meal is meat and two veg. This is a meat dish served together on the same plate with two types of vegetable, one of which is often a type of potato. It is common to eat a dessert (also known as a pudding, or afters) after the main dish.

It is increasingly popular for British people to get a takeaway or go to a restaurant instead of cooking at home, and often this is used as a chance to try different types of food. Most towns have an Indian restaurant and Chinese restaurants are also very common. Many people like Italian pizza and pasta dishes. Fast food restaurants often serve beef burgers or fried chicken. Fish and chip shops are still popular, especially in towns by the coast.

1.8 Holidays and Festivals

People in Britain celebrate a number of holidays throughout the year, among which are religious holidays like Christmas Day and Easter, Bank Holidays and some other public holidays like Easter Monday, the Boxing Day and the New Year's Day.

1.8.1 Religious Holidays

(1) Christmas. The word Christmas comes from the Old English name "Cristes Maesse" and is the celebration of the birth of Jesus. The first recorded observance occurred in Rome in AD 360, but it was not until AD 440 that the Christian Church fixed a celebration date of 25th December. Christmas in England began in AD 596,

when St Augustine[5] landed on her shores with monks who wanted to bring Christianity to the Anglo-Saxons. Christmas has always been the biggest and most attractive festival for both adults and children.

For British people, since Christmas falls in winter rather than in summer when they could get away somewhere, Christmas is basically a home and family festival. It is an excellent time for all the family members to get together no matter how far they live from each other. Purchasing Christmas gifts for friends and relations is so common during the festival that you would never be surprised to see big shops which are gaily decorated and brightly lit, stay open long after dark. A Christmas gift can be a card on which some words of best wishes are written or many other things that may amuse the addressee. Whatever the gift is, it must be beautifully wrapped.

A typical British tradition on Christmas is the Queen's Christmas Message made to the Commonwealth. The tradition began in 1932 with a radio broadcast by King George V on the BBC Empire Service. Today the broadcast is made on television and radio via various providers.

At Christmas, the home is usually decorated with colorful paper chains, leaves of holly and mistletoe, and attractive greeting cards received. The Christmas tree stands in the corner of the room, with the branches and leaves decorated with colorful lights and shining gifts. A big evening dinner provides the whole family not only with delicious food but also a moment for them to gather and communicate. Turkey, duck, goose, chicken, Christmas pudding, and mince pies are the most common food on a Christmas dinner table.

A House with Christmas Decorations

Father Christmas, though only an imaginary figure, has been attractive especially to children who expect wonderful presents from him. In children's opinion, Father Christmas is a merry old man with a long white beard and long coat trimmed with white fur, coming all the way from the cold Northern lands on a magic sleigh drawn by reindeer with jingling bells. Children believe that when they are asleep, Father Christmas comes down silently through the chimney and leaves them presents near the beds, which in fact have been bought and put into stockings by their parents.

(2) Easter is another religious holiday in Britain, which begins on Good Friday—the Friday before Easter and ends on Easter Sunday, celebrating Christ's "resurrection". It is observed with variations of date due to different calendars on the first Sunday after the paschal full moon. It has been a tradition that women wear new clothes on that occasion while children often receive Easter eggs made of chocolate. The egg, originally a Christian symbol of new life, is the main symbol of Easter for most people. Rabbits and chicks are also animals traditionally associated with Easter.

1.8.2 Bank Holidays and Public Holidays

The term Bank Holidays dates back to the Bank Holiday Act of 1871 by which banks are closed on the particular days. In Britain, two Bank Holidays are available, one being the Spring Bank Holiday, the other the Summer Bank Holiday. The former happens on the last Monday in May while the latter the last Monday in August, both of which provide British citizens long weekends to enjoy their leisure.

(1) Boxing Day: The day after Christmas (December 26th), celebrated as a holiday in parts of the British Commonwealth, when Christmas gifts are traditionally given to service workers or household employees. Nowadays, the Boxing Day has been famous for the commercial products that are sold at a discount, which inspire people's passion to go shopping sometimes like crazy.

(2) New Year's Day. England celebrates the New Year from the evening of December 31st into January 1st. Traditionally it is not as widely celebrated as Christmas. More traditionally, on the stroke of midnight, people open the back door (to let the old year out) and ask the first dark-haired man to be seen to come through the front door carrying salt, coal and bread. This means that the following year everyone in the house will have enough to eat (bread), enough money (salt) and be warm enough (coal).

New Year Celebrations in London

In Scotland they always seem to celebrate New Year better than anywhere else. The celebration of New Year's Eve is called "Hogmanay", which comes from a kind of oat cake that was traditionally given to children on New Year's Eve. In Edinburgh, the celebrations always include a massive party from Prince's Street to the Royal Mile and Edinburgh Castle. Unfortunately, due to overcrowding in the past the event is now ticket only. On New Year's Day (actually from the stroke of midnight), the tradition of first footing is observed. This is because the first person to set foot in a residence in a New Year is thought to profoundly affect the fortunes of everyone who lives there. Generally strangers are thought to bring good luck. Depending on the area, it may be better to have a dark-haired or fair-haired stranger set foot in the house, but it does mean Scotland is a very welcoming place for strangers at New Year!

There are many other minor festivals undoubtedly, such as wedding anniversary, Mother's Day, various saints' days and local customs. Remembrance Day, also called Armistice Day, is worth mentioning. It is an important patriotic festival on November 11th when the British remember the millions of people, both British and foreign, who died in two world wars.

Notes

[1] Cumbrian Mountain Range: It refers to mountains of the Lake District, northwestern England. Scafell Pike (978 m) is the highest point. Studded with lakes and narrow valleys, the range extends through Cumberland, Westmorland, and Northern Lancashire.

[2] Bristol Channel: The Bristol Channel is a major inlet in the island of Great Britain, separating South Wales from Devon and Somerset in southwest England, and extending from the lower estuary of the River Severn to the North Atlantic Ocean. It takes its name from the English city of Bristol and is over 30 miles (50 km) across at its widest point.

[3] Gulf Stream: The Gulf Stream, together with its northern extension towards Europe, the North Atlantic Drift, is a powerful, warm, and swift Atlantic ocean current that originates in the Gulf of Mexico, exits through the Strait of Florida, and follows the eastern coastlines of the United States and Newfoundland before crossing the Atlantic Ocean.

[4] Ayrshire: It is a registration county, and former administrative county in southwest Scotland, located on the shores of the Firth of Clyde. Its principal towns include Ayr, Kilmarnock and Irvine. The town of Troon on the coast has hosted the British Open Golf Championship twice in the last seven years and eight times in total.

[5] St Augustine: Augustine of Canterbury (?-604) was a Benedictine monk who became the first Archbishop of Canterbury in the year

598. He is considered the "Apostle to the English" and a founder of the English Church.

Exercises

I. Fill in the following blanks with proper words or expressions.

1. Pennines, the most famous mountain in the middle part of England, has been called "________" ever since the 19th century.
2. As for the central lowlands in Scotland, ________ and ________ are the most significant cities.
3. The longest river in the UK is the ________ River and the most important river in Britain is the ________ River.
4. ________ is a narrow sea that separates Britain from the whole of Europe while ________ is the historic construction that links them.
5. Among the four major parts of the UK, ________ has the largest population and in Scotland, about 70% of the Scottish people live in the part of ________.
6. Three languages are the most widely used in the UK and they are ________, ________, and ________.
7. When children in England have reached the age of ________, they don't have to get their parents' consent to get married.
8. British people usually have their ________ between lunch and supper.
9. A typical British tradition on Christmas is the Queen's ________ made to the whole Commonwealth.
10. ________ is an important patriotic festival on November 11th when the British remember those who died in two world wars.

Ⅱ. Explain the following terms.

1. Lake District
2. Conservativeness
3. High tea
4. Easter

Ⅲ. Discuss the following questions.

1. What are the features of the British climate?
2. What are the possible reasons for British people's arrogance?

Chapter Two

A Brief History (Ⅰ)

The British Isles have a rich history going back thousands of years. It is generally acknowledged that the history of England begins with the Anglo-Saxons, who invaded Great Britain about AD 449. They displaced the previous occupants from the southeastern part of the island and called it Angle-land, or England. Previously, the island, like Europe, was home for a succession of peoples dating from the beginnings of the Old Stone Age. History is an interweaving of events and people, and it is not just about kings and queens, it is about ordinary people and how events influenced them and on occasions how they influenced events. Also one has to realize that Britain is not one nation, but a jumble of different peoples who tend to remain distinct in spite of a millennium or more of intermarriage.

2.1 Early Man and Pre-feudal Society

2.1.1 Early Man

The Ice Age ended about 8000 BC The rising sea level produced the English Channel and made Great Britain an island. In the new environment of forest and swamp the Middle Stone Age came and passed, followed by the New Stone Age, during which the practice of agriculture was begun. This period brought a stream of new people to Britain. By 3000 BC the Iberians, or Long Skulls, were farming the chalk soil of southern England, and by 2500 BC the pastoral Beaker folk had established themselves. The latter, named for their characteristic pottery, are noted for their bronze tools and their huge stone monuments, especially Stonehenge. These monuments attest to their social and economic organization as well as their technical skill and intellectual ability.

Stonehenge is an ancient monument in England that includes a circular setting of massive stones. They were precisely aligned in relation to the rising of the sun on the summer solstice.

Some five or six centuries before the birth of Christ, a tall fair people called Celts came across the channel in small boats. They overran the British Isles, as they did virtually all of western Europe. Then came the Brythons, or Britons (still found in Wales and Cornwall), who gave their name to the island of Britain. The Celts knew how to melt iron and were skilled in arts and crafts. They became the ruling class, and the native folk adopted the Celtic language and the Celts' Druid religion.

2.1.2 Roman Rule

Julius Caesar made a landing in Britain in 55 BC, but only succeeded in establishing a temporary bridgehead. After another abortive attempt the next year, he sailed away and the Romans left Britain alone for another century, until they landed in force in 43 AD. In 43 AD, Emperor Claudius gathered a force of about 40,000 to invade the island. A massive force for those days, and the British tribes were no match for them. Within a year or so the Romans had pushed west to a line from Exeter to Lincoln, and by 60 AD controlled most of Britain south of the Humber. A revolt with the Iceni tribe under Queen Boudica nearly managed to force the Romans out. But their superior military knowledge prevailed, and after that they had no major uprisings in England. Most of the country was under civil, rather than military rule. As they pushed north, the people of Scotland were harder to subdue.

Emperor Hadrian decided conquering them was not worth the trouble, so he built a gigantic wall, Hadrian's Wall, to control the frontier. Today, you can still see large sections of Hadrian's Wall as it snakes across the Northumberland moorland. South of this wall the Romans built more than 50 cities and connected them with military roads. Some of these roads, such as the famous Watling Street, serve as the foundations for modern highways.

Hadrian's Wall, a continuous Roman defensive barrier guarding the province of Britain from barbarian invaders. The wall extends from coast to coast for 73 miles (118 km) from Wallsend on the River Tyne in the east to Bowness on the Solway Firth in the west.

In AD 410 the Goths swept down on Rome, and no more Roman troops came to protect Britannia. The Britons, left to themselves, were unable to form a government. Local chieftains warred with one another. Barbarians from Scotland and pirates from Ireland ravaged the land. In vain a Briton wrote for aid to a Roman consul, saying: "The barbarians drive us to the sea; the sea throws us back on the barbarians." With Roman withdrawal, Britain was to slip into a 600-year period of wars and fragmentation. Of Angles and Saxons invading, the Celts being pushed west, the country was under almost continuous Viking[1] attack.

After nearly four centuries of occupation, it left little that was permanent: a superb network of roads, the best Britain would have for 1,400 years; the sites of a number of towns—London, York, and others bearing names that end in the suffix *-cester* and *-caster*; and Christianity. The Anglo-Saxons, who occupied the country after the Romans left, ignored the towns, chased Christianity into Wales, and gave their own names, such as Watling Street, to the Roman roads.

2.1.3 Anglo-Saxon Invasions

Soon after Roman withdrawal, a more dangerous enemy appeared. Across the North Sea came bands of pirates in long black ships. They were the Teutonic peoples—Angles, Saxons, and Jutes—from the region of modern Denmark. They found the island easy to invade. The invaders plundered city after city and drove the Britons ever farther westward. Farmers and herdsmen followed in the wake of the warriors. The newcomers were pagans and had no use for Roman cities or Roman law. They cleared the forests for farmland and built longhouses grouped around the large log hall of their chief, which was decorated with carving and paint and hung with shining armor.

By 600 AD the ruin of Rome's Britannia was complete. The original Celtic stock survived only in the mountains of Wales and in Cornwall. Except in these areas Christianity and the Celtic language died. Britain came to be called Angle-land (later England) after the Angles, and the people spoke Anglo-Saxon.

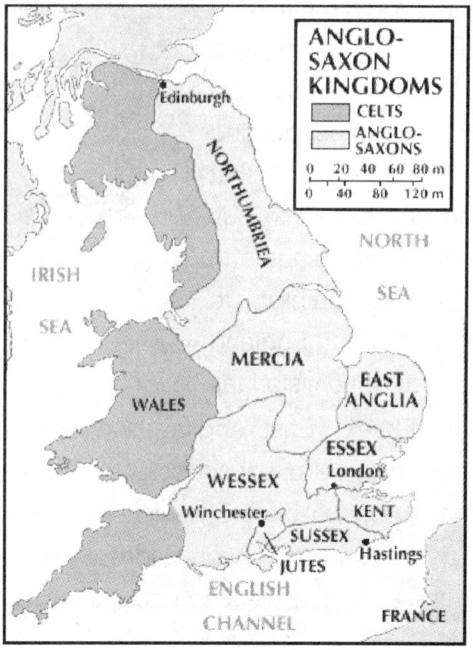

Map of Anglo-Saxon Kingdoms

The small Anglo-Saxon tribes gradually merged into seven or eight little kingdoms. The Jutes, a small tribe, held the Isle of Wight and land to the north. The Saxons established themselves in Wessex on the south coast. The Angles ruled Mercia in the Midlands, East Anglia on the east coast, and Northumbria in the northeast.

2.1.4 Danish Invasion

The new invaders were Scandinavians from Norway and Denmark. The English called them Danes. Summer after summer these bold pirates rowed up the rivers in their longboats, plundered the rich monasteries, and went home with the gold and gems. Soon after 850 a great force remained in England, bent on conquest. Then permanent settlers poured in. The Danes were farmers and traders as well as warriors. When they founded a town—usually a port—they fortified it and opened a market. All of eastern England north of the Thames passed under the rule of the Danish earls, and came to be known as the Danelaw, the part under Danish law.

The Danes would probably have wiped out Christianity in England if it had not been for Alfred the Great, king of Wessex. Alfred, Egbert's grandson, became king of Wessex in one of England's darkest hours. The Danes, part of the Viking forces that had begun to raid the English coasts in the late 8th century, had given up their primary goal of plunder and were now set on conquering England. Wessex and Alfred were all that stood in their way. Alfred at first had to buy a respite, but after his victory at Edington in 878 he forced the Danish king Guthrum to accept baptism and a division of England into two parts, Wessex and what historians later called the Danelaw (Essex, East Anglia, and Northumbria). Alfred began English prose literature by translating Latin books into Anglo-Saxon. He also built schools and ordered the "Anglo-Saxon Chronicle", the first historical record of England, to be begun. By 955, his grandson Eadred, ruled over a united England. Government became centralized, and the king had the infrastructure to rule the whole country.

Alfred the Great

Unfortunately, a century after Alfred's time the Danes started once more to raid England's shores. In 1016 Canute, the king of Norway and Denmark, made himself king of England also. He proved to be a wise and strong ruler, but after his death his empire fell apart, and in 1042 the Danish dynasty in England ended. The English line then returned to the throne with Edward, son of Ethelred. He had been reared by French monks and was called The Confessor.

2.2 Norman Conquest and Decline of Feudalism

2.1.2 Norman Conquest (1066)

While the Danes were invading England, other Norsemen[2] raided the coast of France. On the southern shore of the English Channel they established the Duchy of Normandy. These Norsemen, or Normans, became French in language and culture. In the 11th century the Duchy of Normandy was rich, populous, and powerful. When Edward, the Confessor, died childless, William, duke of Normandy, claimed the English crown. He was a second cousin of Edward, and he had exacted an oath from Harold, earl of Wessex, to support his claim. The English Witan nevertheless elected Harold king. William appealed to the pope. The pope supported William and declared Harold guilty of perjury.

Sculpture of King William I on the Exterior of Lichfield Cathedral

After long preparations William set sail from Normandy. On September 28 he landed his army of 4,000 to 7,000 cavalry and infantry at Pevensey on the English Channel and moved eastward along the coast to Hastings. Harold hurried from the north of England with his army of about 7,000 men, many of whom were half-armed, untrained peasants. On October 13 Harold took a strong position on a hill between the port of Hastings and the present-day village of Battle. At dawn the next day William roused his troops and set out on an 8-mile (13-kilometer) march to join battle before Harold's troops were rested. All day the battle raged. Norman horsemen pressed up the hill. Standing close together and protected by great shields, the English wielded their long-handled battle-axes with terrible effect. Throughout the day William alternated cavalry charges with flights of arrows from his archers.

Pretending retreat, he drew the English from their position and destroyed them. Harold was killed when an arrow pierced his eye. His brothers had already been slain. The English fought on until dusk. Then they fled, leaving the field to William. After the battle William and his army moved northward to isolate London. This is what historians call Battle of Hastings. On Christmas Day, 1066, William was crowned king of England in Westminster Abbey.

Death of Harold in the Battle of Hastings, as Shown on the Bayeus Tapestry

For five years after his coronation, William I was busy putting down revolts in his new kingdom. He seized the land of all Saxons who fought against him and distributed it among his Norman followers—except for vast tracts that he kept for himself as crown lands. In return for the grant of land—called a fief—each lord had to swear loyalty to the king, furnish knights for the king's army, attend the king's court, and aid the king with money on certain occasions. Farmers were reduced to the class of serfs, or villeins, as the Normans called them. A villein could not leave the manor on which he was born. This system of land tenure was the basis of feudalism, which held sway all over Europe in the Middle Ages. The efficiency of William's rule is shown by the survey he had made of all the property in England. His agents visited every manor, found out who owned it, how many people lived there, and reported what the feudal lord ought to pay the king in taxes and feudal service. The findings were recorded in the famous Domesday Book. It was called Domesday (day of doom) because no one could escape its judgment.

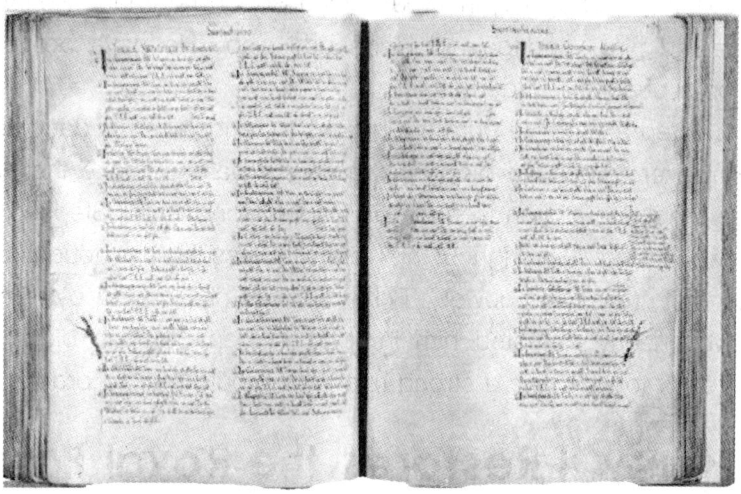

Domesday Book, compiled in 1086 under the direction of William the Conqueror, was a meticulous survey of feudal estates in England.

The date of the Norman Conquest—1066—is one of the most important dates in English history. The Conquest cut England's ties with Scandinavia and connected England with France. French, the language of the Norman rulers, became blended with the Anglo-Saxon speech of the common people, enriching the native language with many new words and ideas. Wooden churches and abbeys were replaced with beautiful stone buildings in the Norman style. Foreign monks and bishops, brought in by the Normans, made the monasteries centers of learning. Anyone who wanted to study went into the church as a matter of course. The king's secretaries, judges, and most of his civil servants were churchmen, because only churchmen had the necessary education.

When he was crowned, William I, the Conqueror, promised to govern according to the laws of Edward the Confessor. The Witan survived in his great council of advisers, which was attended by earls, barons, bishops, and abbots; but the council no longer had the power to choose the king. As feudal overlord of the whole country, William bequeathed England to his second son, William II. He left Normandy to his eldest son, Robert.

2.2.2 William II, Henry I, and Stephen

William II (called William Rufus, the "Red King") came to the throne in 1087. He was a harsh ruler and few mourned him when he was killed by an arrow—shot by an unknown hand—while he was hunting. Robert had gone off on the First Crusade, to recover the Holy Land from the Turks. A third son, Henry I, was therefore able to become king without a struggle, in 1100. When Robert returned, Henry crossed the Channel, defeated him, and gained Normandy also. He gave both England and western France a peaceful, orderly rule.

Henry I exacted a promise from the barons to recognize his daughter Matilda as their ruler. However, when he died, some of the barons broke their promise and instead chose Stephen, a grandson of William the Conqueror. Stephen was a brave knight but a weak king. Throughout his reign lawless barons fought private wars, each seeking to increase his power. Twice he was challenged by Matilda and her supporters, who nearly defeated him in 1141. When Stephen died (1154), the people were ready to welcome a strong ruler who would restore order.

2.2.3 Henry II Restores the Royal Power

The strong ruler was found in Henry Plantagenet, count of Anjou. His mother was Matilda (or Maud), daughter of Henry I of England; his father was Geoffrey of Anjou. He came to the throne of England as Henry II, first of the Plantagenet line of kings, who were to rule England for 245 years. By marriage and inheritance, he came into possession of all western France. He spent most of his long reign, 1154 - 1189, in his French possessions; yet he became one of England's great rulers.

Henry II sent out trained justices on circuit to different towns in England to sit in the county courts. The judges kept records of their cases. When one judge had decided a case, other judges trying the same kind of case were likely to adopt the decision that had been recorded. In the course of years, legal principles came to be based on these decisions. Because this case law applied to all Englishmen equally, it came to be called the common law. The circuit justices also made more extensive use of juries and started the grand jury system in criminal law.

2.2.4 King John and Magna Carta

In 1199 Richard I was succeeded by his brother John, the most despicable of English kings. By a series of blunders John lost almost all his French possessions except the southwest corner. The English barons refused to help him regain his territory. Angered by his tyrannical rule, they drew up a list of things that even a king might not do. On June 15, 1215, they forced him to set his seal to this Great Charter (in Latin, Magna Carta) of English liberties.

Memorial to the Magna Carta 1215

The Magna Carta

Magna Carta is regarded as one of the most notable documents in history. It outlined the barons' customary rights and prohibited the king from changing anything without their consent. More importantly, however, it stated that all free men in England had certain rights that the king had to respect. Thus, for the first time these rights were insisted upon against the king's will. Since then an important principle was established—that the king himself must govern according to law. In later years, whenever a king over-extended his powers, the people could remind him of Magna Carta.

2.2.5 The Rise of Parliament

Henry III, John's eldest son, was crowned at the age of nine and ruled 56 years, 1216 –1272. He was pious and well meaning but incompetent and extravagant. The barons took a strong stand against him in Parliament. In 1264 the barons, led by Simon de Montfort, rose against the king and won a victory over King Henry III in 1264, and took the monarch and his son Edward prisoners. Earl Simon de Montfort ruled the kingdom, and called Parliament in 1265 which not only included knights but representatives from the boroughs. It was known as the "All Estates Parliament". Later, Simon de Montfort was defeated by Henry III's son, Edward I, who ruled England from 1272 to 1307. Edward I wisely accepted the limitations on the king's authority. His parliament of 1295 was called the Model Parliament because it included representatives of shires and towns as well as the Great Council. Many of the laws passed in Edward's reign exist in modified form today. Edward I restored royal control and made several reforms: He limited the barons' right to hold their own courts of law; he reduced the vassals' right to dispose of land to the detriment of their feudal lords; and he gave English common law the direction it was to take for centuries to come. Most important, he used and developed Parliament, which was essentially the king's feudal council with a new name and an enlarged membership. The Model Parliament of 1295, following Montfort's pattern of 1265, consisted of great barons, bishops, abbots, and representatives of counties and towns. In 1297, to get money for his wars, Edward accepted the Confirmation of Charters, agreeing that taxes must have the common assent of the whole realm. This was soon taken to mean assent in Parliament. In the following century, Parliament divided into two houses, Lords and Commons, and made good its claim to control taxation and to participate in the making of statutes. During his reign, Edward conquered northwest Wales, ending the rule of its native princes. He built stone castles, adopted the Welsh longbow as an English weapon, and named his oldest son the Prince of Wales. He intervened in Scottish affairs, even claiming the Scottish throne. Having fought the Scots often but with little effect, Edward died in 1307 without having subdued the northern kingdom. His son, Edward II, gave up the campaign.

2.3 The Decline of Feudalism

2.3.1 The Hundred Years' War

In 1328, the Capetian dynasty in France came to an end with the death of Charles IV, the son of Philip the Fair. An assembly of French barons gave the crown to Philip VI, the nephew of Philip the Fair. Edward III, king of England, asserted that he in fact had a superior claim to the throne because his mother was Philip the Fair's daughter. This, then, was one of the primary causes of the Hundred Years' War. Another cause of the Hundred Years' War was clearly economic conflict. The French monarchy tried to squeeze new taxes from towns in northern Europe which had grown wealthy as trade and cloth-making centers. Dependent as they were on English wool, these towns prospered through their support behind English and Edward III.

The most pressing issue during the Hundred Years' War was the status of Aquitaine, a large province in southwestern France. According to feudal law, Edward III held Aquitaine as part of his fiefdom. Philip attacked this territory, claiming it was rightfully his. Then the war broke out when Edward joined forces with the Flemish in 1337. The war, fought entirely on French soil, raged off and on for more than 100 years. English victories were followed by French victories, then a period of stalemate would follow, until the conflicts again rose to the surface. During periods of truce, English and French soldiers—most of whom were mercenaries—would roam the French countryside killing and stealing. After the battle of Agincourt in 1415, won by the English under Henry V, the English controlled most of northern France. It appeared that England would shortly conquer France and unite the two countries under one crown. At this crucial moment in French history, a young and illiterate peasant girl, Joan of Arc (c. 1412 – 1431), helped to rescue France. She was 13 years old, believing that God had commanded her to drive the English out of France. Joan rallied the demoralized French troops, leading them in battle. Clad in a suit of white armor and flying her own standard she liberated France from the English at the battle of Orleans. Ultimately captured and imprisoned by the English, Joan of Arc was condemned as a heretic and a witch and burned to death by the English in 1431. Encouraged by her heroic efforts, French people finally drove the English out of French territories. By the end of the War in 1453, the English lost all the lands on the Continent except Calais.

The battle of Agincourt in 1415 was Henry V's most famous victory against the French. The English army with the royal standard attacks (left). The French royal standard is to be seen on the ground (bottom right) as French soldiers die. Although the English were outnumbered by more than three to one, Henry's archers destroyed the French feudal cavalry.

The end of the Hundred Years' War was also the end of a long period of economic trouble and declining population in both countries, to which the war had contributed. In France, the war encouraged the emergence of centralized governing institutions. In England, the loss of French territory forced the government to focus on domestic issues. By the end of the war both the French and English peoples began to view themselves as separate and distinctive nationalities, and not merely as members of a feudal empire.

2.3.2 The Black Death and the Peasants' Revolt

The Black Death, an epidemic of plague in Western Europe, that lasted from 1348 to 1349, resulted in the deaths of almost one-quarter of Europe's population. The Black Death was the first in a cycle of plagues in Europe that continued into the 18th century. After the Black Death, more than a fourth of England's population perished. Whole villages were wiped out, and great areas of farmland went to weeds. The serfs who survived demanded higher wages. If their lord refused, they moved to another manor. The government tried to control the rise in wages and bind the laborers to their manors by passing Statute of Laborers. Against this background the immediate cause for popular anger was a poll tax passed in 1381. Then the rebellion started in the southeast of England in May. In June a company of rebels entered London, where they killed the uncle of king Richard II, the duke of Lancaster, and several merchants. While the king was negotiating with others outside the city, the group in London also executed those responsible for the poll tax. The king met with Tyler on June 15. During the meeting, Tyler was killed by the mayor of London, William Walworth and the rebels were sent home by the king's promise that their demands would be met. However, the king broke his promise and the nobles quickly re-established their control with the help of a hastily organized militia of 7,000. A few days later most of the other leaders were pursued, captured and executed, including John Ball and Jack Straw, who were beheaded. Following the collapse of the revolt, the king's concessions were quickly revoked. As soon as the rebels lost, the pledges made by the king were forgotten. The revolt's only success was to keep the poll tax from being levied.

Wat Tyler is killed by Walworth while Richard II watches / Richard II addresses the crowd.

2.3.3 The Wars of Roses

In 1455, two years after the Hundred Years' War ended, the House of York and the House of Lancaster plunged into a long and bloody struggle for the crown. The emblem of the Yorkists was a white rose and that of the Lancastrians a red rose. Because of this the wars were called the Wars of the Roses. The families of York and Lancaster were both descended from King Edward III, but the Yorkists had a better claim to the throne than the Lancastrians. At first Richard of York planned merely to take the government from incapable persons and secure it for himself. Later his ambition was to seize the crown. His ablest supporter was the earl of Warwick with the nickname of "the kingmaker". On the Lancastrian side the real head of the party was Queen Margaret, who fiercely resisted attempts to dethrone her husband, Henry VI, and disinherit her son, Edward. The struggle began when Richard of York won the battle of St. Albans in 1455 and secured control of the government. Four years later the contest was renewed. Richard was finally killed by the forces of Queen Margaret at Wakefield in 1460. His son, however, became king as Edward IV with Warwick's help and imprisoned Henry VI. Then Warwick quarreled with Edward IV and helped Queen Margaret drive him from England and restore Henry VI in 1470. The next year Edward returned and destroyed Margaret's forces. But when Edward IV reentered London and seized the throne, the king himself was assassinated. This ended the first period of the struggle. Fourteen years later war broke out again. Henry Tudor, the last Lancastrian representative, defeated and killed Richard III, the last Yorkist king, at the battle of Bosworth Field on August 22, 1485. The victor became king as Henry VII, thus ending the Wars of the Roses. The following year Henry married Elizabeth of York, the daughter of Edward IV. After this marriage the white and the red roses were united in the rose of the Tudors, the emblem of a new line of English kings.

The White Rose of the House of York

The Red Rose of the House of Lancaster

Tudor Rose

The Wars of Roses dealt a death blow to the feudal power of the nobles and effectively marked the end of the Middle Ages in England. Many of the ruling nobles had been slain during the wars, and their estates were confiscated by the Crown. At the same time, a new aristocracy was pushing up through the broken crust of feudal society. In the towns a rich capitalist class appeared. Country squires—the landed gentry—also grew wealthy. The new aristocracy began to seek political power.

2.3.4 Henry VIII and the English Reformation

The English Reformation started when Henry VIII came to the throne in 1509. The English Reformation was to have far-reaching consequences in Tudor England. Henry VIII decided to rid himself of his first wife, Catherine of Aragon, after she had failed to produce a male heir to the throne. He had already decided who his next wife would be—Anne Boleyn. By 1527, Catherine was considered too old to have any more children.

However, a divorce was not a simple issue. Henry VIII was a Roman Catholic and the head of this church was the pope based in Rome. The Roman Catholic faith believed in marriage for life. It did not recognize, let alone support, divorce. This put Henry VIII in a difficult position. If he went ahead and announced that as king of England he was allowing himself a divorce, the pope could excommunicate him. Another approach Henry used was to make a special appeal to the pope so that he might get a special "Papal Dispensation[3]". But the pope was controlled by Charles V, who was Holy Roman Emperor and king of Spain, and also Catherine's nephew. For both political and family reasons he wanted Henry to stay married to Catherine. The pope did not wish to anger either Charles or Henry, but eventually he was forced to do as Charles V wanted. He forbade Henry's divorce. Henry was so angered that in 1531 he ordered the bishops to make him head of the Church in England, and this became law after Parliament passed the Act of Supremacy[4] in 1534. It was a popular decision. Henry was now free to divorce Catherine and marry his new love, Anne Boleyn. He hoped Anne would give him a son to follow him on the throne.

Henry VIII became Supreme Governor of the Church in England.

These events effectively led to England breaking away from the Roman Catholic Church based in Rome. However, the wealthiest Catholics in England were also the most loyal supporters of the pope, which made them a threat to Henry. Henry decided to shut down the monasteries of England. Between 1536 and 1539, 560 monasteries and other religious houses were closed. Henry did this in order to make money, but he also wanted to be popular with the rising classes of landowners and merchants. As a result, he gained control of the monasteries—the monastic buildings and land were sold off after the dissolution of the monasteries in 1538. Many of the buildings fell into decay, and they lost their farmlands for ever. However, the death of Henry in 1547 did not see an end of the religious problems of England. Henry's elder daughter Mary was a Catholic—and a militant Catholic at that. Her efforts as queen to restore Catholicism to England made her the most unpopular queen in British history and the means that she used to pursue her aims earned her the nickname "bloody Mary". There were 283 Protestant martyrs burnt at the stake in her reign. A loveless marriage of Queen Mary to the King of Spain produced no children. So when she died she was succeeded by her Protestant half-sister Elizabeth.

2.3.5 Era of Elizabeth and the Defeat of the Spanish Armada

Elizabeth's reign brought in one of the most glorious eras of British history. When she became queen in 1558, Elizabeth I wanted to find a peaceful answer to the problems of the English Reformation. She wanted to bring together again those parts of English society which were in religious disagreement. And she wanted to make England prosperous. At the beginning of her reign England was in despair. The country had been weakened by war and religious strife, and the treasury was empty. Spain and France were powerful, and both wanted to rule England. The people hoped their young queen would soon marry a strong man who would guide her. But Elizabeth at once took the government into her own hands. And though she had many suitors and close friendships with several men, she steadfastly refused to marry. When she died at the age of 69, she was still called the Virgin Queen. By then rich and secure, England was enjoying its greatest literary period. English ships were sailing around the world, and the island kingdom had begun to establish its position as a world leader.

In religious matters Elizabeth steered a middle course between the extreme Protestants and the Catholics. She restored the Protestant service but retained many features of Catholicism, including bishops and archbishops. She hoped this compromise would produce unity in the state, but the Catholics, who formed a majority of her subjects, were not reconciled. From time to time some of them plotted with Spain or France to put Mary Stuart on the throne in place of Elizabeth. France and Spain were rivals, and Elizabeth was usually able to play one off against the other. She even used courtship as part of her diplomatic game. She refused to marry Philip II of Spain but held out hopes to more than one of his royal relatives when France seemed to threaten. Later, when Philip turned against England, Elizabeth encouraged French princes. To cut Scotland's ties with France, she gave secret help to the Scottish Presbyterians. She also aided the Protestant Netherlands when they revolted against Spain. Mary Stuart returned to Scotland in 1561 after the death of her husband, Francis, king of France. In 1568 she was compelled to flee across the English border to ask Elizabeth's help. Elizabeth kept her a prisoner for 19 years. Finally Mary was accused of having a part in the so-called Babington Plot to assassinate Elizabeth. Parliament demanded her execution. Elizabeth signed the warrant, and Mary Stuart was beheaded in 1587. In the last years of Elizabeth's reign, Catholics were cruelly persecuted and many were put to death.

Portrait of Elizabeth to commemorate the defeat of the Spanish Armada (1588), depicted in the background. Elizabeth's hand rests on the globe, symbolizing her international power.

During the first 30 years of Elizabeth's reign England was at peace. Commerce revived, and English ships were boldly venturing overseas to the West Indies. There they came into conflict with Spain and Portugal, which owned and ruled the whole New World and claimed a monopoly of trade. English smugglers broke through the blockade and made huge profits by selling, in the West Indies, blacks they had seized in Africa. John Hawkins, Sir Francis Drake, and other English seamen also waylaid Spanish ships on their way home and seized their gold. Elizabeth aided the English privateers with ships and money and shared in their profits and stolen treasure. Philip II finally decided to put an end to these attacks by invading and conquering England. After years of preparation, Philip assembled a great fleet of his best and largest warships, called by the Spanish the Armada[5] (that is, fleet). In

1588 the Armada sailed into the English Channel. The English were waiting for them. Their ships were of newer design, smaller than the Spanish galleons but faster and more heavily armed. In a nine-day battle they inflicted terrible losses on the enemy. The ships that escaped ran into bad weather and only a few returned to Spain. English ships then carried the war to Spain. When the struggle ended—after the deaths of both Elizabeth and Philip—no Spanish fleet dared to challenge England's command of the seas. The defeat of the Spanish Armada established the superiority of English ships and sailors and made the English conscious of their ocean destiny. English merchants began to seek distant markets for their goods. In 1600 the now old queen chartered the famous East India Company, giving it a monopoly of trade with the Far East. From this small start Britain's Indian Empire was to grow.

Defeat of the Spanish Armada, by Philippe-Jacques de Loutherbourg, painted in 1797, depicts the battle of Gravelines.

The most splendid period of English literature, called the Elizabethan Age, began in the later years of Elizabeth's reign. It can be dated back to the Italian Renaissance. "Renaissance" literally means "rebirth". It began in Italy during the 14th century and reached its height in the 15th century. In the 16th and 17th centuries it spread to the rest of Europe. It refers to the rediscovery by scholars (called humanists) of the writings of the ancient Greeks and Romans. In fact, however, the Renaissance was a period of discovery in many fields—of new scientific laws, new forms of art and literature, new religious and political ideas, and new lands,

William Shakespeare (1564 - 1616), the greatest English poet and playwright

including America. However, the effect of the Renaissance was not felt in England until the reign of Elizabeth. Among many great figures of the time Christopher Marlowe, Ben Johnson, and William Shakespeare were the most outstanding representatives in drama, which was characteristics of the epoch and later became known as the Elizabethan drama. Edmund Spenser pushed the English non-dramatic poetry to a new height by his masterpiece *The Faerie Queene* in Elizabeth's honor. John Milton's epic *Paradise Lost*, Thomas More's *Utopia*, Francis Bacon's philosophical and literary works also resulted from the influence of the Renaissance.

2.4 The Bourgeois Revolution

2.4.1 The English Civil War

The Tudor dynasty came to an end when Elizabeth I died in 1603. The crown of England then passed to the Stuart line of Scotland. The new king was called James VI in Scotland and James I in England. The two countries, having the same ruler, were now bound together in a personal union, but for another century they had separate parliaments. James boldly announced that he would rule as an absolute monarch because he received his power from God, and was responsible to Him alone. This view of monarchy was called the divine right of kings. It was generally accepted on the Continent of Europe, but it ran counter to the nature of the English people. Parliament resisted James at every point. So during his reign, James kept quarreling with Parliament over taxation and political matters until his death. As to religious matters he insisted that all people conform to the Church of England and incurred the enmity of the Puritans and the Catholics. Consequently, a small band of Catholic extremists, including Guy Fawkes, placed 36 barrels of gunpowder in the cellar of the Parliament in order to blow up king and Parliament together when the king summoned the Parliament. But the plot was betrayed and Guy Fawkes was arrested on the threshold of the cellar on 5th, November. Since then the very night of November 5th has been celebrated as Bonfire Night[6] with fireworks and burning effigies of Guy Fawkes on a bonfire.

Though tactless and stubborn, James I was quite learned and full of vigor. At his instruction, scholars prepared a new translation of the Bible, called the "King James Version[7]". Published in 1611, it remains in common use today. His quarrel with Parliament over taxation and political matters led him to abolish Parliament in 1610 and he managed to rule without Parliament for 11 years. Upon his death in 1625, James I left the country to his son Charles I. But the young king was not as fortunate as his father for lack of ability and vigor.

Guy Fawkes, a conspirator in the Gunpowder Plot, was arrested while attempting to blow up the Houses of Parliament, November 5, 1605.

Charles was as obstinate a despot as his father. In 1637 Charles' attempt to impose the Anglican liturgy in Scotland led to rioting by Presbyterian Scots. Charles was unable to quell the revolt, and in 1640 he summoned the so-called Short Parliament[8] to raise an army and necessary funds. This body, lasted one month (April – May), and refused his demands, by drawing up a statement of public grievances and insisting on peace with Scotland. Obtaining money by irregular means, Charles advanced against the Scots, who crossed the border, defeated his army at Newburn, and soon afterward occupied Newcastle and Durham.

England's King Charles I is depicted in a proud stance and sumptuous clothing, even though dressed for hunting, by his court painter, Flemish artist Anthony van Dyck, in 1635.

His money exhausted, the king was compelled to call his fifth Parliament, the Long Parliament[9], in 1640 which existed until Cromwell dissolved it in April, 1653. In 1641 Charles agreed to bills abolishing the prerogative courts[10], prohibiting arbitrary taxation, and ensuring that this Parliament would not be dissolved without its own permission. The king also agreed to more religious liberties for the Scots. Soon after, Charles was involved in a plot to murder the leaders of Scottish Presbyterianism. When Charles visited Scotland in August 1641, he promised that he would submit to the demands of the Scottish Parliament.

While still in Scotland, the king received word of a rebellion in Ireland in which thousands of English colonists were massacred. When he returned to London in November, he tried to have Parliament raise an army, under his control, to put down the Irish revolt. Parliament, fearing that the army would be used against itself, refused, and issued the Grand Remonstrance, a list of reform demands, including the right of Parliament to approve the king's ministers. Charles appeared in the House of Commons with an armed force and tried to arrest Pym and four members. The country was aroused, and the king fled with his family from London.

Both sides then raised armies. The supporters of Parliament were called Roundheads, and those of the king, Cavaliers (The Puritans were called Roundheads because they cut their hair short. The Cavaliers wore long flowing locks). The first civil war of the English Revolution, now inevitable, began at Edgehill on October 23, 1642. In general, the early part of the war went well for the Royalists until in 1644 when the Puritans defeated Charles's Cavaliers at Marston Moor. In this battle Oliver Cromwell, the Puritan leader, won the name Ironsides. The next year he gained a decisive victory at Naseby. Soon, Charles gave himself up to the Scottish army on May 5, 1646. Having refused to accept Presbyterianism, he was delivered in June 1647 to the English Parliament. Later he escaped to the Isle of Wight but was imprisoned there. By this time a serious division had occurred between Parliament and its army. The army's leader, Oliver Cromwell and his supporters, the Independents, forced Parliament to pass an act of treason against further negotiation with the king. But the moderate Parliamentarians wanted to negotiate a compromise with the king, which angered the Independents so much that troops were called in and the moderate Parliamentarians were driven out. The remaining legislators formed the so-called Rump Parliament and appointed a court to try the king. On January 27 he was sentenced to death as a tyrant, murderer, and enemy of the nation. Subsequently Charles I was beheaded on January 30, 1649. The Rump then declared England a Commonwealth, i. e. a republic without a king or a House of Lords and Oliver Cromwell became chairman of the council of state.

The Rump Parliament governed England while Cromwell put down revolts in Ireland and Scotland with great cruelty. In 1653 he came back from the wars, dismissed Parliament, and "nominated" a Parliament of his own. The Commonwealth then took the name of Protectorate, with Cromwell as Lord Protector. The Puritans closed the theaters, suppressed horse racing, cockfighting, and bearbaiting, and made Sunday strictly a day of worship. Cromwell's rule was more despotic than the king's. Yet the revolution accomplished its purpose. When the monarchy was revived it became a limited monarchy. The Church of England never again tried to include all Englishmen. When Cromwell died in 1658 his eldest son, Richard Cromwell, became Lord Protector. Too weak to control the army, Tumbledown Dick resigned the next year. In 1660 George Monk, one of Cromwell's generals, brought an army from Scotland and had the Rump of the Long Parliament recalled to dissolve itself. A new Parliament was elected and at once offered the crown to the exiled son of Charles I.

Oliver Cromwell, 1st Lord Protector of the Commonwealth of England, Scotland and Ireland

2.4.2 The Restoration and Glorious Revolution

After Cromwell died in 1658, his son Richard proved unable to carry on the government. A new Parliament, called in 1660, restored the Stuart line, and Charles was recalled from exile to be crowned. Charles's apparent purpose throughout his reign was to make himself an absolute monarch. And this led him to try to raise a standing army, to restore Catholicism. During his reign Charles followed a shifty course, bribing, flattering, and yielding to Parliament whenever opposition proved too strong. However, in 1679 when an "Exclusion Bill" was presented in Parliament to bar James, his brother from the kingship, Charles was angered and dissolved Parliament. The governing classes at once split into bitter factions—the Tories, who opposed the bill, and the Whigs[11], who favored it. Thus were born the first great political parties in history. The Tories, descended from the Cavaliers, represented the landed aristocracy. They upheld the divine right of kings and the Anglican Church. The Whigs, descended from the Roundheads, represented the commercial classes of the cities. They championed Parliament against the king and urged toleration for nonconformists.

The English Restoration restored the monarchy under King Charles II and peace after the English Civil War.

In 1685, Charles II died, and his brother, James II, stepped quietly to the throne. However, when a male heir to James was born, in 1688, Tory and Whig leaders joined together and decided to set aside the Catholic line of kings. They invited Mary, a daughter of James, and her Dutch husband, William of Orange, to occupy the throne as joint sovereigns. After William landed in England with an army, James fled to the Continent. Then a new Parliament declared the throne vacant and appointed William and Mary joint sovereign.

William III, King of England, Scotland and Ireland

Mary II, Queen of England, Scotland and Ireland

In return for this, William and Mary accepted Declaration of Rights proposed by Parliament in 1689. Then Parliament speedily enacted it into law as the famous Bill of Rights. It was a comprehensive piece of legislation with the purpose to make it the king's obligation to govern with the assistance of Parliament. It prohibited taxes or keeping a standing army without the approval of the legislature. It also provided for free speech, free elections, and frequent meetings of Parliament. Among other provisions was one preventing the monarch from being a Roman Catholic. As a result, Parliament, and not inheritance or divine right, would determine the succession to the throne. This was the fruit of the so-called Glorious Revolution—a revolution without bloodshed. Since then, England entered a new period. It not only swept away the obstacles of feudalism and paved the way for the development of capitalism in England in the next two centuries, but also turned into a myth the king's claim to rule by divine right. The English king, instead of controlling Parliament, had left his crown in the control of Parliament. This marked a real beginning of the constitutional monarchy. From then on, the main concern in the kingdom was shifted from internal struggle to economic problems and foreign expansion. The country would soon experience a speedy economic development which led to and promoted the Industrial Revolution.

Notes

[1] Viking: Viking is one of the Norse (Scandinavian) explorers, warriors, merchants, and pirates who raided and colonized wide areas of Europe from the late eighth to the early eleventh century.

[2] Norseman: Norseman was "people from the North" and was applied primarily to Nordic people originating from southern and central Scandinavia. They established states and settlements in areas which today are part of the Faroe Islands, England, Scotland, Wales, Iceland, Finland, Ireland, Russia, Italy, Canada, Greenland, France, Ukraine, Estonia, Latvia, Lithuania and Germany.

[3] Papal Dispensation: It is a reserved right of the Pope that allows for individuals to be exempted from a specific Canon Law.

[4] the Act of Supremacy: It was passed in 1534; this is the piece of legislation which declares that the sovereign is Supreme Head of the Church of England and establishes the Church of England's independence from Rome.

[5] the Armada: The Armada was the Spanish fleet that sailed against England in 1588, with the intention of overthrowing Elizabeth I of England. The mission was a total failure and a landmark in naval history for a poorly planned and badly handled operation.

[6] Bonfire Night: It is also called Guy Fawkes Night.

[7] King James Version: It is an English translation of the Christian Holy Bible begun in 1604 and completed in 1611 by the Church of England and is considered one of the masterpieces of early modern English literature.

[8] the Short Parliament: It refers to a Parliament of England that sat from 13 April to 5 May 1640 during the reign of King Charles I of England, so called because it lasted only three weeks.

[9] the Long Parliament: It was first called by King Charles I on 3 November 1640, six months after the dissolution of the Short Parliament. It sat throughout the First and Second Civil Wars until December 1648, when it was purged by the New Model Army and was reinstated in February 1660 after the fall of Cromwell and was formally dissolved on 16 March 1660.

[10] the prerogative court: A prerogative court is a court through which the discretionary powers, privileges, and legal immunities reserved to the sovereign were exercised. In general, this includes, in the case of England, all courts initially part of the King's Court.

[11] the Tories and the Whigs: They are political parties in England since around 1681—Whigs being supporters of the Catholic James and Tories being their Royalist opponents.

Exercises

I. Fill in the following blanks with proper words or expressions.

1. The Roman soldiers conquered Britain in AD 43 under ________.
2. In the late 8th century, the ________ began to attack the English coasts. Under the leadership of King ________, the West Saxons offered resistance.
3. On Christmas Day, 1066, after the Battle of ________, ____________________ was crowned king of England in Westminster Abbey.
4. On June 15, 1215, the English barons forced ________ to set his seal to ________ (in Latin, Magna Carta) of English liberties.

5. Edward I summoned Parliament in 1295, which is later called ________.
6. By the end of Hundred Years' War in 1453, the English lost all the lands on the Continent except ________.
7. The war between the House of York and the House of Lancaster resulted in the establishment of the House of ________ in 1485.
8. In the First Civil War, the king's men were called ________ and the supporters of Parliament were called ________.
9. Since 1603, the very night of November 5th has been celebrated as ____________ with fireworks and burning effigies of ____________ on a bonfire.
10. In 1688, Tory and Whig leaders joined together and invited ________, a daughter of James, and her Dutch husband, ________, to occupy the throne as joint sovereigns.

II. Explain the following terms.

1. The Hundred Years' War
2. Great Charter
3. The Wars of Roses
4. The Glorious Revolution

III. Discuss the following questions.

1. What are Norman Conquest and its influence?
2. What is a constitutional monarchy? When did it begin in Britain?

Chapter Three

A Brief History (Ⅱ)

3.1 The Industrial Revolution and the Chartist Movement

3.1.1 The Struggle with France

While England was suffering from revolution, France, under Louis XIV, was achieving a dominant position in Europe. With internal conflict ended, England turned its attention abroad. In 1689 it joined with Holland and several German states in the War of the Grand Alliance against France. The war spread to America, where it was called King William's War. It marked the beginning of a long struggle to decide whether France or England was to control India and North America.

When William died, in 1702, Louis XIV proclaimed James Stuart, son of James II, king of England, Scotland, and Ireland. Parliament, however, had provided that if William and Mary had no children, the crown should pass to Anne, a Protestant, daughter of James II by his first wife. As soon as Anne came to the throne in 1702, England entered upon another war with France to break up a threatened combination of France and Spain. This was called in Europe the War of the Spanish Succession. In America it was known as Queen Anne's War. The Duke of Marlborough led the English, Dutch, and Germans to brilliant victories, and the Treaty of Utrecht (1713) gave England important territories (all Nova Scotia and Newfoundland) in the New World. The most notable event in Anne's reign was the union of England with

Scotland. Since 1603 the two nations had been loosely associated under the same king. The Act of Union (1707) united them in a single kingdom, called Great Britain, and joined their parliaments. Thereafter the government and parliament in London were called British rather than English.

The Stuart line came to an end when Anne died, since none of her 17 children survived her. She was succeeded in 1714 by George I, a prince of the House of Hanover, a small state in Germany. George did not speak English, and he was so wrapped up in his beloved Hanover that he took little interest in British affairs. He soon began to stay away from meetings of his inner council, or cabinet, and left the government in the hands of Sir Robert Walpole, the able Whig leader. His son, George II, who ruled 1727 -1760, also stayed away from meetings of his ministers. Walpole made himself supreme in the government, selected his colleagues, and insisted they work with him or leave the cabinet. He thus became the first prime minister. Walpole promoted trade and commerce and strove to avoid war. But in 1739 the British people became aroused over the story of Robert Jenkins, a sea captain, who claimed the Spaniards had boarded his ship and cut off his ear. Walpole was persuaded to declare war against Spain in 1739—the War of Jenkins' Ear. He resigned when this war merged into another Continental war, the War of the Austrian Succession, in America called King George's War. When peace was made, in 1748, the real issue—whether France or Britain was to prevail in India and North America—was still unsettled.

The struggle with France was renewed in the Seven Years' War, which broke out in 1756. This war brought to the fore a leader of genius, William Pitt, earl of Chatham. He carried on the struggle against France in America, Africa, and India, as well as in Europe and on the sea. When the war came to an end, the Treaty of Paris was signed in 1763. According to the Treaty, France ceded Canada and her American possessions east of the Mississippi, with the exception of New Orleans and gave up four of her West Indian islands, as well as her African possessions. Spain, who had joined the war on the sides of France, ceded Florida to England together with all her possessions east of the Mississippi. The war cost France almost all its territory in North

William Pitt the Elder, lauded British leader during the war, confirming Britain's status as the world's dominant colonial power.

America and India and established Britain as the world's chief colonial power.

In 1789 the French Revolution erupted. French citizens rose against their monarch, Louis XVI, eliminated the ancient legal distinctions based on social class, and established a republican government. The French revolutionaries invited all of the peoples of Europe to follow their example. Conservative monarchs throughout Europe were hostile toward the revolution. George III expelled the French envoy. Within a few years wars broke out between France and a number of European powers. In 1793 France declared war on Britain and Britain promptly joined the coalition of European monarchs against the new French republic. The war dragged on without much result until the young general Napoleon Bonaparte began to win amazing victories. By 1797 Britain was left to carry on the war alone. Britain, weak on land, was supreme on the sea. Admiral Horatio Nelson's victory of the Nile (1798) gave the British navy control of the Mediterranean and secured the route to India. At Trafalgar (1805) Nelson destroyed the French fleet. Napoleon, victorious on the Continent, was unable to invade the island kingdom; so he sought to ruin the "race of shopkeepers" by forbidding Europe to trade with Britain. In response Britain instituted a blockade of goods going into or out of European ports controlled by Napoleon. The United States, exasperated by Britain's interference with its commerce, declared war on Britain in 1812[1]. After Napoleon invaded Russia in 1812 and suffered a disastrous defeat, Britain mobilized its forces for a land war and joined a coalition with Russia, Austria, and Prussia. The center of fighting shifted to Spain, where a British force under the Duke of Wellington successfully fought its way across the country and invaded France in 1813. Two years later Wellington led the coalition of forces that decisively defeated Napoleon at the Battle of Waterloo and ended the French revolutionary wars. Before the year ended, a British ship carried off Napoleon to an island prison. The Congress of Vienna, which followed the end of the Napoleonic Wars, was a great diplomatic victory for Britain. France was left intact but its continental neighbors achieved security of their borders. The treaty created a balance of power among the nations of Europe that led to 40 years of peace on the continent. With peace established in Europe, Britain was free to spend its energy and resources on expanding its overseas empire.

Triumph over France brought Great Britain national glory and financial profit. The empire expanded and British control over sea routes was made secure. The increased demand for British goods stimulated commerce and quickened the pace of the Industrial Revolution. British blast furnaces and textile mills supplied munitions and clothes not only for the armies of Great Britain but for its allies as well.

The war swelled the fortunes of landlords, merchants, and manufacturers. Meanwhile, laissez-faire (from a French term, meaning "let it alone"), the rough beginning of a free market economy, was becoming the order of the day in industry.

Portrait of the Duke of Wellington by Francisco Goya , 1812 – 1814

3.1.2 The American Revolution

Before the Seven Years' War ended, George III began his 60-year reign, 1760 – 1820. Determined to "be a king" but quite unfit to be one, he got rid of Pitt and put his own Tory friend, Lord North in power. Britain's role in the imperial wars cost the country a great deal, and the national debt rose higher than it had ever been before. In order to lower the national debt, the Tory government imposed new taxes on the American colonies. The colonists insisted the British Parliament had no right to tax them without their consent. Beginning in 1763 Parliament passed laws to tax colonial commodities such as sugar, glass, cider, and tea. The most controversial of these duties was the Stamp Act of 1765, which taxed legal documents and publications. Americans not only complained about the cost of these taxes, but also questioned the British government's right to impose them. In 1775, 13 American colonies rebelled against British rule. The American Revolution gave France and Spain an opportunity to strike back at the British Empire. Both supported the American colonists with money and ultimately declared war on Britain. The British army was unprepared for war in North America, and it suffered a series of humiliating defeats, culminating in the surrender of British general Charles Cornwallis to American forces at Yorktown, Virginia, in 1781. The Royal Navy fared no better. When hostilities ended, Florida was returned to Spain, and the 13 rebellious colonies achieved independence as the United States of America.

George III in Coronation Robes, Portrait by Allan Ramsay, 1762

The loss of the American colonies came at great cost to Britain's self-image. George III was blamed for the disaster, and he decided to withdraw from direct control of government. Parliament regained its leadership. William Pitt the Younger became prime minister in 1783 and held the position for 17 years. In 1800 Pitt succeeded in bringing Ireland into a union with Great Britain similar to that between England and Scotland. The Act of Union[2] went into force January 1, 1801, creating the United Kingdom of Great Britain and Ireland. The mass of the Irish, however, being Catholics, were still excluded from the government because George III allowed only Church-of-England Irish to sit in Parliament.

3.1.3 The Industrial Revolution and Its Impact

The Industrial Revolution

The development of industry in Britain was a long and gradual process. Industrialization took place earlier and more rapidly in Britain than anywhere else because existing conditions were favorable in England. A system of internal waterways and canals and the absence of physical barriers to trade made the transport of goods less difficult than in other nations. Coalfields and thick forests, located conveniently close to large deposits of metal ores, provided fuel to power the furnaces that produced iron. Thriving commercial banks provided financing for investments in industrial plants and machinery. Advances in agriculture also contributed to the industrialization process.

The first phase of industrialization centered on the production of cotton clothing. At the beginning of the 18th century Britain still imported finished cotton cloth from India. Soon domestic manufacturing reversed this flow, and England became the world's primary supplier of cotton cloth. Two developments made this possible: the availability of cheap raw cotton from Egypt and America, and the invention of new machines that enabled workers to spin more thread and weave more cloth. One of these new machines was known as the spinning jenny invented by James Hargreaves in 1765. It used foot pedals to control the spinning of multiple threads. This device allowed a worker to spin 200 times as much thread in 1815 as could be spun 50 years earlier. Another mechanical device, the flying shuttle, quickly and automatically passed thread through a loom, the device on which cloth is woven. This flying shuttle enabled one person to operate a loom, whereas previously it had taken an entire team of workers. The operation of machinery became more efficient and profitable with the addition of waterpower and later the perfection of the rotary steam engine by Scottish inventor James Watt in 1784. Cotton production soared. By 1815 Britain was exporting 100 times the amount of cotton it had exported half a century earlier. Cotton became its most important product. With the introduction of machinery, factories became the site of organized production of textiles, replacing small-scale manufacture in the home.

A Watt steam engine was fuelled primarily by coal that propelled the Industrial Revolution in Great Britain and the world.

Iron was the miracle product of industrialization. Engineers used it to build the machines that powered production and ultimately the rails and engines that powered distribution. Iron had long been refined in England in furnaces that used charcoal as fuel. This process, known as smelting, involved heating iron ore to high temperatures to remove most of the impurities. However, charcoal left some impurities in the iron, which made it difficult to cast the iron into bars. Abraham

Darby, an English iron manufacturer, discovered that smelting with coke, a purified form of coal, made possible the production of a better product. Newly developed techniques allowed the iron to be heated and stirred in great vats until impurities had been burned off. Factory workers then fed the cooling iron through rolling machines that formed it into bars. By 1850 English manufacturers were producing more than half of the world's iron.

The most important use of this enormous output of iron was in building railroads. The railroads developed as a result of the technological advances made during the Industrial Revolution. The iron factories produced high-grade material suitable for constructing train engines and tracks. Skilled ironworkers provided machine parts of exact sizes. Inventors put Watt's steam engine to use, first to pump water from mines, then to drive pistons up and down, and finally to generate the rotary motion that propelled the wheels of trains. In 1829 engineer and inventor George Stephenson created an engine that could pull three times its weight and outrun a horse. The following year the first important railway opened, carrying coal and bulk goods between Manchester and Liverpool. It soon carried more people than products. Passenger travel by rail was faster, cheaper, and more comfortable than travel by coach. The introduction of the railroad changed forever concepts of speed and distance that were centuries old. Hundreds of independent railway companies sprang up. They invested millions of pounds to employ hundreds of thousands of laborers to lay thousands of miles of iron track. All railroad lines ultimately connected to London, the commercial center of the nation.

George Stephenson of England built the Rocket with his son, Robert, in 1829. It was the fastest steam locomotive of its time, with a speed of 36 miles (58 kilometers) per hour.

The Impact of Industrialization

Industrialization transformed nearly every aspect of British life. Firstly, productivity was greatly increased. By 1830 Britain produced half of Europe's iron and cotton, three-quarters of its coal, and nearly all of its steam engines. The English supplied the technological expertise for engineering in other countries, and they planned the railway systems for nearly all of Europe. Steam-powered ships made the world a smaller place in the same way that railroads had shrunk the British Isles. Bulk cargoes were now easily moved around the globe, and wealth poured into London and the commercial ports in western Britain. By rough estimates, the per capita wealth of England tripled from 1801 to 1851, a remarkable growth considering that the population doubled. Industrialization consolidated Britain's position as the greatest power in the world.

Secondly, with the industrial revolution, population was more and more concentrated in towns and cities. While the population as a whole grew by 100 percent between 1801 and 1851, the population of towns such as Liverpool and Manchester grew by 1,000 percent. London, which had about 1 million inhabitants by 1801, grew to more than 2.3 million by 1850. More remarkably, 9 towns had populations of more than 100,000, and more than 50 had populations of more than 20,000. By 1850 the urban population was half of the whole population of England.

Thirdly, this increase in wealth as the Industrial Revolution, however, did not benefit the poor. The rapid growth of capitalism caused miseries and disasters among the working people. Men and women toiled 12 to 18 hours a day in mines and factories. Wages were at starvation levels. Child labor was widespread. As a result of the introduction of machinery, unskilled workers, mostly women and children displaced handicraftsmen and skilled workers. Working and living conditions were horrible for the workers. Child labor was prevalent in Britain because children were a cheap source of labor for employers and easier to manage. They were forbidden to hold meetings, to organize unions, even to publish pamphlets. When workers rioted and smashed the new machines, the government made machine breaking a capital crime. In 1811, fourteen Luddites were put to death in Yorkshire after their destruction of two stocking frames. In 1819 one of Britain's largest public demonstrations was held in Manchester. Between 50,000 and 60,000 people appealed for political and economic reform. Government cavalry troops attacked the crowd. Eleven people died, and more than 400 sustained injuries in what came to be known as the Peterloo Massacre. This event was critical in the early history of labor organization in Britain; many moderate Britons were outraged at the government's action and gave their support to the emerging labor movement.

3.1.4 The Chartist Movement

The factory system established by industrialization made tremendous changes in the social structure. Two new classes had appeared—the capitalists, who owned the factories and machines, and the mass of the workers, who were dependent upon the capitalists for employment. Large manufacturing cities had risen in the north, close to the coalfields. Many of these cities had no representation in Parliament because no new boroughs had been created to send up members since the time of Charles II. In the south of England Tory proprietors of boroughs with few or no inhabitants (called pocket boroughs or rotten boroughs) continued to send representatives. When William IV began his short reign in 1830, the reform of Parliament had by now become the burning issue. Extreme Tories, led by the Duke of Wellington, stood fast against it. Reform groups in Parliament, including the moderate Tories, drew together and supported Earl Grey, the Whig leader. Wellington's government fell and the Whigs came into power. In 1832 Lord John Russell introduced a strong reform bill which was passed as the Great Reform Act. It created 43 new boroughs and deprived the rotten boroughs of their representatives in Parliament. The battle for universal suffrage, however, was still to be fought. The Reform Act slightly increased the number of voters by lowering the property qualifications; but the mass of the working people were still too poor to vote. Their living and working conditions were made worse by a series of bad harvests from 1837 to 1840. They came to realize that only by securing enough representation in Parliament could they force the government to pass the law in favor of the poor. This led to the outbreak of the Chartist Movement.

The Great Chartist Meeting on Kennington Common, London in 1848

In 1837, workers in London, organized in the London Working Men's Association[3], submitted a petition to Parliament as a result of widespread dissatisfaction with the Reform Bill of 1832 and the Poor Law of 1834. Later the petition became known as the People's Charter, which contained six specific demands, including suffrage for all male citizens 21 years of age and over, the abolition of the property qualification for MPs, elections by secret ballot, annual parliamentary elections, and payment for MPs. When these demands were rejected by the House of Commons, the association launched a nationwide campaign for its program, and about 1,250,000 persons signed a petition to Parliament requesting that the charter be enacted into law. When Parliament again rejected the charter, the Chartists planned direct action in the form of a general strike. The strike failed, but an insurrection broke out in Monmouth shire in November 1839, and many Chartist leaders were arrested and imprisoned. Chartism was in a period of decline until 1848, when another petition was sent to Parliament. Despite a large public demonstration, the charter was again rejected. The Chartist movement gradually disintegrated thereafter, but all the programs it advocated, except the demand for annual parliamentary elections, eventually became law. Meanwhile an Anti-Corn Law League had been formed in 1836, to campaign for the free entry of foreign wheat to feed the hungry poor. Sir Robert Peel, the Conservative prime minister, was finally converted to their view; and in 1846 he put through Parliament the famous bill repealing the Corn Laws[4].

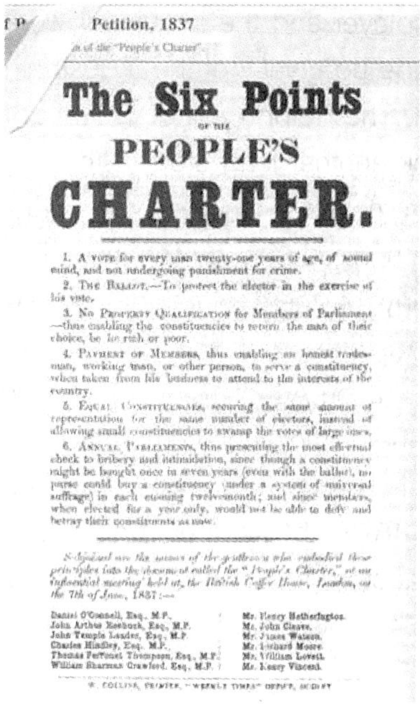
Petition, 1837

The Six Points of the PEOPLE'S CHARTER.

1. A vote for every man twenty-one years of age, of sound mind, and not undergoing punishment for crime.

2. The Ballot.—To protect the elector in the exercise of his vote.

3. No Property Qualification for Members of Parliament—thus enabling the constituencies to return the man of their choice, be he rich or poor.

4. Payment of Members, thus enabling an honest tradesman, working man, or other person, to serve a constituency, when taken from his business to attend to the interests of the country.

5. Equal Constituencies, securing the same amount of representation for the same number of electors, instead of allowing small constituencies to swamp the votes of large ones.

6. Annual Parliaments, thus presenting the most effectual check to bribery and intimidation, since though a constituency might be bought once in seven years (even with the ballot), no purse could buy a constituency (under a system of universal suffrage) in each ensuing twelvemonth; and since members, when elected for a year only, would not be able to defy and betray their constituents as now.

Subjoined are the names of the gentlemen who embodied these principles into the document called the "People's Charter," at an influential meeting held at the British Coffee House, London, on the 7th of June, 1837:—

Daniel O'Connell, Esq., M.P.	Mr. Henry Hetherington.
John Arthur Roebuck, Esq., M.P.	Mr. John Cleave.
John Temple Leader, Esq., M.P.	Mr. James Watson.
Charles Hindley, Esq., M.P.	Mr. Richard Moore.
Thomas Perronet Thompson, Esq., M.P.	Mr. William Lovett.
William Sharman Crawford, Esq., M.P.	Mr. Henry Vincent.

The People's Charter

3.1.5 Parliamentary Reform

The Reform Act created 43 new boroughs and deprived the rotten boroughs of their representatives in Parliament. The battle for universal suffrage, however, was still to be fought. The Reform Act slightly increased the number of voters by lowering the property qualifications; but the mass of the working people were still too poor to vote.

During the 1830s the Tories dropped their somewhat discredited name and became known as the Conservative party. The free-trade Conservatives gradually merged with the Whigs, who were to become the new Liberal party. Liberalism in the 19th century meant individualism. The true Liberal of that day championed freedom of thought and religion, freedom of trade, freedom of contract between the individual employer and the individual workman, and unrestricted competition. The party was made up chiefly of the industrial middle class.

The Reform Act of 1832 had benefited only the middle class. In 1867 Parliament took another long step in the direction of democracy by putting through the second Reform Act. This gave the vote to almost all adult males in the towns. The bill had been introduced by Benjamin Disraeli, a Conservative. Nevertheless the new voters, many of them workingmen, supported William Gladstone, Liberal leader. With Gladstone's first and greatest ministry, 1868 – 1874, an era of reform set in. The Education Act of 1870 set up elementary schools financed in part by the government. In the same year competitive examinations were introduced for employment in the civil service. The Trade Union Act of 1871 gave full legal recognition to trade unions. In 1872 the secret ballot was introduced in parliamentary elections. During Gladstone's second ministry, 1880 – 1885, a third Reform Bill[5] was enacted, in 1884. This gave rural voters the same voting privileges as the townspeople.

3.2 The British Empire and Two World Wars

Imperialism came into the ascendancy in 1874 with Benjamin Disraeli's Conservative ministry. Disraeli obtained for Britain financial control of the Suez Canal, key to Britain's eastern empire. In 1876 he had Queen Victoria declared empress of India. When Russia defeated Turkey and advanced close to Constantinople, he called the Congress of Berlin (1878), which checked Russian ambitions. During the three ministries of Robert Salisbury, the government brought the navy to a high state of efficiency and secured for Britain the lion's share in the partition of Africa. To stimulate interest in the empire, it celebrated the 50th and 60th years of Victoria's rule (1887 and 1897) with magnificent "jubilees" attended by Indian princes and representatives of all the far-flung dominions and colonies. Before the century ended,

Queen of the United Kingdom (1837 – 1901)

the British were engaged in the Boer War (1899 –1902) against the Dutch farmers (Boers) in South Africa. After some humiliating defeats, Britain won the war and annexed the two Boer republics, the Transvaal and the Orange Free State. Following annexation, Britain granted self-government to South Africa under the leadership of Jan Smuts, a Boer. Before the war was over, Queen Victoria died (1901), ending the longest reign in British history. Edward VII, her son, succeeded her.

3.2.1 Britain in World War I

When Edward VII came to the throne, in 1901, Britain was no longer the only "workshop of the world". The Industrial Revolution was now in full swing in other countries. Germany, the United States, and Japan competed strongly with Britain in foreign markets. Unemployment soon became chronic. Serious unrest stirred the working classes. Germany not only competed with British industry but had become the greatest military power on the Continent; and in 1900 it began to expand its navy, challenging British control of the seas. To meet this threat, Britain abandoned its "splendid isolation" and entered into an alliance with Japan in 1902. In 1904 it concluded the Entente Cordiale with France, and in 1907 it reached a similar agreement with Russia. By 1914 an extremely dangerous situation had developed. Germany and Austria-Hungary had made a military alliance. Russia and France, frightened of German ambitions, had made one also. Although Britain had no treaty with France, in practice it had no choice but to stand by France if it was attacked by Germany. A dreadful chain of events took place. In July 1914 Austria-Hungary declared war on its neighbor Serbia following the murder of a senior Austrian Archduke in Sarajevo. [6] Because Russia had promised to defend Serbia, it declared war on Austria-Hungary. Because of Germany's promise to stand by Austria-Hungary, Russia also found itself at war with Germany. France, Russia's ally, immediately made its troops ready, recognizing that the events in Serbia would lead inevitably to war with Germany. Britain still hoped that it would not be dragged into war, but realized only a miracle could prevent it. No miracle occurred. In August 1914 Germany attacked on France when France took its army through Belgium. Britain immediately declared war because it had promised to guarantee Belgium's neutrality by the treaty of 1838. But Britain went to war also because it feared that Germany's ambitions, like Napoleon's over a century earlier, would completely change the map of Europe. In particular Britain could not allow a major enemy power to control the Low Countries. Germany nearly defeated the Allies, Britain and France, in the first few weeks of war in 1914. It had better trained soldiers, better equipment and a clear plan of attack. The French army and the small British force were fortunate to hold back the German army at the River Marne, deep inside France. Four years of bitter fighting followed. When Russia, following the Bolshevik revolution of 1917, made peace with Germany, the German generals hoped for victory against the Allies. But German submarine attacks on neutral shipping drew America into the war against Germany. The arrival of American troops in France ended Germany's hopes, and it surrendered in November 1918. The destruction had been terrible. Over 750,000 had died and another two million had been seriously wounded.

The worldwide economic depression of 1929 struck Britain hard. Unemployment rose to 2.5 million within a year and to 3 million by the beginning of 1933. Ramsay MacDonald, the Labor prime minister, resigned in 1931 but agreed to sit in a national coalition government to handle the worsening crisis. The government put emergency measures into effect to raise income taxes on the wealthy, to reduce salaries of government workers, and to reduce unemployment benefits that were crippling the government. For the first time in a century, Britain abandoned free trade. The government placed duties on imports and encouraged the population to "buy British". Government programs to build houses and automobiles and expand electric utilities ultimately had their effect on the domestic economy. During the 1930s the government began to nationalize utilities, including coal, and to set wages and prices in large industries such as steel. By 1933 unemployment began to decline, especially in the newer industries, and by 1935 most sectors of the economy were recovering. Britain's share of world exports continued to shrink, however, and industries that had failed to modernize no longer remained competitive. Not only had the United States become an international competitor, but Germany, too, had survived the worst of the depression; its economy recovered as the result of a massive program of rearmament.

3.2.2 Britain in World War II

In 1933 Adolf Hitler came to power in Germany and soon began to rearm the country. Britain, absorbed in domestic troubles, was unprepared for war. Hitler seized Austria in March 1938, then made demands on Czechoslovakia. Britain, along with France, adopted a policy of appeasement[7], hoping Hitler's demands could be satisfied short of war. Neville Chamberlain, who had become prime minister in 1937, believed he had achieved "peace in our time" when Hitler pledged at Munich on September 30, 1938 that he had "no further territorial claims in Europe". Six months later Hitler broke the pact and took over most of Czechoslovakia. Britain joined with France in guaranteeing Poland's independence. Hitler took no action until after the Soviet Union signed a peace pact with Germany on August 24, 1939. Eight days later his army marched into Poland. Britain finally took a stand and declared war on Germany, World War II began. Germany quickly occupied France. During the following two years, the British faced the Germans alone in Europe. Other nations eventually entered the war. By 1941 a coalition led by Germany, Italy, and Japan (known as the Axis powers) faced an alliance of Britain, the Union of Soviet Socialist Republics, and the United States (known as the Allied powers).

As the military situation weakened, the will of the British people strengthened. Britain fought back, inspired by Britain's new prime minister, Winston Churchill, one of the greatest orators in the history of the nation. Britain's first important victory was at El Alamein when forces led by General Bernard Montgomery drove the Germans out of the Egyptian desert in 1942. This was followed by a defeat of Axis forces from North Africa and a joint invasion of Italy by Britain and the United States. In 1943 the Royal Air Force began its own bombardment of German cities, as well as German munitions and airplane factories. In the following year British forces participated in the D-Day invasion[8], which landed Allied troops in France. Following the landing, the British and Americans steadily pushed back German troops from the west, while the USSR advanced into Germany from the east. Fighting in Europe ended in May 1945 with the final defeat of Germany.

The war took a toll on British civilians unlike any conflict since the civil wars of the 17th century. For five years, inhabitants of every British city lived under blackout conditions in which lights were extinguished to prevent German bombers from spotting targets. The continual bombings of London and the industrial cities induced a feeling of resignation and helplessness among the population as shells exploded with random destructiveness. Toward the end of the war, rocket bombs created even greater terror—the rockets traveled with such speed that air-raid sirens were unable to warn the population.

Winston Churchill, Prime Minister of the United Kingdom from 1940 to 1945 and from 1951 to 1955

The war was an all-consuming experience for every Briton. More than 4.5 million men and women were in uniform overseas, and another 3 million were part of the Home Guard, which responded to air raids and prepared for the constantly anticipated German invasion. Industry shifted entirely to a war footing, and emergency measures gave the government control over nearly every element of the economy. Rationing of food and clothing created hardships. Even in victory, Britain was exhausted of its financial and industrial reserves. It was estimated that the war wiped out more than a quarter of the wealth of the entire nation.

3.2.3 The Decline of the British Empire

The British Empire suffered severe losses in territory and world influence in the years 1947-1949. India, Pakistan, and Ceylon (now Sri Lanka) became self-governing nations within the Commonwealth, and Burma (now Myanmar) gained complete independence. Eire (southern Ireland) cut all ties with Britain and took the name of the Republic of Ireland. On the continent of Europe, Britain no longer held its historic balance of power. Its status as a world power had declined drastically. Great Britain withdrew its last troops from the Suez Canal zone in June 1956.

The death knell of colonialism sounded in the 1950s and 1960s as most of the foreign territories of the European powers won independence. Throughout the 1960s independence was achieved by more than 20 British colonies and trusteeships in Africa, Asia, South America, and the West Indies. By the mid-1980s almost all of the Pacific and West Indies island units had also become independent. In 1997 Hong Kong returned to complete Chinese control for the first time since the middle of the 19th century.

3.3 Post-war Periods

In October 1963 Macmillan resigned. He was succeeded by another Conservative, Sir Alexander Frederick Douglas-Home. In 1964 Labourite Harold Wilson became prime minister. After a Conservative victory in 1970, Edward Heath took office. A pay strike by coal miners, in the midst of a worldwide energy crisis, led Heath to call a new election in February 1974, and Wilson returned as prime minister. Wilson resigned in March 1976 and was succeeded by another Labourite, James Callaghan. In 1979 Callaghan, who had headed a minority government for two years, became the first British prime minister since 1924 to lose office after a no-confidence motion.

3.3.1 The Thatcher Revolution

Margaret Thatcher, who had been the Conservative Party leader since 1975, became Britain's first woman prime minister in 1979. Thatcher was a strident Conservative, and she was determined not to give in to the unions or change from the course she had charted to revive the British economy. Thatcher based her policy on the theory of monetarism. This theory involved strictly controlling the money supply to reduce inflation, lowering tax rates to encourage investment, and minimizing government intervention in industry to remove restrictions on the expansion of businesses. The Thatcher government began privatizing industry, relaxing government regulation, and removing government subsidies. This was strong medicine and initially led to an even more rapid decline. By 1981 both interest rates and unemployment reached postwar highs, and a growing number of British firms faced bankruptcy. Pressure mounted to reverse government policy, and even members of Thatcher's own party threatened to revolt. Thatcher refused to abandon her policies.

A political crisis was averted only after war broke out when Argentina invaded the Falkland Islands, a British dependency in the South Atlantic that is also claimed by Argentina. The Falkland War released a mood of defiance in Britain in the wake of decades of international setbacks. Following Britain's victory in the war, the Conservatives won a resounding electoral victory in 1983. By the mid-1980s monetarist policy had brought down interest rates and mortgages for an increasing number of homeowners. It had dramatically curbed inflation, and the remaining British industries slowly became internationally competitive. At the same time, social programs came under attack with deep cuts in the National Health Service and in the budgets of local government. Conservative support was now evenly balanced between traditional upper-class Conservative voters and the lower middle classes, including skilled workers who saw their standard of living rise and their values of work, family, and personal responsibility vindicated.

The successes of Thatcherism[9] were tempered by the new social divisions it created. Scotland, Wales, and northern England all became economic backwaters; their industrial bases were in ruins, and an entire generation of workers was unemployed. Moreover, the new wealth that monetarism created—in the financial industry, real estate, and technology—led to many displays of luxury among the newly rich. The new wealth contrasted sharply with the loss of income experienced by many inner-city residents and unemployed middle-aged males. By 1990 she had become the longest-serving British leader of the century, but her 15-year tenure as head of the Conservative Party ended in that year. The reasons for discontent with Thatcherism ranged from her domineering personal style to the abolition of the local property tax in favor of a flat-rate community charge, or poll tax.

Margaret Thatcher was British Prime Minister from 4 May 1979 to 28 November 1990.

3.3.2 The Rise of New Labour

With loss of power, Thatcher resigned in November 1990. Her successor as prime minister was John Major, a top minister in her cabinet. In 1992 elections Major led the Conservatives to victory again, extending their winning streak to four elections since 1979. However, during Major's second term he came under severe scrutiny from opponents inside and outside the Conservative Party. In particular, the question of British integration in the EU split the party. In late 1996 the Conservatives lost their majority in Parliament for the first time since they took control of the government in 1979.

As the Conservatives splintered, they faced a serious threat from popular Labour Party leader Tony Blair. In 1994 the Labour Party elected Tony Blair, a young lawyer, as its leader. Under the title New Labour, Blair insisted that his party abandon its nearly century-old commitment to creating a socialist state. Blair benefited immediately from a series of scandals involving Conservative ministers and Members of Parliament. The public spectacle surrounding Prince Charles and Princess Diana, whose marital infidelities were openly discussed on national television and who were finally divorced in 1996, also hurt the Conservatives, who were strong supporters of the monarchy. Despite the continued economic boom—by 1996 inflation had nearly disappeared, unemployment was the lowest in Europe, and growth the highest—Labour led the Conservatives in polls by a significant margin. The general elections of 1997 gave the Labour Party the greatest landslide victory of the century and its largest-ever majority of 179 seats in Parliament. As the United Kingdom's youngest prime minister since the 19th century, Blair seemed to speak for a new generation and a new Britain. Blair attempted to maintain his centrist approach to government against the demands of the traditional Labour constituencies for social justice and the redistribution of wealth. In a bold beginning, he made the Bank of England independent of government. This move was designed to prevent monetary policy from being affected by political issues. In addition, he supported Parliament's decision to reconstitute the ancient parliaments of Scotland and Wales, giving them more regional control and political independence.

Blair also worked closely with Irish Prime Minister Bertie Ahern to revive the stalled peace negotiations in Northern Ireland. In April 1998 a new peace accord was signed that had strong backing from the British and Irish governments. Known as the Good Friday (or Belfast) Agreement[10], the accord authorized the creation of a semiautonomous assembly for Northern Ireland to replace direct rule of the province by the United Kingdom. The accord won overwhelming endorsement from voters in Ireland and Northern Ireland, and in December 1999 the United Kingdom formally transferred power to the new provincial assembly. However, an impasse between Catholic and Protestant groups over the pace of the Irish Republican Army's disarmament forced the United Kingdom to suspend the assembly in February 2000. Provincial rule was restored in May, but the disarmament issue remained unresolved and a source of persistent political tension.

Tony Blair was Prime Minister of the United Kingdom from 2 May 1997 to 27 June 2007.

Under Blair, the United Kingdom continued to play an active role in the European Union (EU). However, Britain's strong economy and monetary policy provided little incentive to accept the unified European currency, the euro. Blair's government backed away from its commitment to a complete economic union with the other EU countries because of the cost. In addition, the economic union had always been unpopular with many Britons. In early 1998 Blair announced a wait-and-see attitude toward monetary integration, an attitude that he maintained even as 11 EU countries officially adopted the euro in 1999.

In another move to modernize and streamline the government, in November 1999 Blair made good on a campaign promise to strip many of the hereditary peers in the

House of Lords of their right to sit and vote in Parliament. The House of Lords Act[11] eliminated all but 92 of the more than 750 seats held by hereditary members of Parliament's upper house.

Gordon Brown in 2008

Blair stepped down as prime minister in June 2007, and the Labour Party chose Gordon Brown as Blair's successor. Blair's resignation came at a time when Labour popularity was at a low ebb, in part because of the ongoing war in Iraq, in part because of unmet promises to reform and improve healthcare and education, and in part because of party scandals, including accusations that peerages were awarded in return for large contributions to the party. As Chancellor of the Exchequer in Blair's government, Brown was noted for his prudent economic management under which Britain had enjoyed a decade of economic growth.

David Cameron in 2010

At the 2010 general election on 6 May, David Cameron led the Conservatives to their best performance since the 1992 election (the last time the Conservatives had won). The Conservatives won the largest number of seats (306) but still 20 seats were short of an overall majority, resulting in the nation's first hung parliament[12] since February 1974. Talks between David Cameron and Liberal Democrat leader Nick Clegg led to an agreed Conservative/Liberal Democrat coalition, enabling the Queen to invite Cameron to form a government. At the age of 43, Cameron became the youngest British Prime Minister since the Earl of Liverpool 198 years earlier. The Cameron Ministry is the first coalition government in the United Kingdom since World War Ⅱ.

3.3.3 European Union

In 1959 Great Britain helped found the European Free Trade Association (EFTA). The more tightly knit European Economic Community (EEC) made greater economic gains, however, and the Macmillan government sought EEC entry to stimulate Britain's trade. Since the tariff agreements between Commonwealth countries conflicted with EEC regulations, long negotiations and compromises were necessary. France vetoed

Britain's bid for EEC membership in 1963 and again in 1967. On January 1, 1973, Britain finally joined the group, by then renamed the European Communities (EC) and later the European Union (EU). In 1988 Thatcher attacked a plan to establish a European federal economic and political state with a central bank and a common community currency. Her continued hard line against greater EC integration led to the division within her Conservative Party that contributed to her downfall in 1990. Major was chosen as head of the Conservative Party in 1990 after staking his bid to power on the idea of British integration in the EU. Many British Conservatives, however, began to lose confidence in the proposed creation of a single economic currency, known as the euro, on the grounds that the single currency system was a threat to national sovereignty. Some members of the party suggested that Major abandon plans to integrate British currency into the single-currency system. Divisions within the Conservative ranks concerning the question of integration contributed to the party's defeat in 1997. Following his election, Blair, who had described his stance on the EU as a "wait and see" policy during his 1997 campaign, emerged as a strong proponent for the strict continuance of the EU budgetary guidelines.

Notes

[1] war on Britain in 1812: The war was fought between the United States of America and the British Empire. Lasting from 1812 to 1815, it was fought chiefly on the Atlantic Ocean and on the land, coasts and waterways of North America.

[2] the Act of Union: It was passed on July 2, 1800; it united the Kingdom of Great Britain and the Kingdom of Ireland to create the United Kingdom of Great Britain and Ireland. The union came into effect on January 1, 1801.

[3] the London Working Men's Association: It was an organization established in London in 1836. It was one of the foundations of Chartism. They were associated with Owenite socialism and the movement for general education.

[4] the Corn Laws: They were import tariffs designed to protect corn prices in the United Kingdom of Great Britain and Ireland against competition from less expensive foreign imports between 1815 and 1846. These laws are often viewed as examples of British mercantilism, and their abolition marked a significant step towards free trade.

[5] third Reform Bill: It refers to the Representation of the People Act of 1884, which was the third reform to Britain's system of voting in the nineteenth century. It was to target rural areas that had been bypassed by the 1867 act.

[6] In July 1914 Austria-Hungary declared war on its neighbor Serbia following the murder of a senior Austrian Archduke in Sarajevo: On June 28, 1914, Archduke Franz Ferdinand of Austria, heir to the Austro-Hungarian throne, and his wife, Sophie, were shot dead in Sarajevo. The political objective of the assassination was to break Austria-Hungary's south-Slav provinces off so they could be combined into a Greater Serbia or a Yugoslavia. It is accepted by historians as the immediate cause of World War I.

[7] a policy of appeasement: It refers to the foreign policy of avoiding war with Germany by British Prime Minister Neville Chamberlain between 1937 and 1939.

[8] the D-Day invasion: On June 6, 1944, a date known ever since as D-Day, a mighty armada crossed a narrow strip of sea from England to Normandy, France, and cracked the Nazi grip on western Europe. D-Day has come to mean the greatest single allied operation of World War II, the invasion of Normandy.

[9] Thatcherism: Thatcherism describes the conviction politics, economic and social policy, and political style of the British Conservative politician Margaret Thatcher, who was leader of her party from 1975 to 1990. It claims to promote low inflation, the small state and free markets through tight control of the money supply, privatization and constraints on the labor movement.

[10] the Good Friday (or Belfast) Agreement: It refers to the agreement reached between the political parties of Northern Ireland and the British and Irish governments on Good Friday, April 10, 1998. It contained provisions for the resolution of the Northern Ireland conflict and for the shared governance of Northern Ireland between unionists and nationalists.

[11] the House of Lords Act: It was a major constitutional enactment that greatly reformed the House of Lords, one of the chambers of Parliament. For centuries, the House of Lords had included several hundred members who inherited their seats; the Act removed such a right. However, as part of a compromise, the Act did permit ninety-two hereditaries to remain in the House on an

interim basis. Another ten hereditaries were created life peers to be able to remain in the House.

[12] hung parliament: a parliament in which no political party has more elected representatives than the others added together.

Exercises

I. Fill in the following blanks with proper words or expressions.

1. The British Industrial Revolution first began in the ________ industry.
2. ________________ invented the "spinning Jenny" in 1765.
3. In 1800 ________________________ succeeded in bringing Ireland into a union with Great Britain similar to that between England and Scotland.
4. In 1815 ______________ led the coalition of forces that decisively defeated Napoleon at the Battle of Waterloo and ended the French revolutionary wars.
5. In 1837, workers in London, organized in the London Working Men's Association, submitted a petition to Parliament, which was known as ________________.
6. ______________ proposed by Lord John Russell in 1832, created 43 new boroughs and deprived the rotten boroughs of their representatives in Parliament.
7. In 1944, British forces participated in the ____________, which landed Allied troops in France.
8. To meet the threat of Soviet aggression, Britain joined ______________________, formed in 1949 and expanded its armament production.
9. ______________, who had been the Conservative party leader since 1975, became Britain's first woman prime minister.
10. In April 1998 ________________ was signed, which authorized the creation of a semiautonomous assembly for Northern Ireland to replace direct rule of the province by the United Kingdom.

II. Explain the following terms.

1. The Seven Years' War
2. The People's Charter
3. The Industrial Revolution
4. Thatcherism

III. Discuss the following questions.

1. What were the consequences of the British Industrial Revolution?
2. How did the British Empire fall?

Chapter Four

Political System

The politics of the United Kingdom of Great Britain and Northern Ireland takes place in the framework of a constitutional monarchy, in which the Monarch is head of state and the Prime Minister of the United Kingdom is the head of government. Executive power is exercised by the UK government, the devolved governments of Scotland and Wales, and the Executive of Northern Ireland. Legislative power is vested in both the government and the two chambers of Parliament, the House of Commons and the House of Lords, as well as in the Scottish parliament and Welsh and Northern Ireland assemblies. The judiciary is independent of the executive and the legislature, though several senior judges are still members of the House of Lords, which is currently the highest court of the UK for civil cases and the highest court of England and Wales for criminal cases. Starting in 2009 however, the judicial role of the House of Lords will be scrapped under the Constitutional Reform Act 2005.

The UK is a multi-party system and since the 1920s, the two largest political parties have been the Conservative Party and the Labour Party. Though coalition and minority governments have been an occasional feature of parliamentary politics, the first-past-the-post electoral system used for general elections tends to maintain the dominance of these two parties, though each has in the past century relied upon a third party to deliver a working majority in Parliament.

The Liberal Democrats, a party formed by the merger of the former Liberal Party and Social Democratic Party in 1988, is the third largest party in the British parliament. It seeks a reform of the electoral system to address the disproportionate dominance of the two main parties that results from the current system.

Growing support for "Nationalist" parties in Scotland and Wales led to proposals for devolution in the 1970s though only in the 1990s did devolution actually happen.

Today, Scotland, Wales and Northern Ireland each possess a legislature and government alongside that of the United Kingdom, responsible for devolved matters. However, it is a matter of dispute as to whether increased autonomy and devolution of executive and legislative powers have contributed to a reduction in support for full independence. The principal pro-independence party, the Scottish National Party, won 20 extra MSPs at the 2007 Scottish parliament elections and now forms the Scottish Government as a minority administration, with plans to hold a referendum on negotiating for independence, before 2011. In Wales, the nationalist party, Plaid Cymru, is the junior coalition partner in the Welsh Assembly Government although unlike the Scottish National Party it does not officially advocate complete secession from the United Kingdom. In Northern Ireland, the largest Pro-Belfast Agreement party, Sinn Féin, not only advocates Northern Ireland's unification with the Republic of Ireland, but also abstains from taking their elected seats in the Westminister government, as this would entail taking a pledge of allegiance to the British monarch.

The constitution is uncodified, being made up of constitutional conventions, statutes and other elements.

This system of government, known as the Westminster system, has been adopted by other countries as well, such as Canada, India, Australia, New Zealand, Singapore, Malaysia and Jamaica, countries that made up part of the British Empire.

4.1 Constitutional Monarchy

A constitutional monarchy is a form of government in which a monarch acts as head of state within the perimeters of a written (i. e., codified), unwritten (i. e., uncodified) or blended constitution. It differs from absolute monarchy in that an absolute monarch serves as the sole source of political power in the state and is not legally bound by any constitution.

Most constitutional monarchies employ a parliamentary system in which the Monarch may have strictly Ceremonial duties or may have Reserve Powers, depending on the constitution, have a directly or indirectly elected prime minister who is the head of government and exercises effective political power. In the past, constitutional monarchs have co-existed with fascist and quasi-fascist constitutions (Fascist Italy, Francoist Spain) and with military dictatorships.

Contemporary constitutional monarchies include Australia, Belgium, Cambodia, Canada, Denmark, Japan, Jordan, Lesotho, Luxembourg, Malaysia, Morocco,

New Zealand, Netherlands, Norway, Spain, Sweden, Thailand and the United Kingdom.

4.1.1 Monarch

The head of state, theoretical and nominal source of executive, judicial and legislative power in the UK is the British monarch, currently Queen Elizabeth II. However, sovereignty in the UK no longer rests with the monarch, since the English Bill of Rights in 1689, which established the principle of Parliamentary sovereignty. Nonetheless, the monarch is still known as the sovereign.

Queen Elizabeth II, the Current Monarch of the United Kingdom

The British sovereign possesses many powers, including the right to choose any British citizen to be her Prime Minister and the right to call and dissolve Parliament whenever she wishes. However, in accordance with the current uncodified constitution, the Prime Minister is the leader of the largest party in the House of Commons, and Parliament is dissolved at the time suggested by the PM. For a bill to become law the monarch has to grant Royal Assent. Queen Anne was the last monarch who withheld Assent: on March 11, 1708 to a bill "for the settling of Militia in Scotland". Other royal powers called royal prerogative, such as patronage to appoint ministers and the ability to declare war, are exercised by the Prime Minister and the Cabinet, with the formal consent of the Queen.

Historically, the British monarch directly exercised all executive authority in the UK government. However, in the early 18th century, the role of Prime Minister (literally meaning the chief or senior minister in the Cabinet) emerged as a de facto executive authority, by directly implementing executive powers and collectively consulting with other members of his/her Cabinet.

Today the sovereign has an essentially ceremonial role restricted in exercise of power by convention and public opinion. However the monarch does continue to exercise three essential rights: the right to be consulted, the right to advise and the right to warn. As a consequence of these ideals, Prime Ministers hold weekly confidential meetings with the monarch in which the sovereign holds the right to express her opinions.

In formal terms, the Crown in Parliament is sovereign even though in practical terms the political head of the UK is the Prime Minister (David Cameron since May 11, 2010). However, the real powers of position of the monarch in the British Constitution should not be downplayed. The monarch does indeed retain some power, but it has to be used with discretion. She fulfills the necessary constitutional role as head of state, and with the absence of a distinct separation of powers as in the American model and a strong second chamber, acts as a final check on executive power. If a time came to pass, for instance, when a law threatened the freedom or security of her subjects and citizens, the Queen could decline royal assent, free as she is from the eddies of party politics. Furthermore, armed removal of her by Parliament or Government would be difficult, as the monarch remains commander-in-chief of the armed forces, who swear an oath of allegiance to her.

4.1.2 The Constitution

The constitution of the United Kingdom is the set of laws and principles under which the United Kingdom is governed.

The UK has no single constitutional document comparable to those of most other nations. It is therefore often said that the country has an "unwritten", uncodified, or de facto constitution. However, the word "unwritten" is something of a misnomer as the majority of the British constitution does exist in the written form of statutes, court judgments, and treaties. The constitution has other unwritten sources, including parliamentary constitutional conventions and the royal prerogatives.

The bedrock of the British constitution has traditionally been the doctrine of parliamentary sovereignty, according to which the statutes passed by Parliament are the UK's supreme and final source of law. It follows that Parliament can change the constitution simply by passing new Acts of Parliament. There is some debate about whether this principle remains entirely valid today. One reason for the uncertainty derives from the UK's membership of the European Union.

4.2 Three Branches of Power

4.2.1 Executive

The United Kingdom Government

The monarch appoints a Prime Minister as head of Her Majesty's Government, guided by the strict convention that the Prime Minister should be the member of the House of Commons most likely to be able to form a Government with the support of that House. In practice, this means that the leader of the political party with an absolute majority of seats in the House of Commons is chosen to be the Prime Minister. The Prime Minister then selects the other Ministers which make up the Government and act as political heads of the various Government Departments. About twenty of the most senior government ministers make up the Cabinet and approximately 100 ministers in total comprise the government. In accordance with constitutional convention, all ministers within the government are either Members of Parliament or peers in the House of Lords.

Arms of the British Government
(A Variation of the Royal Arms)

As in some other parliamentary systems of government (especially those based upon the Westminster System), the executive (called "the government") is drawn from and is answerable to Parliament—a successful vote of no confidence will force the government either to resign or to seek a parliamentary dissolution and a general election. In practice, members of parliament of all major parties are strictly controlled by whips who try to ensure they vote according to party policy. If the government has a large majority, then they are very unlikely to lose enough votes to be unable to pass legislation.

The Prime Minister and the Cabinet

The Prime Minister, as the label suggests, is the prime or senior minister in the Cabinet. S/he is responsible for chairing Cabinet meetings, selecting Cabinet ministers (and all other positions in Her Majesty's government), and formulating governmental policy. The Prime Minister is the de facto source of executive authority in the UK government, since s/he exercises executive functions that are nominally vested in the sovereign (by way of the Royal Prerogatives). Historically, the British monarch was the sole source of executive powers in the government. However, following the rule of the Hanoverian monarchs, an arrangement of a "Prime Minister" chairing and leading the Cabinet began to emerge. Over time, this arrangement became the effective executive branch of government, as it assumed the day-to-day functioning of the British government away from the sovereign.

Theoretically, the Prime Minister is *primus inter pares* (i. e., Latin for "first among equals") among his/her Cabinet colleagues. While the Prime Minister is the senior Cabinet Minister, s/he is theoretically bound to make executive decisions in a collective fashion with the other Cabinet ministers. The Cabinet, along with the PM, consists of Secretaries of State from the various government departments. Cabinet meetings are typically held weekly, while Parliament is in session.

Government Departments and the Civil Service

The Government of the United Kingdom contains a number of ministries known mainly, though not exclusively as departments, e. g. Ministry of Defence. These are politically led by a Government Minister who is often a Secretary of State and member of the Cabinet. He or she may also be supported by a number of junior Ministers. In practice, several government departments and Ministers have responsibilities that cover England alone, with devolved bodies having responsibility for Scotland, Wales and Northern Ireland (for example, the Department of Health), or responsibilities that mainly focus on England (such as the Department for Children, Schools and Families).

Implementation of the Minister's decisions is carried out by a permanent politically neutral organization known as the civil service. Its constitutional role is to support the Government of the day regardless of which political party is in power. Unlike some other democracies, senior civil servants remain in post upon a change of Government. Administrative management of the Department is led by a head civil servant known in most Departments as a Permanent Secretary. The majority of the civil service staff in fact work in executive agencies, which are separate operational organizations reporting to Departments of State.

"Whitehall" is often used as a synonym for the central core of the Civil Service. This is because most Government Departments have headquarters in and around the former Royal Palace Whitehall.

4.2.2 Legislature

The UK Parliament is the supreme legislative body in the United Kingdom (i. e., there is parliamentary sovereignty), and Government is drawn from and answerable to it. Parliament is bicameral, consisting of the House of Commons and the House of Lords. There is also a devolved Scottish Parliament and devolved Assemblies in Wales and Northern Ireland, with varying degrees of legislative authority.

UK Parliament

▲ House of Commons

The countries of the United Kingdom are divided into parliamentary constituencies of broadly equal population by the four Boundary Commissions. Each constituency elects a Member of Parliament (MP) to the House of Commons at General Elections and, if required, at by-elections. The number of constituencies will increase from the current 646 to 650 at the next general election. Of the current 646 MPs, all but one belong to a political party. In modern times, all Prime Ministers and Leaders of the Opposition have been drawn from the Commons, not the Lords. Alec Douglas--Home resigned from his peerages days after becoming Prime Minister in 1963, and the last Prime Minister before him from the Lords left in 1902 (the Marquess of Salisbury).

Parliament meets at the Palace of Westminster.

One party usually has a majority in Parliament, because of the use of the First Past the Post electoral system, which has been conducive in creating the current two-party system. The monarch normally asks a person commissioned to form a government simply whether it can survive in the House of Commons, something which majority governments are expected to be able to do. In exceptional circumstances the monarch asks someone to "form a government" with a parliamentary minority, which in the event of no party having a majority requires the formation of a coalition government. This option is only ever taken at a time of national emergency, such as war-time. It was given in 1916 to Andrew Bonar Law, and when he declined, to David Lloyd George and in 1940 to Winston Churchill. It is worth noting that a government is not formed by a vote of the House of Commons, merely a commission from the monarch. The House of Commons gets its first chance to indicate confidence in the new government when it votes on the Speech from the Throne (the legislative programme proposed by the new government).

▲ House of Lords

The House of Lords was previously a largely hereditary aristocratic chamber, although including life peers, Law Lords and Lords Spiritual. It is currently mid-way through extensive reforms, the most recent of these being enacted in the House of Lords Act 1999. The house still currently consists of two very different types of member, the Lords Temporal and Lords Spiritual. Lords Temporal include appointed members (life peers with no hereditary right for their descendants to sit in the house) and ninety-two remaining hereditary peers, elected from among, and by, the holders of titles which previously gave a seat in the House of Lords. The Lords Spiritual represent the established Church of England and number 26, the Archbishops of York and of Canterbury and the 24 most senior Bishops of the church.

The House of Lords currently acts to review legislation initiated by the House of Commons, with the power to propose amendments, and can exercise a suspensive veto. This allows it to delay legislation if it does not approve it for twelve months. However, the use of vetoes is limited by convention and by the operation of the Parliament Acts 1911 and 1949: the Lords may not veto the "money bills" or major manifesto promises (see Salisbury convention). Persistent use of the veto can also be overturned by the Commons, under a provision of the Parliament Act 1911. Often governments will accept changes in legislation in order to avoid both the time delay, and the negative publicity of being seen to clash with the Lords. However the Lords still retain a full veto in acts which would extend the life of Parliament beyond the 5-year term limit introduced by the Parliament Act 1911.

The House of Lords is currently also the final court of appeal on civil cases within the United Kingdom, although in practice only a small subset of the House of Lords, known as the Law Lords, hears judicial cases. In accordance with the legal doctrine of stare decisis[1], the House of Lords supersedes all civil and criminal courts in England and Wales. (The House of Lords has no role in criminal case appeals in Scotland.) The Constitutional Reform Act 2005 outlines plans for a Supreme Court of the United Kingdom to replace the role of the Law Lords.

4.2.3 Judiciary

The United Kingdom does not have a single legal system due to it being created by the political union of previously independent countries with the terms of the Treaty of Union guaranteeing the continued existence of Scotland's separate legal system. Today the UK has three distinct systems of law: English law, Northern Ireland law and Scots law. Recent constitutional changes will see a new Supreme Court of the United Kingdom come into being in October 2009 that will take on the appeal functions of the Appellate Committee of the House of Lords. The Judicial Committee of the Privy Council, comprising the same members as the Appellate Committee of the House of Lords, is the highest court of appeal for several independent Commonwealth countries, the UK overseas territories, and the British crown dependencies.

England, Wales and Northern Ireland

Both English law, which applies in England and Wales, and Northern Ireland law are based on common-law principles. The essence of common-law is that law is made by judges sitting in courts, applying their common sense and knowledge of legal precedent (stare decisis) to the facts before them. The Courts of England and Wales are headed by the Supreme Court of Judicature of England and Wales, consisting of the Court of Appeal, the High Court of Justice (for civil cases) and the Crown Court (for criminal cases). The Appellate Committee of the House of Lords (usually just referred to, as "The House of Lords") is presently the highest court in the land for both criminal and civil cases in England, Wales, and Northern Ireland and any decision it makes is binding on every other court in the hierarchy.

Scotland

Scots law, a hybrid system based on both common-law and civil-law principles, applies in Scotland. The chief courts are the Court of Session, for civil cases, and the High Court of Justiciary, for criminal cases. The Appellate Committee of the House of Lords (usually just referred to as "The House of Lords") presently serves as the highest court of appeal for civil cases under Scots law but only if the Court of Session grants leave to appeal or the initial judgement was by a majority decision. Sheriff courts deal with most civil and criminal cases including conducting criminal trials with a jury, known as sheriff solemn court, or with a sheriff and no jury, known as sheriff summary court. The sheriff courts provide a local court service with 49 sheriff courts organised across six Sheriffdoms.

4.3 The Party System

Historically, the United Kingdom had two major political parties, though currently three parties dominate the political landscape. Originally, the Conservatives and the Liberals dominated British politics, but the Liberal Party collapsed in the early twentieth century and was largely replaced by the Labour Party. In the 1980s, the Liberals merged with the Social Democratic Party and, as the Liberal Democrats, they are viewed as the third major party. Other parties, often called minor parties (in UK terms at least) contest elections but few except those which are based in single countries of the United Kingdom win seats in Parliament. The Scottish National Party has had MPs continuously since 1967, and Plaid Cymru, the Welsh nationalists, has had MPs continuously since 1974. All 18 MPs elected from Northern Ireland are from parties that just contest elections in Northern Ireland (or in the case of Sinn Féin, the island of Ireland.)

In the most recent general election in 2005, the Labour Party won re-election on a reduced majority, with both the Conservatives and Liberal Democrats making gains.

Labour

The Labour Party won the majority of seats in the House of Commons at the 2005 general election, with 356 MPs.

The history of the Labour Party goes back to 1900 when a Labour Representation Committee was established which changed its name to the Labour Party in 1906. After the First World War, this led to the demise of the Liberal Party as the main reformist force in British politics. The existence of the Labour Party on the left of British politics led to a slow waning of energy from the Liberal Party, which has consequently assumed third place in national politics. After performing poorly in the elections of 1922, 1923 and 1924, the Liberal Party was superseded by the Labour Party as the party of the left.

Following two brief spells in minority governments in 1924 and 1929 - 1931, the Labour Party had its first true victory after World War II in the 1945 "khaki election". Throughout the rest of the twentieth century, Labour governments alternated with Conservative governments. The Conservatives were in power for most of the time, with the Labour Party suffering the "wilderness years" of 1951 - 1964 (three straight general election defeats) and 1979 - 1997 (four straight general election defeats).

During this second period, Margaret Thatcher, who became leader of the Conservative Party in 1975, made a fundamental change to Conservative policies, turning the Conservative Party into an economic neoliberal party. In the General Election of 1979 she defeated James Callaghan's troubled Labour government after the winter of discontent.

For most of the 1980s and the 1990s, Conservative governments under Thatcher and her successor John Major pursued policies of privatization, anti-trade-unionism, and, for a time, Monetarism, now known collectively as Thatcherism.

The Labour Party elected left-winger Michael Foot as their leader after their 1979 election defeat, and he responded to dissatisfaction with the Labour Party by pursuing a number of radical policies developed by its grass-roots members. In 1981 several right-wing Labour MPs formed a breakaway group called the Social Democratic Party (SDP), a move which split Labour and is widely believed to have made Labour unelectable for a decade. The SDP formed an alliance with the Liberal Party which contested the 1983 and 1987 general elections as a centrist alternative to Labour and the Conservatives. After some initial success, the SDP did not prosper (partly due to its unfavourable distribution of votes in the FPTP electoral system), and was accused by some of splitting the anti-Conservative vote.

The SDP eventually merged with the Liberal Party to form the Liberal Democrats in 1988. Support for the new party has increased since then, and the Liberal Democrats (often referred to as LibDems) in 1997 and 2001 gained an increased number of seats in the House of Commons.

The Labour Party was badly defeated in the Conservative landslide of the 1983 general election, and Michael Foot was replaced shortly thereafter by Neil Kinnock as leader. Kinnock expelled the far left militant tendency group and moderated many of the party's policies. Yet he was in turn replaced by John Smith after Labour defeats in the 1987 and 1992 general elections.

Tony Blair became leader of the Labour party after John Smith's sudden death from a heart attack in 1994. He continued to move the Labour Party back towards the "centre" by loosening links with the unions and embracing many of Margaret Thatcher's liberal economic policies. This, coupled with the professionalising of the party machine's approach to the media, helped Labour win a historic landslide in the 1997 general election, after 18 years of Conservative government. Some observers said the Labour Party had by then morphed from a democratic socialist party to a social democratic party, a process which delivered three general election victories but alienated some of its core base.

Conservatives (Tories)

The Conservative Party won the second largest number of seats (still under 200) at the 2005 general election and remained the official opposition, a position they have held continuously since they lost power at the 1997 general election. The crushing defeat of the 1997 election saw them lose over half their seats from 1992 and saw the party re-align with public perceptions of them.

The Conservative Party can trace its origin back to 1662, with the Court Party and the Country Party being formed in the aftermath of the English Civil War. The Court Party soon became known as the Tories, a name that has stuck despite the official name being "Conservative". The term "Tory" originates from the Exclusion Bill crisis of 1678 - 1681—the Whigs were those who supported the exclusion of the

Roman Catholic Duke of York from the thrones of England, Ireland and Scotland, and the Tories were those who opposed it. Both names were originally insults: A "whiggamore" was a horse drover, and a "tory" was an Irish term for an outlaw, later applied to Irish Confederates and Irish Royalists, during the Wars of the Three Kingdoms.

Generally, the Tories were associated with lesser gentry and the Church of England, while Whigs were more associated with trade, money, larger land holders (or "land magnates"), expansion and tolerance.

The Rochdale Radicals were a group of more extreme reformists who were also heavily involved in the cooperative movement. They sought to bring about a more equal society, and are considered by modern standards to be left-wing.

After becoming associated with repression of popular discontent in the years after 1815, the Tories underwent a fundamental transformation under the influence of Robert Peel, himself an industrialist rather than a landowner, who in his 1834 "Tamworth Manifesto" outlined a new "Conservative" philosophy of reforming ills while conserving the good.

Robert Peel

Though Peel's supporters subsequently split from their colleagues over the issue of free trade in 1846, ultimately joining the Whigs and the Radicals to form what would become the Liberal Party, Peel's version of the party's underlying outlook was retained by the remaining Tories, who adopted his label of Conservative as the official name of their party.

In 2008, the Conservative Party formed a pact with the Ulster Unionist Party to select joint candidates for European and House of Commons elections, this angered the UUP as by splitting the Unionist vote, republican parties would be elected in some areas.

Liberal Democrats

The Liberal Democrats won the third largest number of seats at the 2005 general election, winning 62.

The Liberal Democrats were formed in 1988 by a merger of the Liberal Party with the Social Democratic Party, but can trace their origin back to the Whigs and the Rochdale Radicals who evolved into the Liberal Party. The term "Liberal Party" was first used officially in 1868, though it had been in use colloquially for decades beforehand. The Liberal Party formed a government in 1868 and then alternated with the Conservative Party as the party of government throughout the late 19th century and early 20th century.

4.4 Current Political Landscape

Since the 2005 general election, each of the main political parties has changed party leader: David Cameron was elected leader of the Conservatives in 2005, Gordon Brown was elected unopposed to lead the Labour Party (and therefore become Prime Minister) in June 2007, and Nick Clegg was elected leader of the Liberal Democrats in December 2007.

The Conservatives under David Cameron have seen their popularity grow, as shown by their success at the local elections in May 2008, the London mayoral election and opinion polls which showed a strong lead over Labour. They also won a by-election in Crewe and Nantwich with a swing of 17.6%.

In Scotland, the Scottish National Party (SNP) made some strong advances, winning the Scottish general election in May 2007 and gaining support in most national opinion polls since then. In July 2008, the SNP achieved a remarkable by-election victory in Glasgow East, winning the third safest Labour seat in Scotland with a swing of 22.54%. However, in October of the same year, despite confident public predictions by the SNP's leader Alex Salmond that they would win another by-election in Glenrothes, the seat was comfortably won by Labour with a majority of 6,737 and an increased share of the vote. Given that the SNP won the equivalent Holyrood seat in 2007 this was viewed as a significant step back for the SNP. More recently, the SNP significantly out-polled the Labour Party in the 2009 European election.

David Cameron studied philosophy, politics and economics at Oxford University, gaining a first class honours degree. He then joined the Conservative Research Department and became Special Adviser to Norman Lamont, and then to Michael Howard. He was Director of Corporate Affairs at Carlton Communications for seven years.

A first candidacy for Parliament at Stafford in 1997 ended in defeat, but Cameron was elected in 2001 as the Member of Parliament for the Oxfordshire constituency of Witney. He was promoted to the Opposition front bench two years later, and rose rapidly to become head of policy co – ordination during the 2005 general election campaign. With a public image of a young, moderate candidate who would appeal to young voters, he won the Conservative leadership election in 2005.

In the 2010 general election held on May 6, the Conservatives gained a plurality of seats in a hung parliament and Cameron was appointed Prime Minister on May 11, 2010, at the head of a coalition between the Conservatives and the Liberal Democrats. At the age of 43, Cameron became the youngest British Prime Minister since the Earl of Liverpool 198 years earlier. The Cameron Ministry is the first coalition government [2] in the United Kingdom since the Second World War.

Notes

[1] Stare decisis: It is the legal principle by which judges are obliged to respect the precedents established by prior decisions. The words originate from the Latin phrase *Stare decisis et non quieta movere*: stand by decisions and do not disturb the undisturbed. In a legal context, this is understood to mean that courts should generally abide by precedents and not disturb settled matters.

[2] A coalition government: It refers to a cabinet of a parliamentary government in which several parties cooperate. The usual reason given for this arrangement is that no party on its own can achieve a majority in the parliament. A coalition government might also be created in a time of national difficulty or crisis, for example during wartime, to give a government the high degree of perceived political legitimacy it desires whilst also playing a role in diminishing internal political strife. In such times, parties have formed all - party coalitions (national unity governments, grand coalitions). If a coalition collapses, a confidence vote is held or a motion of no confidence is taken.

Exercises

I. Fill in the following blanks with proper words or expressions.

1. The politics of the United Kingdom of Great Britain and Northern Ireland takes place in the framework of a ____________, in which the Monarch is head of state and the Prime Minister of the United Kingdom is the head of government.
2. Sovereignty in the UK no longer rests with the monarch, since the English ________ in 1689, which established the principle of Parliamentary sovereignty.

3. The UK has no ________ comparable to those of most other nations. It is therefore often said that the country has an "unwritten", uncodified, or de facto constitution.
4. The ________ is the de facto source of executive authority in the UK government.
5. Parliament is bicameral, consisting of the ________ and the ________.
6. Each constituency elects a (n) ________ to the House of Commons at General Elections.
7. The House of Lords was previously a largely ____________ chamber, although including life peers, Law Lords and Lords Spiritual.
8. Historically, the United Kingdom had ________ major political parties, though currently three parties dominate the political landscape.
9. Margaret Thatcher, who became leader of the Conservative Party in 1975, made a fundamental change to Conservative policies, turning the Conservative Party into an ____________ party.
10. Britain is arguably the oldest ____________ in the world.

Ⅱ. Explain the following terms.

1. The Bill of Rights
2. The House of Commons
3. constitutional monarchy
4. general elections
5. The Conservative Party

Ⅲ. Discuss the following questions.

1. What is the significance of Magna Carta to the establishment of British Parliamentary Democracy?
2. How did Constitutional Monarchy of Britain influence the world history?

Chapter Five

Economy

By January 2009, the United Kingdom is the six largest economy in the world by nominal Gross Domestic Product. And in history the UK was the first country in the world to industrialise in the 18th and 19th centuries, and for much of the 19th century possessed a predominant role in the global economy. It used to be the "workshop of the world" Despite the decline of its role in the world economy, at the start of the 21st century Britain still maintains an important role in the global economy, due to its large GDP and the financial importance that its capital, London, possesses in the world.

Though Britain ranks among the countries that first entered the capitalist society, after World War Ⅱ it had entered a stage of nationalization and welfare state. After Thatcher's reforms in the 1980s, it was again termed a liberal economy. But there has long been strife between nationalization and privatization in this country. Today, the UK labor is even making efforts to extend privatization of the National Health Service.

The United Kingdom is one of the world's most globalised countries. The capital, London (especially the district called the City of London), is a major financial centre for international business and commerce and one of three "command centres" for the global economy (along with New York City and Tokyo). In 1973, the UK acceded to the European Economic Community [1]. Moreover, Britain is a member of the World Trade Orgnization and other international organizations related to economy.

5.1 A Historical Overview

British economy declined after reaching its peak at the end of the 19th century.

By 1900 the UK was overtaken by both the United States and Germany. From 1945 until now there has gone the story of an economic decline in Britain. However, the general decline trend as compared with other major states should hide the fact that Britain has constantly been one of the major industrial countries in the world.

With help from the United States the British economy quickly recovered after World War II. For a time it came second in GDP after the US. And there had been a long interval without a major recession (1945 – 1973) and a growth in prosperity in the 1950s and 1960s. The annual rate of growth between 1960 and 1973 averaged 2.9%. The national economy grew steadily. And pursuing the economic policy based on the theory of John M. Keynes [2], the British government gave priority to full employment of all workers. Fiscal and monetary policy was adopted to finetune aggregate demand while prices and incomes policy to suppress inflation at source.

However, following the severe shock of the 1973 oil crisis and the 1973 – 1974 stock market crash, the British economy went into recession in 1974, with GDP falling by 1.1%, recording weaker growth than other European nations in the 1970s. In some years of the period, Britain even had a minus growth and the trade deficits [3] were the highest among the Western countries.

A new period of neo-liberal economics began with the advent of the government of Margaret Thatcher of 1979. The new economic policy featuring the theory of the new classical school of thought turned Keynesianism on its head[4]. Most state-owned enterprises in the industrial and service sectors, which since the 1940s had been nationalised, were privatised. The new government laid emphasis on privatization, deregulation and market liberalization. As a result, the British Government owned very few industries or businesses. GDP fell 5.9% at first then rose to 5% at its peak in 1988.

After a mild recession in the early 1990s, there followed the longest uninterrupted period of growth in 200 years, achieving growth in every quarter between 1992 and 2007, one of the highest economic growth rates of major developed economies during that time. According to John Major, who was Prime Minister between 1990 and 1997, he "inherited a sick economy and passed on a sound one". Peak growth was relatively anaemic compared to past rates of growth, such as the 6.5% peak in the early 1970s, although overall growth was more sustained than earlier. This trend is clearly demonstrated during Tony Blair's 10 years in office, when the economic growth was unspectacular, but steady. A strong world economy, rising immigration and public spending helped to boost growth. Annual growth rates averaged 2.68% between 1992 and 2007, with the finance sector growth contributing a greater part than previously.

In 2007, according to the International Monetary Fund, the United Kingdom had the ninth highest level of GDP per capita [5] in the European Union in terms of PPP (purchasing power parity). The UK economy had been one of the strongest EU economies in terms of inflation, interest rates and unemployment. However, in common with the economies of other English-speaking countries, it has higher levels of income inequality than many European countries. In 2007, the UK had the world's third largest current account deficit, despite significant oil revenues. This was mainly the result of a large deficit in the trade in manufactured goods.

Unfortunately, this boom ended in 2008 when the United Kingdom entered a recession brought about by the global financial crisis. GDP decreased by 0.7% in the second quarter of 2009, after a decrease of 2.4% in the first quarter. In May 2009 the European Commission stated, "The UK economy is now clearly experiencing one of its worst recessions in recent history." The EC expected GDP to decline 3.8% in 2009 and projected that growth will remain negative for the first three quarters of 2009. It predicted two quarters of "virtual stagnation" in late 2009 – early 2010, followed by a gradual return to "slight positive growth by late 2010". Facing the situation, the incumbent Prime Minister Gordon Brown [6] now takes measures both at grass-roots level and of global proportions to curb the aftermath of this global slowdown in economy.

5.2 Natural Resources

Natural resources are things that occur naturally, and that are useful to us. They include fuels such as oil and natural gas, and materials such as iron ore, and timber. There are renewable resources and non-renewable resources. Care is needed to make sure resources are used sustainably and not over-harvested. The non-renewable resources coal, oil and natural gas constitute the fossil fuels.

5.2.1 Fossil fuels

Britain has large deposits of coal, an estimated 243 million short tons [7] in 2003. Important coal areas can be found in Central Lowlands of Scotland, Northeast England, Central England and South Wales around such big cities as Glasgow, Edinburgh, Newcastle, Sheffield, Nottingham, Manchester, Birmingham and Swansea.

Coal has been mined for more than 300 years. For most of the 19th and 20th centuries, coal was Britain's richest natural resource, meeting most of the nation's requirement for energy. In 1970 the UK was the third largest producer of coal but coal production has declined rapidly since then. Decreasing domestic consumption and a surge of low-cost imports have been the principal causes of the production decline. The UK now imports more coal than it produces domestically. In order to meet its obligations under the Kyoto Protocol [8], the UK likely will continue to phase out coal consumption and production.

Oil and gas were discovered under the North Sea during the 1960s and new supplies are still being found today. Gas has been particularly important in replacing coal as a fuel for generating electricity.

The UK had 4 billion barrels of proven crude oil reserves in 2006, the most of any EU member country. The UK Continental Shelf, located in the North Sea off the eastern coast of the UK, contains the bulk of the country's oil reserves. The UK consumed 1.8 million barrels per day of oil in 2005. The importance of oil to the UK economy has declined slightly over the past two decades, with oil's contribution to total energy consumption falling from 37 percent in 1983 to 35 percent in 2003. The UK government expects oil production in the country to continue to decline, reaching 1.38 million barrels per day by 2009.

The UK held an estimated 18.8 trillion cubic feet of proven natural gas reserves in 2006. Most of these reserves occur in three distinct areas: (1) associated fields in the UK continental shelf; (2) non-associated fields in the Southern Gas Basin, located adjacent to the Dutch sector of the North Sea; and (3) non-associated fields in the Irish Sea. In order to take advantage of its domestic reserves, the UK government has encouraged the use of natural gas, including its substitution for coal and oil in industrial consumption and electricity production. With the increase of natural gas consumption, in 2004 the UK became a net importer of natural gas for the first time since 1996.

5.2.2 Hydroelectricity and Wind Power

With the non-renewable resources ever declining, more efforts are made to make use of renewable resources that can be replaced by natural processes at a rate comparable or faster than their rate of consumption by humans, including solar radiation, tides, winds and hydroelectricity.

In the UK, the majority of electricity is generated by a mix of fossil fuels and nuclear power. Moreover, Britain makes use of water and wind power to supply energy. It currently generates about 1.3 percent of its electricity from hydroelectric schemes—most of which are large-scale schemes in the Scottish Highlands. The country saw a large scale of hydroelectricity development in the 1940s and 1950s.

However, opportunities to use this technology on a large scale are now becoming more limited, not only because of environmental concerns, but also because many of the most economically attractive sites for schemes have already been used.

Now the business of generating electricity from the wind is growing fast as the world looks for cleaner ways to produce energy. Wind farms and other forms of renewable energy are expected to eventually replace coal-, oil- and gas-fired power stations. In 1997, there were 550 wind turbines and over 30 wind farms in the UK. The government has made a promise that 10% of the energy of the UK will come from renewable sources by 2010.

Britain is ready for huge wind power increase.

5.2.3 Minerals

Britain has relatively few mineral resources. Zinc, tin, iron ore, and copper are all produced in small quantities.

At one time Cornwall boasted 2,000 tin mines and it was a world leader in tin production.

Britain's main commercial minerals are those used in the construction and building industries such as sand and gravel, limestone and gypsum. They are normally mined from the surface in quarries using heavy machinery. Smaller quarries are also found across England and provide stone for the local building industry.

5.3 Different Sectors

Classified on the basis of its stage in the production chain, a modern economy is divided into three sectors. The first sector involves the extraction and production of raw materials, such as corn, coal, wood and iron. The secondary sector involves the transformation of raw or intermediate materials into goods e. g. manufacturing steel into cars, or textiles into clothing. And the tertiary sector involves the provision of services to consumers and businesses, such as baby-sitting, cinema and banking.

5.3.1 Agriculture

Agriculture provides around 60% of Britain's food needs even though it employs just 1.4% of the country's labour force. Farming contributed £ 5.6 billion to the UK economy in 2006. The total area of agricultural land in 2006 was 18.7 million hectares, about 77% of the total land area in the United Kingdom (excluding inland water).

Different types of farming occur in different regions of Britain. This is due to the influence of relief, climate (especially precipitation and temperature), soil type and to an extent closeness to the market. Upland areas generally lend themselves to sheep farming, flat areas to crop production and wet/warm areas to milk and beef production.

Some parts of Britain have excellent soil for crops, while others are used for cattle, sheep, pigs and poultry. In the northwest of England, Wales and Scotland, farmers keep cattle and sheep. Sheep can survive the cold winters on the hills and moors. In the southwest of England, the rich grass is ideal for feeding dairy cows. In the southeast of England and the lowlands of Scotland, grain, potatoes and sugar beet are grown. And in the east of England (East Anglia), wheat, barley and vegetables are grown in enormous fields.

Agricultural products in Britain mainly include cereals, oilseed, potatoes, vegetables; cattle, sheep, poultry; and fish in a broad sense. These products come from different types of farming, which include arable (growing of crops and cereals), pastoral (rearing and production of animals including pigs, chickens, hill farming sheep, beef and dairy cattle), mixed farming (combination of arable and pastoral), horticulture (production of flowers, fruit, vegetables or ornamental plants), market gardening (production of fruit and vegetables) and viticulture (grapes).

Then the principal crops that grow in Britain are wheat, barley, oats, potatoes, sugar beet, vegetables, oil seed rape, and fruits. The livestock products include poultry, sheep, cattle, milk, meat, eggs, and wool.

5.3.2 Production

The production sector concerns mining and quarrying, manufacturing, electricity, gas and water supply, construction, etc. Of these categories, mining and quarrying and electricity, gas and water supply are directly associated with the natural resources, so they are not going to be discussed here again.

As mentioned above, Britain was the first country to be industrialized. Though it has declined ever since 1900, the manufacturing still accounted for a fair large amount of national output. In 2003, the industry accounted for 16% of national output in the UK and for 13% of employment. This is a continuation of the steady decline in the importance of this sector to the British economy since the 1960s, although the sector is still important for overseas trade, accounting for 83% of exports in 2003. The regions with the highest proportion of employees in manufacturing were the East Midlands and West Midlands (at 19% and 18% respectively). London had the lowest at 6%.

Although the manufacturing sector's share of both employment and the UK's GDP has steadily fallen since the 1960s, manufacturing output in terms of both production and value has steadily increased since 1945. This is a trend common in many mature Western economies. Heavy industry, employing many thousands of people and producing large volumes of low-value goods (such as steelmaking) has either become highly efficient or has been replaced by smaller industrial units producing high-value goods.

Engineering and allied industries comprise the single largest sector, contributing 30.8% of total Gross Value Added in manufacturing in 2003. Within this sector, transport equipment was the largest contributor, with 8 global car manufacturers being present in the UK—BMW (MINI, Rolls-Royce), Tata (Jaguar, Land Rover), General Motors (Vauxhall), Honda, Nissan, Toyota and Volkswagen (Bentley). Also, Britain manufactures railway locomotives, the aerospace and defence equipment. Another important component of engineering and allied industries is electronics, audio and optical equipment, with the UK having a broad base of domestic firms, alongside a number of foreign firms manufacturing a wide range of TV, radio and communications products, scientific and optical instruments, electrical machinery and office machinery and computers.

Chemicals and chemical-based products are another important contributor to the

UK's manufacturing base. Within this sector, the pharmaceutical industry is particularly successful, with the world's second and third largest pharmaceutical firms (GlaxoSmithKline and AstraZeneca respectively) being based in the UK and having major research and development and manufacturing facilities there.

And other important sectors of the manufacturing industry include food, drink, tobacco, paper, printing, publishing and textiles.

5.3.3 Service Industries

The service sector is the dominant sector of the UK economy, a feature normally associated with the economy of a developed country. This means that the tertiary sector jobs outnumber the secondary and primary sector jobs. Service industries include wholesale and retail trade, tourism, communications and logistics, finance and housing services, education and other public services, etc.

Wholesale and retail trade

First, the wholesale and retail trade offers the daily supply of goods to a nation. On one hand, the wholesale sector comprises establishments engaged in wholesaling merchandise, generally without transformation, and rendering services incidental to [9] the sale of merchandise. The wholesaling process is an intermediate step in the distribution of merchandise. Wholesalers sell merchandise to other businesses and normally operate from a warehouse or office. On the other hand, the retail sector comprises establishments engaged in retailing merchandise, generally without transformation, and rendering services incidental to the sale of merchandise. The retailing process is the final step in the distribution of merchandise; retailers are, therefore, organized to sell merchandise in small quantities to the general public.

The retail trade has a direct contact with the consumers. Now the retailing takes different forms, in a store, supermarket or via the Internet. Famous suppliers such as Tesco and Spar now sell almost everything that a customer wants to buy. Tesco, for example, is now the largest British retailer by both global sales and domestic market share, with profits exceeding £ 3 billion. It is currently the third largest global retailer based on revenue, behind Wal-Mart and France's Carrefour. Originally specialising in food and drink, Tesco has diversified into areas such as clothing, consumer electronics, financial services, telecoms, home, health and car insurance, dental plans, retailing and renting DVDs, CDs, music downloads, Internet services and software. What's more, the retail sails have now become the important parameter for a nation's economic performance. To the joy of British retailers, sales volume in the three months July to September 2009 increased by 0.9% when compared to the previous three months.

Tourism

Craigievar Castle

Tourism plays a significant part in the United Kingdom's economy, and as such is one of the largest industries in the UK, accounting for 3.5% of the economy, worth approximately £ 85 billion in 2005. In the same year, the UK ranked fifth in the international tourism earnings lagging behind the USA, Spain, France and Italy. The 32.1 million overseas visitors who came in 2006 spent £ 15.4 billion in the UK.

Over 2 million jobs are sustained by tourism activity in the UK, either directly or indirectly. There are an estimated 1.4 million jobs directly related to tourism activity in the UK, some 5% of all people in employment in the UK. Approximately 130,400 of these jobs are in self-employment.

Finance and housing services

Britain is famous for its financial services. London is the world's largest financial centre, with financial services based around two districts: the City of London and the Docklands. The City of London is a small area within Greater London, England. The City is today a major business and financial centre, ranking on a par with New York City as the leading centre of global finance. The City houses the London Stock Exchange, London Metal Exchange, Lloyds of London, and the Bank of England. The Docklands began development in the 1980s and is now home to the Financial Services Authority, as well as several important financial institutions such as Barclays Bank, Citigroup and HSBC. There are now over 500 banks with offices in the City and Docklands, with the majority of business in London being conducted on an international basis, with established leads in areas such as Eurobonds, foreign exchange markets, energy futures and global insurance.

The financial industry added gross value of £ 86,145 million to the UK economy in 2004, and the country had £ 21 billion of financial exports in 2005, contributing significantly towards the balance of payments. The UK has had an expanding export business in financial service, which has been influenced by a mixture of unique institutions, light regulation, and a highly skilled workforce.

Then come real estate and lettings. This sector includes letting of dwellings and other related business support activities. The lettings industry added gross value of £ 83,037 million to the UK economy in 2004 while other real estate and business support activities added gross value of £ 175,333 million.

The UK property market boomed for the seven years up to 2008 and in some areas property trebled in value over that period. The UK property market initially peaked in July 2004 and was static or falling in the capital and some other areas until late 2005, leading many to worry about the possibility of a house price crash and to predict the end of a major British property bubble. However, the property market strengthened considerably in the first half of 2006, showing particular strength in the capital.

The predicted house price crash did in fact occur, beginning in late 2008, and was all the more damaging because of record levels of household debt. Increasing numbers of bankruptcies and home repossessions[10] have worried some economists. This has led many to propose that the correction in house prices will lead much of the country into a lengthy recession.

5.3.4 Education and Other Public Services

Since 1980s, Britain has implemented the policy of education marketing and privatization. The educational reform act of 1988 and the higher education reform act of 1992 spurred on the development of market mechanism in education. It is reported that in the school year of 2003 - 2004, there were 300,055 overseas students studying in Britain. The non-EU students contributed 10.4 billion to the British revenue.

Other public services include all those services provided by the government directly to the citizen or those from the private sector commissioned by the government. The British government provides its citizens with such social services as welfare, traffic amenities, and broadcasting. All these services contribute to the service sector of Britain's national economy.

Notes

[1] The European Economic Community: It is now known as the European Union after the ratification of the Treaty of Maastricht in 1993.

[2] John M. Keynes: He was a British economist whose ideas have been a central influence on modern macroeconomics, both in theory and practice. He advocated interventionist government policy, by which governments would use fiscal and monetary measures to mitigate the adverse effects of business cycles, economic recessions, and depressions. His ideas are the basis for the school of thought known as Keynesian economics, and its various

offshoots.

[3] trade deficit: It refers to the condition that exists when the value of what a country imports exceeds the value of what it exports; also called an unfavorable balance of trade.

[4] turn something on its head: change something completely.

[5] per capita: for each person in a country or area.

[6] Gordon Brown: He became Prime Minister in June 2007, after the resignation of Tony Blair and three days after becoming leader of the governing Labour Party. Immediately before this he had served as Chancellor of the Exchequer in the Labour government from 1997 to 2007 under Tony Blair.

[7] short ton: It is a unit of weight equal to 2,000 pounds (907.18474 kg).

[8] the Kyoto Protocol: It is a protocol to the United Nations Framework Convention on Climate Change (UNFCCC), aimed at combating global warming. The Protocol was initially adopted on 11 December 1997 in Kyoto, Japan and entered into force on 16 February 2005. As of November 2009, 187 states have signed and ratified the protocol, but unfortunately not including the United States who was responsible for 36.1% of the 1990 emission levels.

[9] incidental to: found in connection with.

[10] home repossession: the action that the mortgage company takes to sell your house to settle the debts due to the company.

Exercises

I. Fill in the following blanks with proper words or expressions.

1. The UK was the first country in the world to ______________ in the 18th and 19th centuries, and for much of ______________ possessed a predominant role in the global economy.
2. Pursuing the economic policy based on the theory of John M. Keynes, the British government gave priority to ______________ of all workers.
3. British economy declined after reaching its peak at the end of the 19th century. By 1900 the UK was overtaken by both ______________ and ______________.
4. Facing the economic recession in 2008 – 2009, the incumbent Prime Minister ______________ take measures both at grass-roots level and of global proportions to curb the aftermath of this global slowdown in economy.

5. Oil and gas were discovered under ____________ during the 1960s and new supplies are still being found today.
6. In the UK, the majority of electricity is generated by a mix of ____________ and ________.
7. Agriculture provides around 60% of Britain's food needs even though it employs just ________ of the country's labour force.
8. ________ is now the largest British retailer by both global sales and domestic market share, with profits exceeding £ 3 billion.
9. In 2005, the UK ranked ________ in the international tourism earnings.
10. The Docklands began development in the 1980s and is now home to ____________, as well as several important financial institutions such as Barclays Bank, Citigroup and HSBC.

Ⅱ. Explain the following terms.

1. Margaret Thatcher's economic policy
2. renewable resources
3. the tertiary sector
4. the retail sector

Ⅲ. Discuss the following questions.

1. What do you learn from the historical development of British economy?
2. Make a suggestion to the British government on how to develop the renewable resources.

Chapter Six

Literature

Literature has been the high skills of writing with imagination, covering literary types such as fiction, poetry, drama, and essays.

British literature refers to literature associated with the United Kingdom, the Isle of Man and the Channel Islands as well as to literature from England, Wales and Scotland prior to the formation of the United Kingdom. Most British literature is in the English language.

British literature is a wonderful realm that possesses characteristic features. With a long history and a glorious tradition, British literature can be traced back to the fifth century when old English literature came into being, and it has produced quite a number of towering literary figures that have made marvelous contribution to the world literature—William Shakespeare, James Joyce, and T. S. Eliot are only a few to mention. British literature has also achieved its fame for its exuberant imagination and innovation, bringing about the emergence of a variety of literary schools (Classicism and Neo-classicism, Romanticism, Realism, Modernism etc.) and the exploration of novel literary techniques (for instance, the technique of Stream of Consciousness). Above all, due to the historical reasons that made English an international language, British literature has exerted great influence upon the world literature, especially literature of the English-speaking nations such as Australia, New Zealand and the United States.

6.1 Literature before the Renaissance

6.1.1 Old English Literature (450 –1066)

Old English literature refers to the literature in the period from 450 to 1066, which began with the settlement of the Anglo-Saxons in Wessex in England and ended with the conquest of England by William Duke of Normandy. *Beowulf*, an Anglo-Saxon epic that is believed to be composed between the year of 700 and 900, is the most important literary work of this period.

An epic is a long narrative poem that operates on a grand scale and deals with the deeds of warriors and heroes. *Beowulf* can properly be called an epic poem in the sense that it celebrates the achievements of a hero in narrative verse. *Beowulf* tells the story of Beowulf, a warrior prince from Sweden, who goes to Denmark and kills the monster Grendel and defeats Grendel's mother, a water-monster, but eventually receives his own death in fighting with a fire dragon.

Structurally, *Beowulf* is built around three fights, each involving a battle between those who live in the royal hall and a monster. In *Beowulf*, the monsters symbolize the dangerous, unpredictable and incomprehensible forces that threaten the security and well being of those in power and the way of life they represent, while the great hall stands for a place of refuge and shared values, providing warmth and protection against the dangers in the darkness outside.

6.1.2 Middle English Literature (1066 –1485)

Middle English literature refers to the literature in the period from 1066 to 1485, which lasted from the Norman Conquest to the end of the Wars of Roses[1]. Geoffrey Chaucer is the representative literary figure of this period.

Geoffrey Chaucer (1340 – 1400) is the first great individual name in English literature. Born in a merchant's family in London, he entered the royal service to become a professional royal servant, holding a series of posts. In succession he served three kings—Edward Ⅲ, Richard II and Henry Ⅱ. He seemed to have prospered, for a large amount of royal favor came his way. He was buried in what came to known as the Poets' Corner in Westminster Abbey. *The Canterbury Tales* is his most popular work for its power of observation, piercing irony, sense of humor and warm humanity.

The Canterbury Tales, which is incomplete to Chaucer's plan, contains twenty-four tales told by a group of pilgrims on their journey to Canterbury. Most of the tales are written in verse which reflects Chaucer's innovation by introducing into the native alliterative verse the French and Italian styles. Chaucer writes in dialect used by Londoners, and by the sheer weight and popularity of his writings he sets it firmly on the way towards Modern English. Chaucer is thus to be regarded as the first short story-teller and the first modern poet in English literature.

6.2 Renaissance Literature

Renaissance, marking a transition from the medieval to the modern world, refers to the period between the 14th and mid-17th centuries which started in Italy with the flowering of painting, sculpture and literature. In essence, the Renaissance is a historical period in which the European humanist thinkers and scholars made attempts to get rid of those old feudalist ideas in medieval Europe, to introduce new ideas that expressed the interests of the rising bourgeoisie, and to recover the purity of the early church from the corruption of the Roman Catholic Church.

Renaissance occurred in different periods in different countries with different emphasis. The emphasis in Italy is on fine arts, in France on literature, and in England on drama. Due to the War of Roses in the country and its geographical isolation from the European continent, Renaissance came later in England than other European countries. But when it did come, it was to produce some towering figures in the English and world literary heritage—Thomas More, William Shakespeare, Edmund Spenser and other humanist thinkers.

6.2.1 Thomas More (1478 –1535)

Lawyer and expert in politics and foreign affairs, Thomas More was an embodiment of the spirit of the Renaissance. More was Lord Chancellor to Henry Ⅷ, but he resigned after refusing to agree to the king's divorce from Catherine of Aragon. Then he was imprisoned, found guilty of treason and beheaded because of his refusal to conform to the *Act of Supremacy*. More left behind some enlightening writings, among which *Utopia* is considered his masterpiece.

Utopia first appeared in 1517 in Latin and it was not translated into English until 1551. It describes an ideal state where everybody lives a simple life and shares the goods in common, possesses a good knowledge of Latin, fights no war and enjoys full freedom in religious belief.

6.2.1 William Shakespeare (1564 –1616)

William Shakespeare, actor, poet and playwright, was a man of late Renaissance who gave the fullest expression to humanist ideals. Born in 1564 at Stratford, a market town on the Avon in Warwickshire, he was the eldest son and the third of eight children of John Shakespeare and Mary Arden. He received his education in the local grammar school. He probably left school at 15, and at 18 he married Anne Hathaway who was eight years senior. In 1592, he was in the London theatre, writing and acting. In his later years, he became quite wealthy, buying a large house in his hometown. He stayed there till his death in 1616, and was buried in the churchyard.

William Shakespeare
(1564 – 1616)

Shakespeare was a prolific writer. In his lifetime, he produced 37 plays, 154 sonnets and 2 long verses. His dramas include historical plays, comedies and tragedies, covering a multiplicity of themes. Shakespeare's principal history plays deal with a line of English monarchs from Richard II through to the defeat of Richard III by Henry VII, the first Tudor monarch. *Henry IV*(1597 –1598) and *Henry V*(1599) are two of the well-known historical plays of Shakespeare.

Most of the comedies were written in the early time of his career when Shakespeare was still young. The keynote of the comedies is the freedom from the feudal fetters. The heroes and heroines fight for their own ideal and mould their life according to their own free will. A case in point is one of his best comedies *The Merchant of Venice* (1597).

Tragedies are the most famous part of Shakespeare's literary achievements, and 4 tragedies are worth mentioning—*Hamlet* (1601), *Othello* (1604), *King Lear* (1605) and *Macbeth* (1605).

Hamlet is often considered to be Shakespeare's greatest tragedy. The story came from an old Danish legend about the young prince Hamlet seeking revenge on his uncle who murders his father, marries his mother and seizes power. The tragedy ends with a bloody scene at which all the major characters are either killed or poisoned.

In addition to the 4 tragedies, *Romeo and Julie*(1595), a story of two young lovers from feudal families which ends in a tragic double suicide, is also popular among readers.

6.3 Literature in the 17th and 18th Centuries

Unmarried and without an heir, Queen Elizabeth died in 1603, thus terminating the three-generation Tudor rule and starting the Stuart dynasty. The century in England was cut into two halves by the English Revolution[2], which brought about disruption and change to society. Francis Bacon and John Milton were two remarkable representatives in British literature in this period.

A broad contrast to the disruption and change of the 17th century, the 18th century presents England with a keynote of a desire for rational agreement and an increasing confidence. The novel appeared in this century, and the dominant spirit of the century was the Enlightenment.

Enlightenment, a name given by historians to a phase succeeding the Renaissance and followed by Romanticism, was an intellectual movement originating in France, which attracted widespread support among the ruling and intellectual classes of Europe and North America in the second half of the 18th century. The Enlightenment believed in the universal authority of reason, and in its ability to understand and explain. It favored toleration and moderation in religion, and was hopeful about the rational perfectibility of man, and optimistic about human future. Enlightenment sometimes is also called the Age of Reason.

British literature produced literary giants such as Alexander Pope, Jonathan Swift and Daniel Defoe at this stage.

6.3.1 Francis Bacon (1561 –1626)

Francis Bacon, English philosopher, essayist and statesmen, was educated at Trinity College at Cambridge. As a politician he went through a complicated experience of rise and fall. Only with the succession of James I did his position improved. He was made Attorney General, Lord Keeper of the Great Seal and Lord Chancellor, but was accused of accepting bribes. He pleaded guilty, and was imprisoned in the tower of London, which led to the end of his political career and his devotion to writing.

As a philosopher, Bacon held that philosophy should be kept separate from theology, not intimately be blended with it. The whole basis of his philosophy was practical: to give mankind mastery over the forces of nature by means of scientific discoveries and inventions.

Essays (1612) is Bacon's most widely read work. First published in 1597, it contained 10 short essays. Later more were added until finally 58 essays included. Dealing with a wide range of topics concerning various aspects of life, *Essays* is noted for its striking, terse style and sharp observation about life. Many of his sayings from *Essays* are still universally acknowledged today. For example:

Knowledge is power.

Reading maketh a full man, conference a ready man, and writing an exact man.

Virtue is like precious odors—most fragrant when they are incensed or crushed.

6.3.2 John Milton (1608 –1674)

A fine classical scholar, Milton first attracted public attention by his Latin verse. During the Civil War Milton was a strong supporter of the parliamentary party, and in 1649, after the execution of Charles I, he became Government Secretary for Foreign Tongues. Milton's late years were spent in the shadow of Restoration, when he was lonely and blind. Yet it was during this period that he wrote his three master epic poems: *Paradise Lost* (1667), *Paradise Regained* (1671) and *Samson Agonistes* (1671).

Paradise Lost is a long epic poem of twelve volumes whose theme is the fall of men: men's disobedience and the loss there upon of Paradise, with its prime cause Satan. In this epic poem Satan is the most successfully portrayed character who was evil, rebellious, courageous, heroic and tragic.

John Milton was viewed as one of the two leaders in the English Revolution (Cromwell was the man of action while he the man of thought), ranking with Chaucer and Shakespeare.

6.3.3 Jonathan Swift (1667 –1745)

Jonathan Swift, churchman, political writer and poet, is the foremost satirist in the English language and one of the satiric masters of all time whose works transcend the limitations of time and place. Born in Dublin, he became a clergyman and later a political pamphleteer. But the satirical tone and the pessimistic view made his works controversial, and his writings have sometimes been attacked as misanthropic.

Gulliver's Travels (1726), his best work, is a social and political prose satire in the form of a book of travels. It consists of four voyages by Lemuel Gulliver, to Lilliput, Brobdingnag, the flying island of Laputa, and finally to the land of the Houyhnhnms, a race of supremely intelligent horses, who are served by the *Yahoos*, reasonless and conscienceless beasts in the shape of human beings.

6.3.4 Daniel Defoe (1660 –1731)

Daniel Defoe was born in London, the son of a butcher. A man of wide learning, Defoe could speak and read six or seven languages, and his interests and activities were many—he was in turn a shopkeeper, manufacturer, journalist and government spy. At the age of 59, he began writing novels, and *The Life and Strange Surprising Adventures of Robinson Crusoe, of York, Mariner* (1719) made him one of the greatest fiction writers of the 18th-century England.

Robinson Crusoe began with Crusoe's account of his birth and parentage, and related that, against his father's advice, he was determined to go to sea. Having shipwrecked on an island, he managed to survive, rescued a black boy whom he named Friday, and eventually got hold of a ship to sail back home.

Robinson Crusoe is the first novel in the complete modern sense; it is not only a masterpiece of story telling but also an interpretation of life. As a novel it has all the essential constituents: unity of theme, of action and of style, character, narrative, dialogue, etc. It is a story told with a combination of minute realism and of the curiosity that keeps the mind to the very end. Dates, places, names and particulars of Crusoe's relative and similar details are given with great exactness, and the method of journalism is followed to the uttermost, giving the impression that everything written is a record of real life. For these reasons, *Robinson Crusoe* is regarded as the first English novel in the history of Western literature.

6.3.5 Alexander Pope (1688 –1744)

The great poet and verse satirist of the 18th century, Alexander Pope was renowned for his translations of Homer and for his biting counter attacks on the criticisms of his literary enemies. He represented the rationalistic neoclassical tendency in literature and has often been considered the spokesman in verse of the Age of Reason.

An Essay on Criticism (1711), Pope's first noteworthy poem, was a clever poem in heroic verse embodying well-worn literary axioms. The lines are very well tuned, and many of them, such as the famous saying "A little learning is a dangerous thing", have passed into current speech.

His later years were poisoned by the attacks of his literary rivals, to whom he retorted in the *Dunciad* (1728), a clever and malicious satire. Pope's *An Essay on Man* (1734) was a philosophical poem which gave memorable expression to ideas about nature and man's place in nature.

6.4 The Age of Romanticism (1790 – 1840)

The Romantic period is also referred to as the Age of Revolution. At the heart of the period and of Romanticism is the French Revolution, with a great deal of the subsequent vocabulary of liberal politics right through to the present day.

Romanticism was a movement in literature, philosophy, music and art which developed in Europe in the late 18th and early 19th centuries. Starting from the ideas of Rousseau in France and from the Storm and Stress movement in Germany, Romanticism laid great emphasis on man's emotional nature and his profound inner forces overlooked by Classicism. Romanticism emphasized individual values and aspirations above those of society. A reaction to the Industrial Revolution, Romanticism looked to the Middle Ages and to direct contact with nature for inspiration. It gave impetus to the national liberation movement in the 19th-century Europe.

Literature took the full force of Romanticism which brought forth a full flowering of literary talents in England such as Wordsworth, Byron, Shelley and Keats. Their works, diversified in character and daring in spirit, all depicted man's eager search for individual freedom, pure sentiments and ideal beauty.

6.4.1 George Gordon Byron (1788 – 1824)

George Gordon Byron may be taken as typical of the spirit of general revolt, who is chiefly known for two long poems, *Chile Harold's Pilgrimag*(1809 – 1818) and *Don Juan* (1818-1823). The heroes of his poems are mostly with fiery passion and unbending will, fighting against tyranny and injustice, but merely fighters striving for personal freedom. In his poems Byron expressed his own ideal of freedom through the creation and depiction of such heroes, who accordingly are called "Byronic heroes".

Even in his own time, Byron's poetry exerted a powerful influence on writers all over Europe because it expressed an ardent love of liberty and a fierce hatred of tyranny. He was admired by Pushkin and Lermontov in Russia and many others in

Western Europe, and the Byronic hero became an idol of the young.

6.4.2 Percy Bysshe Shelley (1792 –1822)

Like Byron, Percy Bysshe Shelley was a rebel against the common conventions of society. Born of a wealthy and aristocratic family, Shelly had developed the most advanced views upon most of the questions that trouble the mind of man in his early age. He spent his late years wandering in Italy, despising the comforts of a settled home. He was drowned in a squall while he was cruising off the coast of Italy, and his ashes were placed in the Protestant cemetery in Rome.

One of the major English Romantic poets, Shelley is critically regarded among the finest lyric poets in the English language. He is most famous for such verse works as *Ode to the West Wind* (1819), *To a Skylark* (1820), and *The Masque of Anarchy* (1819), which are among the most popular and critically acclaimed poems in the English language.

Shelley wrote many other notable works, among which is the lyrical drama *Prometheus Unbound* (1820). Unlike the hero portrayed the Greek tragedian Aeschylus, Shelley depicted a different Prometheus, who, instead of reconciling with Zeus, fought on until he won his freedom.

6.4.3 Jane Austin (1775 –1817)

The second daughter and seventh child of a country rector, Jane Austin spent her girlhood in the rural area of her birthplace. Fortunately, she had a lively and affectionate family circle which provided a stimulating context for her writing. She took up novel writing in 1795, and her first novel, *Sense and Sensibility*, was published in 1811, followed by the publication of her other novels in succession. They are *Pride and Prejudice* (1813), *Northanger Abbey* (1818), *Mansfield Park* (1814), *Emma* (1816) and *Persuasion* (1818). It is *Pride and Prejudice* that has won her worldwide popularity.

Austin's novels are domestic comedies, but she wrote in an objective, realistic manner. She did not talk about her technical methods or moralize upon ethical problems or idealize herself in a beautiful and brilliant heroine, but made brief comments in such a mildly phrased way that one needs to take a second look before recognizing their gentle sarcasm or incisive truth.

Jane Austin's novels are mostly concerned with love and marriage. Her heroines, like herself, have a sense of humor and can smile at their own foibles; and their power of reasoning is strong enough to make them learn by experience.

Jane Austin is considered one of the most important women novelists in the history of British literature, and her novels are best known for their witty writing and subtle characterization.

6.5 Victorian Literature (1837 - 1901)

Victorian literature refers to the English literature from 1837 to 1901 when Queen Victoria reigned in England. The abundance of novel writing was the literary feature of the time. As a matter of fact, novel was so important during the Victorian times that this period might be called the Golden Age of the Novel.

Several factors contributed to the rise of novel writing. First, the development of popular education led to a fresh demand for prose fiction. Next, the decline of historical novels brought forth the rise of domestic novel, and novelists turned their attention to the teeming life around them. Each writer, moreover, tended to specialize in some aspect of domestic life, and so modern society was thoroughly explored. The didactic element was on the increase, and novelists began to use their pens to support or denounce some subjects in which they were interested. Dickens was foremost in this respect. The rise of a standard prose style for the novel was also apparent, which was a kind of prose that is rapid, clear, and flexible.

Charlotte Bronte, Charles Dickens and Thomas Hardy were the outstanding novelists in this period.

6.5.1 Charlotte Bronte (1816 –1855)

Charlotte Bronte suffered a lot in her childhood. Her mother died early, and her father spent most of his time on his duties as vicar and his studies. The death of her two elder sisters when they were small also deeply impressed her. Her experience was comparatively limited to the bleak northern moors and to a few years as pupil and teacher in shabby boarding schools, but she was essentially influenced by her reading of the leading poets of the Romantic Movement. She wrote poems, but geared her attention towards novel writing when her poems failed to gain public notice. Her first novel, *The Professor*, was rejected by several publishers, and did not come out until after her death, but her next novel, *Jane Eyre* (1847), won immediate success, and has enjoyed a long popularity since its publication. It records the experience of a fragile, friendless girl struggling in a hostile society, which could have reflected Charlotte's own painful experience as governess.

Her writing is marked throughout by intensity—intensity of vision in the descriptive passages, and intensity of feeling in the emotional scenes. The two distinctive characteristics of her work are the closely observed factual details and the extravagant adventures of the spirit in a fantasy world. Her constant theme is the struggles of an orphan girl.

Charlotte Bronte is viewed as the forerunner of Feminism[3] since her masterpiece, *Jane Eyre*, advocated the voice that women should be equal in economy, marriage and social status.

6.5.2 Charles Dickens (1812 –1870)

Charles Dickens was the greatest British story-teller in the 19th century. He left us more than 20 novels, most of which are still widely read, such as the *Pickwick Papers* (1837), *Oliver Twist* (1838), *A Tale of Two Cities* (1859), *Great Expectations* (1861), and *David Copperfield* (1850).

The son of an impoverished government clerk, Dickens had little schooling and at the age of 12 he set out to work in a blacking factory. Later he worked as an office boy for a lawyer and taught himself shorthand and became a reporter of debates in Parliament. Soon he started writing fiction in his spare time, and achieved fame at the age of 25 with the publication of *Pickwick Papers*.

Charles Dickens
(1812 – 1870)

After publishing the historical novel *A Tale of Two Cities* whose structural pattern depends upon parallelism and antithesis between London and Paris, Dickens devoted himself to the novel of social conditions. He wrote *Oliver Twist*, *A Christmas Carol* (1843), *Hard Times* (1854) and *Bleak House* (1853), all with a reforming purpose. *David Copperfield*, considered his best book and believed to be his favorite, is a kind of autobiographical romance.

Dickens' novels present a vivid picture of the life in the 19th century England, covering a wide range of themes: social, moral, emotional, psychological. But whatever he wrote, he had some basis on his own experience. Many of his stories were set in the most humble surroundings and the most poverty-stricken districts with which he was familiar in his youth, and the characters depicted in his writings were the ordinary people of his time.

Dickens distinguished himself as a realism novelist for his truthful account of life and for his bitter criticism to the vices of the capitalist society in his novels. He is both the most imaginative and fantastic and the most topical and documentary of great novelists.

6.5.3 Thomas Hardy (1840 –1928)

Thomas Hardy, poet and novelist, was born in a small village near Dorchester. Son of a builder, he practised architecture in his early life, but later tried a life of writing. He devoted himself to novel and poem writing, but his poems mainly came out after he had made great achievements in fiction writing.

According to his own classification, Hardy's novels could be categorized into three groups: Novels of Character and Environment for which he was best known, *Romances and Fantasies*, and *Novels of Ingenuity*. Such novels as *Far from the Madding Crowd* (1874), *The Return of the Native* (1878), *The Mayor of Casterbridge* (1886), and *Tess of D'Urbervilles* (1891) belong to the group called Novels of Character and Environment.

Pessimist and fatalist he was, Hardy depicted his heroes and heroines as human beings who appeared to be crushed by a superior force, a merciless fate, and the indifferences of his fellow creatures. A case in point is *Tess of the D'Urbervilles* which is the most widely read of all his works. It narrates how Tess, the daughter of a poor villager, went hopelessly to her doom after she was seduced by the young master Alec, abandoned by Angel Clare on their wedding night, and driven to become Alec's mistress.

6.6 Literature in the First Half of the 20th Century

The last years of the 19th century and the early decades of the 20th century witnessed the rapid development of science and technology which led on the one hand to great material gains, but on the other hand to the world-wide economic depression and mass unemployment. World War I resulted in the common sentiments of distrust and despair in the whole Western world. Young people who had experienced disillusionment experimented with various styles of life that were beyond imagination of the older generation. In such a background emerged modernism which emphasized the irrationality of the human mind and the illogicality of things in the world.

Modernism was characterized by a conscious rejection of established rules, traditions and conventions. It strove to reflect the social and political changes, the dangers and anxieties, the rapid growth of technological and psychological knowledge of the 20th century, providing fresh ways of looking at man's position and function in the universe.

Modernist writers explored the distorted, alienated and ill relationships between man and nature, man and society, and man and himself. They rejected rationalism, denied external objectivity, paid attention to the inner workings of the human psyche, experimented with all sorts of literary form of expression, with time shifts and spatial transformations.

James Joyce, Thomas Stearns Eliot and George Bernard Shaw were representative figures of this period in terms of fiction, poetry and drama.

6.6.1 James Joyce (1882 –1941)

James Joyce, poet and novelist, was born in a middle class family in Dublin, Ireland. He graduated from University College, Dublin in 1902, and got in touch with some well-known Irish literary figures of that time. He spent most of his years abroad, and died in Zurich in 1941.

James Joyce
(1882 - 1941)

James Joyce is generally regarded as the most important fiction writer in the 20th century. His works are full of experiments with languages and symbolism, well-known for the literary technique called Stream of Consciousness.

Stream of Consciousness is a literary technique which was first used in the late 19th century to evince subjective as well as objective reality. It is employed to reveal the characters' feelings, thoughts and actions, often following an associative rather than a logical sequence, without comments by the author. Stream of Consciousness attempts to portray the remote, preconscious state of consciousness that exists before the mind organizes sensations, hence frequently lacking the unity, explicit cohesion, and selectivity of direct thought.

Dubliners (1914), *A Portrait of the Artist as a Young Man* (1916), *Ulysses* (1922) and *Finnegans Wake* (1939) are James Joyce's major works, each with its own unique literary features. *Dubliners* is a collection of short stories in which the characters are portrayed in naturalistic detail. *A Portrait of the Artist as a Young Man* is an autobiographical novel, depicting the different stages of the developing mind of the hero in the course of seeking identity. What's noteworthy is that the depiction is done within the hero's mind, and the employment of this literary technique marks a turning point in modern English fiction.

James Joyce' masterpiece, *Ulysses*, is considered the single best fiction ever written in the 20th century. Stream of Consciousness technique was employed in this novel to describe the events of a single day (July 16th, 1904) in Dublin. Though difficult to read, the book became a great success. It is so influential that July 16th has become a holiday celebrated annually in Dublin by devotees of literature from all over the world.

More innovative was *Finnegans Wake.* It is taken as the most difficult novel in English language since it is full of puns and allusions in more than 30 languages.

Forerunner in the subjective movement in fiction, James Joyce was perhaps the most important fiction writer in British literature in the 20th century.

6.6.2 Thomas Stearns Eliot (1888 –1965)

Thomas Stearns Eliot, the most modern and most influential poet in the 20th century, was born in St. Louis, Missouri. After school in Boston and Harvard University, he studied philosophy in Marburg, Paris and Oxford. In 1927 he became a British citizen and spent his last half life in Britain.

Eliot's notable achievements in poetry are *The Love Song of J. Alfred Prufrock* (1915), *The Waste Land* (1922), and *Four Quartets* (1944), among which *The Waste Land* is considered his best contribution to English poetry. Eliot was awarded the Nobel Prize in 1949.

The Waste Land is a long poem about the spiritual emptiness and emotional impoverishment common both to the dying genteel world and the new urban materialist world. It consists of five sections—Burial of the Dead, A Game Chess, The Fire Sermon, Death by Water, and What the Thunder Said. In addition to the large number of symbols (which is a characteristic feature of Modernism), the poem drew upon allusions, mythology, classical literature, etc.

Apart from poetry, Eliot was also a playwright and literary critic. *Murder in the Cathedral* (1940) was his important play, and *Traditional and the Individual Talent* (1919) and *The Metaphysical Poets* (1921) are two of his principal critical essays.

6.6.3 George Bernard Shaw (1856 –1950)

George Bernard Shaw is one of the most important dramatists in the 20th century in British literature. He won the Nobel Prize in 1925 for the idealism and humanism embodied in his drama.

George Bernard Shaw
(1856 - 1950)

Born in Dublin, Shaw spent his childhood and early youth in Ireland, which made him understand better the sufferings and bitterness of the Irish people under the English rule. In 1876 he went to London to study by himself and began to take up fiction writing, whose failure in turn made him turn to drama.

Shaw left us 51 plays, covering a wide range of modes. *Widower's House* (1892) is an attack on the slum landlords. *Mrs. Warren's Profession* (1898) is a comic satire exposing the economic incentives to prostitution in a capitalist society. *Heartbreak House*(1913), is about the decadence of pre-war English society. *Saint Joan* (1923) is a romantic historical drama while *Man and Superman* (1904) the philosophical. *The Doctor's Dilemma* (1906) is tragic, *The Apple Cart* (1929) gives an examination of monarchy, and *Pygmalion* (1912) deals with language, love and social class. His best comedies include *Major Barbara*(1905) and *Pygmalion*, upon which the Hollywood film *My Fair Lady* was made.

Shaw presented a vivid picture of the life in the capitalist society. He was a member of the Fabian Society[4] and his writings were greatly influenced by the Fabian Society whose aim was to make a transition from capitalism to socialism without violence.

Shaw visited China in 1933, and he was popular among the Chinese readers.

Notes

[1] War of Roses: War of Roses, or the Thirty Years' War, was a series of civil wars fought between two great families in England which lasted for 30 years (1455 - 1485). Both families, the House of Lancaster with a red rose as its emblem and the House of York with a white rose claimed of the right to the English throne. Thus a war began and didn't come to an end until King Henry VII defeated Richard III (1483-1485) at the Battle of Bosworth. Henry Tudor, or Henry VII (1485-1509) married Elizabeth of the House of York, which brought compromise between the two families, and established a highly consolidated as well as a new English dynasty.

[2] English Revolution: The term has been used to describe two different events in English history. The Glorious Revolution of

1688, whereby James II was replaced by William III and Mary II as monarch and a constitutional monarchy established, was described by Whig historians as the English Revolution. In the twentieth century, however, Marxist historians used the term English Revolution to describe the period of the English Civil Wars and Commonwealth period 1640 - 1660, in which Parliament challenged the authority King Charles I and finally executed him in 1649. This was followed by a ten - year period of republican bourgeois government, the Commonwealth, before monarchy was restored in the shape of Charles' son, Charles II, in 1660.

[3] Feminism: It refers to political, cultural, and economic movements aimed at establishing greater rights, legal protection for women, and/or women's liberation. The history of feminism can be divided into three waves. The first wave transpired in the nineteenth and early twentieth centuries, the second occurred in the 1960s and 1970s, and the third extended from the 1990s to the present. Feminist theory emerged from these feminist movements.

[4] Fabian Society: A socilaism society founded in 1884 by a group of British intellectuals who advocated that socialism be established by gradual reforms within the law. Its memebrs were mostly intellectuals such as scholars, lawyers, journalists and writers, among whom the most famous were Sidney and Beatrice Webb, Bernard Shaw, Graham Wallas, H.G. Wells and Clement Attlee.

Exercises

I. Fill in the following blanks with proper words or expressions.

1. Geoffrey Chaucer is the first great individual name in English literature. ________ is his most popular work. Chaucer writes in ________ used by Londoners, and by the sheer weight and popularity of his writings he sets it firmly on the way towards ____________. Chaucer is thus to be regarded as the first short story-teller and ____________ in English literature.
2. Shakespeare was a prolific writer. In his lifetime, he produced ____________, ____________ and 2 long verses. His dramas include ____________, comedies and tragedies, covering a multiplicity of themes. ____________ are the most famous part of Shakespeare's literary achievements, and 4 tragedies are worth mentioning—*Hamlet*, ________, *King Lear* and ________.

3. John Milton, the man of thought in English Revolution, wrote his three master ____________. They were ____________, *Paradise Regained* and *Samson Agonistes*.
4. Jane Austin's novels are mostly concerned with ____________. Her novels are best known for their witty writing and ____________.
5. Charlotte Bronte is viewed as the forerunner of ____________ since her masterpiece, *Jane Eyre*, advocated the voice that women should be equal in economy, marriage and social status.
6. Charles Dickens was the greatest British story-teller in the 19 th century. His historical novel, *A Tale of Two Cities* depends upon ____________ between London and Paris in structural pattern. ____________, considered his best novel and believed to be his favorite, is a kind of autobiographical romance.
7. Thomas Hardy was a ____________, and he depicted his heroes and heroines as human beings who appeared to be crushed by a superior force, ____________, and ________.
8. James Joyce' masterpiece, __________, is considered the single best fiction ever written in the 20th century. __________ technique was employed in this novel to describe the events of a single day (July 16 th, 1904) in Dublin.
9. Thomas Stearns Eliot is viewed as the most modern and most ____________ poet in the 20th century. His masterpiece, *The Waste Land*, is a long poem about ____________ and emotional impoverishment common both to the dying genteel world and the new urban materialist world.
10. George Bernard Shaw left us __________ plays, covering a wide range of modes. *Widower's House* is an attack on the slum landlords. *Mrs. Warren's Profession* is ____________ exposing the economic incentives to prostitution in a capitalist society. And __________ deals with language, love and social class, upon which the Hollywood film *My Fair Lady* was made.

Ⅱ. Explain the following terms.

1. Epic
2. Romanticism
3. Byronic hero
4. Modernism
5. Stream of Consciousness

Ⅲ. Discuss the following questions.

1. What are the characteristic features of British literature?
2. What's your interpretation of William Shakespeare's contribution to British literature?

Chapter Seven

Education System

Education in England is overseen by the Department for Children, Schools and Families and the Department for Business, Innovation and Skills. At a local level the local authorities take responsibility for implementing policy for public education and state schools.

7.1 Introduction

7.1.1 History

Before 1902, there was no system of publicly funded secondary education in Great Britain, and those students who were educated beyond the primary level attended either privately endowed grammar schools or public schools (which were also privately endowed, but were usually much older than the other grammar schools). The Education Act of 1902 established a system of new, publicly funded grammar schools and also provided government aid for some existing grammar schools. Technical training courses, attended mostly by those students who were not academically qualified for admission to the grammar schools, were also begun.

During the period between the two world wars, this system was modified. Students completing primary school at age 11 were required to take a series of examinations called the eleven-plus. Results of these tests determined a student's placement in a three-track secondary system. The highest scoring students were admitted to grammar schools and were likely to go on to university studies. The other students attended either modern schools, where they completed a course of higher-level elementary studies and did not go on to university, or technical schools, whose most promising graduates were sometimes admitted to university.

Some British educators thought this system to be overly rigid, and after World War II many "comprehensive" schools, which combined elements of grammar, modern, and technical schools, were established, although many highly respected grammar schools have survived. By the late 20th century the eleven-plus exams had become defunct and the vast majority of secondary-school students attended comprehensive schools, with a much smaller proportion attending grammar schools or technical schools. In comprehensives, pupils are placed in A, B, or C "streams" according to their aptitudes and abilities. Comprehensives are similar to the large, multi-purpose American high school, in which the ability grouping system is known as "tracking".

The purpose of the comprehensive school is to democratize education, do away with early selection procedures, and provide equal opportunity for all children. In 1975 legislation was passed in the United Kingdom to hasten the transition to this system, reflecting the long-term policy of the Labour government to organize all secondary education on a comprehensive basis. Although some comprehensive schools have been quite successful, the transition has been slow, and the issue is complicated by mixed attitudes toward the long-revered public schools and strong residual devotion to the traditional grammar school system.

7.1.2 School years

The table below describes the most common patterns for schooling in the state sector in England:

<table>
<tr><th>Age on Sept. 1st</th><th>Year</th><th>Curriculum stage</th><th colspan="3">Schools</th></tr>
<tr><td>3</td><td>Nursery</td><td rowspan="2">Foundation Stage</td><td colspan="3">Nursery school</td></tr>
<tr><td>4</td><td>Reception</td><td rowspan="3">Infant school</td><td rowspan="7">Primary school</td><td rowspan="5">First school</td></tr>
<tr><td>5</td><td>Year 1</td><td rowspan="2">Key Stage 1</td></tr>
<tr><td>6</td><td>Year 2</td></tr>
<tr><td>7</td><td>Year 3</td><td rowspan="4">Key Stage 2</td><td rowspan="4">Junior school</td></tr>
<tr><td>8</td><td>Year 4</td></tr>
<tr><td>9</td><td>Year 5</td><td rowspan="2">Middle school</td></tr>
<tr><td>10</td><td>Year 6</td></tr>
</table>

续表

Age on Sept. 1st	Year	Curriculum stage	Schools		
11	Year 7	Key Stage 3	Secondary school	Secondary school with Sixth form	Middle school
12	Year 8				
13	Year 9				Upper school
14	Year 10	Key Stage 4 / GCSE			
15	Year 11				
16	Year 12	Sixth form / A level	Sixth form college		
17	Year 13				

7.1.3 Two Types of Schools

There are two types of schools: state-run schools and independent schools. State-run schools and colleges are financed through national taxation, and take pupils free of charge between the ages of 3 and 18. More than 93% of students in the UK attend publicly-funded state schools. Primary schools usually include both girls and boys as pupils. Secondary schools may be either single-sex or co-educational.

Approximately 7% of English schoolchildren attend privately run independent schools(public schools). Education at independent schools is usually chargeable. Such schools, some of which are boarding schools, cover primary and secondary education. The independent school system usually teaches separate sciences (biology, chemistry and physics) and takes the highest 50% of pupils in the entrance exam (the 1st form exam). Most independent schools have a prep dept or a pre prep dept of a kindergarten or a sixth form or a senior school. Some may be single-sex.

Education departments in England, Scotland and Wales fund schools through a local education authority (or education authority in Scotland). In Northern Ireland, schools are largely financed from public funds through five education and library boards.

7.1.4 Public schools in the UK

A public school, in common British usage, is a school which is usually prestigious and historic, which charges fees, does not arbitrarily restrict admissions, and is financed by bodies other than the state, commonly as a private charitable trust. Often but not always they are boarding schools. Confusingly to a non-native English speaker a public school is actually a private school! In British usage, a government-run school (which would be called a "public school" in other areas, such as the United States) is called a state school.

Many of the independent schools in the UK do not refer to themselves as public schools. Many choose to use the term independent school. In part this is due to a sense that some "minor" public schools have many of the social associations and traditions of public schools but without the quality of teaching and extracurricular activities.

The term "public" (first adopted by Eton) historically refers to the fact that the school was open to the paying public, as opposed to, a religious school that was only open to members of a certain church, and in contrast to private education at home (usually only practical for the very wealthy who could afford tutors).

Public schools played an important role in the development of the Victorian social elite. Under a number of forward-looking headmasters leading public schools developed a curriculum based heavily on classics and physical activity for boys and young men of the upper and upper middle classes. They were schools for the gentlemanly elite of Victorian politics, armed forces and colonial government. Often successful businessmen would send their sons to public school as a mark of participation in the elite.

Public schools often relied heavily on the maintenance of discipline by older boys, both to reduce staffing costs and as preparation for military or public service.

While under the best circumstances the Victorian public schools were superb examples of education, the reliance on corporal punishment and the prefect system could also make them awful. The classics-based curriculum was criticised for not providing skills in sciences or engineering.

The public school system influenced the school systems of the British empire to an extent. Recognisably "public" schools can be found in many Commonwealth countries.

Today most public schools are highly selective on academic grounds, as well as financial grounds (ability to pay high fees) and social grounds—often a family connection to the school is very desirable in admissions.

7.2 Primary and Secondary Education

The school year begins usually on the 1st of September (sometimes the 2nd or 3rd if the 1st falls on a weekend). Education is compulsory for all children from the term after their fifth birthday to the last Friday in June of the school year in which they turn 16. This will be raised in 2013 to the year in which they turn 17 and in 2015 to the year in which they turn 18.

7.2.1 Primary education

Primary education in England is normally conducted through infant and junior schools or a combined primary school.

Foundation Stage 1 (in a preschool/childcare environment)

Part-time Foundation Stage, age 3 to 4

Full-time Foundation Stage 2 (in an infant or primary school)

Reception, age 4 to 5

Key Stage 1 (in an infant or primary school)

Year 1, age 5 to 6

Year 2, age 6 to 7

Year 3, age 7 to 8

Key Stage 2 (in junior or primary school)

Year 4, age 8 to 9

Year 5, age 9 to 10

Year 6, age 10 to 11

Primary or elementary education is the first years of formal, structured education that occurs during childhood. In most Western countries, it is compulsory for children to receive primary education (though in many jurisdictions it is permissible for parents to provide it).

Primary education generally begins when children are four to seven years of age. The division between primary and secondary education is somewhat arbitrary, but it generally occurs at about twelve years of age (adolescence); some educational systems have separate middle schools for that period. Primary and secondary education together are sometimes (in particular, in Canada and the United States) referred to as "K-12" education (K is for kindergarten, 12 is for twelfth grade).

Typically, primary education is provided in schools , where (in the absence of parental movement or other intervening factors) the child will stay, in steadily advancing classes, until they complete it and move on to secondary schooling. Children are usually placed in classes with one teacher who will be primarily responsible for their education and welfare for that year. This teacher may be assisted to varying degrees by specialist teachers in certain subject areas, often music or physical education. The continuity with a single teacher and the opportunity to build up a close relationship with the class is a notable feature of the primary education system. Over the past few decades, schools have been testing various arrangements which break from the one-teacher, one-class mold.

The major goals of primary education are achieving basic literacy and numeracy amongst all their students, as well as establishing foundations in science, geography, history and other social sciences . The relative priority of various areas, and the methods used to teach them, are an area of considerable political debate.

Traditionally, various forms of corporal punishment were an integral part of early education in the UK. This practice has now been outlawed in the UK.

7.2.2 Secondary education

Secondary education in England is normally conducted through secondaries which cover the two secondary key stages:

Key Stage 3

Year 7, age 11 to 12

Year 8, age 12 to 13

Year 9, age 13 to 14

Key Stage 4

Year 10, age 14 to 15

Year 11, age 15 to 16 (end of compulsory education)

In addition, some secondary schools also make provision for post-compulsory study through sixth form departments.

Year 12, age 16 to 17

Year 13, age 17 to 18

Historically, years 7 to 12/13 used to be known as "first form" to lower/upper sixth form. There now exists a common parallel usage for 6th form only: year 12/lower 6th and year 13/upper 6th, probably due to its separate, voluntary nature and situation as the A-level years.

7.2.3 Secondary school

In some schools, especially for subjects such as mathematics, science and modern languages, schools stream pupils on ability, otherwise pupils are taught with the other members of their form; all students study the same subjects and they are English, Welsh for pupils within Wales as it is compulsory at GCSE level, modern foreign languages, usually French, German or Spanish, geography, history, citizenship/guidance/PSHE, religious education, design technology, music, information and communications technology, drama and physical education. There are also vocational subjects which students may choose to learn, they are: hairdressing and beauty, construction, woodwork, travel and tourism, business studies and other more minor subjects. In grammar and public schools, it is more common for traditional subjects—such as Greek and Latin, to be additionally taught. All students between the ages of fourteen and sixteen in England and Wales sit the General Certificate of Secondary Education (GCSE) examinations, whereas the students in Scotland sit the Standard Grade at the fourth year of their schooling. The Standard Grade is broadly equivalent to that of the English General Certificate of Secondary Education. Students who do the General Certificate of Secondary Education usually sit five examinations at the minimum, generally sit around nine or ten examinations, and sometimes up to twelve or thirteen depending on what the school can provide. At GCSE level the following subjects are mandatory: English, mathematics, science, physical education, religious education, citizenship, information and communications technology. Schools then offer other subjects that the students can choose to do. Students sitting Standard Grade examinations sit eight.

7.2.4 National Curriculum

The UK introduced a national curriculum in 1992 and state schools are required to adhere to it until students reach age 16. However, independent schools are not obliged to do so.

National curriculum core subjects are: English, mathematics and science; Welsh is a core subject in Welsh-speaking schools. Foundation subjects are design and technology, information and communication technology, history, geography, modern foreign languages, music, art and design, physical education, religious education, and citizenship.

Northern Ireland follows a similar framework; however, schools can develop additional curriculum elements to express their particular ethos and meet pupils' individual needs and circumstances. The curriculum also includes the Irish language in Irish-speaking schools.

7.2.5 Examinations

After five years of secondary education, students take examinations in a range of subjects at the level of General Certificate of Secondary Education. The GCSE is a single-subject examination set and marked by independent examination boards. Students usually take up to ten (there is no upper or lower limit) GCSE examinations in different subjects, including mathematics and English.

After taking GCSE s, students may leave secondary schooling; alternatively, they may choose to continue their education at vocational or technical colleges, or they may take a higher level of secondary school examinations known as AS-levels after an additional year of study. Following two years of study, students may take A-level (short for advanced level) examinations, which are required for university entrance in the UK.

Scotland has its own qualification framework that is separate from that in England, Wales and Northern Ireland. After seven years of primary education and four years of compulsory secondary education, students aged 15 to 16 may take the Scottish Certificate of Education (SCE). The Scottish Certificate of Education is recognized throughout the UK as the equivalent to GCE A-levels and is usually the entry qualification for university.

All state-funded schools are regularly inspected by the Office for Standards in Education (Ofsted), which publishes reports of the quality of education at each school. Schools judged by Ofsted to be providing an inadequate standard of education may be placed in special measures, which may include replacing the governing body and senior staff.

Ofsted

The Office for Standards in Education, Children's Services and Skills (Ofsted) is the non-ministerial government department of Her Majesty's Chief Inspector of Schools in England ("HMCI"). [1] All the powers belong to HMCI or to Her Majesty's Inspectors of Schools ("HMI") who are appointed by Order in Council and are thus office holders under the Crown. Ofsted itself has no legal existence or statutory recognition but is identified in the public mind with the functions of HMCI.

HMCI is responsible for inspecting the standards of independent schools and state schools, local education authorities, child day care and childminding in England. It also monitors the work of the Independent Schools Inspectorate. [2] HMI are empowered and required to provide independent advice to the United Kingdom government and parliament on matters of policy and to publish an annual report to parliament on the quality of educational provision in England.

The Office carries out regular inspections of each school in England, resulting in a published evaluation of the effectiveness of the school. An adverse report may include a recommendation for further intervention in the running of the school.

The Education and Training Inspectorate in Northern Ireland, Her Majesty's Inspectorate of Education in Scotland, and Estyn in Wales perform similar functions within their education systems.

Ofsted's head office is in Kingsway, Holborn in central London.

The Department for Children, Schools and Families (DCSF) is a British government department responsible for all issues affecting people up to the age of 19 including child protection and education.

The Department for Business, Innovation and Skills (BIS) is a ministerial department of the United Kingdom Government created on 6 June 2009 by the merger of the Department for Innovation, Universities and Skills (DIUS) and the Department for Business, Enterprise and Regulatory Reform (BERR).

7.3 Higher Education

The autonomy of higher-educational institutions is strikingly pronounced in Great Britain. Its universities enjoy almost complete autonomy from national or local government in their administration and the determination of their curricula, despite the fact that the schools receive nearly all of their funding from the state. Entry requirements for British universities are rather complicated. A student must secure a General Certificate of Education by taking examinations in various subjects and receiving passing marks in them. The greater the number of "advanced level" passes, rather than General Certificate of Secondary Education (formerly "ordinary level") passes, that a student acquires, the better his chances are of entering the university of his choice. Britain has a centralized admissions bureau to which candidates for admission are able to give their choice of universities in an order of preference. This selective admission to universities, combined with the close supervision of students through a tutorial system, makes it possible for most British undergraduates to complete a degree course in three years rather than the standard four years. Great Britain's academic programs are more highly specialized than their European continental counterparts. Most undergraduates follow an "honours" course (leading to an honours degree) in one or, at the most, two subjects, while the remaining minority of students take "pass" courses that cover a variety of subjects. Great Britain's model of higher education has been copied to varying degrees in Canada, Australia, India, South Africa, New Zealand, and other former British colonial territories in Africa, Southeast Asia, and the Pacific.

Students normally enter university from 18 onwards and study for an academic degree. Approximately 1.8 million students are currently enrolled in the UK higher education system; about one third of young people go on to higher education at age 18 (with almost 50% of students in Scotland), and an increasing number of "mature" students are studying either full-time or part-time for university degrees. Higher education is a current policy priority for the government, with a target set to attract 50% of 18- to 30-year-olds to higher education by 2010.

7.3.1 Academic Degrees

Bachelor's degree

The typical first degree offered at British universities is the bachelor's degree (typically three years). During a first degree students are known as undergraduates. The state does not control syllabuses, but it does influence admission procedures. Unlike most degrees, the state still has control over teacher training courses, and uses Ofsted inspectors to maintain standards.

Postgraduate education

Students who have completed a first degree are eligible to undertake a postgraduate degree, which includes master's degree (typically taken in one year) and doctoral degree (typically taken in three years). Postgraduate education is not automatically financed by the state, and so admission is in practice highly competitive.

7.3.2 Adult Education

Adult education, continuing education or lifelong learning is offered to students of all ages. One-or two-year access courses allow adults access to university. The Open University runs a distance learning program which can result in a degree.

Open University Coat of Arms

The Open University is the distance learning university founded and funded by the UK Government. It is notable for having an open entry policy, i. e., students' previous academic achievements are not taken into account for entry to most undergraduate courses. The majority of undergraduate students are based in the United Kingdom, but its courses can be studied anywhere in the world. Most of the postgraduate students (higher education) are based on campus where they take courses and attend the OU facilities for research.

It was established in 1969 and the first students enrolled in January 1971. It is incorporated by Royal Charter as an exempt charity in England and Wales and a registered charity in Scotland.

The administration is based at Walton Hall, Milton Keynes in Buckinghamshire, but has regional centres in each of its thirteen regions around the UK. It also has offices in other European countries. The University awards undergraduate and postgraduate degrees, as well as non-degree qualifications such as diplomas and certificates, or continuing education units.

With more than 180,000 students enrolled, including more than 25,000 students studying overseas, it is the largest academic institution in the UK by student number, and qualifies as one of the world's largest universities. Since it was founded, more than 3 million students have studied its courses. It was rated top university in England and Wales for student satisfaction in the 2005[9] and 2006 UK government national student satisfaction survey, and second in the 2007 survey.

7.3.3 Further Education

Further education (often abbreviated "FE") is a term mainly used in connection with education in the United Kingdom and the Republic of Ireland. It is post-compulsory education (in addition to that received at secondary school), that is distinct from the education offered in universities (higher education). It may be at any level above compulsory education, from basic training to higher national diploma or foundation degree.

A distinction is usually made between FE and higher education ("HE") which is education at a higher level than secondary school, usually provided in distinct institutions such as universities. FE in the United Kingdom therefore includes education for people over 16, usually excluding universities. It is primarily taught in FE colleges (which are similar in concept to United States community colleges, and sometimes use "community college" in their title), work-based learning, and adult and community learning institutions. This includes post-16 courses similar to those taught at schools and sub-degree courses similar to those taught at higher education colleges (which also teach degree-level courses) and at some universities.

Colleges in England that are regarded as part of the FE sector include:

General FE and tertiary colleges

Sixth form colleges

Specialist colleges (mainly colleges of agriculture and horticulture and colleges of drama and dance)

In England, further education is often seen as forming one part of a wider learning and skills sector, alongside workplace education, prison education, and other types of non-school, non-university education and training. Since June 2009, the sector is overseen by the new Department for Business, Innovation and Skills, although some parts (such as education and training for 14 – 19 year olds) fall within the Department for Children, Schools and Families.

Exercises

I. Fill in the following blanks with proper words or expressions.

1. During the period between the two world wars, students completing primary school at age 11 were required to take a series of examinations called ________ .
2. ____________ are similar to the large, multipurpose American high school, in which the ability grouping system is known as "tracking".

3. The purpose of the comprehensive school is to ________ education, do away with early selection procedures, and provide equal opportunity for all children.
4. More than 93% of students in the UK attend publicly-funded ________ .
5. Public schools played an important role in the development of the ________ social elite.
6. Primary and secondary education together are sometimes (in particular, in Canada and the United States) referred to as ________ education.
7. National Curriculum core subjects are: ________ , ________ and ________ .
8. After five years of secondary education, students take examinations in a range of subjects at the level of ________ .
9. All state-funded schools are regularly inspected by the Office for Standards in Education (Ofsted), which publishes reports of the ________ at each school.
10. British universities enjoy almost ________ from national or local government in their administration and the determination of their curricula.

Ⅱ. Explain the following terms.

1. comprehensive schools
2. public schools
3. General Certificate of Secondary Education (GCSE)
4. further education
5. national curriculum

Ⅲ. Discuss the following questions.

1. In what ways is Chinese education different from British education in primary and secondary education?
2. Are there any problems in Chinese high education? What lessons can we learn from British high education?

Chapter Eight
Foreign Relations

Britain has diplomatic relations with 169 countries and is a member of some 120 international organizations. It has a complex pattern of economic, military, social, and cultural links with other countries. As one of five permanent members of the UN Security Council (China, France, Russian Federation, the United Kingdom and the United States), a founding member of the North Atlantic Treaty Organization (NATO)[1], and of the Commonwealth[2], Britain pursues a global approach to foreign policy; it currently is weighing the degree of its integration with continental Europe. A member of the European Union (EU), it chose to remain outside the Economic and Monetary Union for the time being.

The contemporary foreign policy of Britain is greatly influenced by its imperial history. During the 19th century, Great Britain had colonies all over the world and got the name "the sun-never-setting empire" in its history. Britain is no longer an imperial country now; yet, the effect of the "empire" can still be felt in Britain and in the international field in the following three respects. Firstly, it still has close relationships with those countries, which used to be a part of that empire. It maintains links through a voluntary organization called the Commonwealth of Nations. Secondly, it became a member of the European Union in 1973. And thirdly, it remains one of the 7 large developed economies (the UK, the United States, Italy, Germany, Japan, France and Canada) in the world.

8.1 Relations with Commonwealth Countries

8.1.1 The British Empire

The British Empire is the name given to the United Kingdom of Great Britain and Northern Ireland and the former dominions, colonies and other territories throughout the world from the seventeenth century to the middle of the twentieth century. At its height in the early 1900s, the British Empire was the largest empire in human history. It was an empire of 33 million square kilometers, taking up one fifth of the world's total dry land. The territory was about 135 times as large as that of Britain.

In 1900 it was not absurd to regard London as the centre of the world, and children learned certain phrases which expressed in simple terms the "truths" which the British regarded as paramount: The sun never sets on the British Empire; India is the brightest jewel in the Imperial crown; Britannia rules the waves. Such phrases are obviously now unrealistic. The old imperialism has become unfashionable, and the old "jingoism" has become absurd. Britain is merely one of the states of Western Europe, aiming to keep up with the economic progress of the others, and feeling some duty to give material help to former colonies without claiming any sort of power over them.

The history of the British Empire passed through several phases. The loss of the American colonies at the end of the eighteenth century was accepted easily enough, and during the nineteenth century there was a movement towards the granting of self-government to other parts of the world in which large numbers of migrants from Britain had settled permanently. During the late nineteenth and early twentieth centuries the older colonies of Australia, Canada, New Zealand and South Africa and the Irish Free State were given Dominion Status. This enabled them to enjoy internal self-government and a considerable degree of freedom in their foreign relations. The Dominions were seen as: "Autonomous communities within the British Empire, equal in status, in no way subordinate to one another in any aspect of their domestic or external affairs, though united by a common allegiance to the Crown and freely associated as members of the British Commonwealth of Nations."

After gaining independence in 1947, India decided to adopt a republican constitution and yet desired to remain within the Commonwealth. For many years prior to World War Ⅱ, Britain tried to hold on to India, which was regarded as "the jewel in the crown" of the Empire. If India gained independence, it was realized that soon the British Empire would be no more. In the late 1950s more of the colonies in the Caribbean and Africa sought independence. By 1968 most of Britain's colonial territories had been granted formal independence, thus making Britain's withdrawal from her former powerful world role.

8.1.2 The Commonwealth

Commonwealth of Nations is a worldwide voluntary association of independent sovereign states, whose members share a common commitment to promoting human rights, democracy, and economic development. The association was formerly known as the British Commonwealth of Nations, but today is referred to simply as the Commonwealth. There are 50 member nations with about 1. 7 billion people that make up the Commonwealth. All members accept the British monarch as the symbolic head of the Commonwealth. The second Monday in March is celebrated as Commonwealth Day; on that day the British monarch, as the head of the Commonwealth, presents an annual message to all member countries. English is an official language of many members of the Commonwealth. Commonwealth members share many customs and traditions as a result of their association with Britain. Many have parliamentary systems of government on the British model, and their judicial and educational institutions are often similar to those in Britain.

Almost all members of the Commonwealth were once ruled by Britain as part of the British Empire. All but one, Mozambique, were once associated in some constitutional way with either the former British Empire or with another member country. Some of them, such as Australia and Canada, were largely settled by British people. Others, such as India and Nigeria, were areas where British administrators governed a large non-British population.

The Commonwealth is a flexible and informal association. Its main function is to encourage communication and cooperation among its diverse members, with their different needs and concerns. Only independent nations can be considered full members; they are all fully sovereign and in no way subordinate to Britain. Dependencies of Commonwealth nations are also included in the Commonwealth although not as full members, and can participate in many Commonwealth activities. In 1965 the Commonwealth Secretariat was established in London to serve as a clearing house for the exchange of information. The Secretariat is headed by the Commonwealth secretary general and is responsible for carrying out programs formulated during the various meetings. The secretary general is elected by the Commonwealth heads of government from among the many Commonwealth diplomats and ministers. The Commonwealth Foundation provides financial and other support to professional associations and non-government organizations, making these groups able to travel to other Commonwealth countries to work together.

Every two years, the Commonwealth Conference is held, when the heads of Commonwealth governments meet to discuss common problems at Commonwealth Heads of Government Meetings (CHOGM). In addition, ministers and experts in education, health, finance, science, law, women's issues, youth affairs, and various technical fields meet frequently to consult and act on important issues.

So, even though Britain granted its colonial territories independence, it continued to feel close to these new countries and wanted to continue to cooperate with them. Many of these countries, having had similar experiences while being ruled by the British, found they shared similar histories, laws, economic concerns and cultural experiences which made them feel connected to each other. The Commonwealth was set up as a forum for continued cooperation and as a sort of support network.

8.2 Relations with Europe

Britain's links with Europe can be seen mainly from the different perspectives of its cultural and economic interests. Culturally, there is a long common cultural heritage between many of the European countries; some of their languages derive from the same Indo-European family, the landscapes are familiar and similar, and their religions are shared. The opening of the Channel Tunnel in 1994, providing a railway system under the sea linking Britain with France, brought Britain physically closer to Europe. Journeys between the two became quicker and more reliable, thus improving the communications and commercial links with Europe, in turn affecting both the cultural and economic spheres. Economically, today half of Britain's trade is with countries within the European Union whereas formally, in the days of her empire, her economic interests were bound up with her trading partners within the empire. The shift in Britain's economic interests from Commonwealth to Europe has been one of the chief changes observed in Britain's international relations since the 1960s.

In 1973 the United Kingdom joined the European Economic Community (EEC). This was an important psychological decision for the nation because traditionally Britain had looked beyond its European neighbors, feeling that it had more in common with the United States on the one hand, and the Commonwealth on the other. To many Britons, membership in the European Community meant turning its back on these "old friends[3]". In fact, the decision to join the EEC was a natural one given that British economic, political and military interests were already deeply bound up with other European countries.

The European Union (EU) has its roots in the experience of the two world wars which tore Europe apart in the first half of this century. Some of the countries involved, notably France and Germany, decided that they should work together to ensure peace rather than work against each other which seemed to lead to war. The EU was founded in 1958, when six countries signed the Treaty of Rome, their primary concern being to restore their economies which had suffered the aftermath of the two world wars in Europe. Further integration, particularly regarding economic aspects, were achieved with the ratification of the Single European Act in 1986.

The aims of the Union have been to reduce and remove restrictions between the member countries by the removal of internal trade barriers, by enabling a free flow of capital and the eventual introduction of a common currency, and by allowing citizens of all the member states to seek jobs in any of the member countries without having to acquire a work permit.

Because Britain has always been less enthusiastic about giving up its national sovereignty to a European government, the decision to join the EEC was very controversial. Today, Britain's participation in the European Union, as it is now called, remains controversial. At the centre of the controversy is the fact that it is not clear what the European Union (EU) is and what it will become. Britain likes to think of the EU as a place where economic cooperation is possible, with the free movement of goods and people. That is to say, while Britons are happy to have other European countries as trading partners, they are reluctant to think about them as fellow citizens belonging to the same state. Thus it has been said that while the British have their minds in Europe, their hearts have not followed. Even though Britain is deeply committed to the EU by accepting EU policies which it does not entirely agree with, it did not choose to use the euro in 2002.

8.3 Britain's Special Relationship with the US

It is quite natural that Britain and the United States hold a good relationship, as the two were closely allied during World War II, and continued to work together closely in the post war years because they shared many of the same worries about the Soviet Union. They also shared many secrets with each other, particularly in the areas of intelligence gathering and defense so that some analysts of international relations conclude that the relationship is "special". Some of the reasons for the "special" relationship are that both countries speak the same language and have a broadly similar culture, that their economic interests have been similar, and that both countries have agreed upon their main security interests, with the formation of the North Atlantic Treaty Organization (NATO) being the most concrete manifestation of this shared concern. Although the two countries do generally enjoy a good relationship, particularly since World War II, they are also distinct communities with their own identities.

However, the "special relationship" with the United States has gone through many ups and downs. The major test of Anglo-American relations occurred during the 1956 Suez Crisis. On July 26th, 1956, the Egyptian nationalist president Gamel Nasser[4], tried to nationalize the Suez Canal[5], which harmed British and French economic interests, so together British and French forces invaded, trying to take the canal back by force. To the surprise of the British, the Americans did not support this action and used America's economic power to force the Anglo-French forces to withdraw. Humiliated, the British began to realize that to a large extent their own foreign policy actions could be limited by the United States. It is regarded as Britain's last attempt to act out an imperial role on the world stage, and since then, Britain and the United States have worked hard to maintain good relations.

As a part of its NATO commitments, the British host a large American military presence. There are 63 American military bases in Britain. Since the collapse of the Soviet Union, some people have suggested that NATO is no longer necessary. However, all the main political parties in Britain see NATO as an important defense commitment, and feel that it is very necessary for the USA and Europe to stand together in this respect.

8.4 Britain's Security and Defense Policy

The end of the British Empire left Britain a medium-sized European country. The British economy ranks about sixth in the world. Lacking the all-powerful navy of its imperial past, Britain is no longer what it used to be. However, the UK still possesses independent nuclear deterrent and advanced armed forces. It maintains not only naval nuclear-armed submarines, but also air nuclear Tornado squadrons and ground-based nuclear missiles and weapons.

Britain spends more on defense than most other advanced industrial countries. It is the third largest spender in the world and is ranked fifth or sixth in terms of its military power. It is a member of the nuclear "club", maintaining an extensive nuclear capability which makes it a little brother to the nuclear superpowers. Britain also spends money on civil defense which is a significant part in its security, the purpose of which is to improve the quality and readiness of emergency system and to increase training opportunities arranged by the Home office.

The essential part of British defense policy is its participation in the North Atlantic Treaty Organization known as NATO, which aims to protect member states against aggression, to provide a foundation for security in Europe, and to provide a forum for transatlantic defense cooperation . NATO has promised that it is a threat to no country and that its weapons will only be used in self-defense. Britain takes pride in leading the newly-established Rapid Reaction Corps[6] in NATO, and it has established a land-based force which is designed to provide an early military response to a crisis. In addition to its NATO commitments, the UK retains an independent nuclear weapons capability. Since Britain is a traditional sea power, naturally its nuclear force is a naval one. Britain has three or four nuclear-armed submarines. In spite of being assigned to NATO, this nuclear force is fully under the command of the British government, and could be used independently if the British government ever thought it was necessary. All of the five permanent UN Security Council members have independent nuclear weapons capabilities. Nuclear weapons are important for the prestige of a country as well as its protection, though it is highly unlikely that Britain would ever use, or need to use it.

Notes

[1] the North Atlantic Treaty Organization(NATO): It was set up in 1949. It originally consisted of Belgium, Canada, Denmark, France, Iceland, Italy, Luxembourg, Netherlands, Norway, Portugal, UK, and USA. Now it has increased to nineteen member states. The purpose of NATO is to protect member states against aggression, to provide a foundation for security in Europe, and to provide a forum for transatlantic defense cooperation.

[2] the Commonwealth: It is a voluntary association of states which is made up mostly of former British colonies. There are 50 members of the Commonwealth: Many of these are developing countries like India and Cyprus; others are developed nations like Australia, Canada and New Zealand. The Commonwealth was set up as a forum for continued cooperation and as a sort of support network.

[3] old friends: "Old friends" here refers to the United States and

the Commonwealth countries.

[4] Gamel Nasser: He is the Egyptian army officer and statesman, who was born in 1918 and died in 1970. He and Neguib led the military coup and overthrew the monarchy. He was Prime Minister from 1954 to 1956 and he nationalized the Suez Canal in 1956. He was president of the United Arab Republic from 1958 to 1970.

[5] the Suez Canal: It is a shipping canal connecting the Mediterranean at Port Said with the Red Sea. The canal provides the shortest route for sea traffic between Europe and Asia. It was built between 1859 and 1869 by Ferdinand de Lesseps with the French and Egyptian capital, but Britain bought a major interest in the company and controlled it in 1875. It was nationalized by Nasser in 1956.

[6] Rapid Reaction Corps: RRC is a land-based military force which was established by the NATO to meet the emergency. The British troops dominated the corps, which they are proud of. Nowadays many countries have established such troops in order to deal with terrorists and emergencies.

Exercises

I. Fill in the following blanks with proper words or expressions.

1. The contemporary foreign policy of the UK is greatly influenced by its ________ history.
2. During the 19th century, Great Britain had colonies all over the world and got the name "____________" in its history.
3. During the late nineteenth and early twentieth centuries, some older colonies were given Dominion status. Name two of these colonies: __________ and ____________.
4. For many years prior to World War II, Britain tried to hold on to ________, which was regarded as "the jewel in the crown" of the Empire.
5. The opening of the ____________ in 1994, providing a railway system under the sea linking Britain with France, brought Britain physically closer to Europe.
6. The shift in Britain's economic interests from Commonwealth to ________ has been one of the chief changes observed in Britain's international relations since the 1960s.
7. The UK joined the European Economic Community in ________.
8. The major test of Anglo-American relations occurred during the 1956 ___________.
9. Britain is a member of ________ "club", maintaining an extensive nuclear capability

which makes it a little brother to the nuclear ________.

10. Since Britain is a traditional sea power, it's not surprising that Britain has three or four nuclear armed ____________.

Ⅱ. Explain the following terms.

1. The British Empire
2. The Commonwealth
3. The European Union
4. NATO

Ⅲ. Discuss the following questions.

1. How did the British Empire end? How did the British react to this reality?
2. How is the relationship between Britain and Europe? What do they have in common?

Chapter Nine

Religion

9.1 General Introduction

The United Kingdom has one of the most religiously diverse populations in the European Union. Each religion has a considerable internal diversity of traditions, movements, cultures and languages.

Religious practice cuts across ethnic groups and ethnic groups are multi-religious. Indians for example may be Sikhs, Hindus, Muslims, Christians or others. The largest religious minority in the UK are the Muslims. It is estimated that there are over two million Muslims in the UK today. Jews, Hindus and Sikhs are also large religious minorities in the UK.

Religion in the United Kingdom is about the development of religion in the United Kingdom since its formation in 1707. The Treaty of Union that led to the formation of the United Kingdom of Great Britain (which became the United Kingdom of Great Britain and Ireland in 1801 when Great Britain signed an Act of Union with Ireland) ensured that there would be a Protestant succession as well as a link between church and state that still remains.

According to the 2001 UK census, Christianity remains the major religion, followed by Islam, Hinduism, Sikhism, Judaism and Buddhism in terms of number of adherents. In the 2001 census, 71.6% of the population put themselves down as Christian. Though each country that makes up the UK has a long tradition of Christianity that pre-dates the UK itself, in practice all have relatively low levels of religious observance and today are secular societies.

Religions in the United Kingdom, 2001

Religion/Denomination	Current religion	Percent
Christian	42,079,000	71.6
No religion	9,104,000	15.5
Muslim	1,591,000	2.7
Hindu	559,000	1.0
Sikh	336,000	0.6
Jewish	267,000	0.5
Buddhist	152,000	0.3
Other religions	179,000	0.3
All religions	45,163,000	76.8
Not answered	4,289,000	7.3
No religion + Not answered	13,626,000	23.2
Base	58,789,000	100

Source: UK 2001 Census

Denominations in Great Britain

Religion/Denomination	Percent
No religion	45.7
Church of England	20.9
Roman Catholic	9.0
Presbyterian/Church of Scotland	2.8
Methodist	1.9
Other Protestant	2.7
Christian (no denomination)	10.3
Other Christian	0.4
Muslim	3.3
Hindu	1.4
Jewish	0.4
Sikh	0.4
Other religions	0.4
Refused / NA	0.5

Source: BSA Survey 2007

Religions of Ethnic Groups

Ethnic group	Christian	Buddhist	Hindu	Jewish	Muslim	Sikh	Others	No religion	Not stated
White British	75.94%	0.11%	0.01%	0.48%	0.14%	0.01%	0.24%	15.45%	7.62%
White Irish	85.42%	0.19%	0.02%	0.18%	0.14%	0.02%	0.26%	6.35%	7.42%
Other White	62.67%	0.33%	0.09%	2.39%	8.61%	0.04%	0.57%	15.91%	9.38%
Mixed	52.46%	0.70%	0.87%	0.47%	9.72%	0.42%	0.58%	23.25%	11.54%
Indian	4.89%	0.18%	45.00%	0.06%	12.70%	29.06%	1.75%	1.73%	4.63%
Pakistani	1.09%	0.03%	0.08%	0.05%	92.01%	0.05%	0.04%	0.50%	6.16%
Bangladeshi	0.50%	0.06%	0.60%	0.05%	92.48%	0.04%	0.01%	0.43%	5.83%
Other Asian	13.42%	4.85%	26.76%	0.30%	37.31%	6.22%	0.93%	3.44%	6.79%
Black Caribbean	73.76%	0.17%	0.29%	0.10%	0.79%	0.02%	0.59%	11.23%	13.04%
Black African	68.87%	0.07%	0.21%	0.05%	20.04%	0.09%	0.21%	2.31%	8.14%
Other Black	66.61%	0.20%	0.36%	0.13%	5.97%	0.07%	0.65%	12.09%	13.93%
Chinese	25.56%	15.12%	0.07%	0.05%	0.33%	0.03%	0.49%	9.75%	52.60%
Other	32.98%	15.49%	1.32%	1.05%	25.68%	1.02%	0.90%	14.08%	7.48%

Source: UK 2001 Census

9.2 England and Wales

Christianity is the most widely practiced and declared religion in England. The Anglican Church of England is the established church of England holding a special constitutional position for the United Kingdom. After Christianity, religions with the most adherents are Islam, Hinduism, Sikhism, Judaism, Buddhism, the Bahá'í Faith, the Rastafari movement and Neopaganism. There are also organisations which promote irreligion, atheist humanism, and secularism.

Many of England's most notable buildings and monuments are religious in nature, including Stonehenge, the Angel of the North, Westminster Abbey, St Paul's Cathedral and Canterbury Cathedral. The festivals of Christmas and Easter, both of which are religious in origin, are still widely commemorated in the country.

Stonehenge is a prehistoric monument located in the English county of Wiltshire, about 3.2 kilometres (2.0 mi) west of Amesbury and 13 kilometres (8.1 mi) north of Salisbury. Archaeologists had believed that the iconic stone monument was erected around 2500 BC.

Westminster Abbey

St Paul's Cathedral

The Collegiate Church of St Peter at Westminster, which is almost always referred to popularly and informally as Westminster Abbey, is a large, mainly Gothic church, in Westminster, London, just to the west of the Palace of Westminster. It is the traditional place of coronation and burial site for English, later British and later still (and currently) monarchs of the Commonwealth Realms.

St Paul's Cathedral is an Anglican cathedral on Ludgate Hill, the highest point in the City of London, and is the seat of the Bishop of London. The present building dates from the 17th century and was designed by Sir Christopher Wren.

Canterbury Cathedral

Canterbury Cathedral in Canterbury, Kent, is one of the oldest and most famous Christian structures in England and forms part of a World Heritage Site.

It is the cathedral of the Archbishop of Canterbury, leader of the Church of

England and symbolic leader of the worldwide Anglican Communion. Its formal title is the Cathedral and Metropolitical Church of Christ at Canterbury.

9.2.1 Christianity

Christianity was first introduced through the Romans, who invaded England under the leadership of Julius Caesar in 55 BC and ruled England till their withdrawal in early 5th century when Roman Empire faced serious threats from the normadic tribes from central Asia steppes. Archaeological evidence for Christian communities began to appear in the 3rd and 4th centuries. The Romano-British population after the withdrawal of the Roman legions was mostly Christian.

Christianity was re-introduced into England through missionaries from Scotland and from Continental Europe; the era of St Augustine (the first Archbishop of Canterbury) and the Celtic Christian missionaries in the north (notably St Aidan and St Cuthbert). The Synod of Whitby in 664 ultimately led to the English Church being fully part of Roman Catholicism.

Norman nobles and bishops had influence before the Norman Conquest of 1066, and Norman influences affected late Anglo-Saxon architecture. Edward the Confessor was brought up in Normandy, and in 1042 brought masons to work on Westminster Abbey, the first Romanesque building in England.

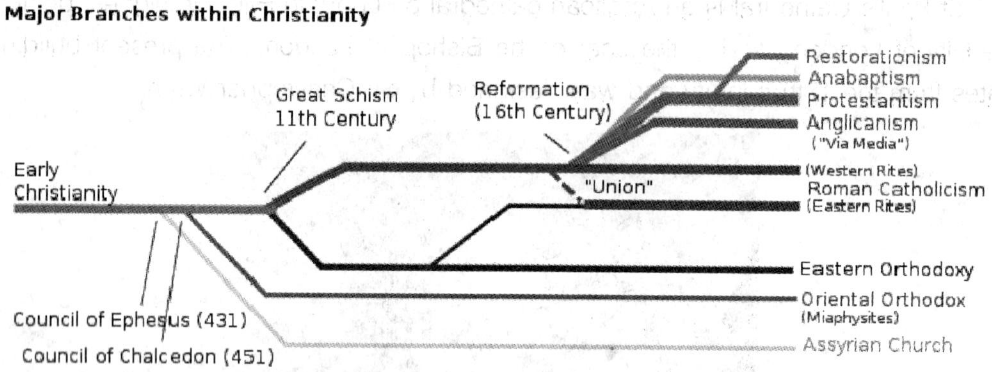

The initial differences between the East and West traditions stemmed from socio-cultural and linguistic divisions in and between the Western Roman and Byzantine Empires. Since the West (that is, Western Europe) spoke Latin as its lingua franca and the East (Eastern Europe, the Middle East, Asia, and northern Africa) largely used Koine Greek to transmit writings, theological developments were difficult to translate from one branch to the other. In the course of ecumenical councils (large gatherings of Christian leaders), some church bodies split from the larger family of Christianity. Many earlier heretical groups either died off for lack of followers and/or suppression by the church at large.

The first significant, lasting split in historic Christianity came from the Church of the East, who left following the Christological controversy over Nestorianism in 431. Today, the Assyrian and Roman Catholic Church view this schism as largely linguistic, due to problems of translating very delicate and precise terminology from Latin to Aramaic and vice versa. Following the Council of Chalcedon in 451, the next large split came with the Syrian and Alexandrian churches dividing themselves, with the dissenting churches becoming today's Oriental Orthodoxy (A similar Christological statement was made between Pope John Paul II and Syriac patriarch Ignatius Zakka II, as well as between representatives of both Eastern and Oriental Orthodoxy).

There has been a claim that the Chalcedonian Creed restored Nestorianism, however this is refuted by maintaining the following distinctions associated with the *person* of Christ: two hypostases, two natures (Nestorian); one hypostasis, one nature (Monophysite); one hypostasis, two natures (Orthodox/Catholic).

Although the church as a whole didn't experience any major divisions for centuries afterward, the Eastern and Western groups drifted until the point where patriarchs from both families excommunicated one another in about 1054 in what is known as the Great Schism. The political and theological reasons for the schism were complex, but one major controversy was the inclusion and acceptance in the West of the filioque clause into the Nicene Creed, which the East viewed as erroneous. Another was the definition of papal primacy. Both West and East agreed that the patriarch of Rome was owed a "primacy of honour" by the other patriarchs (those of Alexandria, Antioch, Constantinople and Jerusalem), but the West also contended that this primacy extended to jurisdiction, a position rejected by the Eastern patriarchs. Various attempts at dialogue between the two groups would occur, but it was only in the 1960s, under Pope Paul VI and Patriarch Athenagoras, that significant steps began to be made to mend the relationship between the two.

In Western Christianity, there were a handful of geographically isolated movements that preceded the spirit of the Protestant Reformation. The Cathars were a very strong movement in medieval southwestern France, but did not survive into modern times. In northern Italy and southeastern France, Peter Waldo founded the Waldensians in the 12th century. This movement has largely been absorbed by modern-day Protestant groups. In Bohemia, a movement in the early 15th century by Jan Hus called the Hussites defied Roman Catholic dogma and still exists to this day (alternately known as the Moravian Church).

The Protestant Reformation began with the posting of Martin Luther's *Ninety-Five Theses* in Saxony on October 31, 1517, written as a set of grievances to reform the pre-Reformation Western Church. Luther's writings, combined with the work of Swiss theologian Huldrych Zwingli and French theologian and politician John Calvin sought to reform existing problems in doctrine and practice. However, due to the reactions of ecclesiastical office holders at the time of the reformers, the Roman Catholic Church separated from them, instigating a rift in Western Christianity. In England, Henry VIII of England declared himself to be supreme governor of the Church of England with the Act of Supremacy in 1531, founding the Church of England, repressing both Lutheran reformers and those loyal to the pope.

The Old Catholic Church split from the Roman Catholic Church in the 1870s because of the promulgation of the dogma of Papal Infallibility as promoted by the First Vatican Council of 1869 – 1870. The term "Old Catholic" was first used in 1853 to describe the members of the See of Utrecht that were not under Papal authority. The Old Catholic movement grew in America but has not maintained ties with Utrecht, although talks were under way between independent Old Catholic bishops and Utrecht.

The Liberal Catholic Church started in 1916 via an Old Catholic bishop in London, bishop Matthew, who consecrated bishop James Wedgwood to the Episcopacy. This stream has in its relatively short existence known many splits, which operate worldwide under several names.

9.2.2 The Reformation in England

These events were, in part, associated with the wider process of the European Protestant Reformation, a religious and political movement which affected the practice of Christianity across most of Europe during this period. Many factors contributed to the process: the decline of feudalism and the rise of nationalism, the rise of the common law, the invention of the printing press and increased circulation of the Bible, the transmission of new knowledge and ideas among scholars and the upper and middle classes. However, the various phases of the English Reformation, which also covered Wales and Ireland, were largely driven by changes in government policy, to which public opinion gradually accommodated itself.

England was peculiar in that its government broke with the Roman church before adopting any Protestant principles. Henry VIII in fact prided himself on his orthodoxy. When a few obscure persons, about 1520, began to whisper Luther's ideas in England, Henry himself wrote a *Defense of the Seven Sacraments* in refutation, for which a grateful pope conferred upon him the title "Defender of the Faith". But the king had no male heir. Recalling the violent anarchy from which the Tudor dynasty had extricated England, and determined as a New Monarchy to build up a durable monarchy, he decided that he must remarry in order to have a son. He therefore requested the pope, Clement VII, to annul his existing marriage to Catherine of Aragon. Popes in the past had obliged monarchs in similar situations. The pope now, however, was embarrassed by the fact that Cathrine, who objected, was the aunt of the Emperor Charles V, whom the pope was in no position to offend. Henry, not a patient man, drove matters forward. He appointed a new archbishop of Canterbury, repudiated the Roman connection, secured the annulment of his earlier marriage, and married the youthful Anne Boleyn. In 1534 English Parliament passed the Act of Supremacy, which declared the English king to be the "Protector and Only Supreme Head of the Church and Clergy of England". All subjects were required to take the oath of supremacy acknowledging the religious headship of Henry and rejecting that of the pope. For refusing this oath Sir Thomas More, a statesman and humanist best known as the author of *Utopia*, was executed for treason. Henry, in the next few years, closed all the monasteries in England, seized the extensive monastic lands, and passed them out to numerous followers. He thus strengthened and reconstituted a landed aristocracy which had been seriously weakened in the Wars of Roses. The new landed gentry remained firm supporters of the house of Tudor and the English national church, whatever its doctrines.

Henry died in 1547 and was succeeded by his 10-year-old son, Edward VI. The Protestant party now came to the fore. But Edward died in 1553 and was succeeded by his much older half-sister, Mary, the daughter of Catherine of Aragon and a devout Roman Catholic whose whole life had been embittered by the break with Rome. Mary tried to re-Catholicize England, but she actually made Catholicism more unpopular with the English. She was succeeded by Elizabeth. Under Elizabeth the English became Protestant, gradually and in their own way. The Church of England took on a form of its own: English replaced Latin as the language of the liturgy, there was no cult of the saints, and the clergy married. In doctrine, it was Elizabeth's policy to make the dogmas broad and ambiguous, so that persons of all shades of belief could be more readily accommodated. The Thirty-nine Articles, composed by a committee of bishops, defined the creed of the Anglican church.

Timeline of the English Reformation

- Act of Supremacy (1534): declared that Henry VIII was "the only supreme head on earth of the Church in England" and required the nobility to swear an oath recognising Henry's supremacy.
- Six Articles (1539): although the organisation of the church in England was reformed, the articles reaffirmed Catholic doctrine.
- Book of Common Prayer and Book of Common Order
- Prayer Book Rebellion

- Marian Persecutions and Marian exiles: during the re-establishment of Roman Catholicism in England under Mary I, some Protestants were persecuted and some upheld their faith in exile.
- Elizabethan Religious Settlement: under Elizabeth I political and religious stability was maintained by means of a compromise in both doctrine and practice between the Anglicanism of Henry VIII and that of Edward VI.
    - Act of Supremacy 1559: it restored religious affairs in England to the state at the death of Edward VI, and imposed the Oath of Supremacy on those holding office.
    - Thirty-Nine Articles (1563): the defining statements of Anglican doctrine were made a legal requirement in England in 1571 and were imposed by the Test Act of 1673 (until 1824).
    - Regnans in Excelsis
- Priest hole: wealthy Roman Catholics constructed hiding places in their houses for priests.
- James I of England and religious issues
    - Gunpowder Plot: a conspiracy by a small group of Catholic extremists to blow up king James I and his parliameut on 5 November 1605.
- The Vicar of Bray: the changes of political and religious regime required office holders to show flexibility in their declared convictions, as satirised in the popular song *The Vicar of Bray*.
- Westminster Assembly (1643): it was appointed by the Long Parliament to restructure the Church of England, drew up the Westminster Confession of Faith (which became, and remains, the "subordinate standard" of doctrine in the Church of Scotland and has been influential within Presbyterian churches worldwide).
- 1689 Baptist Confession of Faith: it was written by Calvinistic Baptists in England to give a formal expression of the Reformed and Protestant Christian faith with an obvious Baptist perspective.
- Royal Declaration of Indulgence (1672): Charles II attempted to extend religious liberty to Protestant nonconformists in his realms.
- Declaration of Indulgence (1687 – 1688): James II attempted to establish freedom of religion in England.
    - Seven Bishops: bishops of the Church of England who petitioned James II against the Declaration of Indulgence were imprisoned.
- Popish Plot (1678 – 1681): a conspiracy to discredit Catholics in England accused Catholics of plotting.
- Exclusion Bill: it sought to exclude the Charles II's brother and heir

presumptive, James, Duke of York, from the throne of England because he was Catholic.

- Penal law: a specific series of laws that sought to uphold the establishment of the Church of England against Protestant nonconformists and Roman Catholics, by imposing various forfeitures, civil penalties, and civil disabilities upon these dissenters.
  - Test Act: it required a religious test of officials to ensure conformity with the established church.
  - Act of Uniformity 1662: it required the use of all the rites and ceremonies in the Book of Common Prayer in Church of England services, and episcopal ordination for all ministers.
  - Conventicle Act 1664: it forbade religious assemblies of more than five people outside the auspices of the Church of England.
  - Five Mile Act 1665: it forbade clergymen from living within five miles (8 km) of a parish from which they had been banned.
- Nonjuring schism: the Anglican Church split in the aftermath of the Glorious Revolution of 1688, over whether William of Orange could legally be recognized as King of England.

Today, the Church of England is the established church in England. It regards itself as in continuity with the Pre-Reformation State Catholic Church (something the Roman Catholic Church does not accept), but has been a distinct Anglican Church since the settlement under Elizabeth I (with some disruption during the 17th-century Commonwealth period). British Monarch is formally Supreme Governor of the Church of England, but its spiritual leader is the Archbishop of Canterbury, who is regarded by convention as the head of the worldwide communion of Anglican Churches. In practice the Church of England is governed by the General Synod, under the authority of Parliament.

9.2.3 Roman Catholicism

The English Church was heavily influenced by Rome from the arrival of St Augustine of Canterbury who arrived in AD 598, until the final break with Roman control at the accession of Elizabeth I in 1558.

The early years of the UK were difficult for English adherents of the Roman Catholic Church, although the persecution was not violent as they had experienced in the recent past, for instance under the Popery Act 1698, that affected adherents in England and Wales. The civil rights of adherents to Roman Catholicism were severely curtailed, and there was no longer, as once in Stuart times, any Catholic presence at court, in public life, in the military or professions. Many of the Catholic nobles and gentry who had preserved on their lands among their tenants small pockets of Catholicism had followed James II into exile, and others at last conformed to Anglicanism, meaning that only very few such Catholic communities survived.

In the late 18th and early 19th centuries most restrictions on Catholic participation in public life were relaxed under acts such as the *Papists Act* 1778, *Roman Catholic Relief Act* 1791 and *Catholic Relief Act* 1829. This process of Catholic Emancipation met violent opposition in the Gordon Riots of 1780 in London. In the 1840s and 1850s, especially during the Great Irish Famine, while the bulk of the large outflow of emigration from Ireland was headed to the United States, thousands of poor Irish people also moved to England, establishing communities in cities and towns up and down the country such as London and Liverpool, thus giving Catholicism a huge numerical boost. In 1850, the Roman Catholic Church in England and Wales re-established a hierarchy.

9.2.4 Methodism

A strong tradition of Methodism developed from the 18th century onwards. The Methodist revival was started in England by a group of men including John Wesley and his younger brother Charles as a movement within the Church of England, but developed as a separ.

9.2.5 Pentecostal

Pentecostal churches are continuing to grow and, in terms of church attendance, are now third after the Church of England and the Roman Catholic Church. There are three main denominations of Pentecostal churches:

- Assemblies of God in Great Britain are part of the World Assemblies of God Fellowship.
- Apostolic Church.
- Elim Pentecostal Church.

There is also a growing number of independent, charismatic churches that encourage Pentecostal practices at part of their worship, such as Kingsgate Community Church in Peterborough which started with 9 people in 1988 and now has a congregation in excess of 1,500.

9.2.6 Islam

Islam in England is the second largest religion, with most Muslims being immigrants from South Asia (in particular Pakistan, Bangladesh and India), or being descendants of immigrants from that region. Many others are from Muslim-dominated regions such as the Middle East, Somalia, Malaysia and Indonesia, while fewer come from other African countries such as Nigeria, Uganda and Sierra Leone.

London Central Mosque in Regents Park, London

Although Islam is generally thought of as being a recent arrival to the country, there has been contact with Muslims for many centuries. An early example would be the decision of Offa, the eighth-century King of Mercia (one of the Anglo-Saxon kingdoms existing at that time), to have coins minted with an Islamic inscription on them—copies of coins issued by the near-contemporary Muslim ruler Al-Mansur. It is thought that they were minted to facilitate trade with the expanding Islamic empire in Spain.

Muslim scholarship was well known among the learned in England by 1386, when Chaucer was writing. In the Prologue to the *Canterbury Tales*, there is among the pilgrims wending their way to Canterbury, a "Doctour of Phisyk" whose learning included Razi, Avicenna. Ibn Sina's canon of medicine was a standard text for medical students well into the 17th century.

Islam today is the second largest religion in England with 40% of Muslims living in London, where they make up 8.5% of the population. There are also large numbers of Muslims in Birmingham, Manchester, Bradford, Luton, Slough, Leicester and the mill towns of Northern England.

Notable mosques include the London Central Mosque, Al-Rahma Mosque, Birmingham Central Mosque, East London Mosque, Finsbury Park Mosque, London Markaz and Markazi Mosque.

9.2.7 Judaism

The first written records of Jewish settlement in England date from the time of the Norman Conquest, mentioning Jews who arrived with William the Conqueror in 1066 although it is believed that there were Jews present in Great Britain since Roman times. The Jewish population lived in England from the Norman Conquest until they were expelled in 1290 by a decree of King Edward I. England had no official Jewish presence, save for isolated individuals who practiced Judaism secretly, until the reign of Oliver Cromwell. While Cromwell never officially readmitted Jews to Britain, the small colony of Sephardic Jews living in London was unmasked in 1656, and, because of Cromwell's need of their financial assistance, they were allowed to stay. While the Jewish community in Britain remained comparatively small until the late nineteenth century, there had long been efforts to integrate Jews into British life legally. The Jewish Naturalisation Act of 1753 was in force for only a few months and would not have allowed for the naturalization of many, save a few wealthy businessmen. Historians commonly date Jewish Emancipation to 1858 when Jews were finally allowed to sit in Parliament though a few other minor pieces of legislation continued into the 1890s. Due to the lack of anti-Jewish violence in Britain in the nineteenth century, it acquired a reputation for religious tolerance. Britain became a haven for some Jews fleeing the Holocaust in the 1930s – 1940s, and the Jewish community in Britain continues to be vibrant today.

9.2.8 Hinduism

Hinduism in England is particularly found in London where the majority of the country's Hindu population lives. Within London, Hinduism is found in Brent and Harrow where Hindus make up a fifth of the population, and to a lesser extent, in Southall, Hounslow, Hendon, and Wembley. Outside London, Leicester has a significant concentration of Hindus, largely from East Africa, with over 40,000 living in the city. England has a number of Hindu temples, including the Hindu temple at Neasden which is the largest Hindu temple in Europe. Recently the largest Hindu Mandir in the North of England, the Bradford Lakshmi Narayan Hindu Temple opened in Bradford, West Yorkshire.

Neasden Temple

Early Hindus in England were mostly students during the 19th century. There have been three waves of migration of Hindus to England since then.

Before India's Independence in 1947, Hindu migration was minuscule and largely temporary. The second wave of Hindu migration occurred in the 1970s after the expulsion of Gujarati Hindus from Uganda. Initially, Hindu immigration was limited to Punjabi and Gujarati Hindus, but, by 2000, small Hindu communities of every ethnicity could be found in England. England is also host to a large immigrant community of Sri Lankan Hindus who are mostly Tamils. The last wave of migration of Hindus has been taking place since the 1990s with refugees from Sri Lanka and professionals from India. However, there is becoming an increasing number of English Western Hindus in England, who have either converted from another faith or been an English Hindu from birth.

9.2.9 Sikhism

The first Sikh migration came in the 1950s. It was mostly of men from the Punjab seeking work in industries like foundries and textiles. These new arrivals mostly settled in London, Birmingham and West Yorkshire. Thousands of Sikhs from East Africa soon followed, this mass immigration was caused by Idi Amin's persecution of ethnic groups in Uganda, thousands forced to flee the region in fear of losing their lives.

9.2.10 Buddhism

The earliest Buddhist influence on England came through the UK's imperial connections with South East Asia, and as a result the early connections were with the Theravada traditions of Burma, Thailand, and Sri Lanka. The tradition of study resulted in the foundation of the Pali Text Society, which undertook the task of translating the Pali Canon of Buddhist texts into English.

In 1924 London's Buddhist Society was founded, and in 1926 the Theravadin London Buddhist Vihara. The rate of growth was slow but steady through the century, and the 1950s saw the development of interest in Zen Buddhism.

9.3 Scotland

Christianity is the largest religion in Scotland. At the 2001 census 65% of the Scottish population was Christian. The Church of Scotland, often known as the Kirk, is recognised in law as the national church of Scotland. It is not an established church and is independent of state control. However, it is the largest religious grouping in Scotland, with 42% of the population. The other major denomination is the Roman Catholic Church, which claims around 16% of the population, and is especially important in west central Scotland. There are also around 15,000 each of Baptists, Episcopalians and conservative Presbyterians, with smaller numbers of Quakers, Pentecostal, Gospel Hall. The only churches to witness an increase in attendance are independent churches, which include the popular evangelical wing. Judaism has been established in Scotland since at least the High Middle Ages. In recent years other religions have established a presence in Scotland, mainly through immigration, though also partly through the attraction of converts. Those with the most adherents are Islam (mainly among immigrants from South Asia), Buddhism, Sikhism and Hinduism. Other minority faiths include the Bahá'í Faith, Rasta and small Neopagan groups. There are also various organisations which actively promote humanism, rationalism and secularism, reflecting the 28% who claim to have no religious beliefs, or did not state a religion.

9.4 Northern Ireland

Christianity remains by far the largest religion in the country, though several other religions have also established a presence. The Church of Ireland in recent years has seen a drop in members along with many other church such as the Methodist. The Presbyterian Church has seen a minor increase, the Roman Catholic Church has increased by up to 3%. Though dwarfed by the Christian churches, the country also has small Muslim, Hindu, Sikh, Buddhist and Jewish communities. There is a Muslim Mosque, Jewish Synagogue, Sikh Gurdwara and two Hindu Temples in Belfast. There is another Sikh Gurdwara in Derry. The Muslim community is one of the fastest growing non-Christian faith in Northern Ireland. Jews in Northern Ireland are small in number, about 500, down from 1,310 in 1967, but in recent years the population has seen a small growth.

9.5 Future Trends

According to reporter Ruth Gledhill, the document *Religious Trends* published by *Christian Research* in 2008 estimates that:

- By 2035, 1.96 million Muslims—double the number attending today—will be attending mosques. They will outnumber Christians who attend churches.
- Church attendance in Britain is declining so fast that the "Church of England, Catholicism and other denominations will become financially unviable". By 2030, the number of Anglican churches in the UK will drop to 10,000 with an average attendance of 35 persons.
- By 2050 only about 0.9 million Christians will go to church. There will be only 3,600 churchgoing Methodists, 87,899 members of the Church of England, 101,700 Roman Catholics, 4,400 Presbyterians, 123,000 Baptists, and 168,000 independent Christians.
- Calls for disestablishment of the Church of England, which has been the official church, will likely result.

In general, such future trends will present the UK many challenges in near future and, thus, provide another prospect to approach this country.

Exercises

I. Fill in the following blanks with proper words or expressions.

1. ___________ and _______ are the two religions that have most adherents in the UK.
2. The ___________ is the established church of England holding a special constitutional position for the United Kingdom.
3. Christianity was first introduced into England through ___________.
4. In 1536, the Church in England split from Rome over the issue of the divorce of ___________ from Catherine of Aragon. The split led to the emergence of a separate ecclesiastical authority.
5. The initial differences between the East and West traditions stem from ___________ and _______ divisions in and between the Western Roman and Byzantine Empires.
6. The Protestant Reformation began with the posting of Martin Luther's ___________ in Saxony on October 31, _______, written as a set of grievances to reform the pre-Reformation Western Church.
7. Under ___________ the English became Protestant, gradually and in their own way.
8. ___________, often known as the Kirk, is recognised in law as the national church of Scotland.
9. ___________ declared that Henry VIII was "the only supreme head on earth of the Church in England" and required the nobility to swear an oath recognising Henry's supremacy.
10. In the future, calls for ___________ of the Church of England, which has been the official church, will likely result.

II. Explain the following terms.

1. Protestant Reformation
2. English Reformation
3. Act of Supremacy
4. Westminster Abbey

III. Discuss the following questions.

1. What were the major factors which contributed to the English Reformation?
2. What are the situations of Muslims in the UK?

Chapter Ten

News Media

The United Kingdom has a wide diversity of news media with an almost unparalleled number of outlets. If you live in this country, you will find a plentiful of ways to keep yourself well-informed and divert yourself in your leisure time. You can pick up your morning paper at breakfast table, you can turn on the car radio on your way to work, you can enjoy a favorite television show with your family after a tiring day of work, and also you can surf on the Internet as a perfect way to end the day.

10.1 The Press

Britain has one of the world's oldest published newspaper industries. Published in the year 1513, *Trewe Encountre* is known as the earliest printed newspaper in Britain. In the late 18th and 19th centuries, an increasing number of newspapers began to appear along with the industrialization of economy and the enhanced literary levels due to mass education. *The Observer*, a popular Sunday newspaper, first published in 1791, rendering it the world's oldest national newspaper, while *The Times*, launched in 1785, is Britain's oldest daily newspaper. London's Fleet Street and Manchester remained the center of the newspaper printing and publishing until the 1980s, but now all of the national newspapers have moved their headquarters to other parts of London or away from the capital.

The period from 1860 to 1910 was considered a "golden age" of newspaper publication, with technical advances in printing and communication combined with a professionalization of journalism and the prominence of new owners. Then newspapers became more partisan[1] and there was the rise of new or yellow journalism. Socialist and labor newspapers also proliferated and in 1912 *the Daily Herald* was published as the first daily newspaper of the trade union and labor movement.

There are about 130 daily and Sunday newspapers, over 2,000 weekly newspapers and 7,000 periodical publications in Britain today. The newspapers are traditionally categorized into two types: the quality newspapers (qualities or broadsheets) and popular newspapers (populars or tabloids). Following the tradition of the press of the 18th and 19th centuries, broadsheets are larger in size and are seen as being more intellectual and upmarket. Largely composed of in-depth articles of particular political and social importance, as well as reviews and feature articles about "high culture", the kind of newspapers are generally read by a well-educated, middle-class audience. *The Times*, *The Guardian* and *The Daily Telegraph* are referred to as Britain's "Big Three". Tabloids, on the other side, are smaller in size and seen as being more downmarket than broadsheets, catering to gossip and stories about celebrities, whether in politics, sports or entertainment. They carry lots of crime, sports and sensational human interest stories and thus gain the name "the gutter press". Since the term "tabloid" has become a synonym for down-market newspapers in Britain, some small-format papers which claim a higher standard of journalism refer to themselves as "compact" newspapers instead.

The circulation of newspapers, in relation to the population, is higher in Britain than in any other developed countries except Sweden. About 60 percent of adult Britons read a national newspaper daily, and more than 65 percent buy a Sunday newspaper. Even more Britons read local or regional newspapers.

The press in Britain is at liberty to comment on matters of public interest, subject to law. There is no censorship and it is completely free to say exactly what it likes about anybody or anything, but the publishers can be prosecuted for insult if they deliberately tarnish a person's reputation with fabricated stories. As to political stance, these papers are almost always financially independent of any political party and are not obliged to follow any specific party line.

10.1.1 National Daily Newspapers

The Times
Here for you
DEPTH PERCEPTION
Sculpture park focusing on photographers focusing on sculpture

theguardian
Backlash over Blair's school revolution

The Daily Telegraph
£10,500 fees if Oxford is to stop the rot
12 SECTIONS
Private Diana video to be shown on TV
£35m saves Raphael for nation

The Times (circulation approximately 692,581)

This is one of Britain's most famous and influential newspapers, and has long been recognized as one of the world's greatest papers. It is still popular among the British people, and they use it for announcements of births, marriages and deaths on the back page, and also for notices of engagement to be married, which are still put on the Court page, arranged in order of state precedence.

The Times was founded by John Walter on January 1, 1785 as *The Daily Universal Register*, with Walter in the role of editor. It became *The Times* on January 1, 1788, publishing commercial news and notices, along with some scandals. In 1803, John Walter handed ownership and editorship to his son, John Walter II, whose pioneering endeavors to obtain Continental news, especially from France, helped build the paper's reputation among policy makers and financiers. He also expanded the paper from 4 pages to 12 large pages, and by the time when John Walter III took over the control of the paper in 1848, the foundations of *The Times*'s fame as Britain's prominent national journal and daily historical record had been solidly laid. By the mid-1800s it had become a widely respected influence on British public opinion, and its circulation had increased from 5,000 in 1815 to 40,000 in 1850. A companion weekly with its own editorial staff, *The Sunday Times*, began publishing in 1822. *The Times* was also the first to hire war correspondent, William Howard Russell, to cover the Crimean War[2].

The paper remained the most significant until around 1860 when a number of more competitive titles appeared, each differentiated by its political biases and interests. It was Sir William Haley, then the director general of the BBC, who made *The Times* once again a great newspaper when he became the editor in the 1950s. In 1966, news was put permanently on its front page in place of advertisements. When taken over by the Thomson group in 1967, it became much less serious than before, and thus gained an increasing circulation. Though the newspaper was printed in broadsheets format for 200 years, it switched to compact size in 2004 in the hope of appealing to younger readers. *The Times* was named as the Britain's leading daily newspaper for business people by The British Business Survey 2005, an independent survey sponsored by *The Financial Times*, *The Guardian*, *The Daily Telegraph*, *The Economist*, and *The Times*. In November 2006 *The Times* began printing headlines in its new font, Times Modern.

Renowned for its cautious attitude, *The Times* often reflects the view held by the government. Though politically a moderately centre-right newspaper and traditionally a supporter of the Conservative Party, it supported the Labour Party in the 2001 and 2005 general elections.

The Guardian (circulation approximately 358,844)

Founded in 1821 as *The Manchester Guardian* by the non-conformist businessmen,the paper was considered unique among all the other major British newspapers for the arrangements which vested ownership of the undertaking in a trustee (the Scott Trust, via the Guardian Media Group). In 1959, "Manchester" was dropped from the name to reflect its success as a national daily newspaper with an established cosmopolitan reputation.

The Guardian once had a reputation as "an organ of the middle class", or in the words of C. P. Scott's son Ted "a paper that will remain bourgeois to the last". But now its stance in politics is described as centre-left or radical, holding a favorable attitude towards the Liberal Party and being rather closer in sympathy to the Labour Party than to the Conservatives.

The Daily Telegraph (circulation approximately 1,400,000)

The paper was founded in 1855 with the title *The Daily Telegraph and Courier*, later to be known simply as *The Daily Telegraph*. As the first penny paper in London, it has built a large readership, remaining the market leader for broadsheets, with a circulation of 1,400,000 copies, owing to over 300,000 discount subscribers each day.

A feature of special reporting has been made throughout the paper's history. Its correspondents have covered virtually every major war since 1860s when the American Civil War burst out.

The year 2004 saw the tenth anniversary of the launch of the *Telegraph*'s website *Electronic Telegraph*. Now re-launched as telegraph. co. uk, the website was the UK's first national newspaper online.

Theoretically independent, the paper has been politically conservative in modern times. According to a MORI survey conducted in 2005, 64% of the *Telegraph* readers intended to support the Conservative Party in the coming elections. The personal links between the paper's editors and the leadership of the Conservative Party, also known by the term Tories, along with the paper's influence over Conservative activists, has resulted in the paper commonly being referred to, especially in *Private Eye*, as the *Torygraph*.

The Daily Mirror (circulation approximately 4,400,000)

The Daily Mirror was founded in 1903 as a newspaper for women. With the highlight of photo-rich tabloid format, the paper carries many sensational and personal types of stories as well as strip cartoons. The paper is printed in half the normal size and frequently has the largest circulation in the western world. For a period during the 1990s it was renamed *The Mirror*, but reverted to its original name in 2002. It is politically independent and caters for readers who are not much concerned with politics, though sometimes very moderate and sensible comments are made in simple language.

The Sun (circulation approximately 7,900,000)

The Sun is a daily tabloid newspaper published both in the United Kingdom and Ireland (where it is known as *The Irish Sun*). It was launched by IPC (International Press Corporation) to replace the failing *Daily Herald*, which was committed to the Labour Party. In 1969 *the Sun* was taken over by the tycoon Mr. Rupert Murdoch, who had already bought *The News of the World*, a sensationalist Sunday newspaper.

Politically, *The Sun* remained nominally Labour in the early Murdoch years. It supported Labour in the 1970 general election. However, the paper caused a small stir by changing tack politically, supporting Margaret Thatcher in the 1979 general election. From then on, *The Sun* became an ardent supporter of Margaret Thatcher and her policies. Throughout the 1980's, its stance, on many issues, was to the right of *The Daily Mail*, and it maintained close to the Conservatives when Thatcher was succeeded by John Major in 1990.

In 1978 *The Sun* surpassed *The Daily Mirror* in circulation, partly due to actor Christopher Timothy for the extensive advertising on ITV. Between 1994 and 1996, *The Sun's* circulation climbed to the peak, with its highest average sale in the week ending July 16, 1994, when the daily figure was 4,305,957. Now its circulation becomes the second highest in the world and the biggest within the UK.

Morning Star

The *Morning Star* is a communist British daily newspaper in tabloid format. It is devoted to foreign and domestic news, away from the perceived pro-business stance of other publications. It first appeared in 1930 as the *Daily Worker*, the organ of the Communist Party of Great Britain and the name was changed into *Morning Star* in 1966. The circulation of the *Morning Star* is about 60,000, and has doubled to 150,000 in the past ten years. An online version of the paper was launched on April 1, 2004. Initially only some parts of the site were free, and this policy was changed on 1 January 1, 2009 with all the content freely available now.

10.1.2 National Sunday Newspapers

Most Britons enjoy reading daily papers on their breakfast tables, but the dailies have no Sunday editions, which leaves the gap to be filled by Sunday newspapers. Sunday papers also fall into the two categories as broadsheets and tabloids. The broadsheets contain some famous titles like *The Observer* (1791), *The Sunday Times* (1822), *Sunday Telegraph* (1961) and *The Independent on Sunday* (1990), etc., while *News of the World* (1843), *The People* (1881), *Sunday Express* (1918), *Sunday Mirror* (1963) and *The Mail on Sunday* (1982) compose the list of tabloids.

The Sunday press has long been noted for their extremes of good and bad quality. At its best, it may enjoy worldwide renown for their responsible journalism like *The Observer*, which devotes extensive space to the arts, government, education, and politics. At its worst, it can also be as infamous as the *News of the World*, specializing in extensive crime-reports where sex is the focus of interest.

As the leading example of Britain's quality Sundays, *The Observer* was first published on December 4, 1791 by W. S. Bourne, which renders it the world's oldest Sunday newspaper. The paper, reporting on news and background pieces, mostly aims at well-educated readers, including a large international audience. It stands on the same political spectrum as its daily sister paper *The Guardian*, and takes a left-liberal or social democratic line on most issues. There is a visitor centre in London known as The Newsroom, where members of the public are allowed access to the archives of *The Observer* and *The Guardian*, including bound copies of old editions, a photographic library and other items such as diaries, letters and notebooks. The Newsroom also mounts temporary exhibitions and runs an educational program for schools.

The *News of the World*, on the contrary, is the most popular among Britain's Sunday tabloids, and has attracted more readers than any other Sunday paper for more than a century. With an averaging circulation of 3,445,459 copies per week in October 2006, the paper is the best-selling English-language newspaper in the world. One of the factors that can account for the large circulation is its fondness for sex scandals which has won it the nicknames "News of the Screws" and "Screws of the World". Like the other tabloids, the *News of the World* uses aggressive and usually mean-spirited tactics to sell its issues. Also, its allegations about the sexual practices, drug use, or private conduct of celebrities are usually defamatory, which often gets the paper involved into libel actions. England footballer David Beckham and his wife Victoria, for example, brought a legal action against the paper seeking libel damages over an article that carried the headline: "Posh and Becks on the Rocks" in 2005. The legal action was withdrawn in 2006 and "resolved on a confidential basis", according to the couple's spokeswoman Jo Milloy.

In 1990, the British government asked a committee to examine the situation. "A published code of practice was drawn up and a new Press Complaints Commission[3] enforced it. According to the code, journalists should not try to obtain information by subterfuge, intimidation or harassment and they should not photograph people without their consent." (张奎武, 177 - 178)

10.1.3 Periodicals

There are a wide array of different types of periodicals published in Britain, from magisterial quarterlies to coterie art periodicals, from scholarly and professional organs to penny weeklies and illustrated family magazines. Almost every field of study has its own journal published either weekly or monthly. Among them, the most important are *The Economist*, *New Statesman*, *Spectator*.

The Economist is a weekly magazine published in London and generally reckoned as one of the world's prominent journals of its kind. It provides world coverage of news and particularly of international and political developments and prospects bearing on the world's economy. Being right-wing in political attitude, the journal has a circulation of about 725,000, with North America accounting for about half of total readership. The *New Statesman* was founded in 1913 as a literary weekly magazine, famous for its aggressive and often satirical analysis of the British and world political scenes. Inclining towards the left wing of the Labour Party, it has become politically an independent socialist forum for serious intellectual discussion, political commentary, and criticism. The *Spectator* is moderately conservative in its editorial stance, and widely noted for its critical reviews and essays on political, literary, and economic issues.

In brief, you can read a variety of newspapers and periodicals in Britain, but their quality can be extremely good or extremely bad. At their worst they can be irresponsible, tasteless and lacking in consideration for individuals. The British press has a great impact on public views and opinions, even the government has sometimes paid money to newspaper publishers to buy their support. While generally speaking the press is "free" from government control and censorship, many British laws limit the freedom of the newspapers. For example, there are laws restraining newspapers from revealing the information about people tried on court because this can prejudice the judicial system. Other laws of libel and defamation prevent the press from printing fabricated stories about people. When it comes to government information, the papers are not allowed to reveal it unless the government says it can be released according to the Official Secrets Act.

10.2 Radio and Television

Once playing the most important role in Britons' leisure life, the broadcast media—radio and television—still remains a vital form of entertainment, regardless of the fierce challenge from online media. There are mainly three companies that run the business of radio and television in Britain. They are the British Broadcasting Corporation (BBC), the Independent Television Commission (ITC), and the Radio Authority. Although ultimately accountable to Parliament, the companies have virtually complete independence in the conduct of their business. Of course, the independence is endowed on the premise of certain obligations that the programmes display a proper balance and wide range of subject, impartiality in matters of controversy and accuracy in news coverage, and also the programmes can not pander to vulgar taste.

10.2.1 Radio

The British radio market has a history of over 80 years of radio broadcasting and 30 years of commercial radio broadcasting. There are more than 250 radio stations in the United Kingdom, among them, the most prominent are the national networks run by the BBC.

- BBC Radio 1 broadcasts mostly current pop music output on FM and digital radio, with live music throughout the year.
- BBC Radio 2 is the UK's most listened-to radio station, with 12.9 million weekly listeners. It features presenters Terry Wogan and Jonathan Ross, and playing

popular music from the last 5 decades as well as special interest programmes in the evening.

- BBC Radio 3 is a classical music station, broadcasting high-quality concerts and performances. At night, it transmits a wide range of jazz and world music.
- BBC Radio 4 is a current affairs and speech station, with news, debate and radio drama.
- BBC Radio 5 Live broadcasts 24 hours live news and sports commentary with phone-in debates and studio guests.

The BBC also provides 40 local radio services, mainly broadcasting a mix of local news and music aimed at an older audience. Also available nationwide are three national commercial channels, namely Absolute Radio, Classic FM and talk SPORT.

Commercial radio licenses are awarded by Office of Communication, a government body which advertises a license for an area and holds a so-called beauty contest to determine which station will be granted permission to broadcast in that area. Most local commercial stations in the United Kingdom broadcast to a city or group of towns within a radius of 20 – 50 miles. The predominant format is pop music, but many other tastes are also catered for, particularly in London and the larger cities, and on digital radio.

Rather than operating as independent entities, many local radio stations are owned by large radio groups which broadcast a similar format to many areas. The largest operator of radio is Global Radio which bought the former media group, Gcap Media. It owns Classic FM and London's most popular commercial station, 95. 8 Capital FM. Other owners are Bauer Radio and UTV Radio, which mainly own stations that broadcast in highly populated city areas.

Many of these stations, including all the BBC stations, are also available via digital television services.

Community radio stations broadcast to a small area, normally within a 3-mile (5-kilometre) radius, and are mostly not-for-profit organizations, owned by local people, on which the broadcasters are volunteers. They are recognized under the Communications Act 2003 as a distinct third tier of radio in the UK. The community radio movement in the UK was founded in the mid-1970s, broadcasting through Restricted Service Licence[4], the Internet and cable.

10.2.2 Television

30.15 million viewers watched Den Watts serve Angie divorce papers (Christmas 1986).

British television broadcasting started in 1932, when the BBC broadcasted its first television programme, which rendered Britain the first country that had a regular daily television schedule directed to homes. They were also the first to have technical professions to work on TVs, though only 9 percent of British households owned a TV during the first four years of its existence. Now it has a collection of free and subscription services over various distribution media, and the Britons who find entertainment in watching TV can switch among almost 600 channels which provide all kinds of programmes.

Television viewing is the most popular leisure pastime in Britain. It is reported that British people spend an average of 4 hours a day watching TV and one of the most frequently read parts of the newspaper is the TV listings. People are allowed access to the latest news and information over the airwaves, and conversations among friends and family will frequently center around programmes that were watched the evening before. So an exclusion from British television viewing may lead to an exclusion from British culture and society as well.

British people watch news, entertainment, sport, sitcoms, drama series and soap operas on TV. Among them, soap operas are one of the most popular genres, which are mostly broadcast during prime time. Unlike American soap operas, which focus on rich, famous and exciting characters, most UK soap operas feature realistic accounts of the daily life of working-class communities. The most popular soaps are *Coronation Street*, *EastEnders*, *Emmerdale*, *Hollyoaks*, *Doctors*, *Neighbours and Home and Away*, the first two of which are consistently among the highest-rated shows on British television week-on-week. With its setting located in the northern city of Manchester, *Coronation Street* is the oldest and the most watched show on British television, which began in the 1960s. Its rival, *EastEnders* was first broadcast on BBC 1 on February 19, 1985. Its storylines touch on the domestic and professional lives of the people who live and work in the fictitious east London Borough of Walford. The 1986 Christmas Day episode of *EastEnders* was the highest-rated UK soap opera episode ever, with 30.15 million viewers. This episode was also the most watched program in UK television for the 1980s, compared to the records set by the 1970 splashdown of Apollo 13 (28.6 million viewers), and Princess Diana's funeral in 1997 (32.1 million viewers). The two soaps are renowned as the "flagship", as they are the highest rating programmes for ITV and the BBC respectively.

Daily news and weather forecasts are also popular viewing. The Broadcasting Act[5] is designed to keep ownership of broadcast media widely spread so there are no concentrations of media power in the hands of a few, and foreign ownership (that is ownership outside the European Union) is mainly prohibited. The same legislation also contains safeguards to maintain certain standards of decency, taste, accuracy and balance.

10.2.3 The British Broadcasting Corporation

The British Broadcasting Corporation, more familiarly known as the BBC, was founded in 1927 to work with radio and later became involved in TV. With its headquarters located in the Greater London borough of Westminster, the BBC held a monopoly on British television from its inception until 1954 and on radio until 1972.

The Headquarters of the BBC

When it was established in 1922 as a private service radio station, the Corporation was known as the British Broadcasting Company, Ltd. However, the government worried that broadcasting was too important to be left to the market and set up the 1926 Crawford Committee for an enquiry. In his speech delivered to the committee, John Reith (later Lord Reith) stated that "Broadcasting must be conducted in the future as it has been in the past, as a Public Service with definite standards." The next year, upon recommendation of the committee, the company was liquidated and replaced by a public corporation, the British Broadcasting Corporation.

In the early history of the Corporation, John Reith played a vital role as general manager from 1922 and director general from 1927 to 1938. He developed radio broadcasting throughout Great Britain, inaugurated the empire of shortwave broadcasting, and introduced the world's first regular television service in 1936. His concept of public service broadcasting prevailed in Britons and also impacted broadcasting service in many other countries.

British television service was interrupted by World War II, and resumed in 1946. In 1964, a second BBC channel was established, and three years later regular colour television service was introduced by the BBC, which was the first in Europe. It retained the sole broadcasting corporation in Britain until the passage of the Television Act in 1954 and the subsequent creation of a commercial channel run by the Independent Broadcasting Authority in 1955. The BBC's monopoly of radio was broken when the government decided to permit local commercial broadcasting service starting in the early 1970s.

The constitution and finances of the BBC are governed by the Royal Charter, which is reviewed every 10 years. The Charter enables the Queen, with the advice of the Government, to appoint the members of the BBC Trust, an independent 12-member panel, including a chairman, a vice-chairman and separate national governors for Scotland, Wales and Northern Ireland. The 2007 Charter specifies that the mission of the Corporation is to "inform, educate and entertain". It claims that the Corporation exists to serve the public interest and to promote its public purposes (http://en.wikipedia.org/wiki/BBC).

- Sustaining citizenship and civil society;
- Promoting education and learning;
- Stimulating creativity and cultural excellence;
- Representing the UK, its nations, regions and communities;
- Bringing the UK to the world and the world to the UK;
- Helping to deliver to the public the benefit of emerging communications technologies and services, and taking a leading role in the switchover to digital television.

The BBC is run on the basis of television license, which is charged to all owners of equipment capable of receiving live television broadcasts. The level of the fee is determined by the Government under a multi-year agreement with the Corporation. The license fee costs as much as £ 142.50 per year per household (as of April 2009), but a discount is available for owners with only black-and-white television sets. Because of the revenue from the license, all the BBC channels and its radio are free of any commercial advertisements. The BBC is also closely related to government because of their financial support to the broadcasts, but the station has the independence to decide what to do with money.

The Corporation offers five radio networks and national television channels in Britain, with a variety of programmes ranging from popular music to news and entertainment. Under the Royal Charter, the BBC is required to refrain from broadcasting any opinion of its own on current affairs and issues of public policy and to be disinterested in matters of controversy. Its free-to-air networks include BBC 1 and BBC 2. BBC 1 specializes in shows with broad appeal, such as entertainment, sport, current affairs, drama, and kids shows. BBC 2 caters for audiences with special interest and so broadcasts documentaries and shows geared toward particular social groups, such as the elderly, the handicapped, homosexuals and so on.

Older UK audiences usually refer to the BBC as "the Beeb", a nickname originally used by Peter Sellers in *The Goon Show* in the 1950s. It also has another nickname "Auntie", which is said to originate from the old-fashioned "Auntie knows best" attitude.

Nowadays the BBC is no longer just about TV shows, and it has become instead a multimedia business with wide publishing and educational interests. Not only can you watch BBC shows about cars, pop music, cooking, holidays and gardening, but you can buy magazines which complement the shows by providing further information. It broadcasts in English and 43 other languages all over the world. Its global weekly audience is estimated to be at least 140 million people.

10.2.4 The Independent Broadcasting Authority

The Independent Broadcasting Authority (IBA) was the regulatory body in Great Britain for commercial television and commercial/independent radio broadcasts. In this context, "independent" indicated freedom from the BBC, rather than the government. The British television network regulated by the IBA consisted of a band of private companies in competition with the BBC. The IBA came into existence when the Sound Broadcasting Act 1972 endowed the Independent Television Authority responsibility for organizing the new Independent Local Radio (ILR) stations. Governed by the Independent Broadcasting Authority legislation and a license, the IBA was composed of a chairman, a deputy chairman and ten other members appointed by the Home Secretary.

Instead of producing its own radio and television programs, the IBA had all these provided by commercial program companies. Then the main functions of the IBA were to regulate television network, appointing the companies, supervising program arrangements, controlling advertisements and operating transmitting stations.

In the late 1980s the IBA was appointed as regulator and transmitter operator for the first DBS (Direct Broadcasting by Satellite) service for the UK and awarded the franchise to BSB (British Satellite Broadcasting). However, as a part of the Broadcasting Act 1990, it reassigned its regulatory duties of the Independent

Broadcasting Authority and Cable Authority to two newly formed bodies, the Independent Television Commission (ITC) and the Radio Authority in 1991.

From January 1, 1991, ITC began its duty of licensing and regulating all non-BBC television services, including ITV and Channel 4 (run by the Channel Four Television Corporation established under the 1990 Act). The ITV network is the oldest commercial television network in Great Britain. It was authorized by act of Parliament in 1954, permitting a single channel to operate by selling airtime to advertisers, which was a quite different way of practice compared with that of the BBC. Since the Broadcasting Act 1990, it has been renamed as Channel 3. The number 3 has no real meaning other than to distinguish it from BBC 1, BBC 2 and Channel 4. Unlike most of the TV channels in the UK, ITV is not owned by one single company, but instead it is operated by four companies which have been licensed to provide regional Channel 3 services. Another national commercial broadcaster is Channel 4, which was first launched in 1982 as a state-owned television channel.

In the early 2000s, the Communications Act 2003 gave rise to a White Paper issued by the British government, declaring the intention to merge the ITC with the Radio Authority, Office of Telecommunications, and Radiocommunications Agency. This merger took effect on December 29, 2003, with most powers of the ITC being taken over by the Office of Communications.

10.3 Digital Broadcasting

In the United Kingdom, the development of digital audio broadcasting (DAB) started from the inception of test transmissions by the BBC in 1990. The British digital radio network is unparalleled in that it is the biggest in the world, including 103 transmitters, two national DAB ensembles and forty-eight regional and local DAB ensembles broadcasting over 250 commercial and 34 BBC radio stations across the country.

Transmitters Including Emley Moor (Pictured) Broadcast Digital Radio via DAB and Digital Terrestrial Television

With the introduction of digital radio technology, many new stations have been launched. Among them, the most influential are several new BBC stations listed as follows.

- BBC 6 Music is a music station broadcasting

predominantly less mainstream genres of music like alternative rock.

● BBC 1Xtra transmits black, urban and gospel music (like rap, RnB and drum'n'bass, etc.).

● BBC Radio 7 uses the BBC's large archive of speech programming to broadcast classic comedy, drama and children's programming mainly originally from Radio 4.

● BBC Asian Network—geared toward the large South Asian community in the UK (a station evolved from BBC Local Radio origins in the 1970s).

● BBC Radio 5 Live Sports Extra—a companion to Five Live for additional events

In addition the BBC World Service is also broadcast nationally on DAB. The BBC's national DAB ensemble broadcasts on frequency block 12B (225.648 MHz) across the country, covering currently 87% of the population of the Great Britain. With ongoing procedures, it plans to extend its coverage to 90%.

Digital radios were first sold as car radios in 1997, with a price settled around £ 800. In the Great Britain, 32.1% of the population own a DAB digital radio set and 58% of people are allowed access to digital radio either through a radio set, television or the Internet.

Television broadcasting system also benefits from the digital broadcasting technology. The traditional way of receiving television in the United Kingdom was analogue terrestrial television, however it has now largely been superseded by digital providers. Digital terrestrial television (DTT) was established in Great Britain on November 15, 1998. DTT is usually received by means of a compatible Set-top box or Integrated Digital Television (IDTV), connected to an appropriate receiving antenna. In most cases, programmes can be received by using existing aerials originally used for analogue terrestrial television.

The British government licenses the broadcast of channels in six groups, also called multiplexes, labeled 1, 2, A, B, C, and D. The BBC has a multiplex to their own (Multiplex 1), ITV and Channel 4 share Multiplex 2, and Five and S4C share Multiplex A. The remaining spectrum (Multiplexes B, C and D) are auctioned off.

In the digital world, the BBC has started three new television services, known as BBC Choice (Established on September 23, 1998, it is the first British TV channel to broadcast exclusively in digital format.), BBC News 24 (a 24-hour rolling news television channel) and BBC Parliament (broadcasts all the work of the parliamentary and legislative bodies of the United Kingdom). Meanwhile, ITV has launched ITV2 in England and Wales, You2 (later UTV2) in Northern Ireland and S2 in Scotland, as well as GMTV2 during the early mornings. ITV2 started from December 7, 1998, broadcasting 24 hours a day as a division of ITV plc. It is available on digital television via satellite, cable, IPTV and terrestrial (Freeview) platforms. UTV2 closed on January 22, 2002, and S2 just over two years after its inception. Both were replaced by ITV2, following their deals with ITV Digital. Channel 4 has expanded greatly after gaining greater independence from the IBA, especially in the multi-channel digital world. Using its space of Multiplex 2, Channel 4 has also set up digital channels like FilmFour (a free digital channel screening films), and E4 which is run as a pay-TV companion to Channel 4. The "E" stands for entertainment, and the channel is mainly geared toward the lucrative group with an average age from 15 to 35. Five sold its half of Multiplex A to the owner of the other half of the multiplex, S4C, who established a subsidiary channel called S4C Digital Networks (SDN).

10.4 News Agencies

In the UK, there are several news agencies supplying news reports to organizations in the news trade. Of all these news agencies, Reuters, the Press Association and Extel Financial are the major ones.

The Reuters Building in Canary Wharf, London Borough of Tower Hamlets

Founded by Paul Julius Reuter in 1851, Reuters is one of the leading newswire services in the world. At its very beginning, the company's news service was built up by using electric telegraphy as well as carrier pigeons in its network. Commercial news was the major concern of the company in the early days and its headquarters were located in London to serve banks, brokerage houses and leading business firms. Its first newspaper client was *Morning Advertiser*, a London paper devoted to trade interests. Since the subscription of *Morning Advertiser* in 1858, the Reuters' clientele list has seen a rapid increase of its newspapers clients. The steady expansion of Reuters's newspaper business could be well accounted for by its reputation for being the first to report on news scoops from abroad, like the news of Abraham Lincoln's assassination.

In the 1960s Reuters became one of the first news agencies that use computers to transmit financial news overseas, and in 1973 it began making computer-terminal displays of foreign-exchange rates available to clients. In 1981 Reuters started providing service of making electronic transactions over its network, and it went on to develop a wide range of electronic trading and brokering services. In the quest to secure the company's tradition for objective reporting, Reuters Founders Share Company Limited was formed in 1984 as part of the share float. It held one "Founders Share" which could outvote all other shares to prevent any attempt to alter the rules relating to the Reuters Trust Principles, which set out the company's aim to preserve its independence, integrity, and freedom from bias in its news reporting. In 2008 Reuters incorporated with Canadian electronic publisher Thomson Corporation to form Thomson Reuters. Today the company employs over 10,335 full-time staff and about 13, 000 journalists and photographers, operating in at least 200 cities in 94 countries and supplying news text in about 20 languages. The principal news agency in every country in the world is affiliated to Reuters and almost every major news outlet in the world subscribes to the Reuters's services.

Reuters operates under a very strict policy towards upholding objectiveness. In the enforcement of this objective policy, Reuters has been careful not to use the word terrorist except in quotes when major global events are reported. As Stephen Jukes (Reuters global news editor) puts it, "We all know that one man's terrorist is another man's freedom fighter, and that Reuters upholds the principle that we do not use the word terrorist." Of course, this policy of Reuters has caused quite a few unfavorable responses from journalists and newspapers.

The Press Association is a news agency in the United Kingdom and Ireland, providing London-based service of news-collecting to almost all national and local newspapers, television and radio, as well as many websites. It was founded by provincial newspaper proprietors on a co-operative basis in 1868, consisting two subsidiaries, the Scottish Press Association and the Press Association of Ireland (covering Northern and the Republic of Ireland). Legend has it that they came up with the idea in the back of a Hansom Cab during a traffic jam as a result of London smog. When it was founded the committee who organized it said "The Press Association is formed on the principle of co-operation and can never be worked for individual profit, or become exclusive in its character". Now the PA produces 150 to 200 stories on weekdays, which have a large impact on coverage in UK media. A survey shows that 70% of British news articles in five London newspapers of the most notable quality are largely influenced by the PA version. It is also reckoned a highly reliable source of news by organizations such as the BBC which treats it as "a confirmed, single source". With the development of new technology of media, the company has gone from a news and sport supplier to traditional media, to a service of providing multimedia news, sport, weather and information to thousands of different organizations. A full history of the Press Association was written by Chris Moncrieff, the former Political Editor of the PA in 2001 entitled "Living on a Deadline".

Extel Financial is also a London-based news agency and has a network of offices in Europe and the United States and direct representation in Japan and Southeast Asia. It was originally established in 1872 as the Exchange Telegraph company (Extel), with its initial business of laying the first telegraphic cable on the Atlantic seabed to electronically connect London and New York. In the following years, the company gradually grew into one of the leading news agencies, supplying financial information and associated businesses. Extel Cards, first produced in 1922, are one of the notable achievements of the company. The Cards contain brief data on profit and loss, employees, business activities and executive management. Another is the Extel Survey started by Geoffrey Osmint, an independent consultant, in 1974. The Survey focuses on collecting views and votes from fund managers on the services and advice they are getting from research analysts at stock broking houses. The Survey was run independently by Geoffrey Osmint until it became the Extel Survey in 1985.

10.5 Online Media

The United Kingdom has been involved with the Internet since the latter's creation. The revolution in information technology (IT) and the introduction of the Internet have resulted in innovations that are having increasingly visible effects not only on the lifestyle of the average Britons, but also on the form of traditional print and broadcast media. With the World Wide Web pages operated by major news organizations, the Internet is quickly becoming the center of news media. Information of all kinds is becoming accessible via the Internet. Instead of picking up a newspaper, or watching the 10 o'clock news, people will log onto the Internet to get the news they want whenever they want it. Many workers listen to the radio through the Internet while sitting at their desk. According to Office of Communication's 2007 report the average UK citizen uses the Internet for 36 minutes every day.

The Britons have cultivated an increasing taste for browsing the websites of the newspapers and magazines whose print editions were most read before. Now almost all of the newspapers and magazines have launched their online editions so as to survive in the fierce competition. Some local newspapers, like the *Southport Reporter*, even go online fully and stop the publication of their printed paper. Local news websites are also emerging in the form of web forums and blog sites. This new trend has reduced the consumption of paper and ink in the UK.

The same trend has become prevailing in the radio industry, as "online" has been regarded as a promised land by most station owners. There are over 350 British radio stations streaming their stations online, not including Restricted Service Licenced radio stations, Hospital radio stations and stations who solely broadcast online. The figures taken by Radio Joint Audience Research (RAJAR) between April and May in 2008 showed that 14.5 million people have listened to radio online, with 9.4 million people listening every week. In 2006, the Phonographic Performance Limited (PPL) proclaimed that it would charge additional royalty fees on British Internet radio stations if they broadcasted outside the United Kingdom. In response to this, radio stations which streamed online had to implement IP blocking to prevent listeners outside the UK from listening to their radio programmes and therefore avoided the increased fees. In March 2007, the PPL was reported to re-negotiate royalty fees paid by British Internet radio stations, and the result of the negotiations was that fees would increase.

The BBC launched BBC Online (renamed as bbc.co.uk in 2004) on May 11, 1994 as a paid subscription service. It is a large network of websites including high profile sites such as *BBC News and Sport*, the video and radio services co-branded *BBC iPlayer*, the pre-school site *Cbeebies*, and learning services like *Bitesize*. Among them, *BBC iPlayer* was launched in December 2007 as a special service, which allows users to download both radio and TV programmes for up to seven days after broadcast. The television version allows users to either stream programmes or to download them using peer-to-peer and DRM[6] technology. Following its old tradition, the BBC Online was initially entirely free from advertisements, due to its funding derived from compulsory television licence fees from British audiences. However, recently some major online companies have complained that the BBC website receives too much funding from the television license, charging that it is impossible for other websites to compete with the vast range of advertising-free content available on the BBC site.

As an emerging form of news medium, the Internet allows its viewers access to a huge quantity of information, but simultaneously it is also overflowing with news reports at tension with objectivity, information open to question, and even false rumors with harmful effects. Therefore, it is essential for the Internet viewers to take in information online selectively based on their own judgment.

Conclusion

The function of news media is more than to entertain the readers. Newspapers, radio, television and websites for example, supply Britons with weather forecasts; provide information about political and social issues; carry advertisements; cater for educational programmes; and allow people to express their opinions or seek advice via some interactive columns or programs. What is more important is the role of news media as the watchdog of public interest. It is the obligation of news media to inform the British citizens about issues the country may be facing and what the government is doing to solve these issues. Keeping an eye on the government, the press and broadcast in the UK can secure the objectivity of government reports and parliamentary democracy. This function can be traced in the names of some dominant newspapers, like *The Times*, *The Observer* and *The Guardian*, which are still popular among the British readers today.

Combined with the watchdog function, news media are also endowed with the power of shaping public opinion. As a powerful propaganda tool, the news media may affect the general public's attitudes by focusing attention on some national problems and political issues while ignoring others. Media coverage of an issue increases the national importance that Britons ascribe to it. If the media do, indeed, shape what individuals consider important, they may also alter the bases of judgments about governmental and parliamentary performance. By focusing on some issues and not others, the news may determine the standards by which the governmental and parliamentary performances are evaluated and may, as a result, provoke surges and declines in the popularity of government and parliament.

This powerful persuasive impact of news media on Britons' political attitudes and behavior, according to many analysts, can be misleading and even present a huge threat to liberal democracy. Specifically, when a media bias is involved, it is practically impossible for the public to attain an impartial perception of government and its policies. Some even point out that the power of the press and broadcast has surpassed that of parliament. Contemporary politicians prefer to speak directly to the news media rather than to parliament. They all spend a lot of time and money improving their public image and try to secure favorable coverage on newspapers and TV.

The news media also play a vital role in cultivating a nationwide culture. By reading through their daily papers, tuning on their radio or TV, or surfing online, all Britons may find the same contents, share the same experience and have the same concerns. Regardless of the regional differences and geographical gaps between them, they are the group of people living in the same country, and immersed in the same culture.

Notes

[1] Partisan: (Newspapers become) prejudiced in favor of a particular cause.

[2] the Crimean War: The war was fought (October 1853 - February 1856) between the Russian Empire on one side and an alliance of the British Empire, France, the Ottoman Empire and the Kingdom of Sardinia on the other. It was part of a long-running contest between the major European powers for influence over territories of the declining Ottoman Empire.

[3] Press Complaints Commission: PCC is the successor of the Press Council, established with its Code of Practice. It is a regulatory body for British printed newspapers and magazines, consisting of representatives of the major publishers.

[4] Restricted Service Licence (RSL): It refers to a licence typically granted by Office of Communication to radio stations and television stations broadcasting within the UK to serve a local community or a special event.

[5] the Broadcasting Act (1990): It is a law of the British parliament, regarded by both its supporters and its critics as a quintessential example of Thatcherism. The aim of the Act was to reform the entire structure of British broadcasting. It led directly to the abolition of the Independent Broadcasting Authority and its replacement with the Independent Television Commission and Radio Authority (both now replaced by Office of Communication).

[6] DRM: DRM is the abbreviation for digital rights managemeat. It is a generic term for access control technologies that can be used by hardware manufacturers, publishers, copyright holders and individuals to try to impose limitations on the usage of digital content and devices.

Exercises

I. Fill in the following blanks with proper words or expressions.

1. The newspapers are traditionally categorized into two types: the quality newspapers (qualities or ____________) and popular newspapers (populars or ____________).

2. There is no ________ and it is completely free to say exactly what it likes about anybody or anything, but the publishers can be prosecuted for insult if they deliberately tarnish a person's reputation with fabricated stories.
3. ________________, ________________ and ________________ are referred to as the "Big Three" among Britain's newspapers.
4. When it comes to government information, the papers are not allowed to reveal it unless the government says it can be released according to the ________________.
5. There are mainly three companies that run the business of radio and television in Britain. They are ________________, ________________ and ________________.
6. Commercial radio licenses are awarded by ______________, a government body which advertises a license for an area and holds a so-called beauty contest to determine which station will be granted permission to broadcast in that area.
7. The ____________ is designed to keep ownership of broadcast media widely spread so there are no concentrations of media power in the hands of a few, and foreign ownership (that is ownership outside the European Union) is mainly prohibited.
8. In his speech delivered to the committee, John Reith (later Lord Reith) stated that "Broadcasting must be conducted in the future as it has been in the past, as a ________ Service with definite standards."
9. Older UK audiences usually refer to the BBC as "________________", a nickname originally used by Peter Sellers in *The Goon Show* in the 1950s.
10. Following its old tradition, the BBC Online was initially entirely free from advertisements, due to its funding derived from compulsory ____________________ from British audiences.

Ⅱ. Explain the following terms.

1. *The Times*
2. The BBC
3. Digital terrestrial television
4. Reuters

Ⅲ. Discuss the following questions.

1. What are the differences between quality papers and popular papers?
2. How does the British news media exert its watchdog function? And what are the negative effects of news media?

Bibliography

Bell, Daniel. (1973). *The Coming of the Post-industrial Society.* NY: Basic Books.

Bromnead, P. (1978). *Life in Modern Britain.* London: Longman.

Chaffey, John. (1994). *A New View of Britain.* Bath: Hodder & Stoughton.

Ruth, Gledhill. (2008). *Religious Trends.* Christian Research

McDowall, David. (1989). *An Illustrated History of Britain.* London: Pearson Education Limited.

Mutz, C. D. & Sniderman, P. M. & Brody, R. A. (1996). *Political Persuasion and Attitude Change.* Michigan: University of Michigan Press.

Palmer, R. R. (2008). *A History of the Modern World.* McGraw-Hill Companies, Inc

Trevelyan, George Macaulay. (1959). *A Shortened History of England.* Baltimore: Penguin Books.

Britannica Encyclopedia. http://www.britannica.com

Britannica Online Encyclopedia. http://www.britannica.com/

BSA Survey 2007

Economy of the United Kingdom. http://en.wikipedia.org/wiki/Economy_of_the_United_Kingdom

http://en.wikipedia.org/wiki/

http://wwrn.org/article.php/

http://www.answers.com

http://www.learnenglish.de/culture/newyear.htm

http://www.wikipedia.org

Microsoft Encarta, http://www.microsoft.com/uk/encarta/default.mspx

UK 2001 Census, 2001

Wikipedia, the free encyclopedia, http://en.wikipedia.org/wiki/Main_Page

陈德. (2008). 新编英语国家概况. 西安: 西安交通大学出版社.

段洁云.（2007）. 英语国家社会与文化. 昆明：云南大学出版社.
高继海.（2006）. 简明英国文学史. 开封：河南大学出版社.
来安方.（2008）. 英美文化与国家概况. 上海：复旦大学出版社.
来安方主编.（1995）. 英美概况. 郑州：河南教育出版社.
李延年.（2004）. 英美概况. 长沙：国防科技大学出版社.
刘炳善.（1985）. 英国文学简史. 上海：上海外语教育出版社.
罗选民主编.（1996）. 英美社会与文化. 武汉：华中科技大学出版社.
苏立昌.（2008）. 英国社会与文化. 长春：南开大学出版社.
隋铭才.（2003）. 英美概况. 北京：高等教育出版社.
汪尧田，陈治刚.（1984）. 英美概况. 上海：上海外语教育出版社.
王恩铭主编.（2003）. 美国文化与社会. 上海：上海外语教育出版社.
王九萍等主编.（2009）. 英美概况（21世纪英语专业系列教材）. 西安：西安交通大学出版社.
王佐良等.（1992）. 欧洲文化入门. 北京：外语教学与研究出版社.
温洪瑞、李学珍.（2008）. 英美概况. 济南：山东大学出版社.
肖惠云主编，王义副主编.（2003）. 当代英国概况. 上海：上海教育出版社.
谢福之.（2007）. 英语国家概况. 北京：外语教学与研究出版社.
《新编英美概况》编委会.（2004）. 新编英美概况. 汕头：汕头大学出版社.
徐晓晴，张红岩，王威.（2008）. 英语国家社会与文化. 苏州：苏州大学出版社.
许鲁之.（2007）. 新编英美概况. 青岛：中国海洋大学出版社.
余志远.（2000）. 英语国家概况. 北京：外语教学与研究出版社.
张奎武.（2000）. 英美概况. 长春：吉林科学技术出版社.
周静琼.（2003）. 当代美国概况. 上海：上海教育出版社.
周叔麟主编.（2004）. 新编英美概况教程. 北京：北京大学出版社.
朱永涛著.（2005）. 英语国家社会与文化入门. 北京：高等教育出版社.

高等院校特色课程英语系列教材

新编英美国家社会与文化

美国篇

主　编：范建华　毛启红
副主编：秦志红　何　玲　张明权
编　者：(按姓氏笔画排列)
毛启红　石莉莉　邝增乾　朱　婧
刘长城　关世民　李　飒　李　萍
何　兖　何　玲　张明权　陆巧玲
范建华　秦志红　徐小丽　徐　佳
唐永辉

苏州大学出版社

图书在版编目(CIP)数据

新编英美国家社会与文化. 美国篇/范建华,毛启红主编. —苏州:苏州大学出版社,2010.8(2013.1 重印)
ISBN 978-7-81137-567-1

Ⅰ.①新… Ⅱ.①范…②毛… Ⅲ.①英语-阅读教学-高等学校-教材②美国-概况 Ⅳ.①H319.4:K

中国版本图书馆 CIP 数据核字(2010)第 163235 号

新编英美国家社会与文化
美国篇
范建华 毛启红 主编
责任编辑 王 娅

苏州大学出版社出版发行
(地址:苏州市十梓街 1 号 邮编:215006)
丹阳市兴华印刷厂印装
(地址:丹阳市胡桥镇 邮编:212313)

开本 787mm×1 092mm 1/16 印张 22.25(共两册) 字数 555 千
2010 年 8 月第 1 版 2013 年 1 月第 2 次印刷
ISBN 978-7-81137-567-1 定价: 48.00 元
(共两册)

苏州大学版图书若有印装错误,本社负责调换
苏州大学出版社营销部 电话:0512-65225020
苏州大学出版社网址 http://www.sudapress.com

前 言

“英美国家概况”课程是为高等学校英语专业学生开设的专业知识必修课。按照教育部21世纪我国高等学校英语专业人才的培养目标和要求，在打好扎实的英语语言基本功和牢固掌握英语专业知识的前提下，要拓宽学生的人文学科知识，扩大知识面，对西方不同的政治、经济、文化、历史和科技教育等有较全面的了解，其中重点是对英国和美国国情的梳理和掌握。同时，注重培养学生独立思考、分析问题、解决问题的能力和创新能力，培养学生跨文化交际意识和能力，提高思想道德素质、文化素养，并对今后从事英美问题的研究打下坚实的基础。

一直以来，在这样一门重要课程的教材选择方面，存在着诸多难点：

1. 由于“英美国家概况”课程的知识覆盖面广，涉及历史、政治、经济、文化等方方面面，所选教材在内容上应做到有详有略，既全面翔实，又重点突出。

2. 英美两国在政治、地域、风俗等方面与中国有很大差异，这种差异会对学生的认知和理解造成一定的困难。教材编写者应充分考虑到这种客观存在的文化差异，并在编排上加以妥善考虑。

3. 英文版的教材中存在大量历史事件、地理位置等专有名词和术语，这对于学生的英文水平是一个很大的挑战。教材的语言在地道通畅外还应做到难易适中。

4. 网络时代，学习方式呈多样化，教材的内容不应显得过于陈旧，应能满足网络时代的学习需求。

为此，我们组织国内诸多高校的一线“英美国家概况”课程教师，从实际授课需求出发，在他们多年教学经验的基础上，编写了《新编英美国家社会与文化》(英文版)一书。本书充分考虑了以上提及的问题，综合考量了教师的教学需要和学生的学习需求，对于应该让中国学生掌握的英美国家社会文化知识作了详尽介绍，而对一些只需要了解的知识简要介绍，使教材在有限的篇幅里较为全面地向中国学生展示“尽可能真实的英国和美国”。本教材既可作为大中专院校相关课程的教材，满足人才培养需求，也可以作为英语爱好者的普及性读物。

希望读者通过本套教材的学习，了解英美国家简史，以及英美两国的政治、经济、文化发展状况，了解中国与英美两国国际关系演变的基本情况与信息，进一步认识借鉴外国经验对我国经济社会发展的重要意义，从而增强自己的跨文化交际能力，丰富自己的知识结构,为今后的工作打下良好的文化知识基础。

本书由泰州师范高等专科学校范建华老师和南京人口管理干部学院毛启红老师担任主编。分为英国篇和美国篇两册,共20章。其中英国篇第1章由南京林业大学吴雪峰老师编写,第2章和第3章由南京信息工程大学张厚振老师编写,第4章由南京人口管理干部学院毛启红、刘长城老师编写,第5章由江苏大学张明权老师编写,第6章由广西师范大学陆巧玲、何玲老师编写,第7章由常熟理工学院何兖老师编写,第8章由浙江传媒学院陈欣老师编写,第9章由宿迁学院张子通老师编写,第10章由南京医科大学徐畅老师编写。美国篇第1章由淮北师范大学唐永辉老师编写,第2章和第3章由泰州师范高等专科学校范建华、徐小丽和徐佳老师编写,第4章由南京人口管理干部学院毛启红、刘长城老师编写,第5章由江苏大学张明权老师编写,第6章由广西师范大学陆巧玲、何玲老师编写,第7章由常熟理工学院何兖老师编写,第8章由海南师范大学关世民老师编写,第9章由桂林电子科技大学邝增乾老师编写,第10章由南京医科大学秦志红老师编写。泰州师范高等专科学校李萍、石莉莉、朱婧、李飒等老师协助收集材料,并审读了全部书稿,提出了许多建设性意见。

成书之际,我们衷心感谢苏州大学外国语学院衡仁权博士帮助审校书稿,感谢苏州大学出版社对此书的大力支持,感谢编辑为此书付出的大量辛劳!

由于编者水平有限,书中一定存在不少瑕疵和谬误,敬请读者和同行批评、指正!

编　者

2010 年 8 月

目 录

Chapter One

General Introduction

The full name of the United States of America (USA) is sometimes abbreviated to the United States (US), or just to America. Since the establishment of the US, the number of states expanded from 13 to 50. Washington, D. C., the capital city of the US, is in the District of Columbia, not, as many Chinese students might expect, in the State of Washington. The flag of the US (the American flag) consists of thirteen equal horizontal stripes of red (top and bottom) alternating with white, with a blue rectangle in the canton bearing 50 small, white, five-pointed stars arranged in 9 offset horizontal rows of 6 stars (top and bottom) alternating with rows of 5 stars. The 50 stars on the flag represent the 50 US states and the 13 stripes represent the original 13 colonies that rebelled against the British monarchy and became the first states in the Union. Nicknames for the flag include the Stars and Stripes, Old Glory, and the Star-Spangled Banner (also the name of the national anthem).

The US has established a highly developed national economy within a matter of about two hundred years, counting from the time of its independence. Perhaps no other country has left as great an impression on the contemporary world as the US—a big achievement for such a relatively young nation. Lauded as a beacon of freedom, where over the centuries millions of immigrants have come to better their lives, and reviled as an international bully, perhaps never more so than in recent years, it's a place you have to explore in order to understand and appreciate.

The images of the country that named itself after a continent are embedded in the mind of people from all over the world: endless highways cutting through shimmering deserts; forests of skyscrapers towering over urban jungles; acres of beaches dotted with surfboards and suntanned skin; high mountain peaks and green river valleys; magnificent feats of engineering, from the Brooklyn Bridge to the

Hoover Dam. The country's emblems are so familiar that they constitute as much a part of the world's culture as its own—Lady Liberty, the Grand Canyon, the Empire State Building, the US Capitol, the "Hollywood" sign ... the list goes on.

1.1 Topography

1.1.1 Physiographic Divisions

The US is a country in the Western Hemisphere. Bounded on the east by the Atlantic Ocean and on the west by the Pacific Ocean, the US occupies a territory of 95,220,572 km^2 primarily in the mid-latitude region of the North American continental landmass. The non-contiguous territory comprising the state of Alaska is located in the extreme northwestern part of the continent and is separated from the 48 contiguous states by Canada. The Hawaii islands in the mid-Pacific form the 50th state of the US.

The territory comprised of the 48 contiguous states is bordered by Canada on the north and Mexico on the south. Alaska is bordered by Canada on the east and the Bering Sea on the west, which also separates it from Russia and Asia. The US is the second largest country in North America after Canada and the fourth largest in the world after Russia, Canada and China.

The location of the US in the mid-latitude region of the North American landmass flanked by the Atlantic and Pacific Oceans on either side and its vast territorial extension especially from the west to the east imparts it with a diverse physical environment. The country boasts of a varying range of climatic regions that are as far apart as the Arctic conditions in the far corners of Alaska and the subtropical climatic conditions in the state of Florida. The natural vegetation of the US can also be as varied as tropical rain forests to arid desert scrubland, and its physical landscape can be as diverse as the high and rugged mountain peaks of the Appalachians and the flat expanses of the prairie lowlands.

Despite New York's status as the cultural and economic center of the US, the federal capital is in Washington, D. C., which doesn't even rank among the top twenty cities in terms of population (though officially, it is a district, not a city). The US government is divided into three branches: the executive, headed by the president; the legislative, which comprises the Senate and the House of Representatives; and the judicial, with the Supreme Court as its highest office.

The eastern US has a varied topography. A broad, flat coastal plain lines the Atlantic and Gulf shores from the Texas-Mexico border to New York City, and includes the Florida Peninsula. Areas further inland feature rolling hills and temperate forests. The Appalachian Mountains form a line of low mountains separating the eastern seaboard from the Great Lakes and the Mississippi Basin. The five Great Lakes are located in the north-central portion of the country, four of them forming part of the border with Canada. The southeast US contains subtropical forests and, near the gulf coast, mangrove wetlands, especially in Florida. West of the Appalachians lies the Mississippi River Basin and two large eastern tributaries, the Ohio River and the Tennessee River. The Ohio and Tennessee Valleys and the Midwest consist largely of rolling hills and productive farmland, stretching south to the Gulf Coast.

The Great Plains lie west of the Mississippi River and east of the Rocky Mountains. A large portion of the country's agricultural products are grown in the Great Plains. Before their general conversion to farmland, the Great Plains were noted for their extensive grasslands, from tall-grass prairie in the eastern plains to short-grass steppes in the western High Plains. Elevation rises gradually from less than a few hundred feet near the Mississippi River to more than a mile high in the High Plains. The generally low relief of the plains is broken in several places, most notably in the Ozark and Ouachita Mountains, which form the US Interior Highlands, the only major mountainous region between the Rocky Mountains and the Appalachian Mountains. The Great Plains come to an abrupt end at the Rocky Mountains. The Rocky Mountains form a large portion of the western US, entering from Canada and stretching nearly to Mexico. The Rocky Mountains generally contain fairly mild slopes and low peaks compared to many of the other great mountain ranges, with a few exceptions (such as the Teton Mountains in Wyoming and the Sawatch Range in Colorado). In addition, instead of being one generally continuous and solid mountain range, it is broken up into a number of smaller, intermittent mountain ranges, forming a large series of basins and valleys.

West of the Rocky Mountains lies the Inter-Montana Plateaus (also known as the Intermountain West), a large, arid desert lying between the Rockies and the Cascades and Sierra Nevada Ranges. The large southern portion, known as the Great Basin, consists of salt flats, drainage basins, and many small north-south mountain ranges. The southwest is predominantly a low-lying desert region. A portion known as the Colorado Plateau, centered around the Four Corners Region, is considered to have some of the most spectacular scenery in the world. It is accentuated in such national parks as Grand Canyon, Arches, and Bryce Canyon, among others.

The Inter-Montana Plateaus come to an end at the Cascade Range and the

Sierra Nevada. The Cascades consist of largely intermittent, volcanic mountains rising prominently from the surrounding landscape. The Sierra Nevada, further south, is a high, rugged, and dense mountain range. It contains the highest point in the contiguous 48 states, Mount Whitney (14,505 ft; 4,419.19 m). These areas contain some spectacular scenery as well, as evidenced by such national parks as Yosemite and Mount Rainier. West of the Cascades and Sierra Nevada is a series of valleys, such as the Central Valley in California and the Willamette Valley in Oregon. Along the coast is a series of low mountain ranges known as the Pacific Coast Ranges. Much of the Pacific northwest coast is inhabited by some of the densest vegetation outside of the tropics, and also the tallest trees in the world (the redwoods).

Alaska contains some of the most dramatic and untapped scenery in the country. Tall, prominent mountain ranges rise up sharply from broad, flat tundra plains. On the islands off the south and southwest coast are many volcanoes. Hawaii, far to the south of Alaska in the Pacific Ocean, is a chain of tropical, volcanic islands, popular as a tourist destination for many from East Asia and the mainland US.

The geography of the US varies across its immense area. Within the continental US, eight distinct physiographic divisions exist, though each is composed of several smaller physiographic subdivisions. These major divisions are:

Laurentian Upland—part of the Canadian Shield that extends into the northern US Great Lakes area.

Atlantic Plain—the coastal regions of the eastern and southern parts which include the continental shelf, the Atlantic Coast and the Gulf Coast.

Appalachian Highlands—lying on the eastern side of the US, Which includes the Appalachian Mountains, the Watchung Mountains, the Adirondacks and New England Province originally containing the Great Eastern Forest.

Interior Plains—part of the interior continental US, which includes much of what is called the Great Plains.

Interior Highlands—also part of the interior continental US, and this division includes the Ozark Plateau.

Rocky Mountain System—one branch of the Cordilleran system lying far inland in the western states.

Inter-Montana Plateaus—also divided into the Columbia Plateau, the Colorado Plateau and the Basin and Range Province, it is a system of plateaus, basins, ranges and gorges between the Rocky and Pacific Mountain Systems. It is the setting for the Grand Canyon, the Great Basin and Death Valley.

Pacific Mountain System—the coastal mountain ranges and features in the west coast of the US.

The Atlantic coast of the US is, with minor exceptions, low. The Appalachian Highland owes its oblique northeast-southwest trend to crustal deformations which in very early geological time gave a beginning to what later came to be the Appalachian mountain system. This system had its climax of deformation so long ago (probably in Permian time) that it has since then been very generally reduced to moderate or low relief. It owes its present day altitude either to renewed elevations along the earlier lines or to the survival of the most resistant rocks as residual mountains. The oblique trend of this coast would be even more pronounced but for a comparatively modern crustal movement, causing a depression in the northeast resulting in an encroachment of the sea upon the land. Additionally, the southeastern section has undergone an elevation resulting in the advance of the land upon the sea.

1.1.2 The Two Major Cities

Washington, D. C.

Washington, D. C., formally the District of Columbia and commonly referred to as Washington, the District, or simply D. C., is the capital of the US, founded on July 16, 1790. The City of Washington was originally a separate municipality within the Territory of Columbia until an act of Congress in 1871 effectively merged the City and the Territory into a single entity called the District of Columbia. It is for this reason that the city, while legally named the District of Columbia, is known as Washington, D. C.

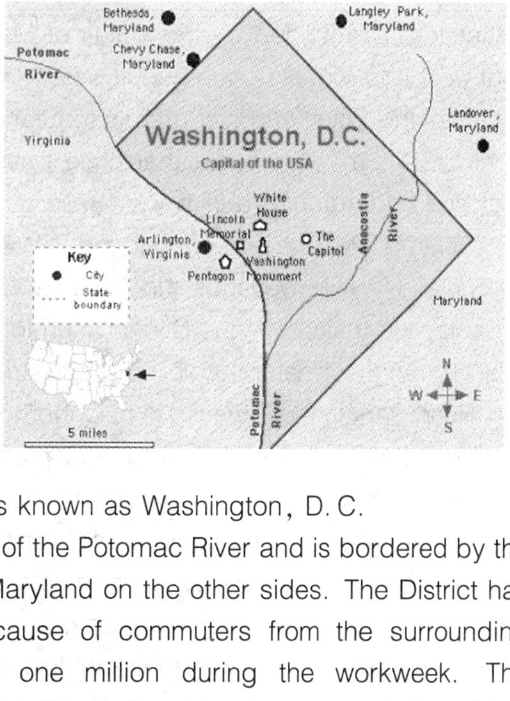

The city is located on the north bank of the Potomac River and is bordered by the states of Virginia on the southwest and Maryland on the other sides. The District has a resident population of 599,657; because of commuters from the surrounding suburbs, its population rises to over one million during the workweek. The Washington Metropolitan Area, of which the District is a part, has a population of 5.3 million, the ninth largest metropolitan area in the country.

Article One of the US Constitution provides for a federal district, distinct from the states, to serve as the permanent national capital. The centers of all three branches of the federal government of the US are located in the District, as are many of the nation's monuments and museums. Washington, D. C. hosts 174 foreign embassies as well as the headquarters of the World Bank, the International Monetary Fund (IMF), the Organization of American States (OAS), the Inter-American Development Bank, and the Pan-American Health Organization (PAHO). The headquarters of other institutions such as trade unions, lobbying groups, and professional associations are also located in the District.

The city is governed by a mayor and a thirteen-member city council. However, the US Congress has supreme authority over Washington, D. C., and may overturn local laws. Residents of the District therefore have less self-governance than residents of the states. The District has a non-voting at-large Congressional delegate, but no senators. D. C. residents could not vote in presidential elections until the ratification of the Twenty-third Amendment to the US Constitution in 1961.

The District has a total area of 68.3 square miles (177 km^2), of which 61.4 square miles (159 km^2) is land and 6.9 square miles (18 km^2) is water. The District is no longer 100 square miles (260 km^2) due to the retrocession of the southern portion of the District back to the Commonwealth of Virginia in 1846. The District's current area consists only of the territory ceded by the state of Maryland. Washington is therefore surrounded by the states of Maryland on the southeast, northeast, and northwest and Virginia on the southwest. The District has three major natural flowing streams: the Potomac River and its tributaries, the Anacostia River and Rock Creek. Tiber Creek, a watercourse that once passed through the National Mall, was fully enclosed underground during the 1870s.

Contrary to the urban legend, Washington was not built on reclaimed swampland. While wetlands did cover areas along the two rivers and other natural streams, the majority of the District's territory consisted of farmland and tree-covered hills. The highest natural point in the District of Columbia is Point Reno, located in Fort Reno Park in the Taneytown neighborhood, at 409 feet (125m) above sea level. The lowest point is sea level at the Potomac River.

Approximately 19.4% of Washington, D. C. is parkland, which ties New York City for the largest percentage of parkland among high-density US cities. The US National Park Service manages most of the natural habitat in Washington, D. C., including Rock Creek Park, the Chesapeake and Ohio Canal National Historical Park, the National Mall, Theodore Roosevelt Island, the Constitution Gardens, Meridian Hill Park, and Anacostia Park. The only significant area of natural habitat not managed by the National Park Service is the US National Arboretum, which is operated by the US Department of Agriculture. The Great Falls of the Potomac River are located upstream (northwest) of Washington. During the 19th century, the Chesapeake and Ohio Canal, which starts in Georgetown, was used to allow barge traffic to bypass the falls.

New York City

New York City is located in the northeastern US, in southeastern New York State, approximately halfway between Washington, D. C. and Boston. The location at the mouth of the Hudson River, which feeds into a naturally sheltered harbor and then into the Atlantic Ocean, has helped the city grow in significance as a trading city. Much of New York is built on the three islands of Manhattan, Staten Island, and Long Island, making land scarce and encouraging a high population density.

The Hudson River flows through the Hudson Valley into New York Bay. Between New York City and Troy, New York, the river is an estuary. The Hudson separates the city from New Jersey. The East River, actually a tidal strait, flows from Long Island Sound and separates the Bronx and Manhattan from Long Island. The Harlem River, another tidal strait between the East and Hudson Rivers, separates Manhattan from the Bronx.

The city's land has been altered considerably by human intervention, with substantial land reclamation along the waterfronts since Dutch colonial times. Reclamation is most notable in Lower Manhattan, with developments such as Battery Park City in the 1970s and 1980s. Some of the natural variations in topography have been evened out, particularly in Manhattan.

New York City's total area is 468.9 square miles (1,214km^2). 164.1 square miles (425km^2) of this is water and 304.8 square miles (789 km^2) is land. The highest point in the city is Todt Hill on Staten Island, which at 409.8 feet (124.9m) above sea level. The summit of the ridge is largely covered in woodlands as part of the Staten Island Greenbelt.

New York is the most populous city in the US, and the center of the New York metropolitan area, which is one of the most populous urban areas in the world. A leading global city, New York exerts a powerful influence over worldwide commerce, finance, culture, fashion and entertainment. As host of the United Nations headquarters, it is also an important center for international affairs. The city is often referred to as New York City to differentiate it from the state of New York, of which it is a part.

Many districts and landmarks in the city have become well-known to outsiders. The Statue of Liberty greeted millions of immigrants as they came to America in the late 19th and early 20th centuries. Wall Street, in Lower Manhattan, has been a dominant global financial center since World War Ⅱ and is home to the New York Stock Exchange. The city has been home to several of the tallest buildings in the world, including the Empire State Building and the twin towers of the former World Trade Center.

The City is the birthplace of many cultural movements, including the Harlem Renaissance in literature and visual art; abstract expressionism (also known as the New York School) in painting; hip hop, punk, salsa, disco and Tin Pan Alley in music; and is the home of Broadway theater.

New York is notable among American cities for its high use of mass transit, most of which runs 24 hours per day, and for the overall density and diversity of its population. In 2005, nearly 170 languages were spoken in the city and 36% of its population was born outside the US. Sometimes referred to as "the City That Never Sleeps", the city has also been nicknamed the Capital of the World, Gotham, and the Big Apple.

New York City has a humid subtropical climate and enjoys an average of 234 days with at least some sunshine annually. It is the northernmost major city in North America that features a humid subtropical climate using the 0℃ (American scientist standard) isotherm as criteria.

The building form most closely associated with New York City is the skyscraper, whose introduction and widespread adoption saw New York buildings shift from the low-scale European tradition to the vertical rise of business districts. As of August 2008, New York City has 5,538 high-rise buildings, with 50 completed skyscrapers taller than 656 feet (200 m). This is more than any other city in the US, and second in the world behind Hong Kong.

New York City has over 28,000 acres (110 km^2) of municipal parkland and 14 square miles (23 km^2) of public beaches. This parkland is augmented by thousands of acres of Gateway National Recreation Area, part of the National Park system, which lies within city boundaries. The Jamaica Bay Wildlife Refuge alone, the only wildlife refuge in the National Park System, is over 9,000 acres (36 km^2) of marsh islands and water taking up most of Jamaica Bay.

1.2 Rivers, Lakes and Coast

1.2.1 The Atlantic Seacoast

The Atlantic Seacoast, also known as the Eastern Coastal Plain, is a wide strip of fairly level country between the Atlantic and the Appalachians. It is the country of the first European immigrants and the original 13 states. Broad in the south, about 300 kilometers, the coastal plain narrows towards the north and gives way to rocky coastlines in New England. The coastal plain is made of low land and the tides from the sea can be seen rushing up the streams for many miles. Therefore, it is also called by some people as the tide-water region. A large part of Georgia and Florida is low-lying swampy land. The Okefenokee Swamp in southern Georgia and the Everglades in southern Florida are huge swamps which have become tourist attractions. But the Atlantic beaches are well-known for their fine sand which has given birth to famous summer playgrounds such as Atlantic City and Miami Beach.

As the Coastal Plain extends westwards, it gives way to a series of hills where rivers and streams suddenly fall to a lower level, resulting in the so-called Fall Line running along the west border of the plain. The abundant water powers supplied by the rapids and falls have led to the rise of some cities along the Fall Line, such as Columbia, Richmond, and Washington.

1.2.2 The Great Mississippi River

The Mississippi River is the largest river system in the US and the largest of North America. About 2,320 miles (3,730 km) long, the river originates at Lake Itasca, Minnesota and flows slowly southwards in sweeping meanders, terminating 95 river miles below New Orleans, Louisiana where it begins to flow to the Gulf of Mexico. Along with its major tributary, the Missouri River, the river drains 31 US states stretching from the Rocky Mountains in the west to the Appalachian Mountains in the east to the Canada-US border on the north, including most of the Great Plains, and is the fourth longest river in the world and the tenth most powerful river in the world.

From its origin at Lake Itasca to St. Louis, Missouri, the flow of the Mississippi River is moderated by 43 dams. Fourteen of these dams are located above Minneapolis in the headwaters region and serve multiple purposes including power generation and recreation. The remaining 29 dams beginning in downtown Minneapolis all contain locks and were constructed to permit commercial navigation of the upper river. Taken as a whole these 43 dams significantly shape the geography and influence the ecology of the upper river. Beginning just below Saint Paul, Minnesota and continuing throughout the upper and lower river, the Mississippi is further controlled by thousands of wing dikes that moderate the river's flow in order to maintain an open navigation channel and prevent the river from eroding its banks.

The Mississippi River runs through 10 states and was used to define portions of these states' borders. The middle of the riverbed at the time when the borders were established was the line to define the borders between states. The river has since shifted, but the state borders of Wisconsin, Iowa, Illinois, Missouri, Kentucky, Arkansas, Tennessee, and Mississippi have not changed; they still follow the former bed of the Mississippi River as of their establishment.

The widest point of the Mississippi River is Lake Winnibigoshish, near Grand Rapids, Minnesota, at over 7 miles (11 km) across. Also of note is Lake Onalaska, near La Crosse, Wisconsin, where the river is over 4 miles (6.4 km) wide (created by Lock and Dam No. 7) and Lake Pepin at more than 2 miles (3.2 km) wide. However, the first two areas are lakes or reservoirs rather than free flowing water. In other areas where the Mississippi is a flowing river (other than Lake Pepin), it exceeds 1 mile (1.6 km) in width in several places in its lower course.

The Missouri River flows from the confluence of the Jefferson, Madison and Gallatin Rivers and is the longest river in the US. Taken together, the Jefferson, the Missouri, and the Mississippi form the longest river system in North America. If measured from the source of the Jefferson at Brower's Spring to the Gulf of Mexico, the length of the Mississippi-Missouri-Jefferson combination is approximately 3,900 miles (6,300 km), making the combination the fourth longest river in the world. The uppermost 207 miles (333 km) of this combined river are called the Jefferson, the lowest 1,352 miles (2,176 km) are part of the Mississippi, and the intervening 2,341 miles (3,767 km) are called the Missouri.

The Arkansas River is the second-longest tributary of the Mississippi River. Measured by water volume, the largest of all Mississippi tributaries is the Ohio River.

The Mississippi River is divided into the upper Mississippi, from its source south to the Ohio River, and the lower Mississippi, from the Ohio to its mouth near New Orleans.

The current form of the Mississippi River Basin was largely shaped by the Cordilleran Ice Sheet of the most recent Ice Age. The southernmost extent of the enormous glaciations extended well into the present-day US and Mississippi Basin. When the ice sheet began to recede, hundreds of feet of rich sediment were deposited, creating the flat and fertile landscape of the Mississippi Valley. During the melt, giant glacial rivers found drainage paths into the Mississippi watershed, creating such features as the Minnesota River, James River, and Milk River valleys. When the ice sheet completely retreated, many of these "temporary" rivers found paths to Hudson Bay or the Arctic Ocean, leaving the Mississippi Basin with many features "oversized" for the existing rivers to have carved in the same time period. The Mississippi River Delta has shifted and changed constantly since the formation of the river, but the construction of dams on the river has greatly reduced the flow of sediment to the delta. In recent years, the Mississippi's mouth has shown a steady shift towards the Atchafalaya River channel, but because of flood works at the river's mouth, this change of course—which would be catastrophic for seaports at the river mouth—has been held at bay.

Throughout its history, whether for Native Americans, explorers, or modern commerce, the Mississippi has always been a major navigation route through the center of North America. In the 19th and 20th centuries, despite its slow current and relative depth, a series of dams were constructed on the river, one of the most notable of which is at St. Anthony Falls on the border between Minneapolis and St. Paul. These dams facilitate navigation for a steady stream of barge traffic carrying agricultural products from the fertile Mississippi Basin to the Gulf Coast, and like the Columbia River, most of the Mississippi also is a cascade of reservoirs. Most of its big tributaries—the Missouri and Ohio Rivers—have also been developed for navigation. However, the development of the 20th and 21st centuries has also come with environmental problems, the most infamous of which is the enormous Gulf of Mexico dead zone that extends hundreds of miles out to sea from the river's mouth. Because of dredging activity to deepen the Mississippi River channel, many natural features such as sandbars and meanders no longer exist. Efforts are being made to clean up the river and its tributaries, including the establishment of National Park Service sites on the river and the prevention of agricultural waste from flowing into the river.

1.2.3 The Great Lakes

The most important lakes in America are the Great Lakes. The Great Lakes are a collection of freshwater lakes located in eastern North America, on the Canada-US border. Consisting of Lakes Superior, Michigan, Huron, Erie, and Ontario, they extend about 1,600 kilometers from east to west, forming the largest group of freshwater lakes on Earth by surface. Of the five great lakes, only Lake Michigan belongs to America completely while the other four are shared with Canada. They are sometimes referred to as "the Third Coast" by some citizens of the US. Because of their size, types of ecosystems, and large abundances of beaches and coastal wetlands along their coasts, some regard them as inland seas or as one sea.

The five lakes slope downward towards the east. Lake Erie is over 100 meters higher than Lake Ontario and the steep water flow gives birth to the world-famous Niagara Falls which attract large numbers of visitors from around the world.

The Great Lakes contain roughly 22% of the world's fresh surface water. This is enough water to cover the 48 contiguous US states to a uniform depth of 9.5 feet (2.9 m). However, only 2% of this volume is replaced each year, causing water levels to fall in recent years as the water undergoes heavy human use. Although the lakes contain a large percent of the world's fresh water, the Great Lakes supply only a small portion of America's drinking water (roughly 4.2%).

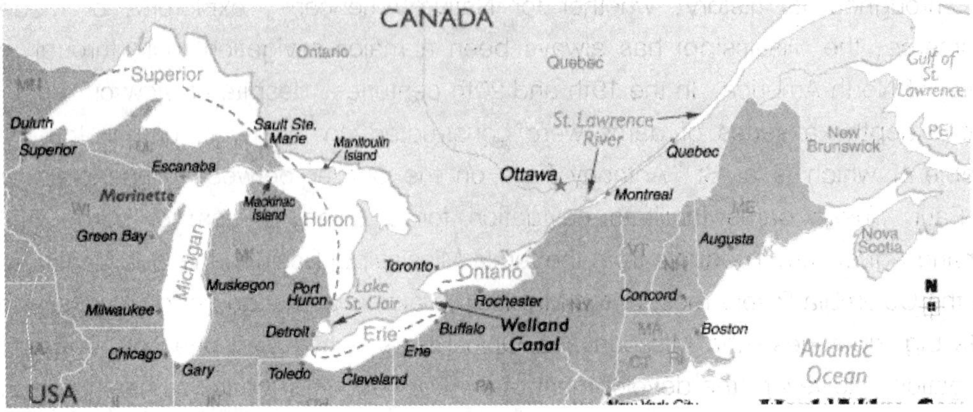

The lakes are extensively used for transport, though cargo traffic has decreased considerably in recent years. The Great Lakes Waterway makes each of the lakes accessible.

1.2.4 The Pacific Coast

The West Coast, Western Seaboard, or Pacific Coast are terms for the westernmost coastal states of the US. The term most often refers to the states of California, Oregon and Washington. Although not part of the contiguous US, Alaska and Hawaii do border the Pacific Ocean and can also be included in the West Coast. The US census groups the five states of California, Oregon, Washington, Alaska, and Hawaii together as the Pacific region.

As of 2008, the estimated population of the West Coast (the Census Bureau's Pacific Region) was approximately 49 million (47 million if only California, Oregon and Washington are included).

The term Left Coast is sometimes used, a form of word-play relating the region's position on the left of a conventionally displayed map of the US to its reputation for being more politically left-wing than some other parts of the US.

Major coastal cities on the West Coast include Los Angeles, San Diego, San Francisco, Oakland, Seattle, Anchorage, Honolulu, and Long Beach. Major non-coastal cities in West Coast states include Las Vegas, San Jose, Sacramento, Fresno, and Portland.

1.3 Climate

Due to its large size and wide range of geographic features, the US contains examples of nearly every global climate. The climate is temperate in most areas, subtropical in the Deep South, tropical in Hawaii and southern Florida, polar in Alaska, semiarid in the Great Plains west of the 100th meridian, Mediterranean in coastal California and arid in the Great Basin. Its comparatively favorable agricultural climate contributes (in part) to the country's rise as a world power, with infrequent severe drought in the major agricultural regions, a general lack of widespread flooding, and a mainly temperate climate that receives adequate precipitation.

The main influence on US weather is the polar jet stream, which brings in large low pressure systems from the northern Pacific Ocean. The Cascade Range, Sierra Nevada, and Rocky Mountains pick up most of the moisture from these systems as they move eastward. Greatly diminished by the time they reach the High Plains, much of the moisture has been sapped by the geographic effect as it is forced over several mountain ranges. However, once it moves over the Great Plains, uninterrupted flat land allows it to reorganize and can lead to major clashes of air masses. In addition, moisture from the Gulf of Mexico is often drawn northward. When combined with a powerful jet stream, this can lead to violent thunderstorms, especially during spring and summer. Sometimes during late winter and spring these storms can combine with another low pressure system as they move up the East Coast and into the Atlantic Ocean, where they intensify rapidly. These storms are known as nor'easters and often bring widespread, heavy snowfall to the Mid-Atlantic and New England. The uninterrupted flat grasslands of the Great Plains also lead to some of the most extreme climate swings in the world. Temperatures can rise or drop rapidly and winds can be extreme, and the flow of heat waves or Arctic air masses often advance uninterrupted through the plains.

The Great Basin and Columbia Plateau (the Inter-Montana Plateaus) are arid or semiarid regions that lie in the rain shadow of the Cascades and Sierra Nevada. Precipitation averages less than 15 inches (38 cm). The Southwest is a hot desert, with temperatures exceeding 100℉(38℃) for several weeks at a time in summer. The Southwest and the Great Basin are also affected by the monsoon from the Gulf of California from July to September, which brings localized but often severe thunderstorms to the region.

Much of California consists of a Mediterranean climate, with sometimes excessive rainfall from October to April and nearly no rain for the rest of the year. In the Pacific Northwest rain falls year-round, but is much heavier during winter and spring. The mountains of the west receive abundant precipitation and very heavy snowfall. The Cascades are one of the snowiest places in the world, with some places averaging over 600 inches (1,520 cm) of snow annually, but the lower elevations closer to the coast receive very little snow. Another significant (but localized) weather effect is lake-effect snow that falls south and east of the Great Lakes, especially in the hilly portions of the Upper Peninsula of Michigan and on the Tug Hill Plateau in New York. The lake effect dumped well over 5 feet of snow in the Buffalo, New York area throughout the 2006 to 2007.

In northern Alaska, tundra and arctic conditions predominate, and the temperature has fallen as low as minus −80℉ (−62℃). On the other end of the spectrum, Death Valley, California once reached 134℉ (56.7℃), the second-highest temperature ever recorded on Earth.

On average, the mountains of the western states receive the highest levels of snowfall on Earth. The greatest annual snowfall level is at Mount Rainier in Washington, at 692 inches (1,760 cm); the record there was 1,122 inches (2,850cm) in the winter of 1971–1972. This record was broken by the Mt. Baker Ski Area in northwestern Washington which reported 1,140 inches (2,900 cm) of snowfall for the 1998–1999 snowfall season. Other places with significant snowfall outside the Cascade Range are the Wasatch Mountains, near the Great Salt Lake, and the Sierra Nevada, near Lake Tahoe. In the east, while snowfall does not approach western levels, the region near the Great Lakes and the mountains of the Northeast receive the most. Along the northwestern Pacific coast, rainfall is greater than anywhere else in the continental US, with Quinault Ranger in Washington having an average of 137 inches (350cm). Hawaii receives even more, with 460 inches (1,200cm) measured annually on Mount Waialeale, in Kauai. The Mojave Desert, in the southwest, home to the driest locale in the US Yuma, Arizona, has an average of 2.63 inches (6.7 cm) of precipitation each year.

In central portions of the US, tornadoes are more common than anywhere else on Earth and touch down most commonly in the spring and summer. Deadly and destructive hurricanes occur almost every year along the Atlantic seaboard and the Gulf of Mexico. The Appalachian region and the Midwest experience the worst floods, though virtually no area in the US is immune to flooding. The Southwest has the worst droughts; one is thought to have lasted over 500 years and to have decimated the Anasazi people. The West is affected by large wildfires each year.

1.4 Natural Resources

The US is a land rich in natural resources. Some of these resources, such as water, iron ore, coal, oil, silver, and gold, are especially plentiful in the country.

The US has a large deposit of iron ore. The nation produces more than 80 million tons of iron a year. For many years, iron ore came primarily from the Great Lake region of Minnesota and Michigan, but the mines were severely depleted during the two World Wars. The richer ores are exhausted, though large amounts of lower-grade materials remain and form the basis of a thriving industry. Iron ores are also mined in Missouri, New York, Utah and Wyoming.

Coal is another major natural resource found in large quantities in the US which can last for hundreds of years. Coal deposits are widely distributed in the country. Most of coal reserves are to be found in the Appalachians, the Central Plain, and the Rockies.

The US, very rich in oil, was once the largest oil producing country in the world. Oil wells in the US produce more than 3,200 million barrels of petroleum a year. The production, processing and marketing of such petroleum products as gasoline and oil make up one of its largest industries. Most domestic production of oil and natural gas comes from offshore areas of Louisiana and Texas, and from onshore areas of Texas, Oklahoma, and California. Although the oil production in the US is very large, the big consumption has made America insufficient in oil supply. The shortage of domestic supplies of energy was forcefully publicized by the Arab oil embargo of 1973 -1974. Until this embargo most Americans did not realize that the US does not have enough energy to meet its ever-growing needs.

Other basic metals and minerals mined on a large scale in the US include zinc, copper, silver, and phosphate rock.

The US enjoys abundant water resources. Today the rivers and streams of the US furnish 63% of the water supply for cities, towns and farmlands, 93% of the water used by industry, and almost all of the water used to generate electric power. Unlike some other countries, the US as a whole has little trouble as caused by the shortage of fresh water.

The US has also plenty of fertile soil. Farmlands in the US make up about 12% of the arable lands in the world, and they are among the richest and most productive. Of the 2.3 billion acres of land in the 50 states, an estimated 300 million acres are planted annually. The country's very large acreage of highly productive farmlands could be expected to continue to supply the nation generously, with substantial surplus for export.

1.5 Population and Language

For centuries, the US has attracted people in search of a share of "the American

Dream" from all corners of the world. In fact, the US history is one of immigration. In 1620, about 100 English colonists, so-called "Mayflower Pilgrims" left for America seeking religious freedom. They landed near Plymouth, Massachusetts, marking an early successful European migration to North America, which had been inhabited by Amerindian people for more than 16,000 years. The immigration flow to the US first accelerated after the French Revolution, and during the 19th century, population pressure, fragmentation of land in rural Europe and famines drove millions of Europeans to the New World. Throughout the 19th and 20th centuries, American ports teemed with German, Chinese, Irish, Italian, Polish and immigrants from all over the world.

The US is called the melting pot because there are people from everywhere around the world. They have different cultures, different customs, but when they come to the US, they are one, one nation. Americans take pride in their "melting pot" society that encourages newcomers to assimilate into the American culture. But the melting pot imagery has been contested by the idea of multiculturalism, the "salad bowl theory", or as it is known in Canada, the "cultural mosaic", whereby the immigrants retain their own national characteristics while integrating into a new society.

In 1790, the year of the first census of the US population, there were only 3,929,214 Americans. By 1900, the US population jumped to 75,994,575. In 1920 the census counted more than a hundred million people (105,710,620). Another 100 million people were added to the US population in just fifty years when the two hundred million barrier was reached in 1970 with 203,302,031 counted in the census. The current US population is over 300 million people (303,500,000 in early 2008), so the US has the world's third largest population (following China and India).

As the world's population is approximately 6.6 billion, the current US population represents a mere 4.5% of the world's population so about one in every twenty people on the planet is a resident of the US.

The US does not have an official language; however, the majority of the population speaks English as a native language (some 82%). The variety of English spoken in the US is known as American English; together with Canadian English it makes up the group of dialects known as North American English. 96% of the population of the US speaks English "well" or "very well". There have been several proposals to make English the national language in amendments to immigration reform bills. None of these bills have become law with the amendment intact.

Spanish is the second most common language in the country, and is spoken by over 12% of the population. The US holds the world's fifth largest Spanish-speaking population, outnumbered only by Mexico, Spain, Argentina, and Colombia. Throughout the southwestern US, long-established Spanish-speaking communities coexist with large numbers of more recent Spanish-speaking immigrants. Although many new Latin American immigrants are less fluent in English, second-generation Hispanic Americans commonly speak English fluently, while only about half still speak Spanish.

According to the 2000 US census, people of German ancestry make up the largest single ethnic group in the US, and the German language ranks fifth. Italian, Polish, and Greek are still widely spoken among populations descending from immigrants from those countries in the early 20th century, but the use of these languages is dwindling as older generations pass away. Russian is also spoken by immigrant populations.

Tagalog and Vietnamese have over one million speakers in the US, almost entirely within recent immigrant populations. Both languages, along with the varieties of the Chinese language, Japanese, and Korean, are now used in elections in Alaska, California, Hawaii, Illinois, New York, Texas, and Washington.

There is also a small population of Native Americans who still speak their native languages, but these populations are decreasing, and the languages are almost never widely used outside of reservations. Hawaiian, although having few native speakers, is an official language along with English at the state level in Hawaii. The state government of Louisiana offers services and documents in French, as does New Mexico in Spanish. Besides English, Spanish, French, German, Navajo and other Native American languages, all other languages are usually learned from immigrant ancestors that came after the time of independence or learned through some form of education.

1.6 The American Dream

The term is not easily defined, and a unitary definition does not exist—the American Dream probably has a different meaning to every US citizen. For some it is the dream of freedom and equality, for others it is the dream of a fulfilled life or even the dream of fame and wealth. In general, the American Dream can be defined as being the opportunity and freedom for all citizens to achieve their goals and become rich and famous if only they work hard enough.

The American Dream is often associated with immigration, as the dream of religious freedom, economic prosperity, and meritocracy has historically driven immigrants to the US. The term is used by many modern Americans to signify success in life as a result of hard work (as in, "living [or pursuing] the American Dream").

The origin of the American Dream, a term coined by James Truslow Adams in his book *The Epic's of America* (1931), stems from the departure in government and economics from the models of the Old World. Additionally, from the American Revolutionary War well into the latter half of the 18th century, many of America's physical resources were unclaimed and held out the promise of land ownership and lucky investment in land or industry in the 19th century. The development of the Industrial Revolution combined with the great natural resources of the enormous and as yet unsettled (by Europeans) continent created the possibility of achieving wealth and transitioning "from rags to riches".

The living conditions in Europe and the hope of a better standard of living in America led to the migration of hundreds of thousands to the new world. Impoverished Western Europeans escaping the Irish potato famines in Ireland, the Highland clearances in Scotland and the aftermath of Napoleon in the rest of Europe came to America to escape a poor quality of life at home. They had heard about the government in America and hoped for an escape from their old life.

The Industrial Revolution was one of the great forces that developed the American Dream. The Industrial Revolution, amidst all the government corruption of the Gilded Era, resulted in the creation of hundreds of thousands of jobs. The development of big business, the Transcontinental Railroad, and the increase in oil production greatly increased the American standard of living. "Rags to riches" stories of business tycoons like Andrew Carnegie and John D. Rockefeller led to the belief that if you had talent, intelligence, and a willingness to work extremely hard, you were more likely to live a successful life.

The American Dream has always had a major influence on immigration, and has therefore resulted in wide cultural diversity. Throughout its history, America has been viewed as a country of opportunity, where entrepreneurship flourishes relative to other regions of the world. By the turn of the 18th century, the promise of the American Dream had begun to lure substantial numbers of immigrants from Eastern and Southern Europe. Huge numbers of Italians, Poles, Greeks, Jews, Russians and others came to find work in large industrial and financial centers such as New York, Chicago, Philadelphia and Detroit in the hope of escaping the class boundaries of their home countries. The system of meritocracy distinguished America from other countries because it allowed the members of the lower classes to exceed their social boundaries through hard work and determination.

In the 20th century, the American Dream had its challenges. The Great

Depression caused widespread hardship during the 1930s, and was almost a reverse of the dream for those directly affected. Racial inequality and legal discrimination prevented African Americans across the country from attaining the American Dream.

Since the end of World War II, young American families have sought to live in relative comfort and stability in the suburbs that were built up around major cities. This led to the rise of the relatively conservative 1950s, when many pursued "the perfect family" as a part or consequence of the American Dream. This period was shattered by a new generation of young people who embraced the hippie values of the 1960s, denying traditional values such as the American Dream. In modern times, the American Dream is seen as a possible accomplishment, as all children can go to school and get an education. Though the drive to it waned during those years, the dream itself has never died out.

There are many books, plays and other forms of literature which have defined, explored or denounced the American Dream. F. Scott Fitzgerald's *The Great Gatsby* and Arthur Miller's *Death of a Salesman* are very good examples exploring the theme of the American Dream.

1.7 American Family Life

In the US, the family is still very much alive, despite its many defects. The vast majority of Americans live with people to whom they are related by blood or marriage. Most American couples have two or three children, though larger families are not unusual.

Typically, the family consists of parents and their unmarried children. Middle-aged and elderly people generally do not live with their married children. However, parents usually keep in close contact with their grown children and take great interest in their grandchildren.

Although the majority of families live in houses, many live in apartment buildings. These range in size from two to six apartments to high-rise elevator buildings that may have more than 100 apartments. Some high-rise apartments are very expensive and elegant, but many are built for moderate or even low-income families.

More than 7 million Americans live in mobile homes—living quarters built with wheels. They can be moved, but generally they are brought to a site that is intended to be more or less permanent. Then the wheels are removed, and the home is fastened to the ground. Because they cost much less than conventional homes, mobile homes are especially popular among young couples and elderly retired couples.

About 87 percent of American families are headed by a married couple. We like to think of the typical American household as being closer to a democracy than to a dictatorship. Ideally, mother and father have an equal voice in decision-making. That is the ideal, but obviously not all households are run this way. Many families still live by the old principle that father's word is law. In many others, father is rarely home when the children are awake, and, as far as the children are concerned, mother is the dominant personality and major decision-maker.

Then, there are about 3 million households (with about 8 million children) in which one parent is absent as a result of separation, divorce, or desertion. Almost 90 percent of these households are headed by women whose children spend relatively little time with their fathers. In these families, mother is boss.

Parental roles have altered somewhat since the advent of the working mother. Today, about 10 million American mothers with children under eighteen years of age have jobs. In some families, the working mother is a necessity because the father is unable to find jobs or cannot earn enough for all the family's basic needs. In other households, the mother may work to supplement the father's income so the family can enjoy a higher standard of living. Many working mothers have to employ a cleaning woman one or more days a week to help with housework and childcare.

When a working mother has no household help, her husband often takes a more active part in housekeeping and childrearing. But even in families where the mother does not have an outside job, the father typically spends a significant amount of his leisure time with his children.

No other century promoted such rapid change in American families than the 20th century did. Though most of the first half of the century families were two-parent plus children units, by the 1980s and 1990s divorce was common in half of the homes and many families were single-parent or included step-parents, step-siblings and half-siblings. The major changes in opinions and even some laws on race, gender and sexuality during the 1960s and 1970s brought change to families as well. Some families were headed by gay parents, lived in communes or other non-traditional homes, were of mixed race, or had adopted children. Family life had changed dramatically in less than 50 years. The change in the core make-up of what was considered a family ushered in new celebrations and holidays, ways of cooking, eating, and entertainment, and even daily activities.

1.8 Holidays and Festivals

Referring most broadly to periods of time free from work, the word "holiday" is derived from the word "holyday", and refers generally to special days of celebration and commemoration. There are many holidays and festivals in America. Holidays are days that are set apart for public, religious or special observances. On many of these special occasions, schools, banks and business are closed. Holidays are also a relief from daily toil and a major source of recreation for common people. These can be based on religion, politics, or regional, ethnic, or racial affiliation, and may or may not be officially recognized. For instance, neither Halloween (October 31) nor Valentine's Day (February 14) are official holidays in the sense that businesses and government agencies close down or that the government acknowledges them as special. However, both are widely celebrated in the US. Other holidays receive government recognition at the local level (such as Evacuation Day, March 17, in Suffolk County, Massachusetts), the state level (such as Juneteenth, June 19, in Texas), or the national level (for example, Independence Day, July 4).

Some holidays, such as Halloween and Valentine's Day, have been celebrated in Europe and America for centuries and a number of them are related to pre-Christian celebrations. Among those on the American calendar having ancient origins is Valentine's Day. Moreover, many distinctly American holidays were heavily influenced by preexisting festivals. The American Thanksgiving, for instance, commemorates a feast at Plymouth Colony in 1621 that was most likely inspired by British harvest home traditions. Other holidays, however, are created in America as social circumstances demand. Examples are Martin Luther King Jr.'s birthday and the African American holiday of Kwanzaa.

Holidays are frequently contested. The holiday for Martin Luther King Jr.'s birthday, for instance, was resisted by President Ronald Reagan and the officials of several states. Likewise, while Kwanzaa is regarded by its participants as reinforcing a sense of community, it is seen as divisive by those not participating.

The adaptation of traditional celebrations in the US indicates that they serve different purposes under different circumstances, and that meanings change with personal, social, and cultural contexts. Still, even the major, long-standing holidays such as Independence Day, Thanksgiving, and Christmas are sites of identity politics and contestation. For instance, in the 18th and 19th centuries, African Americans held counter-celebrations near the fourth of July as an ironic commentary on the celebration of freedom in a land of slaves. Subsequently, Native Americans declared Thanksgiving a National Day of Mourning.

The following are some of the most important holidays observed in the USA:

Christmas

The Puritans of Massachusetts believed that holidays were not biblically justified, and therefore did not observe them or allow others to do so. Christmas, for example, was banned in Massachusetts from 1659 to 1681. It was in the middle colonies, where Anglicanism held sway, that Christmas developed. At first a rowdy occasion, Christmas was in the 17th and early 18th centuries a carnivalesque celebration. During the 19th century, however, Christmas changed into a more demure and domestic family holiday. The Christmas tree tradition was borrowed from Germany. Santa Claus derived from European traditions of St. Nicholas, the British Father Christmas, and other mid-winter gift bearers. But the American Santa Claus also owes much to American authors such as Washington Irving, who described him in *Knickerbocker Tales* (1809); Clement Moore, who is said by some to have written "A Visit from St. Nicholas"; and cartoonist Thomas Nast.

Independence Day

Independence Day was celebrated from the day on which *The Declaration of Independence* was adopted and read before the population of the colonies: July 4, 1776. Before independence and as late as 1800, British customary holidays such as Guy Fawkes Day were observed in New England, as were official commemorations in honor of the monarchy. The fourth of July continued the bonfire and fireworks customs of those celebrations. Soon, it became an occasion for lengthy oratory, picnics, sports, and a reading of *The Declaration.*

African American Celebrations

African Americans celebrated these holidays by putting their own historically and culturally derived spin on them. Africans in bondage, for instance, were usually allowed Christmas or New Year's as a holiday. From all accounts, the celebrations were very much African in nature, with masquerading and musical performances. Such festivals were found throughout the African diaspora. Similarly, a Dutch Easter celebration in New York State known as Pinkster became an occasion for an African

American celebration in the African-derived style. For African Americans as well as whites, the fourth of July entailed speech making, feasting, and sports, but might be celebrated on a different day, perhaps in implicit protest. In addition, emancipation celebrations were held. The first of August recognized the abolition of slavery in Haiti in 1837. Since the Civil War, emancipation celebrations have been held at different times around the country. In Texas, June 19, known as Juneteenth, is a legal holiday.

Other Holidays

The Civil War Begat Memorial Day. The period between the Civil War and World War I gave rise to many other holidays, including Flag Day and Labor Day. Along with these official holidays, the US hosts a wide variety of festivals that reflect its multiculturalism. Some ethnic celebrations, such as St. Patrick's Day, have become nationally celebrated; some, such as the Mexican Cinco de Mayo, are growing in popularity.

Exercises

I. Fill in the following blanks with proper words or expressions.

1. Bounded on the east by the ________ Ocean and on the west by the ________ Ocean, the US occupies a territory of 95,220,572km^2 primarily in the mid latitude region of the North American continental landmass.
2. ________ in the mid-Pacific form the 50th state of the US.
3. The US is the second largest country in North America after Canada and the fourth largest in the world after ________, ________ and ________.
4. The cultural and economic center of the US is ________.
5. The territory comprised of the 48 contiguous states is bordered by ________ to the north and ________ to the south.
6. The Great Plains lie west of the ________ River and east of the ________ Mountains.
7. New York City is located at the mouth of the ________ River, which feeds into a naturally sheltered harbor and then into the Atlantic Ocean.
8. ________ is the largest river system in the US and the largest of North America.
9. Of the five great lakes, only Lake ________ belongs to America completely while the other four are shared with Canada.
10. Lake Erie is over 100 meters higher than Lake Ontario and the steep water flow gives birth to the world-famous ________ Falls which attract large numbers of visitors from around the world.

Ⅱ. Explain the following terms.

1. the flag of the US
2. American Dream

Ⅲ. Discuss the following questions.

1. What are the features of the Atlantic Seacoast?
2. Why is the US called "the melting pot"?

Chapter Two

A Brief History (Ⅰ)

2.1 The Discovery of America

2.1.1 The Personal History of Columbus

Christopher Columbus (or Columbo in Italian) was the son of Dominico Columbo and Susannah Fontanarossa. The father was a wool carder, a business which seems to have been followed by the family through several generations. He was the oldest of four children, having two brothers and one sister. Of the early years of Columbus little is known. It is asserted by some that Columbus was a wool comber—no mean occupation in that day—and did not follow the sea. On the other hand, it is insisted that, whether or not he enlisted in expeditions against the Venetians and Neapolitans (and the whole record is misty and uncertain), Columbus at an early age showed a marked inclination for the sea, and his education was largely directed along the lines of his tastes, and included such studies as geography, astronomy, and navigation. It is certain that when Columbus arrived at Lisbon he was one of the best geographers and cosmographers of his age, and was accustomed to the sea from infancy. Happily his was at an age favorable for discovery. The works of travel were brought to the front. The closing decade of the 15th century was a time of heroism, of deeds of daring, and discovery. Rude and unlettered to some extent, yet it was far more fruitful, and brought greater blessings to the world than are bestowed by the effeminate luxury which often characterizes a civilization too daintily pampered, too tenderly reared. Life then was at least serious.

2.1.2 Columbus' Approaching the Spanish Court

Arriving at Cordova, Columbus found the city a great military camp, and all Spain aroused in a final effort to expel the Moors. Fernando, the Confessor, was a very different man from Perez, and instead of treating Columbus kindly, received him coolly, and for a long while actively prevented him from meeting the king. The Copernican theory, though held by some, was not at this time established.

At length, through the friendship of de Quintanilla, Comptroller of the Castilian Treasury, Geraldini, the Pope's nuncio, and his brother, Allessandro, tutor of the children of Ferdinand and Isabella, Columbus was made known to Cardinal Mendoza, who introduced him to the king. Ferdinand listened to him patiently, and referred the whole matter to a council of learned men, and it was not until 1491 (six years later) that the Commission reported the project "vain and impossible, and not becoming great princes to engage in on such slender grounds as had been adduced".

The report of the Commission seemed a death blow to the hopes of Columbus. Disappointed and sick at heart, and disgusted at six years of delay, Columbus turned his back on Spain, "indignant at the thought of having been beguiled out of so many precious years of waning existence". Determined to lay his project before Charles Ⅶ, of France, he departed, and stopped over at the little Monastery of La Rabida, from whose Prior, Juan Perez, six years before, he had departed with such sanguine hopes, for Cordova.

Columbus before Queen Isabella and the Spanish Court

2.1.3 Isabella's Agreeing to Support Columbus' Voyage

But no sooner had Columbus gone, than the queen, who we may believe regretted the loss of possible glory of discovery, hastily dispatched a messenger after him, who overtook him when two leagues away and brought him back.

Although Ferdinand was opposed to the project, Isabella concluded to yield to Columbus his terms and agreed to advance the cost, 14,000 florins, about $7,000, from her own revenues, and so to Spain was saved the empire of a New World. On May 12 Columbus took leave of the king and queen to superintend the fitting out of the expedition at the port of Palos. The hour and the man had at last met.

2.1.4 Fitting out the Expedition

What thoughts and apprehensions filled the heart and mind of Columbus as he at last saw the yearning desires of years about to be met, may be to some extent conceived; they certainly cannot be expressed. Not a general at the head of his great army who, at a critical moment in battle, sees the enemy make the false move which insures him the victory, could feel more exultant than Columbus must have felt when he left the presence of the Spanish Court, and, after seven years of weary and all but hopeless waiting at last saw the possibilities of the great unknown opening up before him, and beheld, in a vision to him as clear and radiant as the sun shining in the heavens, a New World extending its arms and welcoming him to her embrace. It would seem as if everything now conspired to atone for the disappointing past. His old tried friend, Perez, prior of the La Rabida monastery, near Palos, received him with open arms, and well he might, for had not his kind offices made success possible? And the authorities, as if to make good the disappointments of seven years, could not now do too much. All public officials, of all ranks and conditions in the maritime borders of Andalusia were commanded to furnish supplies and assistance of all kinds. Not only so, but as superstition and fear made ship owners reluctant to send their vessels on the expedition, the necessary ships and men were to be provided, if need be, by impressments, and it was in this way vessels and men were secured.

In three months the expedition was ready to sail. The courage of Columbus in setting sail in untried waters becomes more evident when we consider the size of the ships comprising the little expedition. They were three in number; the largest of them, the Santa Maria, was only ninety feet long, being about the size of our modern racing yachts. Her smaller consorts, the Pinta and the Nina, were little caravels, very like our fishing smacks, without any deck to keep the water out. The Santa Maria had four masts, of which two were square rigged, and two fitted with lateen sails like those used on the Nile boats; this vessel Columbus commanded. Martin Alonzo Pinzon commanded the Pinta, and his brother, Vincente Yanez Pinzon, the Nina. The fleet was now all ready for sea; but before setting sail Columbus and most of his officers and crew confessed to Friar Juan Perez, and partook of the Sacrament. Surely such an enterprise needed the blessing of heaven, if any did!

It was before sunrise on Friday morning, August 3, 1492, that Columbus, with 30 officers and adventurers and 90 seamen, in all 120 souls, set sail, "in the name of Christ", from behind the little island of Saltes. Those inclined to be superstitious regarding Friday will do well to note that it was on a Friday Columbus set sail from Palos; it was on Friday, the 12th of October, that he landed in the New World; on a Friday he set sail homeward; on a Friday, again, the 15th of February, 1493, land was sighted on his return to Europe, and that on Friday, the 15th of March, he returned to Palos. The story of that eventful trip has never ceased to charm the world, nor ever will so long as the triumphs of genius, the incentives of religion, and the achievements of courage have interest for mankind.

Columbus bidding farewell to the Queen of Spain on
his departure for the New World, August 3,1492

2.1.5 Columbus' Reaching the New World

That night, the ever memorable night of Thursday, opening into the morning of Friday, the 12th of October, not a soul slept on any vessel. The sea was calm and a good breeze filled the sails, moving the ships along at twelve miles an hour; they were on the eve of an event the world had never seen and could never see again. The musical rippling of the waves and the creaking of the cordage were all the sounds that were audible, for the birds had retired to rest. The hours passed slowly by. It was just past midnight when the admiral, with restless eye, sought to penetrate the darkness. Then a far-off light came to his vision. Calling Guiterrez, a court officer, he also saw it. At two in the morning a gun from the Pinta, which led the other boats, gave notice that land was at last found. A New World had indeed been discovered. The hopes of years had attained their fruition. It was Rodrigo de Triana, a seaman, who first saw land. He received neither promised doublet nor pension. Friday, the 12th of October, 1492, corresponding to the 21st of October, 1492, of the present calendar, was the ever memorable day.

The first sight of the new world—Columbus discovering America

It is not possible within the limits of this chapter to follow Columbus from day to day as he sailed a sea now turbulent and tempestuous, as if to show its other side, in marked contrast to the soft airs and smooth waters that had greeted the voyagers when their purpose held "to sail beyond the sunset and the baths of all the western stars".

Nor can we follow with minuteness Columbus in his subsequent career. He had made the greatest discovery of his or any other ages: He had found the New World, and this, more than anything else, has to do with "The Story of America".

2.2 Overview of Colonial America 1607-1754

From the foundation of the colonies beginning with the founding of Jamestown until the beginning of the Revolutionary War, different regions of the eastern coast had different characteristics. Once established, the thirteen British colonies could be divided into three geographic areas: New England, Middle, and Southern. Each of these had specific economic, social, and political developments that were unique to the regions.

2.2.1 The New England, Middle, and Southern Colonies

New England

Colonies: New Hampshire, Massachusetts, Rhode Island, and Connecticut. These were known for being rich in forests and fur trapping. Harbors were located throughout the region. The area was not known for good farmland. Therefore, the farms were small, mainly to provide food for individual families. New England flourished instead with fishing, shipbuilding, lumbering, and fur trading along with trading goods with Europe. The famous Triangle Trade occurred in the New England colonies where slaves were sold in the West Indies for molasses. This was sent to New England to make rum which was then sent to Africa to trade for slaves.

In New England, small towns were the centers of local government. In 1643, Massachusetts Bay, Plymouth, Connecticut, and New Haven formed the New England Confederation to provide defense against Indians, Dutch, and the French. This was the first attempt to form a union between colonies.

A group of Massasoit Indians organized themselves under King Philip to fight the colonists. King Philip's War lasted from 1675 to 1678. The Indians were finally defeated at a great loss.

Middle Colonies

Colonies: New York, New Jersey, Pennsylvania, and Delaware. This area was excellent for farming and included natural harbors. Farmers grew grain and raised livestock. The Middle Colonies also practiced trade like New England, but typically they were trading raw materials for manufactured items.

One important event that happened in the Middle Colonies during the colonial period was the Zenger Trial in 1735. John Peter Zenger was arrested for writing against the royal governor of New York. Zenger was defended by Andrew Hamilton and found not guilty of helping to establish the idea of freedom of the press.

Southern Colonies

Colonies: Maryland, Virginia, North Carolina, South Carolina, and Georgia. Southern colonies grew their own food along with growing three major cash crops: tobacco, rice, and indigo. These were grown on plantations typically worked by slaves and indentured servants. The main commerce of the South was with England. Plantations kept people widely separate which prevented the growth of many towns.

An important event that occurred in the southern colonies was Bacon's Rebellion. Nathaniel Bacon led a group of Virginia colonists against Indians who were attacking frontier farms. The royal governor, Sir William Berkeley, had not moved against the Indians. Bacon was labeled a traitor by the governor and ordered arrested. Bacon attacked Jamestown and seized the government. He then became ill and died. Berkeley returned, hanged many of the rebels, and was eventually removed from office by King Charles Ⅱ.

2.2.2 The Thirteen Colonies

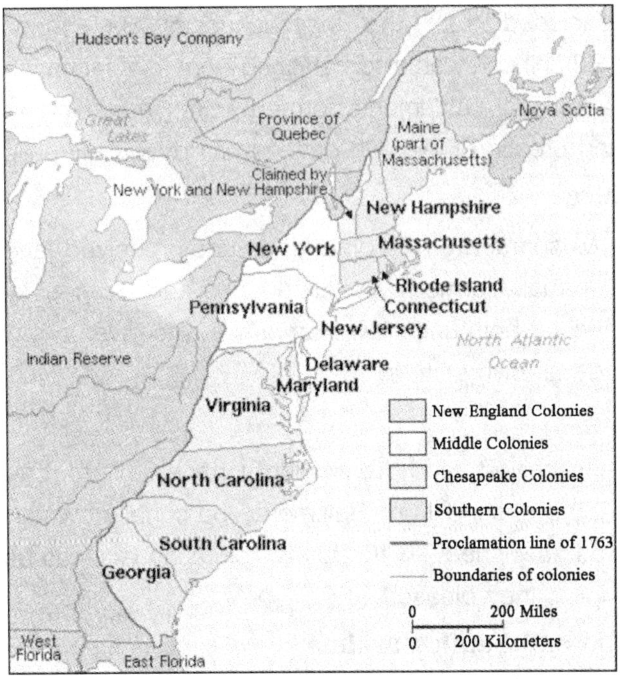

The thirteen colonies

Virginia

Jamestown was the first English settlement in America (1607). It had a hard time at first and didn't flourish until the colonists received their own land and the tobacco industry began flourishing. People continued to arrive and new settlements arose. In 1624, Virginia was made a royal colony.

Massachusetts

Pilgrims wishing to flee persecution and find religious freedom traveled to America and formed the Plymouth Colony in 1620. Before landing, they established their own government, the basis of which was the Mayflower Compact. In 1628, Puritans formed the Massachusetts Bay Company and many Puritans continued to settle in the area around Boston. In 1691, Plymouth joined with the Massachusetts Bay Colony.

Connecticut

A group of individuals led by Thomas Hooker left the Massachusetts Bay Colony due to dissatisfaction with harsh rules and settled in the Connecticut River Valley. In 1639, three settlements joined to form a unified government creating a document called the Fundamental Orders of Connecticut, the first written constitution in America. King Charles II officially united Connecticut as a single colony in 1662.

Rhode Island

Roger Williams argued for freedom of religion and separation of church and state. He was banished from the Massachusetts Bay Colony and founded Providence. Anne Hutchinson was also banished from Massachusetts and she settled Portsmouth. Two additional settlements formed in the area and all four received a charter from England creating their own government eventually called Rhode Island.

New Hampshire

In 1622, John Mason and Sir Ferdinando Gorges received land in northern New England. Mason eventually formed New Hampshire and Gorges' land led to Maine. Massachusetts controlled both until New Hampshire was given a royal charter in 1679 and Maine was made its own state in 1820.

Maryland

Lord Baltimore received land from King Charles I to create a haven for Catholics. His son, the second Lord Baltimore, personally owned all the land and could use or sell it as he wished. In 1649, the Toleration Act was passed allowing all Christians to worship as they pleased.

North Carolina and South Carolina

Eight men received charters in 1663 from King Charles II to settle south of

Virginia. The area was called Carolina. The main port was Charles Town (Charleston). In 1729, North and South Carolina became separate royal colonies.

New York

The Dutch owned a colony called New Netherland. In 1664, Charles II granted New Netherland to his brother James, Duke of York. He just had to take it from the Dutch. He arrived with a fleet. The Dutch surrendered without a fight.

New Jersey

The Duke of York granted some land to Sir George Carteret and Lord John Berkeley who named their colony New Jersey. They provided liberal grants of land and freedom of religion. The two parts of the colony were not united into a royal colony until 1702.

Pennsylvania

The Quakers were persecuted by the English and wished to have a colony in America. William Penn received a grant which the King called Pennsylvania. Penn wished to begin a "holy experiment". The first settlement was Philadelphia. This colony quickly became one of the largest in the New World.

Delaware

When the Duke of York got New Netherland, he also received New Sweden which had been founded by Peter Minuit. He renamed this area Delaware. This area became part of Pennsylvania until 1703 when it created its own legislature.

Georgia

James Oglethorpe received a charter to create a colony between South Carolina and Florida. He founded Savannah in 1733. Georgia became a royal colony in 1752.

1754 marked a changed era in America with the beginning of the French and Indian War. From this period on, the colonists became more discontent with British rule as new acts and sanctions were created. The increasing tension between Britain and the colonies would lead to the Revolutionary War.

2.3 Mayflower Compact

The Mayflower Compact is often cited as one of the foundations of the US Constitution. The story of its creation begins with the Pilgrims in England.

Pilgrims were separatists from the Anglican Church in England. They were protestants who did not recognize the authority of the Anglican Church and formed their own Puritan Church. To escape persecution and possible imprisonment, they actually fled England for Holland in 1607. They lived in Holland for a while before deciding to create their own colony in the New World. They received a land patent from the Virginia Company and created their own joint-stock company for the enterprise.

Aboard the Mayflower

The Pilgrims left aboard the Mayflower in 1620. There were 102 men, women, and children aboard including some non-puritan settlers like John Alden and Miles Standish. They were headed for Virginia but got blown off course and instead decided to found their colony in Cape Cod in what would become the Massachusetts Bay Colony. They called the colony Plymouth after the harbor in England from which they departed for the New World.

Since the new location for their colony was outside the areas claimed by the two chartered joint-stock companies, they considered them-selves technically independent and created their own government under the Mayflower Compact.

Creating the Mayflower Compact

In basic terms, the Mayflower Compact was a social contract whereby the forty-one men who signed it agreed to abide by the new government's laws in exchange for shared protection. Unfortunately, the original document has been lost. William Bradford included a transcription of the document in his book, *Of Plymouth Plantation*. In part his transcription states:

"*Having undertaken, for the Glory of God and advancement of the Christian Faith and Honor of our King and Country, a Voyage to plant the First Colony in the Northern Parts of Virginia, do by these present solemnly and mutually in the presence of God and one of another, Covenant and Combine ourselves together into a Civil Body Politic, for our better ordering and preservation and furtherance of the ends aforesaid; and by virtue hereof to enact, constitute and frame such just and equal Laws, Ordinances, Acts, Constitutions and Offices, from time to time, as shall be thought most meet and convenient for the general good of the Colony, unto which we promise all due submission and obedience.*"

The Mayflower Compact was the foundational document for the Plymouth Colony. The fact that it was a covenant whereby the settlers would subordinate their rights to follow laws passed by the government to ensure protection and survival made it a unique document. As previously stated, it set a precedent and was indeed an influential document for the founding fathers as they created the US Constitution.

2.4 The American War of Independence

The War of the Revolution from 1775 to 1783

On the outbreak of the war the American colonies were, from North to South, Maine, New Hampshire, Massachusetts, Rhode Island and Connecticut (making up New England), New York, Pennsylvania, New Jersey, Delaware, Maryland, Virginia, North Carolina, South Carolina and Georgia.

The principal cities were Boston in Massachusetts, New York, Philadelphia, the colonial capital of Pennsylvania, and Charleston, the capital of South Carolina.

Map of the American Colonies at the outbreak of war in 1775

To the north of the colonies lay the British province of Canada, with its mainly French-speaking population, and to the west the hinterland of the American landmass.

The American colonies differed widely. The New England colonies had been established and settled largely by English Presbyterians and comprised small close knit farming communities, with fishing and trading centers along the coast. The populations were inward looking and intolerant of outsiders.

Boston was a busy port, reputed to be one of the wealthiest in the English-speaking world.

New York contained a polyglot population of Dutch, Swedes and English. Upstate New York contained large estates. The Hudson River, a main communications artery, was the centre of considerable trading activity. The large state area contained a considerable Indian presence from the Six Nations confederation, particularly the Mohawks.

Pennsylvania, established by the Quaker Penn family, had been hamstrung in the early part of the 18th century by the stranglehold the Quakers maintained on government. The population, particularly in the west of the colony, was largely German and Scotch-Irish with little commitment to the British Crown. The colony was a prosperous community of small farmers. In the east lay Philadelphia, the largest city in the American colonies and the first capital of the US.

Virginia and the southern colonies were different in character. Tobacco growing along the Tideway's coastline was the backbone of the Virginian economy. Ships from England collected the tobacco and delivered in exchange goods that enabled the most successful planters to maintain the lavish lifestyle of English country gentlemen. More than 50 percent of the colony's population comprised African slaves. In the remote western regions of the colony colonists cut farmsteads from the forests and maintained a precarious existence in the face of resistance from the native American tribes.

The Carolinas and Georgia, the most recently established colonies, were similar in character and outlook to Virginia.

The relationship between the American colonies and the British Crown was complex and turbulent. In each colony the Royal Governor had historically been at odds with the assembly of elected leading colonials, usually over taxation. Pennsylvania, where the Penn family exempted themselves from financial contribution to the running of the colony, is a good illustration of the almost unworkable system that had grown up.

The main element that kept the colonies and the British Crown in uneasy alliance was the threat from France with its powerful base along the St Lawrence seaway in Canada and along the western borders of New York, Pennsylvania and Virginia.

The long and agonizing French and Indian War between 1755 and 1762 saw the French forced out of Canada, with Britain assuming government of the French population, and the American colonies released from the threat of French invasion and dominance.

That war, fought in Europe, India and the West Indies, left Britain with considerable debt. The British government considered the American colonies should contribute to the reduction of that debt and many of the measures that brought about the Revolutionary War were to that end.

General George Washington

Following the war a substantial British garrison remained in America. The 18th century armies were not easy guests, particularly with their practices of enforced and fraudulent recruitment. The redcoats became as unpopular in the towns and villages of New England as they were in "Old" England. The relationship between the royal troops and their provincial colleagues in the war against the French had been far from easy. The royal officers tended to be contemptuous of the professionalism of the provincials and the colonies resented the loss of life in battles like Ticonderoga brought about by the incompetence of Royal officers. A dispute that simmered throughout the French and Indian War arose from the ranking of provincial officers beneath royal officers of the same grade. George Washington had found this particularly galling.

General Braddock's disastrous defeat in July 1755 in Western Pennsylvania struck a major blow to the prestige of the British Crown. The withdrawal of Colonel Dunbar with the survivors of Braddock's regular troops to Philadelphia, leaving Pennsylvania, Maryland, Virginia and even western New York to be ravaged by Indian raiding parties, encouraged by the French, led many in those colonies to question the worth of the link with Britain and to look to their own colonial governments to fill the vacuum left by the Royal Forces.

Braddock's campaign provides a looming portent for the future of the colonies. Many of the participants went on to take major parts in the Revolutionary War: George Washington, Gage, Gates, Mercer, Lee and several others.

The war began with the attempt by Gage to seize the armaments held by Congress at Concord and the exchange of shots at Lexington.

The signing of *The Declaration of Independence*

2.5 The American Civil War

The American Civil War was the most costly of all American wars in history. A savage war that split the country in half, the Civil War cost the US over 600,000 lives, and led to over 1,000,000 casualties. In many instances the victors were the few left standing on the battlefield. Raging through the country, it affected everyone in the US and even other countries. Abolishing slavery was accomplished at the highest price possible, the Civil War.

The American Civil War (1861–1865), also known as the War Between the States and several other names, was a civil war in the US. Eleven Southern slave states declared their secession from the US and formed the Confederate States of America (the Confederacy). Led by Jefferson Davis, they fought against the US (the Union), which was supported by all the free states and the five border slave states. The Union states were loosely referred to as "the North".

In the presidential election of 1860, the Republican Party, led by Abraham Lincoln, had campaigned against the expansion of slavery beyond the states in which it already existed. The Republican victory in that election resulted in seven Southern states declaring their secession from the Union even before Lincoln took office on March 4, 1861. Both the outgoing and incoming US administrations rejected the legality of secession, considering it rebellion.

Abraham Lincoln, the 16th President of the United States

Hostilities began on April 12, 1861, when Confederate forces attacked a US military installation at Fort Sumter in South Carolina. Lincoln responded by calling for a volunteer army from each state, leading to declarations of secession by four more Southern slave states. Both sides raised armies as the Union assumed control of the Border States early in the war and established a naval blockade. In September, 1862, Lincoln's *Emancipation Proclamation* made ending slavery in the South a war goal, and dissuaded the British from intervening. The *Proclamation* went into effect on January 1,1863.

The Emancipation Proclamation was of great importance. It was a progressive event, helping to end the war sooner. After it was issued many Negroes actually took part in the war and made great contribution to the victory of the North. The North began to gain advantage in the war. Karl Marx said it was "the most important document in American history since the founding of the United States".

Confederate Commander Robert E. Lee won battles in the east, but in 1863 his northward advance was turned back after the Battle of Gettysburg and, in the west, the Union Gained control of the Mississippi River at the Battle of Vicksburg, thereby splitting the Confederacy. Long-term Union advantages in men and material were realized in 1864 when Ulysses S. Grant fought battles of attrition against Lee, while Union General William Sherman captured Atlanta, Georgia, and marched to the sea. Confederate resistance collapsed after Lee surrendered to Grant at Appomattox Court House on April 9, 1865.

The American Civil War was the deadliest war in American history, resulting in the deaths of 620,000 soldiers and an undetermined number of civilian casualties. It legally abolished slavery in the US, restored the Union and strengthened the role of the federal government. The social, political, economic and racial issues of the war decisively shaped the reconstruction era that lasted to 1877, and brought changes that helped make the country a united superpower.

Exercises

I. Fill in the following blanks with proper words or expressions.

1. It was Christopher Columbus who first ________ American continent.
2. The history of the US is generally agreed to have begun in ________.
3. The First Continental Congress was held in ________ in September, 1774.
4. The American War of Independence started in ________ and ended in ________.
5. Washington won the great victory on December 26, 1776 in ________.
6. After the Federal Government was established, the city ________ was chosen as the capital for the time being.
7. The pamphlet "Common Sense" was written by ________.
8. As the result of the US-Mexican War, nearly ________ of the entire territory of Mexico was lost.
9. The Battle of ________ was the turning point of the American Civil War.
10. During the Civil War Lincoln issued the ________, which declared the abolition of slavery.

II. Explain the following terms.

1. Christopher Columbus
2. Mayflower

3. *the Declaration of Independence*
4. Abraham Lincoln

Ⅲ. Discuss the following questions.

1. How was the New World discovered? Why was it important?
2. What was the significance of the Civil War?

Chapter Three

A Brief History(Ⅱ)

3.1 World War Ⅰ

President Woodrow Wilson

In 1914, World War Ⅰ erupted across Europe. Soon after the war's outbreak, Wilson proclaimed US neutrality designed to keep the US out of the conflict. The US attempted to remain neutral, but its resolve was tested by German submarine warfare. In 1915, Germany announced a U-boat blockade of the Allies' ports and, in the ensuing months, killed a number of Americans in torpedo attacks on British vessels and one US tanker. On May 7, 1915, a U-boat sank the British ocean liner, killing close to 1,200 people, including 128 Americans. In late January, 1917, Germany proclaimed the resumption of unrestricted submarine warfare: Germany vowed to sink all ships, belligerent or neutral, in a wide zone around the Allies. In response, Wilson cut diplomatic relations with Germany. In the next few months, five US ships were sunk.

In the meantime, British intelligence intercepted the Zimmenrman Telegram. Sent from the German foreign secretary to the German ambassador to Mexico, the Zimmerman Telegram suggested that Mexico enter the war against the US. In return for a German pledge to aid in the restoration of Mexico's former territories of Texas, Arizona, and New Mexico. Germany also promised to help Japan if Japan went to war against the US. The telegram and the continued aggression towards US ships convinced Wilson to break US neutrality and call for war.

In April 1917, the US declared war on Germany. Wilson, who had been elected six months earlier on the slogan, "He kept us out of war", now charged into the war, proclaiming it necessary "to make the world safe for democracy".

American involvement in World War Ⅰ lasted from the summer of 1917 to the armistice that ended the war in November, 1918—just over one year. American involvement helped to secure Allied victory: American troops overran heavily fortified German trenches and reinvigorated the British and French war efforts. At the war's end, the American death toll exceeded 110,000.

For America the war was relatively brief, and the casualties, while large, could not be compared with those of the other major nations. For America, however, the Great War was a turning point: For the first time American soldiers in significant numbers crossed the Atlantic to fight in a foreign war; for the first time America became deeply embroiled in European affairs; for the first time an American president helped shape the fate of a postwar world; for the first time America was part of the Western family of nations in the fullest sense, and the impact of the two million soldiers who fought in France as well as President Wilson and the diplomats who negotiated the peace treaty in Versailles in 1919 changed the course of American diplomacy forever.

From the beginning of World War Ⅰ, Wilson had hoped for a peaceful settlement promoting America's democratic ideals. He saw the Allied victory as a victory over autocratic government, and therefore as an opportunity to advance democracy and liberalism worldwide. He wanted to end the war through a liberal peace agreement. On January 8, 1918, Wilson made his famous "Fourteen Points" address, introducing the idea of a League of Nations—a league that would guarantee all nations "fundamental rights, equal sovereignty, freedom from aggression, freedom of the seas, and eventual disarmament". The League of Nations, he announced, would "insure peace and justice throughout the world".

But Wilson's effort to reshape the world according to his plan to "make the world safe for democracy" was ultimately a failure. After the war, Wilson devoted all of his abundant energy and talents and brainpower to achieving that dream. The rest of the world, however, was not ready to see thing his way. *The Treaty of Versailles* was vindictive and harsh, and few historians doubt that it was a direct contributor to the outbreak of World War Ⅱ. The US Senate rejected *the Treaty of Versailles.* The League of Nations, which Wilson cherished as his dream to achieve worldwide peace and stability, was also rejected by the Senate.

But in the longer view Wilsonian democracy did not die. His progressive ideas lived on among his most able sub-cabinet members, including his very capable Assistant Secretary of the Navy Franklin Delano Roosevelt. And in the longterm Wilson's failed League of Nations found a new life in the United Nations, which, although it remains a controversial entity whose achievements have been mixed, has, it must be said, kept the world from being an even more violent and dangerous place than it otherwise would have been. Many of those who worked for and with Wilson to achieve his ideals were young men who came of age a generation later, leading the US through World War II and beyond. All of them, one way or another, were touched by the impact of Woodrow Wilson.

3.2 Prosperity and Depression

After World War I, the US entered a consumer society, with booming markets for radios, home appliances, synthetic textiles, and plastics. One of the most admired men of the decade was Henry Ford, who had introduced the assembly line into automobile factories. Ford could pay high wages and still earn enormous profits by mass-producing the Model T, a car that millions of buyers could afford.

But the superficial prosperity masked deep problems. With profits soaring and interest rates low, plenty of money was available for investment. Much of it, however, went into reckless speculation in the stock market. Frantic bidding pushed prices far above stock shares' real value. Investors bought stocks "on margin", borrowing up to 90 percent of the purchase price. The bubble burst in 1929. The stock market crashed, triggering a worldwide depression. The Great Depression that followed after the crash was the most devastating economic blow that the nation had ever suffered. It lasted for ten years, dominating every aspect of American life during the 1930s. Intractable and all-encompassing, the Depression loosened its grip on the nation only after the outbreak of World War II.

3.2.1 Prosperity: the Roaring Twenties

At the beginning of the 1920s, the US was converting from a wartime to peacetime economy. When weapons for World War I were no longer needed, there was a temporary stall in the economy. After a few years, the country prospered, in part because there was a great demand for American goods from war-torn European countries. In this decade, America became the richest nation on Earth and a culture of consumerism was born.

During the 1920s, there was a "golden age" for radio. The radio found its way into virtually every home in America. It became a national pastime; many listeners would gather in their living rooms to tune in sports, concerts, sermons, and news much like we gather around the TV. Broadcasting was more than a business or a job ... it was considered to be a very glamorous profession. Radio was a formal affair; announcers dressed up for work in tuxedos and evening gown, even if there was no studio audience. Many local stations had a staff orchestra, and some had their own dramatic groups. Each station had its own group of fans who tuned in each week to listen to their favourite programs. Radio was at its peak, and its influence is much like that of TV or the Internet today.

The year 1922 introduced the first movie made with sound, *The Jazz Singer*. And in 1926, the advent of Technicolor made movies more entertaining and memorable. Consequently, the movie industry became a major part of American industry in general.

Science, medicine and health advanced remarkably during the same period. Albert Einstein was awarded the Nobel Prize in physics in 1921. Diphtheria became better controlled in 1923 by newly introduced immunization. An interest developed in nutrition, caloric consumption and physical vitality.

During the 1920s government policies, progress in technology, and a new consumer society produced a booming economy. Radio helped transform the US into a single national market, and a mass popular culture developed based largely on the consumption of luxury items.

3.2.2 The Great Depression

After World War I, America saw a short-term development in the 1920s, but unexpectedly, the Great Depression broke out. The revolution in consumer goods disguised the decline of many traditional industries in the 1920s. Railroads suffered from poor management and from the competition of the growing trucking industry. Coal was being replaced by petroleum and natural gas. Cotton textiles declined with the development of rayon and other synthetic fibers.

On the lower end of that spectrum, many had incomes that were too small for much buying beyond bare subsistence. People working in coal mining and the textile for leather industries were suffering.

The ability to produce had increased, but the ability to consume was limited. This had happened with grain production and the tractor in the early twenties. The supply was so great that the drop in grain prices hurt farmers. And the farmers responded by increasing production even more.

In manufacturing, by 1927 production in the US had begun to decline, most notably in automobiles and in building materials such as steel, rubber and other materials for the automobile. Home buying and home building were also down. Not enough people could afford to buy a house. Too many people were paying rent rather than making payments on their own house ... a benefit to landlords, but for common people an unfortunate distribution of wealth upwards.

By 1933, the value of the stocks on the New York Stock Exchange was less than one fifth of what it had been at its peak in 1929. Businesses closed, factories shut down, banks failed and farm income fell by some 50%. By 1932, about one in every four Americans was unemployed.

During the Great Depression, many people had to receive relief supplies

The unequal distribution of wealth, saturation of the market for consumer goods, and growing speculation all created economic instability. The boom of the 1920s would end in a great crash; yet the achievements of the decade would survive even that dire experience.

Optimism prevailed throughout much of the US in the 1920s. Many believed that the new Federal Reserve System and other advances had freed the country from the recurring business cycles that had plagued earlier generation. But signs of a failing economy were evident in the late 1928 and into the following year. In fact Herbert Hoover, Secretary of Commerce, under President Coolidge warned him in 1925 about the dangers of excessive stock market speculation. And after Hoover took office on March 4, 1929, he continued what had been his criticism of excessive speculation and excessive use of borrowed money in buying stocks. Hoover remained an economic conservative in so far as he believed that little government intervention in the economy was necessary in peacetime, but he believed that too much money was being put into unproductive speculation rather than into productive investment.

Franklin Delano Roosevelt

In the election of 1932, Hoover lost the presidency to the Governor of New York, Franklin Delano Roosevelt. Only 6 of 48 states voted for Hoover. The Democratic Party became the majority party in the House of Representatives and the Senate by huge margins.

3.3 The New Deal and World War II

Franklin D. Roosevelt (FDR) was elected President in 1932. In order to deal with economic depression, in the first three months he brought forward more than 70 acts to Congress, which were generally called Roosevelt's "New Deal".

Though determined to maintain its neutrality, the US was gradually drawn into the war in Europe. American isolationism shifted to full involvement after Japan bombed Pearl Harbor on December 7, 1941. America sided with Britain, France and the Soviet Union against Germany, Italy, and Japan. The European part of the war ended with Germany's surrender in May, 1945. Japan surrendered in September, 1945, after the US dropped atomic bombs on Hiroshima and Nagasaki.

3.3.1 The New Deal

FDR came to office convinced of the economic theories of John Maynard Keynes, who argued that government spending could revive a faltering economy. FDR's New Deal embodied this strategy.

The First Hundred Days and the First New Deal

In his inauguration speech of 1933, FDR pledged to devote his presidency to helping the poor and promoting recovery, claiming "the only thing we have to fear is fear itself". During the first hundred days of his presidency, FDR set forth his plan for national recovery, known as the New Deal. The New Deal ushered in an unprecedented era of government intervention in the economy.

The first problem FDR faced during the early months of 1933 was a rash of bank closures in 38 states. In response, he called for a bank holiday, during which he met with the heads of many suffering banks and developed the Emergency Banking Relief Act, passed on March 9. This act provided a framework under which banks could reopen with federal support. Other important reforms of "the first hundred days" include:

Civilian Conservation Corps (CCC), Agricultural Adjustment Administration (AAA), the Federal Emergency Relief Act (FERA), the Tennessee Valley Authority (TVA), the Federal Securities Act (FSA), the National Recovery Administration (NRA), the Public Works Administration (PWA), the Federal Deposit Insurance Corporation (FDIC).

After June 16, Congress recessed, officially ending "the first hundred days" of reform which created the framework for heavy government involvement to help bring the US out of the Depression.

FDR's first hundred days in office saw unprecedented government intervention in the economy, industry, and agriculture. Democrats in Congress, at FDR's behest, passed measures creating a massive structure of agencies under executive control.

Challenges to the New Deal

After the first hundred days, continued economic distress and mounting opposition to FDR's programs cast doubt upon the New Deal. The first sign that the New Deal was in danger was trouble with the NRA. Opposition to the NRA came to a head in 1935, when the conservative Supreme Court declared the agency unconstitutional, claiming the NRA gave the executive branch regulatory powers that belonged exclusively to Congress. This decision began a series of court decisions that overturned key elements of the New Deal.

The efforts of the AAA, combined with a severe drought in the American heartland, effected a drop in farm production, prompting a rise in farm prices. However, while the AAA did much to help large landowners and commercial farmers, it did little for landless laborers and tenant farmers who populated the rural Midwest. This large group of dispossessed farmers made up the majority of those who participated in the western immigration from the dust bowl to California in search of land and employment. As the plight of the dust bowl poor became more widely recognized, questions arose about the effectiveness of the AAA. In 1936, the Supreme Court ruled the AAA unconstitutional, claiming it enforced illegal taxation.

Another source of criticism was the conservative American Liberty League, composed of elites who claimed that the New Deal restricted democratically guaranteed freedom to earn and save money and acquire property. Other challenges to the New Deal arose from those appealing to the discontented lower and middle classes.

These challenges passed, at least in part, with the midterm elections of 1934. Despite a vocal minority of dissenters, FDR remained a popular president because of his efforts at relief, his charismatic leadership, and his connection with the citizens symbolized by his frequent fireside chats-radio broadcasts that he used to rally the support of the people and to offer assurances of economic recovery. FDR's popularity and public confidence in the New Deal resulted in a resounding approval of the Democratic program in the elections of 1934. Democrats gained seats in both the House and Senate.

The Second New Deal

Reassured by the overwhelming Democratic victory in the midterm elections of 1934, FDR laid out his plans for the Second New Deal in the January, 1935 State of the Union Address. He outlined six ways in which the administration would renew and intensify the efforts begun under the first New Deal. These plans included an enlarged unemployment relief program, assistance to the rural poor, support for organized labor, social welfare benefits for the elderly and disadvantaged, strict regulation of business and finance, and heavier taxes on the wealthy.

In April, 1935, Congress passed the Emergency Relief Appropriation Act. This act granted FDR $5 billion to use on whatever programs he chose. The majority of that funding went to the Works Progress Administration (WPA). Over eight years, the WPA pumped $11 billion into the economy and supported the unemployed of all backgrounds, from industrial engineers to authors and artists. The unemployment rate fell over 5 percent from 1935 to 1937, partially due to the WPA's efforts.

To regulate the economy, FDR empowered the Federal Reserve Board to exert tighter control over the money supply, and called for strict enforcement of the Securities Exchange Act of 1934, which required that a detailed and truthful prospectus be publicized for each company issuing stock on the US market.

One of the most lasting achievements of the Second New Deal was the creation of social security benefits for the elderly through the Social Security Act of 1935.

Changes of Party Alignments

FDR's landslide victory in the 1936 election confirmed his and his party's success in becoming the representatives of the downtrodden and disadvantaged. Farmers appreciated FDR's consistent efforts to forge an effective agricultural plan. Urban voters and organized labor, great sources of funding for FDR's 1936 campaign, valued his support of union rights and his efforts to cope with rampant unemployment. Many women recognized that FDR's programs attacked the concept of inequality and appreciated that he had appointed the first female cabinet member, Frances Perkins, as Secretary of Labor. Black Americans, as the group most devastated by unemployment, had benefited extensively from New Deal measures. Black support gradually shifted toward FDR and the Democratic Party away from Republican Party, which had consistently won the black vote since the late 1800s.

The election of 1936 saw the rise of a new Democratic coalition, including farmers, urban workers, women, and blacks. This coalition helped FDR win the 1936 election by a landslide.

FDR's presidency and the New Deal thus brought about a realignment of the Democratic and Republican parties. As Democrats won the support of blacks, urban workers, and farmers, they lost the support of the white South, a traditional Democratic stronghold. The Republican Party, meanwhile, lost its long-held black vote.

New Deal Fades

The stage seemed set for FDR's continued success in pushing through the New Deal, but he faced a host of political challenges that hindered his efforts. The first element in the downturn was his involvement in the Court Packing scheme. Early in 1937, Roosevelt proposed a court-reform bill allowing the president to appoint an additional Supreme Court justice for each current justice over the age of seventy. FDR claimed that the bill addressed concerns about the justices' workload, but it was clear that the proposal was meant to dilute the power of the conservative justices of the Supreme Court who had been hostile to New Deal legislation (they had ruled that the AAA and NRA were unconstitutional, among other decisions). The Senate vetoed the scheme in July, 1937. Several justices retired shortly after or announced their intention to do so, and the Supreme Court resisted less during the final years of the Second New Deal than it had during earlier years, but the Court Packing scheme was a blemish on Roosevelt's record. A more direct factor in the decline of the Second New Deal was the inability of FDR's programs to revive the economy. In August, 1937, the nation plunged into the 1937 recession, also known as the "Roosevelt Depression". By early 1938 unemployment had again risen above 20 percent.

The final obstacle to the extension of the Second New Deal came from within Congress, where critics of FDR were growing in power. A conservative coalition legislated cuts in relief programs and blocked further legislation proposed by New Deal supporters. As a result, FDR proposed few new reform measures during his second term in office. That he proposed no new domestic programs in his January

1939 State of the Union address signaled the end of the New Deal.

The New Deal had effectively ended by 1939, owing, in part, to the embarrassing Court Packing scheme, the 1937 recession, and growing congressional opposition.

3.3.2 World War Ⅱ

World War Ⅱ began on September 1, 1939, when Germany, without a declaration of war, invaded Poland. Britain and France declared war on Germany on September 3, and all the members of the Commonwealth of Nations, except Ireland, rapidly followed suit. The fighting in Poland was brief. The German, with its use of new techniques of mechanized and air warfare, crushed the Polish defenses, and the conquest was almost complete when Soviet forces entered Poland on September 17.

Again neutrality was the initial American response to the outbreak of war in Europe. But the bombing of Pearl Harbor naval base in Hawaii by the Japanese in December 1941 brought the US into the war, first against Japan and then against its allies, Germany and Italy.

Neutrality and Isolationism

In the early days of World War Ⅱ, the US Government adopted a sit-on-the-fence policy. The American capitalists wanted to continue their profitable trade with the warring countries, including the aggressors. Many common Americans clung to their belief in "glorious isolation". Between 1935 and 1937, the Congress passed three Neutrality Acts whose aim was to keep the US from being involved in the war, but in fact, these laws encouraged the aggressive nations and made them believe that the US would not lend a hand to the countries attacked.

Opposition to war continued to fade as Hitler's troops invaded and conquered Denmark and Norway in April 1940, Belgium and the Netherlands in May, and France in June, followed by the Battle of Britain throughout the summer and fall, in which German planes bombed British cities.

In this atmosphere of growing alarm, FDR decided to run for an unprecedented third term in office. During his 1940 campaign, Roosevelt appointed a Council for National Defense to oversee defense production, appointed Republican Henry Stimson Secretary of War, and approved a peacetime draft by signing the Selective Service and Training Act. Although he approved the draft, FDR pledged never to "send an American boy to fight in a European war". Isolationists opposed to FDR's reelection sponsored the Committee to defend America by aiding the Allies, urging neutrality and claiming that the US could stand alone regardless of Hitler's advances in Europe. FDR won reelection in spite of the committee's efforts.

Entry into War

After winning reelection, FDR felt confident in stepping up American aid to the Allies. He pushed for passage of the Lend-Lease Act in March, 1941, which allowed the president to lend or lease supplies to any nation deemed "vital to the defense of the United States", such as Britain. FDR extended lend-lease aid to the Soviet Union after Germany invaded in November, 1941. The US also helped the Allies by tracking German submarines and warning the British of their location, and by convoying British ships carrying lend-lease supplies—that is, surrounding British ships with US navy vessels ordered to attack any menacing vessel.

In August, 1941, FDR met with British Prime Minister Winston Churchill on a British ship off Newfoundland. The two leaders discussed military strategy and issued the *Atlantic Charter*, which outlined their ideal postwar world: Among other provisions, it called for disarmament and freedom of the seas. In response to a German attack against a US destroyer, Roosevelt issued the shoot-on-sight order in September 1941, which authorized American naval patrols to fire on all Axis ships found between the US and Iceland. After American destroyers were twice attacked in October, Congress authorized the arming of merchant ships.

FDR signs declaration of war against Japan, 1941

The final provocation for American entry into the war came from Japan, which had joined the Rome-Berlin-Tokyo Axis in September, 1940 by signing the Tripartite Pact. Japan's desire to build an East Asian empire had alarmed the US since Japan's invasion of China in 1931. In September, 1940, Japanese forces continued their invasion into French Indochina. The US responded to this invasion as it had to other invasions in the past: It added items to a lengthy list of embargoed Japanese goods, and eventually froze all trade with Japan. In 1941, US intelligence became aware of plans for a Japanese attack and sent out warnings to commanders of US bases in the Pacific, but most American officials did not believe that the threat was immediate. These officials were proved wrong on December 7, 1941, when, in an attempt to destroy American sea power in the Pacific, Japanese planes bombed the US base at Pearl Harbor. 2,400 Americans died. On December 8, the Senate voted unanimously in favor of FDR's request for a declaration of war on Japan. The House passed the declaration over only one dissenting vote. On December 11, Germany and Italy declared war on the US, completing the entry of the US into World War Ⅱ.

On January 1, 1942, representatives of 26 nations signed the *Declaration of the United Nations*, pledging support for the *Atlantic Charter* and vowing not to make separate peace agreements with the Axis powers.

Wartime Economy

America's involvement in the war lasted a long time—from 1941 to 1945. During these four years, the US sent more than $50 billion worth of war material to the Allies. Although the US had begun preparing for war during the summer of 1940, war production comprised only 15 percent of the nation's industrial output in 1941, and US armed forces were seriously understaffed and undersupplied. During the next four years, war production on the home front churned into high gear.

The US mobilized industry to assist in the war effort. The War Production Board, created in 1942, oversaw the production of thousands of planes, tanks, and artillery pieces required for the war. The War Production Board allocated scarce resources and offered incentives for civilian firms to produce military goods. Factories converted from civilian to war production with amazing speed. Firms that had made vacuum cleaners before the war began to produce machine guns. Due to this shift in production, heavy investment, and new efficient techniques, the US produced more war material than all of the Axis powers combined. The last civilian car was produced in the US in 1942, after which plants were redesigned to produce tanks, planes, weapons, and munitions. By the end of the war, the US had built about 300,000 aircraft, 85,000 tanks, 375,000 artillery pieces, 2.5 million machine guns, and 90,000 sea ships—more war material than the four Axis powers, combined, had produced. This feat was accomplished through substantial investment of capital and the development of new, highly efficient manufacturing techniques.

War spending, accompanied by the draft, ended the high rate of unemployment which had not rebounded from the Great Depression. Organized labor grew strong and wealthy during World War Ⅱ, with union membership growing by about 60 percent. Although most unions abided by a no-strike policy, unions secured new benefits for their members, partially as a concession from the National War Labor Board, which limited wage increases to avoid inflation. Union power suffered a setback when a series of coal miners' strikes provoked Congress to pass the Smith-Connolly War Labor Disputes Act in June, 1943, which limited the right to strike in key industries and allowed the president to take control of any firm beset by strikes.

During World War Ⅱ, women were encouraged to enter the workforce, and women aiding in the war effort were glorified. War advertising encouraged women to actively participate in the war effort. During World War II, even more so than in World War I, women entered the workforce to fill the vacancies left by men at war and aid in the production of war materials. Officials discovered that women could perform the duties of eight of every ten jobs normally done by men. By 1943, more than two million women were working in American war industries. Increasing numbers of women entered the workforce to perform all sorts of jobs. The roles women played in the armed forces helped create new respect for the working woman. Women, however, were paid far less than working men, and traditional notions of gender roles prevailed throughout the war.

Winning the War

In June, 1944, American and British forces landed on the beaches of Normandy, opening the long-delayed western front to attack the Germans. Paris was liberated in August. In May, 1945, Germany surrendered. Three months later, Russia declared war against Japan. On August 6 and 9, American airplanes dropped two atomic bombs on Hiroshima and Nagasaki. On August 14, Japan surrendered and World War II ended.

At the Crimean Conference Churchill, Roosevelt, and Stalin planned the final assault on Germany

In April, 1945, at the end of the war, a conference was called in San Francisco to organize the United Nations. Forty-eight countries altogether attended the conference. Thus, the United Nations was established. During the war, the development of the American economy reached a higher stage. As a result, America became the strongest power in the Western world.

3.4 The Modern Era

The modern era has been a time of great changes in the US. The Great Depression, and World War II devastated the American people. Yet there were also times of prosperity, such as the decade after World War Ⅱ. The development and growth of the US during this era was influenced by helping Europe recover from World War Ⅱ and the US involvement in other wars—mainly the Cold War with the Soviet Union. During this time, Americans went to the moon, ushered in the Civil Rights Movement and the fight for equal rights for women, established relations with China, and witnessed the disintegration of the Soviet Union.

Another topic that is synomous with modern America is technology. American technology has exponentially grown to reach heights people fifty years ago would not have dreamed of. People of this era made immense technological advancements, including the inventions of television, modern computers, the Internet, the CD players and so on. Perhaps the biggest accomplishment in technology in the past few years is the Internet, a worldwide computer network used for entertainment, commerce, education, and communication. Modern American history changed from decade to decade and continues its rapid evolution into the 21st century.

3.4.1 The US in the 1950s

The Cold War

The conflict in ideologies between capitalism and communism resulted in one of the greatest conflicts of the 20th century. The belief that freedom and democracy would die under communist rule caused the US to start a conflict that would last for decades. The decisions made by the US in WW Ⅱ caused tensions to rise between the US and the Soviet Union. Fear of Communism in capitalist nations, caused the US government to use propaganda to raise Cold War anxieties. Furthermore, the American media influenced the attitudes of Americans, making a hatred of communism spread through the nation. Thus, the US caused the conflict known as the Cold War. During then, President Harry S. Truman tooled a strong stance against the Soviet territorial advances in Eastern Europe, advocating a policy of containment. Under this policy, the US would not attempt to change the post-World War Ⅱ situation in Europe, but it would work to prevent further Soviet expansion through peaceful or military means. Germany became a divided country, with a Western zone under joint British, French, and American occupation and an Eastern zone under the Soviet

Harry S. Truman

occupation. In the spring of 1948 the Soviets sealed off West Berlin in an attempt to starve the isolated city into submission. The Western powers responded with a massive airlift of food and fuel until the Soviets lifted the blockade in May, 1949. A month earlier the US had allied with Belgium, Canada, Denmark, France, Iceland, Italy, Luxembourg, the Netherlands, Norway, Portugal, and the United Kingdom to form the North Atlantic Treaty Organization(NATO).

Postwar Prosperity

The decade following World War II was characterized by affluence in much of American society, giving rise to high levels of consumption and a boom in population. For the first time a majority of Americans enjoyed a comfortable standard of living. In 1960, 55 percent of all households owned washing machines, 77 percent owned cars, 90 percent had television sets, and nearly all had refrigerators. The postwar prosperity helped propel the creation of suburbs and the popularization of the automobile. Prosperity also led to a baby boom and the promotion of conservative values. Beneath this widespread prosperity, however, lay deepening poverty for some Americans, and the gap between the rich and poor widened.

3.4.2 The US in the 1960s

The Space Race

The struggle for nuclear dominance begot a battle between the superpowers to exhibit technological prowess in all fields. During the mid-1950s most Americans were aware that the government was doing research on the exploration of space and that one day, probably in the far distant future, men would go to the moon and beyond. But when the Soviet Union launched *Spuntnik*, an artificial satellite, into Earth orbit in 1957, Americans were stunned. Russian scientists had been portrayed as less capable than their American counterparts, and Soviet successes were supposedly based on borrowing of Western ideas. But when the Soviets leaped out on front in space exploration, even with a primitive vehicle, Americans reacted with a combination of disbelief and panic. The US educational system was hauled into court and placed under scrutiny. Reflecting people's attitudes, Congress passed legislation that the National

Neil Armstrong on the moon

Aeronautics and Space Administration (NASA) and passed additional laws meant to improve American science and math curricula. The Space Race was seen as part of the Cold War, and Americans felt they had to win.

No one played this theme more strongly than President John F. Kennedy. Early in his administration he dedicated that nation to putting a man on the moon and returning him safely by the end of the decade, defined as January 1, 1970. With the assistance of former German V-weapon rocket scientists and an aviation industry with much talent, the American caught up with and passed the Soviets and reached Kennedy's goal when astronaut Neil Armstrong stepped out of the Apollo 11 Spacecraft and onto the moon's surface on July 20,1969.

The Civil Rights Movement

As the Cold War raged during the 1950s and 1960s, great changes occurred in American society. With two Democratic presidents in the White House in the 1960s, domestic politics revolved around liberal reforms, especially concerning civil rights.

The modern Civil Rights Movement is said to have begun in 1954 to 1955 with the Supreme Court decision in *Brown v. Board of Education of Topeka* and Rosa Park's refusal to give up her seat to a white man on a bus in Montgomery, Alabama. Led by Dr. Martin Luther King, the Civil Rights Movement achieved its greatest successes, culminating in the 1964 Civil Rights Act and the 1965 Voting Rights Act.

3.4.3 The US in the 1970s

In the 1970s, the Cold War gave way to detente and a more complicated pattern of international relations in which the world was no longer clearly split into two clearly opposed blocs. Less powerful countries had more room to assert their independence, and the two superpowers were partially able to recognize their common interest in trying to check the further spread and proliferation of nuclear weapons. US-Soviet relations would deteriorate once again in the late 1970s and early 1980s.

Nixon's Visit to China

Improved relations with the People's Republic of China are often cited as the most successful diplomatic achievements of Nixon's presidency. One of the main reasons Richard Nixon became the 1952 Vice President candidate on the ticket was his strong anti-communism stance. Despite this, in 1972 Nixon became the first US President to visit China.

In July, 1971, President Nixon's Secretary of State secretly visited Beijing during a trip to Pakistan, and laid the groundwork for Nixon's visit to China.

From February 21 to February 28, 1972, US President Richard Nixon traveled to Beijing, Hangzhou and Shanghai. Almost as soon as the American president arrived in the Chinese capital he was summoned for a meeting with Chairman Mao who, unknown to the Americans, had been ill nine days earlier but was at that point feeling strong enough to meet Nixon. Secretary of State William P. Rogers was excluded from this meeting and the only other American present was National Security Council staffer (and later US Ambassador to China) Winston Lord. To avoid embarrassing Rogers, Lord was cropped out of all the official photographs of the meeting.

Nixon held many meetings with Chinese Premier Zhou Enlai during the trip, which included visits to the Great Wall, Hangzhou, and Shanghai. At the conclusion of his trip, the US and the PRC Governments issued the *Shanghai Communiqué*, a statement of their foreign policy views and a document that would remain the basis of Sino-American bilateral relations for many years. Kissinger stated that the US also intended to pull all its forces out of the island of Taiwan. In the communiqué, both nations pledged to work toward the full normalization of diplomatic relations.

The US acknowledged the notion that all Chinese on both sides of the strait maintain that there is only one China. Nixon and the US government reaffirmed their interests in a peaceful settlement of the Taiwan question agreed by the Chinese themselves. The statement enabled the US and PRC to temporarily set aside "the crucial question obstructing the normalization of relations" concerning the political status of Taiwan and to open trade and other contacts. However, the US continued to maintain official relations with the government of the Republic of China in Taiwan until 1979 when the US broke off relations with the Republic of China and established full diplomatic relations with the PRC.

Detente with the Soviet Union

In May 1972, President Nixon was invited to talks with General Secretary Leonid Brezhnev in Moscow that resulted in the Strategic Arms Limitation Talks, commonly known as SALT, and the first arms limitations treaty was signed in 1972. SALT I limited each of the superpowers to 200 antiballistic missiles and set quotas for intercontinental and submarine missiles. Though largely symbolic, the agreement sparked hope for cooperation between the two superpowers.

The Watergate Scandal

In 1972, Nixon easily won the reelection. During that presidential campaign, however, the Watergate Scandal was revealed. Five men had been arrested for breaking into Democratic Party headquarters at the Watergate office building in Washington, D. C. Two *Washington Post* reporters investigated the incident and discovered that the burglars had been employed by Nixon's reelection committee.

The White House made matters worse by trying to conceal its connection with the break-in. Eventually, tape recordings made by the president himself revealed that he had been involved in the cover-up. By the summer of 1974, it was clear that Congress was about to impeach and convict him. On August 8, Nixon became the only US President to resign from office.

3.4.4 The US from 1980 to 2000

The Reagan Administration

In the 1980 election, Ronald Reagan was elected President. At 69, Reagan was the oldest person ever to become president in American history. Soon after taking office, Reagan presented to Congress a four-part economic program in which he called for reductions in income taxes and business taxes in order to encourage investment, and proposed deep cuts in federal spending in every area except defense. He requested that many government regulations be eliminated to reduce the federal government's role in the day-to-day operation of business.

President Reagan

With his support of the Federal Reserve's tight money policy, inflation was finally brought under control and by 1983, a recovery was under way. Although many Americans were better off financially than they had been in 1980, Reagan's policies led to an increasing gap between the rich and the poor, and social welfare programs had been drastically curtailed. Despite this, Reagan overwhelmed the Democratic Party and won the 1984 election.

At the end of his administration, the nation was enjoying its longest recorded period of peacetime prosperity without a recession or depression.

The Bush and Clinton Administration

President Reagan enjoyed unusually high popularity at the end of his second term in office, but in the terms of the US constitution, he could not run again in 1988. The Republican nomination went to Vice President George H. W. Bush.

In the first two years in office, Bush followed Reagan's economic program and concentrated on solving social and economic problems. His greatest test came when Iraqi President Saddam Hussein invaded Kuwait, and threatened to move into Saudi Arabia. On August 20, 1990, President Bush signed the National Security Directive

45, "US Policy in Response to the Iraqi Invasion of Kuwait", outling US objectives which included the "immediate, complete, and unconditional withdrawal of all Iraqi forces from Kuwait". Vowing to free Kuwait, Bush rallied the United Nations, the US people, and Congress, sending 425,000 American troops to the region. They were joined by 118, 000 troops from allied nations. After weeks of air and missile bombardment, the 100-hour land battle called Operation Desert Storm defeated Iraq's million-man army.

Despite unprecedented popularity from this military and diplomatic triumph, Bush was unable to withstand discontent at home from a faltering economy, rising violence in inner cities, and continued high deficit spending. In 1992, he lost his bid for reelection to Democrat Bill Clinton.

At the age of 46, Clinton was elected president. He acted on many important issues that affected the US and other countries. Measures for economic recovery were taken, and developments began to take shape during Clinton's first term. His second term was a vigorous economic development. His domestic priorities included legislation to upgrade education, to restrict handgun sales, to strengthen environmental rules, and to protect the jobs of parents who must care for sick children. Internationally, his priorities included reducing trade barriers and mediating the Northern Ireland and Israeli-Palestinian conflicts.

Although the economy was strong in the mid-1990s, two phenomena were troubling many Americans. Corporations were resorting more and more to a process known downsizing—trimming the work force to cut costs despite the hardships this inflicted on workers. And in many industries the gap between the annual compensations of corporate executives and common laborers had become enormous. Even the majority of Americans who enjoyed material comfort worried about a perceived decline in the quality of life, in the strength of the family, in neighborliness and civility. Americans probably remained the most optimistic people in the world, but with the century drawing to a close, opinion polls showed that trait in shorter supply than usual.

3.4.5 The US in the 21st Century

In the presidential election of 2000, George W. Bush, son of the former President Bush, became the 43rd President of the US. During his campaign, Bush's foreign policy platform included support of a stronger economic and political relationship with Latin America, especially Mexico, and a reduction in involvement in "nation-building" and other small-scale military engagements. On September 11, 2001, Islamic terrorists attacked the World Trade Center and Pentagon. The

September 11, 2001 terrorist attacks irrevocably altered the direction of the Bush presidency. Bush took drastic steps to protect the homeland and its interests abroad. He created a new cabinet-level agency, the Department of Homeland Security. The new entity consolidated 20 agencies under one cabinet umbrella.

However, in 2008, the financial crisis broke out and the Bush administration can't deal with it well. In the following presidential election of the US, after a hard-fought campaign, Democratic Senator Barack Obama won the US presidential election, and became the 44th president of the US—the first African American in the country's history to do so. After Obama took office, he focused on diplomatic engagement and mended tied frayed by the war in Iraq and other unpopular Bush administration policies. From November 15 to November 18, 2009, Obama made his visit to China, during which the leaders of two countries changed their opinions on the current Sino-American relationship and key international issues. "The relationship between the US and China will shape the 21st century, which makes it as important as any bilateral relationship in the world," US President Barack Obama said. "That reality must underpin our partnership."

President Barack Obama

Exercises

I. Fill in the following blanks with proper words or expressions.

1. In ________, the US declared war on Germany and made the involvement in the first world war officially.
2. In 1929, the bubble burst, the stock market crashed, ________ that followed after the crash was the most devastating economic blow that the nation had ever suffered.
3. Franklin D. Roosevelt was selected President in 1932. In the first three months he brought forward more than 70 acts to Congress, which were generally called Roosevelt's ________.
4. The bombing of Pearl Harbor naval base in Hawaii by the Japanese in ________ brought the US into World War Ⅱ.
5. In April, 1945, at the end of the war, a conference was called in ________ to organize the United Nations. Forty-eight countries altogether attended the

conference. Thus, the United Nations was established.

6. The US caused the conflict known as the Cold War. During then, President ________ tool a strong stance against the Soviet territorial advances in Eastern Europe.
7. In May, 1949, the US allied with Belgium, Canada, Denmark, France, Iceland, Italy, Luxembourg, the Netherlands, Norway, Portugal, and the United Kingdom to form ________.
8. In 1972 ________ became the first US president to visit China.
9. On ________ during Bush administration, Islamic terrorists attacked the World Trade Center and Pentagon.
10. In 2008, ________ won the US presidential election, and became the 44th President of the US—the first African American in the country's history.

Ⅱ. Explain the following terms.

1. the New Deal
2. the Cold War
3. NATO
4. Watergate Scandal
5. 9/11 Incident

Ⅲ. Discuss the following questions.

1. What made the US a powerful country by the end of World War Ⅱ?
2. What were the contents of Reagan's economic program?

Chapter Four

Political System

The US is a presidential, federal republic, in which the president of the US (the head of state and head of government), Congress, and judiciary share powers reserved to the national government, and the federal government shares sovereignty with the state governments. Federal and state elections generally take place within a two-party system, although this is not enshrined in law.

The executive branch is headed by president and is independent of the legislature. Legislative power is vested in the two chambers of Congress, the Senate and the House of Representatives. Judicial power is exercised by the judicial branch (or judiciary), composed of the Supreme Court and lower federal courts. The judiciary's function is to interpret the US Constitution as well as federal laws and regulations. This includes resolving disputes between the executive and legislative branches. The federal government of the US was established by the Constitution. American politics has been dominated by two parties, the Democratic Party and the Republican Party, since the American Civil War, although other parties have also existed.

Major differences between the political system of the US and that of most other developed democracies are the power of the Senate as the upper house of the legislature, the wide scope of power of the Supreme Court, the separation of powers between the legislature and the executive government, and the dominance of the two main parties.

4.1 The Political Culture of America

Most schools in the US teach the *Declaration of Independence*, *Constitution*, *Bill of Rights*, and the writings of the Founding Fathers as the definition of the country's governing ideology. Among the core tenets of this ideology are the following:

· Democracy: The government is answerable to citizens, who may change it through elections.

· Equality before the law: The laws should attach no special privilege to any citizen. Government officials are subject to the law just as others are.

· Freedom of religion and separation of church and state: The government can neither support nor suppress religion.

· Freedom of speech: a marketplace of ideas.

At the time of the United States' founding, the economy was predominantly one of agriculture and small private businesses, and state governments left welfare issues to private or local initiative. As in the UK and other industrialized countries, laissez-faire ideology was largely discredited during the Great Depression. Between the 1930s and 1970s fiscal policy was characterized by the Keynesian consensus, a time during which modern American liberalism dominated economic policy virtually unchallenged. Since the late 1970s and early 1980s, however, laissez-faire ideology has once more become a powerful force in American politics. While the American welfare state expanded more than threefold after WW II, it has been at 20% of the GDP since the late 1970s. Today, modern American liberalism and modern American conservatism are engaged in a continuous political battle, characterized by what the economist describes as "greater divisiveness [and] close, but bitterly fought elections".

Prior to World War II the US pursued a policy of noninterventionism in foreign affairs by not taking sides in conflicts between foreign powers. The country abandoned this policy when it became a superpower, and the country mostly supports internationalism.

4.2 The 1787 Constitution

The Constitution of the US is the supreme law of the US. It is the foundation and source of the legal authority underlying the existence of the US of America and the federal government of the US. It provides the framework for the organization of the US government and for the relationship of the federal government to the states, to citizens, and to all people within the US.

The Constitution defines the three main branches of government: a legislature, the bicameral Congress; an executive branch led by the president; and a judicial branch headed by the Supreme Court. The Constitution specifies the powers and duties of each branch. The Constitution reserves all unenumerated powers for the respective states and the people, thereby establishing the federal system of government.

The US Constitution was adopted on September 17, 1787, by the Constitutional Convention in Philadelphia, Pennsylvania, and ratified by conventions in each US state in the name of "The People". The Constitution has been amended twenty-seven times; the first ten amendments are known as the Bill of Rights.

The US Constitution is the shortest and oldest written constitution still in use by any nation in the world today.

The Constitution has a central place in US law and political culture. The handwritten original document penned by Jacob Shallus is on display at the National Archives and Records Administration in Washington, D. C.

Articles of the Constitution

The Constitution consists of a preamble, seven original articles, twenty-seven amendments, and a paragraph certifying its enactment by the constitutional convention.

Preamble: Statement of Purpose

"*We the People of the US, in order to form a more perfect Union, establish Justice, insure domestic Tranquility, provide for the common defence, promote the general Welfare, and secure the Blessings of Liberty to ourselves and our Posterity, do ordain and establish this Constitution for the US of America.*"

—United States Constitution, Preamble

The preamble does not grant any particular authority to the federal government and it does not prohibit any particular authority. It establishes the fact that the federal government has no authority outside of what follows the preamble, as amended. "We the People", is one of the most-quoted sections of the Constitution. It was thought by the federalists during this time that there was no need for a bill of rights as they thought that the preamble explained the people's rights.

Article One: Legislative Power

Article I describes the Congress, the legislative branch of the federal government. The US Congress is a bicameral body consisting of two co-equal houses: the House of Representatives to represent the people, and the Senate to represent the States.

The article establishes the manner of election and the qualifications of members of each body. Representatives must be at least 25 years old, be a citizen of the US for seven years, and live in the state they represent. Senators must be at least 30 years old, be a citizen for nine years, and live in the state they represent.

Article Section I, reads, "All legislative powers herein granted shall be vested in a Congress of the United States, which shall consist of a Senate and House of Representatives." This provision gives Congress more than simply the responsibility to establish the rules governing its proceedings and for the punishment of its members; it places the power of the government primarily in Congress.

Article I Section VIII enumerates the legislative powers. The powers listed and all other powers are made the exclusive responsibility of the legislative branch:

The Congress shall have power ... To make all laws which shall be necessary and proper for carrying into execution the foregoing powers, and all other powers vested by this Constitution in the government of the United States, or in any department or officer thereof.

Article I Section IX provides a list of eight specific limits on congressional power and Article I Section X limits the rights of the states.

The United States Supreme Court has interpreted the Commerce Clause and the Necessary and Proper Clause in Article I to allow Congress to enact legislation that is neither expressly listed in the enumerated power nor expressly denied in the limitations on Congress. In *McCulloch v. Maryland* (1819), the United States Supreme Court fell back on the strict construction of the necessary and proper clause to read that Congress had "[t]he foregoing powers and all other powers ..."

Article Two: Executive Power

Section I creates the presidency. The section states that the executive power is vested in a president. The presidential term is four years and the vice president serves the identical term. This section originally set the method of electing the president and vice president, but this method has been superseded by the Twelfth Amendment.

· Qualifications. The president must be a natural born citizen of the United States, at least 35 years old and a resident of the United States for at least 14 years. An obsolete part of this clause provides that instead of being a natural born citizen, a person may be a citizen at the time of the adoption of the Constitution. The reason for this clause was to extend eligibility to citizens of the United States at the time of the adoption of the Constitution, regardless of their place of birth, who were born under the allegiance of a foreign sovereign before the founding of the United States. Without this clause, no one would have been eligible to be president until thirty-five years after the founding of the United States.

· Succession. Section Ⅰ specifies that the vice president succeeds to the presidency if the president is removed, unable to discharge the powers and duties of office, dies while in office, or resigns. The original text ("the same shall devolve") left it unclear whether this succession was intended to be on an acting basis (merely taking on the powers of the office) or permanent (assuming the Presidency itself). After the death of William Henry Harrison, John Tyler set the precedent that the succession was permanent; this practice was followed when later presidents died in office. Today the 25th Amendment states that the vice president becomes president upon the death or disability of the president.

· Pay. The president receives "compensation" for being the president, and this compensation may not be increased or decreased during the president's term in office. The president may not receive other compensation from either the United States or any of the individual states.

· Oath of office. The final clause creates the presidential oath to preserve, protect, and defend the Constitution.

Section Ⅱ grants substantive powers to the president:

· The president is the Commander in Chief of the armed forces, and of the state militias when these are called into federal service.

· The president may require opinions of the principal officers of the federal government.

· The president may grant reprieves and pardons, except in cases of impeachment (i. e., the president cannot pardon himself or herself to escape impeachment by Congress).

Section Ⅱ grants and limits the president's appointment powers:

· The president may make treaties, with the advice and consent of the Senate, provided two-thirds of the Senators who present agree.

· With the advice and consent of the Senate, the president may appoint ambassadors, other public ministers and consuls, judges of the Supreme Court, and all other officers of the United States whose appointments are not otherwise described in the Constitution.

- Congress may give the power to appoint lower officers to the president alone, to the courts, or to the heads of departments.
- The president may make any of these appointments during a congressional recess. Such a "recess appointment" expires at the end of the next session of Congress.

Section Ⅲ opens by describing the president's relations with Congress:

- The president reports on the state of the union.
- The president may convene either house, or both houses, of Congress.
- When the two houses of Congress cannot agree on the time of adjournment, the president may adjourn them to some future date.

Section Ⅲ adds:

- The president receives ambassadors.
- The president sees that the laws are faithfully executed.
- The president commissions all the offices of the federal government.

Section Ⅳ provides for removal of the president and other federal officers. The president is removed on impeachment for, and conviction of, treason, bribery, or other high crimes and misdemeanors.

Article Three: Judicial Power

Article Ⅲ describes the court system (the judicial branch), including the Supreme Court. The article requires that there be one court called the Supreme Court; Congress, at its discretion, can create lower courts, whose judgments and orders are reviewable by the Supreme Court. Article Ⅲ also creates the right to trial by jury in all criminal cases, defines the crime of treason, and charges Congress with providing for a punishment for it. This Article also sets the kinds of cases that may be heard by the federal judiciary, which cases the Supreme Court may hear first (called original jurisdiction), and that all other cases heard by the Supreme Court are by appeal under such regulations as the Congress shall make.

Article Four: States' Powers and limits

Article Ⅳ describes the relationship between the states and the federal government and amongst the states. For instance, it requires states to give "full faith and credit" to the public acts, records, and court proceedings of the other states. Congress is permitted to regulate the manner in which proof of such acts, records, or proceedings may be admitted. The "privileges and immunities" clause prohibits state governments from discriminating against citizens of other states in favor of resident citizens (e. g. having tougher penalties for residents of Ohio convicted of crimes within Michigan). It also establishes extradition between the states, as well as laying down a legal basis for freedom of movement and travel amongst the states. Today, this provision is sometimes taken for granted, especially by citizens who live near state borders; but in the days of the Articles of Confederation, crossing state lines was often a much more arduous and costly process. Article Ⅳ also provides for the creation and admission of new states. The Territorial Clause gives Congress the power to make rules for disposing of federal property and governing non-state territories of the United States. Finally, the fourth section of Article Ⅳ requires the United States to guarantee to each state a republican form of government, and to protect the states from invasion and violence.

4.3 The Federal System

The federal government of the US is the central government entity established by the US Constitution, which shares sovereignty over the United States of America with the governments of the individual US states. For official purposes in US courts, the government is sued as (and sues others as) the United States of America, and is referred to simply as "the Government".

The US federal regime dates from 1790 and is considered to be the first modern national federation in the world. Even so, the details of American federalism have been debated since the establishment and ordination of the Constitution, with some parties arguing for expansive national powers, while others have narrowly and strictly interpreted the Constitution's enumeration of the national government's powers.

Since the US Civil War, the powers of the federal government have generally expanded greatly, although there have been periods when states' rights proponents have succeeded in limiting federal power through legislative action, executive prerogative or by constitutional interpretation of the courts.

The seat of the federal government is in the District of Columbia.

4.3.1 The Executive Power

The executive power in the federal government is vested in the president of the United States, although power is often delegated to the Cabinet members and other officials. The president and vice president are elected as running mates for a maximum of two four-year terms by the Electoral College, for which each state, as well as the District of Columbia, is allocated a number of seats based on its representation (or ostensible representation, in the case of D. C.) in both houses of Congress.

President

The executive branch consists of the president and delegates. The president is both the head of state and government, as well as the military commander-in-chief and chief diplomat. The president, according to the Constitution, must "take care that the laws be faithfully executed", and "preserve, protect, and defend the Constitution". The president presides over the executive branch of the federal government, a vast organization numbering about 4 million people, including 1 million active-duty military personnel. The forty-fourth and current president is Barack Obama, the first African American president of the US.

The president may sign legislation passed by Congress into law or may veto it, preventing it from becoming law unless two-thirds of both houses of Congress vote to override the veto. The president may, with the consent of two-thirds of the Senate, make treaties with foreign nations. The president may be impeached by a majority in the House and removed from office by a two-thirds majority in the Senate for "treason, bribery, or other high crimes and misdemeanors". The president may not dissolve Congress or call special elections but does have the power to pardon, or release, criminals convicted of offenses against the federal government (except in cases of impeachment), enact executive orders, and (with the consent of the Senate) appoint Supreme Court justices and federal judges.

Vice President

The vice president is the second-highest executive official of the government. As first in the US presidential line of succession, the vice president becomes president upon the death, resignation, or removal of the president, which has happened nine times in the US history. Under the Constitution, the vice president is president of the Senate. By virtue of this role, he or she is the nominal head of the Senate. In that capacity, the vice president is allowed to vote in the Senate, but only when necessary to break a tied vote. Pursuant to the Twelfth Amendment, the vice president presides over the joint session of Congress when it convenes to count the vote of the Electoral College. While the vice president's only constitutionally prescribed functions, aside from presidential succession, relate to his role as president of the Senate, the office is now commonly viewed as a member of the executive branch of the federal government. The US Constitution does not expressly assign the office to any one branch, causing scholars to dispute whether it belongs to the executive branch, the legislative branch, or both. The current vice president of the US is Joseph Biden, of the Democratic Party.

Secretary of State

The Secretary of State is the Chief Executive Officer of the United States Department of State, the most senior of all federal executive departments. The Secretary of State is the third-highest official of the executive branch of the federal government of the US, after the president and vice president. The Secretary is a member of the president's Cabinet and the highest-ranking cabinet secretary both in the presidential line of succession and order of precedence. The Secretary has many duties and responsibilities. The Secretary serves as the president's chief adviser on US foreign policy and as such negotiates, interprets, and terminates treaties and agreements, personally participates in or directs US representatives to international conferences, organizations, and agencies, conducts negotiations relating to US foreign affairs, and is responsible for the administration and management of foreign embassies and consulate offices. Foreign trade missions and intelligence assets report directly to the Secretary of State. The Secretary is also responsible for overall direction, coordination, and supervision of interdepartmental activities of the US government overseas. The Secretary answers directly to the president of the US.

Cabinet, Executive Departments, and Agencies

The day-to-day enforcement and administration of federal laws is in the hands of the various federal executive departments, created by Congress to deal with specific areas of national and international affairs. The heads of the 15 departments, chosen by the president and approved with the "advice and consent" of the US Senate, form a council of advisers generally known as the president's "Cabinet". In addition to departments, there are a number of staff organizations grouped into the Executive Office of the president. These include the White House staff, the National Security Council, the Office of Management and Budget, the Council of Economic Advisers, the Office of the US Trade Representative, the Office of National Drug Control Policy and the Office of Science and Technology Policy. The employees in these US government agencies are called federal civil servants.

There are also independent agencies such as the United States Postal Service, the National Aeronautics and Space Administration (NASA), the Central Intelligence Agency (CIA), the Environmental Protection Agency, and the United States Agency for International Development. In addition, there are government-owned corporations such as the Federal Deposit Insurance Corporation and the National Railroad Passenger Corporation.

4.3.2 The Legislative Power

Congress is the legislative branch of the federal government. It is bicameral, comprising the House of Representatives and the Senate. The House of Representatives consists of 435 voting members, each of whom represents a congressional district and serves for a two-year term. In addition to the 435 voting members, there are five non-voting members, consisting of four delegates and one resident commissioner. There is one delegate each from the District of Columbia, Guam, Virgin Islands, and American Samoa, and the resident commissioner is from Puerto Rico. House seats are apportioned among the states by population; in contrast, each state has two senators, regardless of population. There are a total of 100 senators (as there are currently 50 states), who serve six-year terms (one third of the Senate stands for election every two years). Each congressional chamber (House or Senate) has particular exclusive powers—the Senate must give "advice and consent" to many important presidential appointments, and the House must introduce any bills for the purpose of raising revenue. The consent of both chambers is required to pass any legislation, which then may only become law by being signed by the president; if the president vetoes such legislation, however, both houses of Congress must then re-pass the legislation, but by a two-thirds majority of each chamber, in order to make such legislation law without the need for the president's signature. The powers of Congress are limited to those enumerated in the Constitution; all other powers are reserved to the states and the people. The Constitution also includes the "Necessary and Proper Clause", which grants Congress the power to "make all laws which shall be necessary and proper for carrying into execution the foregoing powers". Members of the House and Senate are elected by first-past-the-post voting in every state except Louisiana and Washington, which have runoffs.

The US Constitution gives each chamber the power to "determine the rules of its proceedings". From this provision were created congressional committees, which do the work of drafting legislation and conducting congressional investigations into national matters. The 108th Congress (2003 –2005) had 19 standing committees in the House and 17 in the Senate, plus 4 joint permanent committees with members from both houses overseeing the Library of Congress, printing, taxation, and the economy. In addition, each house may name special, or select, committees to study specific problems. Today, much of the congressional workload is borne by subcommittees, of which there are some 150.

Powers of Congress

The Constitution grants numerous powers to Congress. These include the powers to levy and collect taxes, coin money and regulate its value, provide for punishment for counterfeiting, establish post offices and roads, promote progress of science by issuing patents, create federal courts inferior to the Supreme Court, define and punish piracies and felonies, declare war, raise and support armies, provide and maintain a navy, make rules for the regulation of land and naval forces, provide for, arms, and discipline the militia, exercise exclusive legislation in the District of Columbia; and to make laws necessary to properly execute these powers.

Congressional Oversight

Congressional oversight is intended to prevent waste and fraud, protect civil liberties and individual rights, ensure executive compliance with the law, gather information for making laws and educating the public, and evaluate executive performance.

It applies to cabinet departments, executive agencies, regulatory commissions, and the presidency. Congress' oversight function takes many forms:

- Committee inquiries and hearings
- Formal consultations with and reports from the president
- Senate advice and consent for presidential nominations and for treaties
- House impeachment proceedings and subsequent Senate trials
- House and Senate proceedings under the 25th Amendment in the event that the president becomes disabled or the office of the vice president falls vacant
- Informal meetings between legislators and executive officials.

4.3.3 The Judiciary Power

The Supreme Court is the highest court in the federal court system. The court deals with matters pertaining to the federal government, disputes between states, and interpretation of the US Constitution, and can declare legislation or executive action made at any level of the government as unconstitutional, nullifying the law and creating a precedent for future law and decisions. Below the Supreme Court are the courts of appeals, and below them in turn are the district courts, which are the general trial courts for federal law.

Separate from, but not entirely independent of, this federal court system are the individual court systems of each state, each dealing with its own laws and having its own court rules and procedures.

The supreme court of each state is the final authority on the interpretation of that state's laws and constitution. A case may be appealed from a state court to the US Supreme Court only if there is a federal question (an issue arising under the US Constitution, or laws/treaties of the US). The relationship between federal and state laws is extremely complex and confusing as a result of the unique nature of American federalism. For example, a state supreme court is bound only by the US Supreme Court's interpretation of federal law, but is not bound by interpretation of federal law by the federal court of appeals for the circuit in which the state sits, or even the federal district courts located in the state. Conversely, a federal district court hearing a matter involving only a question of state law (usually through diversity jurisdiction) must apply the substantive law of the state in which the court sits, as if the federal court were a court of that state (but at the same time, the case is heard under the Federal Rules of Civil Procedure instead of local rules, which may be quite different).

The federal judiciary consists of the US Supreme Court, whose justices are appointed for life by the president and confirmed by the Senate, and various "lower" or "inferior courts", among which are the courts of appeals and district courts.

The first Congress divided the nation into judicial districts and created federal courts for each district. From that beginning has evolved the present structure: the Supreme Court, 13 courts of appeals, 94 district courts, and 2 courts of special jurisdiction. Congress retains the power to create and abolish federal courts, as well as determining the number of judges in the federal judiciary system. It cannot, however, abolish the Supreme Court.

There are three levels of federal courts with general jurisdiction, meaning that these courts handle criminal cases and civil law suits between individuals. The other courts, such as the bankruptcy courts and the tax court, are specialized courts handling only certain kinds of cases. The bankruptcy courts are branches of the district courts, but their judges do not have lifetime tenure.

The US district courts are the "trial courts" where cases are filed and decided. The US courts of appeals are "appellate courts" that hear appeals of cases decided by the district courts, and some direct appeals from administrative agencies. The Supreme Court hears appeals from the decisions of the courts of appeals or state supreme courts (on constitutional matters), as well as having original jurisdiction over a very small number of cases.

The judicial power extends to cases arising under the Constitution, an Act of Congress, or a US treaty; cases affecting ambassadors, ministers, and consuls of foreign countries in the US; controversies in which the US government is a party; controversies between states (or their citizens) and foreign nations (or their citizens or subjects); and bankruptcy cases. The Eleventh Amendment removed from federal jurisdiction cases in which citizens of one state were the plaintiffs and the government of another state was the defendant. It did not disturb federal jurisdiction in cases in which a state government is a plaintiff and a citizen of another state the defendant.

The power of the federal courts extends both to civil actions for damages and other redress, and to criminal cases arising under federal law. Federal courts can sometimes hear cases arising under state law pursuant to diversity jurisdiction, state courts can decide certain matters involving federal law, and a handful of federal claims are primarily reserved to the state courts (for example, those arising from the Telephone Consumer Protection Act of 1991). Both court systems thus have exclusive jurisdiction in some areas and concurrent jurisdiction in others.

The Constitution safeguards judicial independence by providing that federal judges shall hold office "during good behaviour"; in practice, this usually means they serve until they die, retire, or resign. A judge who commits an offence while in office may be impeached in the same way as the president or other officials of the federal government. US judges are appointed by the president, subject to confirmation by the Senate. Another constitutional provision prohibits Congress from reducing the pay of any judge. Congress is able to set a lower salary for all future judges that take office after the reduction, but may not decrease the rate of pay for judges already in office.

4.4 The Party System

This article presents the historical development and role of political parties in the US politics and outlines more extensively the significant modern political parties. The modern political party system in the US is a two-party system consisting of the Democratic Party and the Republican Party.

4.4.1 Modern US Political Party System

The modern political party system in the US is a two-party system dominated by the Democratic Party and the Republican Party. These two parties have won every US presidential election since 1852 and have controlled the US Congress since at least 1856. Several other third parties from time to time achieve relatively minor representation at the national and state levels.

4.4.2 Democratic Party

The Democratic Party is one of the two major political parties in the US. It is the oldest political party in the US and among the oldest in the world.

The Democratic Party, since the division of the Republican Party in the election of 1912, has consistently positioned itself to the left of the Republican Party in economic as well as social matters. The economically left-leaning philosophy of Franklin D. Roosevelt, which has strongly influenced American liberalism, has shaped much of the party's economic agenda since 1932. Roosevelt's New Deal coalition usually controlled the national government until the 1970s. The Civil Rights Movement of the 1960s has continued to inspire the party's liberal principles, despite having lost the more conservative South in the process.

In 2004, it was the largest political party, with 72 million voters (42.6% of 169 million registered) claiming affiliation. The president of the United States, Barack Obama, is a Democrat, and since the 2006 midterm elections, the Democratic Party is the majority party for the 110th Congress. The party holds an outright majority in the House of Representatives and the US Senate. Democrats also hold a majority of state governorships and control a plurality of state legislatures.

4.4.3 Republican Party

The Republican Party is one of the two major contemporary political parties in the US. It is often referred to as the Grand Old Party (GOP), and "Gallant Old Party".

Founded in 1854 by anti-slavery expansion activists and modernizers, the Republican Party rose to prominence with the election of Abraham Lincoln, the first Republican president. The party presided over the American Civil War and Reconstruction and was harried by internal factions and scandals toward the end of the 19th century. Today, the Republican Party supports a conservative platform (as far as American politics are concerned), with further foundations in economic liberalism, fiscal conservatism, and social conservatism.

Former president George W. Bush is the 19th Republican to hold that office. Republicans currently fill a minority of seats in both the US Senate and the House of Representatives, hold a minority of state governorships, and control a minority of state legislatures. The party's nominee for president of the US in the 2008 presidential election was Senator John McCain of Arizona. It is currently the second largest party with 55 million registered members, encompassing roughly one third of the electorate.

4.4.4 Major Third Parties

Constitution Party

The Constitution Party is a conservative US political party. It was founded as the US Taxpayers Party in 1992. The party's official name was changed to the Constitution Party in 1999; however, some state affiliate parties are known under different names.

According to ballot access expert Richard Winger, the editor of *Ballot Access News*, who periodically compiles and analyzes voter registration statistics as reported by state voter agencies, it ranks third nationally amongst all the US political parties in registered voters, with 366,937 registered members as of November, 2006. This makes it currently the largest third party in the US.

The Constitution Party advocates a platform that claims to reflect the Founding Fathers' original intent of the US Constitution, principles found in the US *Declaration of Independence*, and morals taken from the Bible.

In 2006, Rick Jore of Montana became the first Constitution Party candidate elected to a state-level office, though the Constitution Party of Montana had disaffiliated itself from the national party a short time before the election.

The Constitution Party's 2008 presidential nominee was Chuck Baldwin.

Green Party

In the US, the Green Party has been active as a third party since the 1980s. The party first gained widespread public attention during Ralph Nader's presidential runs in 1996 and 2000. Currently, the primary national Green Party organization in the US is the Green Party of the US, which has eclipsed the earlier Greens/Green Party USA. There are Green Parties in many nations. The Green Party in the US has won elected office mostly at the local level; most winners of public office in the US who are considered Greens have won nonpartisan-ballot elections (that is, the winning Greens won offices in elections in which candidates were not identified on the ballot as affiliated with any political party). In 2005, the Party had 305,000 registered members in states that allow party registration. During the 2006 elections the party had ballot access in 31 states.

Greens emphasize environmentalism, non-hierarchical participatory democracy, social justice, respect for diversity, peace and nonviolence.

The 2008 Green Party presidential nominee was Cynthia McKinney.

Libertarian Party

The Libertarian Party was founded on December 11, 1971. It is one of the largest continuing third parties in the US, claiming more than 200,000 registered voters and more than 600 people in public office, including mayors, county executives, county-council members, school-board members, and other local officials. It has more people in office than all other third parties combined.

The political platform of the Libertarian Party reflects that group's particular brand of libertarianism, favoring minimally regulated, laissez-faire markets, strong civil liberties, minimally regulated migration across borders, and non-interventionism in foreign policy that respects freedom of trade and travel to all foreign countries.

The most recent Libertarian Party nominee for the US president was Bob Barr.

Exercises

I. Fill in the following blanks with proper words or expressions.

1. The city where *the Declaration of Independence* was signed and where the US Constitution was made is ________.
2. The Constitutional Convention was held in the year of ________ and the president of the Convention was ________.
3. The Constitution set up a federal system with ________.
4. A federal system is one in which power is shared between ________ and ________ with some rights reserved to each.
5. The US federal government consists of the following three branches: the executive, ________ and ________.
6. The Congress is divided into ________ with 435 members who serve two-year terms, and ________ with 100 lawmakers who serve six-year terms.
7. Groups who try to persuade Congressmen to vote for or against a bill are known as ________.
8. The Supreme Court is composed of ________ chief justice and ________ associate justices.
9. The Supreme Court has the function of determining whether Congressional legislative or executive action violates the Constitution. This power is called ________.
10. The two major political parties are ________, which is thought to be more liberal, and ________, which is believed to be more conservative.

II. Explain the following terms.

1. a federal system
2. the making of the US Constitution

3. the executive
4. the Bill of Rights

Ⅲ. Discuss the following questions.

1. What is a federal system? What are some of the major differences between a federal system and a confederation?
2. What are some of the major powers of the three branches of the US government? How are the three branches supposed to check and balance each other?

Chapter Five

Economy

The US is the largest national economy in the world. It has been termed "the engine of world economy". The US nominal GDP was estimated as $14.4 trillion in 2008, which is about three times that of Japan, the world's second largest economy. The US economy maintains a very high level of output per capita. It has maintained a stable overall GDP growth rate, a low unemployment rate, and high levels of research and capital investment funded by both national and foreign investors. In 2008, consumer spending made 72% of the economic activity in the US.

The US economy is highly diversified, for it has many technologically advanced industries, such as petroleum, automobile, aerospace, telecommunications, chemicals, electronics, food processing, lumber and mining. The US is also the most important agricultural producer in the world, exporting to other countries a wide range of agricultural products. Moreover, the tertiary industry is no less developed than other countries. No doubt New York is the most important financial center in the world. Share indexes of the New York Stock Market have for a long time been the barometer of world economy. The recent occurrence of financial crisis in the US has encumbered the economy in other countries.

The US has benefited from the excellent composition of its labor force. Of its 139.4 million people, approximately 30.3 percent are managerial and professional; 29.2 percent technical, sales and administrative support; 13.4 percent services; 24.5 percent manufacturing, mining, transport, and crafts; and merely 2.6 percent farming, forestry and fishing. This is a highly productive labor force. However, due to the gradual development of a "two-tier labor market" those at the bottom who lack the education and the professional skills of those at the top, more and more, fail to get comparable pay raises, health insurance coverage, and other benefits. Since

1975, practically all the gains in household income have gone to the top 20% of households.

The US economy maintains a relatively high GDP per capita (estimated at $46,900 in 2009), a low to moderate GDP growth rate, and a low unemployment rate, making it attractive to immigrants worldwide. Since the 1970s, the US economy has absorbed savings from the rest of the world. As one of the best-performing developed countries, the American labor market has attracted immigrants from all over the world and has one of the world's highest migration rates. Americans have the second highest income per hour worked. Despite the financial crisis that started in the middle of 2007, the US is still the biggest industrial country in the world.

However, the American economy is facing stiff competition from the new economic wonders like China and India. These countries are coming together along with Brazil and Russia, in business terms, to form BRIC[1]. The US economy is constantly observing an increasing trend in international deficit in goods and services. This deficit was above 57 billion dollars in February, 2007. Long-term problems include inadequate investment in economic infrastructure, rapidly rising medical and pension costs of an aging population, sizable trade and budget deficits, and stagnation of family income in the lower economic groups. The global economic downturn, the subprime mortgage crisis[2], investment bank failures, falling home prices, and tight credit pushed the US into a recession by mid-2008.

5.1 The Economic System

The economy of the US is characterized by private sector and market factors. For the most part, it has a market economy in which the private sector is allowed to make the majority of economic decisions in determining the direction and scale of what the US economy produces. Most corporations in the US are privately owned and subject to the market force in their management. They buy all materials from the market and sell products on the same market that has now been globalized.

A guiding principle of the US economy, dating back to the colonial period, has been that individuals own the goods and services they make for themselves or purchase to consume. Individuals and private businesses also control the factors of production. They own buildings and equipment, and are free to hire workers, and acquire things that businesses use to produce goods and services. Individuals also own the businesses that are established in the US. The laissez-faire[3] is held as the golden rule by most entrepreneurs. Compared with other countries, the American economy features relatively low levels of regulation and government involvement, as well as a court system that generally protects property rights and enforces contracts.

The US business firms enjoy greater flexibility than their counterparts in Western Europe and Japan in decisions to expand capital investment, to lay off surplus workers, and to develop new products. Producers decide which goods and services to make and sell, and how much to ask for those products. At the same time, consumers decide what they will purchase and how much money they are willing to pay for different goods and services. The interaction between competing producers, who attempt to make the highest possible profit, and consumers, who try to pay as little as possible to acquire what they want, ultimately determines the price of goods and services.

The US does not have a pure market economy, and the government plays an important role in the national economy. It provides services and goods that the market cannot provide effectively, such as national defense, assistance programs for low-income families, and interstate highways and airports. The government also provides incentives to encourage the production and consumption of certain types of products, and discourage the production and consumption of others. It sets general guidelines for doing business and makes policy decisions that affect the economy as a whole. The government also establishes safety guidelines that regulate consumer products, working conditions, and environmental protection. The government control has become more and more conspicuous after Franklin D. Roosevelt implemented "the New Deal" during the Great Depression in the American history.

5.2 A Historical Overview

The economic history of the US has its roots in European settlements in the 16th, 17th, and 18th centuries. The American colonies went from marginally successful colonial economies to a small, independent farming economy, which in 1776 became the US. In 230 years the US grew to a huge, integrated, industrialized economy that makes up over a quarter of the world economy. The economy has maintained high wages, attracting immigrants by the millions from all over the world.

The US was principally an agricultural country when the American Revolution of 1776 took place. After the new nation was founded, a protective tariff was implemented on the imports to protect the domestic production. A century later, the Industrial Revolution came across the Atlantic Ocean to the US from Britain. In 1793 the first factory was built on this new continent. The US soon became a major cotton producer. Due to the innovative spirit of the immigrants, the "American system" of mass production was developed to produce interchangeable parts of machinery that would be assembled in stages by workers specializing in a specific operation. Moreover, with the application of new technologies to industrial task and the emergency of new forms of business, the American economy grew by leaps and bounds. By 1913, more than one third of the world's industrial production came from the US.

By the turn of the century, a middle class had developed that was distrustful of both the business elite and the somewhat radical political movements of farmers and laborers in the Midwest and West. Known as Progressives, these people favored government regulation of business practices to, in their minds, ensure competition and free enterprise. With the efforts of President Theodore Roosevelt and Woodrow Wilson, regulatory laws and agencies were created in favor of these Progressives. Then came the Muckrakers, journalists who encouraged readers to demand more regulation of business. The exposure of Chicago Slaughterhouse's filthy state by Upton Sinclair[4] prompted the federal government to establish the new regulatory Food and Drug Administration.

The economic development up until the Great Depression in 1929 was boosted mainly by the tax reforms and the adoption of assembly line. In 1913, the 16th Amendment to the Constitution made the income tax a permanent fixture in the US tax system. And in the same year, Henry Ford adopted the moving assembly line, with each worker doing one simple task in the production of automobiles. Taking his cue from developments during the progressive era, Ford offered a very generous wage—$5 a day—to his workers, arguing that a mass production enterprise could not survive if average workers could not buy the goods.

Then under Republican President Warren G. Harding, Secretary of the Treasury Andrew Mellon raised the tariff, cut other taxes, and used the large surplus to reduce the federal debt by about a third from 1920 to 1930. Secretary of Commerce Herbert Hoover worked to introduce efficiency, by regulating business practices. The rapid growth of the automobile industry stimulated industries such as oil, glass, and road-building. Tourism soared and consumers with cars had a much wider radius for their shopping. Small cities prospered, and large cities had their best decade ever, with a boom in construction of offices, factories and houses. The new electric power industry transformed both business and everyday life. Telephones and electricity spread to the countryside, but farmers never recovered from the wartime bubble in land prices. Millions migrated to nearby cities.

However, in October, 1929, the stock market crashed and banks began to fail in the Wall Street Crash of 1929. For many years following the Great Depression of the 1930s, when the danger of recession appeared most serious, government sought to strengthen the economy by spending heavily itself or cutting taxes so that consumers would spend more, and by fostering rapid growth in the money supply, which also encouraged more spending. In the 1970s, economic woes brought on by the costs of the Vietnam conflict[5], major price increases, particularly for energy, created a strong fear of inflation. As a result, government leaders came to concentrate more on controlling inflation than on combating recession by limiting spending.

Since the stagflation of the 1970s, the US economy has been characterized by somewhat slower growth. The worst recession in recent decades, in terms of lost output, occurred in the 1973–1975 period of oil shocks, when GDP fell by 3. 1 percent, followed by the 1981–1982 recession, when GDP dropped by 2. 9 percent. And since the 1970s the US has sustained trade deficits with other nations. Output fell by 1. 3 percent in the 1990–1991 downturn, and a tiny 0. 3 percent in the 2001 recession. The 2001 downturn lasted just eight months.

2007–2009 saw the global financial crisis called by the leading economists the worst one since the Great Depression. In 2008 a perfect storm of economic disasters hit the country. The most serious began with the collapse of housing bubbles in California and Florida, and the collapse of housing prices and the construction industries. A series of the largest banks in the US and Europe collapsed; some went bankrupt, such as Lehman Brothers with $690 billion in assets; others such as the leading insurance company AIG, the leading bank Citigroup, and the two largest mortgage companies were bailed out[6] by the government. By late 2008 distress was spreading beyond the financial and housing sectors, especially as the "Big Three" of the automobile industry (General Motors, Ford and Chrysler) were on the verge of bankruptcy, and the retail sector showed major weaknesses.

5.3 Natural Resources

5.3.1 Energy

The US is the largest energy consumer in terms of total use. The majority of this energy is derived from fossil fuels: in 2005, it was estimated that 40% of the nation's energy came from petroleum, 23% from coal, and 23% from natural gas. Nuclear power supplied 8.4% and renewable energy supplied 6.8%, which was mainly from hydroelectric dams although other renewables were included such as geothermal and solar energy.

Oil is the lifeblood of America's economy. Currently, it supplies more than 40% of its total energy demands and more than 99% of the fuel the Americans use in their cars and trucks. The US is much concerned about an immediate readiness to respond to oil supply disruptions and keeping America's oil fields producing in the future.

Coal is one of the true measures of the energy strength of the US. One quarter of the world's coal reserves are found within the US. Coal is also the workhorse of the nation's electric power industry, supplying more than half the electricity consumed by Americans. To tap the full potential of the nation's enormous coal supplies, the US Department of Energy's Office of Fossil Energy is working with the private sector to develop innovative technologies for an emission-free coal plant of the future.

Recently natural gas has also become increasingly popular as an alternative transportation fuel in the US. The Office of Fossil Energy invests in research and development of technologies in the areas of natural gas supply, delivery reliability, and utilization. Natural gas is clean burning and produces significantly fewer harmful emissions than reformulated gasoline.

In the aspect of electricity, more than half of the electricity generated in the US comes from coal today. For the foreseeable future, coal will continue to be the dominant fuel used for electric power production. The low cost and abundance of coal is one of the primary reasons why consumers in the US benefit from some of the lowest electricity rates of any free-market economy. The key challenge is to remove the environmental objections to the use of coal in tomorrow's power plants. New technologies being developed are expected to virtually eliminate the sulfur, nitrogen, and mercury pollutants released when coal is burned. It may also be possible to capture greenhouse gases[7] emitted from coal-fired power plants and prevent them from contributing to global warming concerns.

While coal is the nation's major fuel for electric power, natural gas is the fastest growing fuel. More than 90 percent of the power plants to be built in the next 20 years will likely be fueled by natural gas. Nuclear energy is America's largest source of emission-free electricity. The 103 nuclear units supply about 20 percent of the electricity produced in the US—second only to coal as a fuel source. Cost-efficient technologies are being developed to further enhance nuclear safety, minimize the generation of nuclear waste, and further reduce the risk of proliferation.

Finally, hydropower facilities in the US can generate enough power to supply 28 million households with electricity, the equivalent of nearly 500 million barrels of oil. The total US hydropower capacity is about 95,000 megawatts. Researchers are working on advanced turbine technologies that will not only help maximize the use of hydropower, but also minimize bad environmental effects.

5.3.2 Land and Minerals

The US is rich in mineral resources and fertile farm soil, and it is fortunate to have a moderate climate. It also has extensive coastlines on both the Atlantic and Pacific Oceans, as well as on the Gulf of Mexico. Rivers flow from far within the continent, and the Great Lakes provide additional shipping access. These extensive waterways have helped shape the country's economic growth over the years and helped bind America's 50 individual states together in a single economic unit.

Fertile soil is one of the most important natural resources in the US. The rich soils of the interior plains produce crops of wheat and corn. One fifth of the total area in the US is arable land, 13% of the world total and second only to Russia. For a time prairies covered 40% of the US. Now they are reduced to 26.5%, but still 7.9% of the world total.

America's forest resources are among the world's largest. Softwood forests including white pines are found in the east and redwood trees and Douglas firs are found throughout the coast ranges of the Pacific Ocean. Wood, resin and other forest products are the basic materials of several of the nation's largest industries.

The US is rich in most of the minerals to supply its basic industries. Mineral resources of the US are well developed. Coal, iron ore, copper, oil, sulfur, lead and zinc are found in large quantities. Other minerals, such as uranium, gold, silver, potash and building stone, are also found in large quantities in the US.

5.4 Different Sectors

Divided into three different sectors, the services sector now is the primary economic sector of the US. It contributes nearly 67.8% towards the GDP of the country. The industrial sector contributes 20.5% towards the US's GDP. The country generates a yearly industrial output of about $2,696,880 million (2006 data). Though agriculture is a major industry, yet its contribution is only 1% towards the GDP.

5.4.1 Agriculture

Agriculture is a major industry in the US and the country is a net exporter of food. As of the last census of agriculture in 2007, there were 2. 2 million farms, covering an area of 922 million acres (373 million hectares), an average of 418 acres (170 hectares) per farm. Fifty percent of the US is cropland, pastureland, and rangeland owned and managed by farmers and ranchers and their families. Income of the farm sector in America was 60 billion dollar in 2006.

Agricultural products include wheat, corn, other grains, fruits, vegetables, cotton; beef, pork, poultry, dairy products; forest products; fish. Of all the crops, corn is the most important. There is the Corn Belt in the midwestern US. In this country, two farmers out of every three, and one hectare out of every four grow corn. The annual crop is greater than the nation's yield of wheat, rice and other small grains combined.

Food prices are lower for Americans than they are for citizens of any other industrial country. And the US is the world's largest agricultural exporter. The exports now account for 20 percent to 30 percent of farmers' income.

In the US, each farm family usually lives separately on its own fields, often beyond the sight of its neighbors. The village or town is predominantly a place where the farm family travels to buy supplies, to attend church, and to go for entertainment or political, social or business meetings. In most such areas, special buses pick up children every day to take them to the schools which are usually in the town.

An American farm

5.4.2 Manufacturing

The US is the leading manufacturer in the world with an industrial output of US $2,696,880 millions in 2007. Standing alone, the US manufacturing sector would represent the fifth largest economy in the world—larger than China's economy as a whole. Investments in technology create new industries and careers in manufacturing as US firms introduce products and manufacturing techniques. Perhaps most importantly, productivity in manufacturing has continued to rise significantly.

The US manufacturing sector leads in innovation, accounting for more than 90 percent of all US patents registered annually. American firms are at or near the forefront in technological advances, especially in computers and in medical, aerospace, and military equipment. However, the US manufacturers now face unprecedented challenges in global competition.

Boeing's headquarters in Chicago

Main industries are petroleum, steel, motor vehicles, aerospace, telecommunications, chemicals, electronics, food processing, consumer goods, lumber, mining. Big businesses have arisen in these areas. For example, the Boeing Company, founded by William E. Boeing in Seattle, is a major aerospace and defense corporation. Boeing has later expanded and moved its international headquarters to Chicago, Illinois, in 2001. Boeing is the largest global aircraft manufacturer by revenue, orders and deliveries, and the second largest aerospace and defense contractor in the world.

5.4.3 Service Industries

The service industries have played and continue to play an important role in the US economy. From cutting the grass to providing health care to delivering packages, service industries deeply engage the daily activities of millions of people and businesses. Information, retail, scientific, technical and professional services form the major parts of this sector. Out of all the services, wholesale and retail trade comes up as the leading business areas. Considering the net income, finance and insurance services feature as the top business option.

Finance and Insurance

The financial services industry includes investment banks, security brokerages[8], insurance companies, and banking institutions. They provide a broad array of products such as investment counseling. During the 1990s in the US, the financial service industry experienced substantial consolidation as many banks merged with other traditional banks, investment banks, and insurance companies to form multi-function financial institutions.

The New York Stock Exchange (NYSE) is a stock exchange located at 11 Wall Street in lower Manhattan, New York City. It is the largest stock exchange in the world by US dollar value of its listed companies' securities. As of October, 2008, the combined capitalization of all domestic NYSE listed companies was US $10.1 trillion.

Automobile Service

The automobile service industry maintains and repairs automobiles. It has become increasingly important as the rising cost of new automobiles necessitates maintaining presently owned vehicles for longer periods of time. Furthermore, given the increasing level of technology built into automobiles, even the most basic vehicle maintenance requires work by skilled automotive service technicians.

In addition, about 250 million vehicles are in use in the US. And the US produces such famous brands of cars as the General Motors, Chrysler and Ford. However, they all face hardships during the Financial Crisis of 2007 – 2009. By filing for bankruptcy, the General Motors has had a new start.

Amusement and Recreation

Amusement and recreation is another service industry that continues to grow at a rapid pace. With disposable income on the rise, Americans are increasing their spending on various forms of amusement such as movies, live theatres, and theme parks. Furthermore, recreational services are expanding as Americans enjoy more active lifestyles, joining health clubs and other sports-related clubs.

Since the 1920s, the American film industry has grossed more money every year than that of any other country. And the US film industry has largely been based in and around Hollywood, Los Angeles, California. The major film studios of Hollywood are the primary source of the most commercially successful movies in the world, such as *Star Wars* (1977) and *Titanic* (1997), and the products of Hollywood today dominate the global film industry.

International Trade

The US is the most significant nation in the world when it comes to international trade. For decades, it has led the world in imports while simultaneously remaining one of the top three exporters of the world.

As the major epicenter of world trade, the US enjoys leverage that many other nations do not. For one, since it is the world's leading consumer, it is the number one customer of companies all around the world. Many businesses compete for a share of the US market. In addition, the US occasionally uses its economic influence to impose economic sanctions on different regions of the world.

Since it is the world's leading importer, there are many US dollars in circulation all around the planet. The stable US economy and fairly sound monetary policy has led to faith in the US dollar as the world's most stable currency.

In order to fund the national debt (also known as public debt), the US relies on selling US treasury bonds to people both inside and outside the country, and in recent times the latter have become increasingly important. Much of the money generated for the treasury bonds came from US dollars which are used to purchase imports in the US.

Notes

[1] The initialism of Brazil, Russia, India and China.

[2] An ongoing real estate crisis and financial crisis triggered by a dramatic rise in mortgage delinquencies and foreclosures in the US. After US house prices peaked in mid-2006 and began their steep decline thereafter, refinancing became more difficult for the subprime borrowers. With mortgage delinquencies soaring, securities backed with subprime mortgages, widely held by financial firms, lost most of their value. The result has been a large decline in the capital of many banks and the US government tightened credit around the world.

[3] Laissez-faire means allowing industry to be free of government restriction, especially restrictions in the form of tariffs and government monopolies. The phrase is French and literally means "let do".

[4] Upton Sinclair (1878–1968) is a Pulitzer Prize-winning prolific American author who wrote over 90 books in many genres. He gained particular fame for his 1906 muckraking novel *The Jungle*. The book dealt with conditions in the US meat packing industry, causing a public uproar that partly contributed to the passage of the Pure Food and Drug Act and the Meat Inspection Act in 1906.

[5] Vietnam conflict also known as the Vietnam War, the Second Indochina War, is a Cold War military conflict that may be said to have occurred in Vietnam, Laos, and Cambodia from September 26, 1959 to April 30, 1975. The war was fought between the communist North Vietnam, supported by its communist allies, and the government of South Vietnam, supported by the US and other anti-communist nations.

[6] To give capital to a company in danger of failing in an attempt to save it from bankruptcy and ruin.

[7] It is gases in the atmosphere that absorb and emit radiation within the thermal infrared range.

[8] The business of buying and selling stocks, securities and bonds for clients.

Exercises

I. Fill in the following blanks with proper words or expressions.

1. As the largest national economy in the world, the US has been termed "________".
2. The new economic wonders like China and India from which the American economy is facing stiff competition are, together along with Brazil and Russia, in business terms, to form ________.
3. The economy of the US is characterized by ________ and ________.
4. The government control of economy has become more and more conspicuous after ________ implemented "the New Deal" during the Great Depression in the American history.
5. Since the ________ of the 1970s, the US economy has been characterized by somewhat slower growth.
6. In 2005, it was estimated that ________ of the American energy came from petroleum, 23% from coal, and 23% from natural gas.
7. America's forest resources are among the world's largest. ________ including white pines are found in the east and redwood trees and Douglas firs are found throughout the coast ranges of the Pacific Ocean.
8. Though agriculture is a major industry in the US, yet its contribution is only ________ towards the GDP.
9. Considering the net income, ________ services feature as the top business option in America.
10. The US film industry has largely been based in and around ________, Los Angeles, California.

II. Explain the following terms.

1. mass production
2. characteristics of the American economy
3. global financial crisis
4. Boeing Company
5. NYSE

III. Discuss the following questions.

1. What characterizes the American energy consumption?
2. Suggest measures to help the US out of the financial crisis.

Chapter Six

Literature

Comparatively speaking, the US is a young country. But when it comes to its literature, people are awed by its exuberance in production and uniqueness in theme.

American literature may be the youngest national literature in the world. Its real history, if calculated from the end of the American Revolution[1], is only over 200 years. Yet within a short period, American literature grew rapidly, began to receive international recognition, and has exerted great influence upon the world literature. Literary masters such as Walt Whitman, Emily Dickenson, Mark Twain, William Faulkner, and Earnest Hemingway together with their masterpieces have helped American literature gain world attention and achieve worldwide fame.

American literature is well-known for its uniqueness in theme, though before the American Revolution, American literature could hardly be called American or literature due to the fact that writings of that period were either travel accounts or records of rough life experience in the new land, and European literary styles were commonly adopted. With individualism as the thread throughout American literature, personal ability and hard work, which are treated as the key factors to success, are emphasized, and American Dream has been the repeated focus of literary works.

American literature is an important part of English literature and world literature as well.

6.1 Literature and American Revolution(1746-1815)

6.1.1 Historical Background

American literature of this period covers a period of more than 60 years, during which the American nationhood transformed from its colonial status to that of independence and federation. Literature in the period of American Revolution (before, during and after) was predominantly public and utilitarian, and the characteristic forms of writing include essays, pamphlets, and political documents for purposes of social reform, revolutionary agitation and philosophical declaration. Benjamin Franklin, Thomas Jefferson and Philip Freneau were the outstanding literary figures of this period.

Many factors have contributed to the transition of the American nationhood to the status of independence and federation, and the shaping of American literature in its true sense.

Enlightenment. The 18th century in America is known as the Age of Reason and Enlightenment. The ideas of Enlightenment, whose focus is a form of rationalism, produced new types of men which included scientists, political philosophers, and religious rationalists. Under the influence of Enlightenment, Americans believed that more reasonable political and social orders should be established, and actions should be taken to resist oppressive power and to reform government.

The American Culture. Before the 1760s, American culture was a composite of Native American tribal cultures and European cultures brought to the New World by European traders and colonists. The 13 colonies which later became the first United States were primarily English which followed English traditions, but the English influence was not the only cultural influence. French settlers, Swedes, Dutch, Germans and Scotch-Irish and Africans all contributed to what is known as the American culture.

The American Revolution. By 1763 the colonies had attained a certain degree of maturity in political expression and economic development, and a discontentment against the colonial policy of the British government grew. American pamphleteers and newspaper writers focused on the British atrocities and the depravity of the English, which prepared the public opinion for *The Declaration of Independence* and sustained the will for revolution among Americans.

6.1.2 Voices of the Enlightenment and American Revolution

(1) Benjamin Franklin (1706–1790)

Benjamin Franklin

Benjamin Franklin was an author, inventor, scientist, printer, political statesman, diplomat, and a revolutionary hero. His achievements in all these roles were remarkable. As far as Franklin's literary achievements are concerned, *Poor Richard's Almanacs* (1735) and *The Autobiography* (1788–1789) are his representatives.

Poor Richard's Almanacs drew upon collections of proverbs, anthologies of poetry, and sayings, among which "Early to bed and early to rise, makes a man healthy, wealthy and wise" has become a most frequent quotation.

The Autobiography is considered the earliest American autobiography which remained unfinished at his death in 1790. It is a humorous and fascinating record of an old man's reflections on his rise from a poor boy to a rich and famous personage through self-examination, which has become the core of American Dream.

Benjamin Franklin was viewed as the spokesman of American Enlightenment.

(2) Thomas Jefferson (1743–1826)

Thomas Jefferson was an architect, a scholar and an educator who served the president of the US from 1801 to 1809. He drafted *The Declaration of Independence* (1776), which proved to be a monument to Jefferson as a statesman and author. The document expressed the conviction in the hearts and minds of the American people, and the most famous saying "all men are created equal" comes from the second part of *The Declaration*—the preamble:

"*We hold these truths to be self-evident, that all men are created equal, that they are endowed by their Creator with certain unalienable Rights, that among these are Life, Liberty and the pursuit of Happiness.*"

(3) Philip Freneau (1752–1832)

Philip Freneau was a poet and a transitional figure towards Romanticism. He was important in American literary history for two reasons. First, his enthusiastic celebration of all things American produced some exceptional poems, making him a forerunner of American Romanticism. Second, he used satire as a main poetic device and a political weapon against the British during the war. He was well-known for his patriotic poems and regarded as Father of American Poetry.

His poems included political poems and poems anticipating Romanticism. *To the*

Memory of the Brave Americans (1781) is a political poem and a solemn elegy to the revolution heroes. *The Beauties of Santa Cruz* (1776) is an excellent lyric poem with concrete nature image, which is proof that he was the forerunner of a new poetic style. *To a Wild Honeysuckle* (1786) is a lyrical lament for the mutability of nature and an expression of faith in man's ability to learn universal truths from nature.

6.2 American Romanticism (1815-1865)

6.2.1 Historical Background

Romanticism was a movement in literature, philosophy, music and art which developed in Europe in the late 18th and early 19th centuries, which laid great emphasis on man's emotional nature and his profound inner forces. But in exploring Romanticism, we need to remember that its manifestations varied as widely as the individualistic talents and perspectives of romantic writers. Generally speaking, Romanticism has features as follows:

First and foremost, Romanticism celebrates the triumph of feeling and intuition over reason. Next, Romanticism views the Middle Ages[2] as a source of fascination. Exalting the individual over society, Romanticism shows a strong disliking for the bondage of convention and customs. Nature is believed to be the source of goodness. Cultural nationalism, or the proud belief in one's own cultural genius and heritage, is also a striking attribute of Romanticism.

American Romanticism did not achieve its most powerful articulations until Edgar Ellen Poe, Ralph waldo Emerson, Henry David Thoreau, Nathaniel Hawthorne, Herman Melville, Walt Whitman, and Emily Dickinson. Slightly earlier there were Washington Irving, James Fenimore Cooper and William Bryant who are regarded as pioneers of American Romanticism. Thus, their works constituted what is called "Early Romanticism".

Transcendentalism is an intensified expression of Romanticism, hence sharing the romantic characteristics: the importance of intuition, the exaltation of the individual over society, the new and thrilling delight in nature, fascination with the Gothic and the "Oriental", and the desire to build a national literature and culture. Transcendentalism believes that individuals can intuitively receive higher truths otherwise unavailable through common methods of knowing, thus transcending the limits of rationalism. When it is translated into literature, this belief became an emphasis on symbolic representation.

Emerson, Thoreau, Hawthorne, Melville, Poe, Whitman, and Dickinson are outstanding writers of Transcendentalism and symbolic representation.

6.2.2 Early Romanticism Writers

(1) Washington Irving (1783–1859)

Washington Irving was the first American writer to achieve international recognition, who, accordingly, was known as Father of American Literature. Two of Irving's best known stories are *Rip Van Winkle* and *The legend of Sleepy Hollow*, which are taken from *The Sketch Book of Geoffrey Crayon*, *Gent* (1819–1820), a collection of sketches and stories.

Besides writing fiction, Irving also devoted to history and biography writing. *A History of New York* (1809) and *A History of the Life and Voyages of Christopher Columbus* (1829) are two of such masterpieces. In his imaginative and historical works, Irving has established a literary style known for his humor, his vivid characterization and his sense of irony.

(2) James Fenimore Cooper (1789–1851)

James Fenimore Cooper was best-known for his introduction of "west", "wildness" and "pioneering" into American literature in his Leather-stocking series.

Cooper was born in Burlington, New Jersey, in 1789. He went to Yale at thirteen where he studied with great interest Shakespeare and the major 18th century poets, but he was sent to sea two years later when he was dismissed from Yale because of his rowdy behaviors. In 1820, he published *Precaution*, and *The Spy*, with the Revolutionary War as the background, was published in the following year. This best-selling novel, with its unique American flavor, made Cooper the popular American writer in Europe. Cooper's third novel was *The Pioneers* (1823), which started the Leather-stocking series of five novels—*The Pioneers* (1823), *The Last of the Mohicans* (1826), *The Prairie* (1827), *The Pathfinder* (1840), and *The Deerslayer* (1841). "Leather-stocking" is the nickname for Natty Bumppo who is in the habit of wearing long deerskin leggings. A type of mythic hero, the character of Natty Bumppo is based on the legend of Daniel Boone (a folk hero), which is the idealized image of American manhood.

Cooper started a new kind of fiction which was different from the traditional moral and sentimental tales. He set out to write something that was purely American, and he took the daring frontiersmen and the Indians as the heroes in his books.

6.2.3 Writers of Transcendentalism and Symbolic Representation

(1) Ralph Waldo Emerson (1803–1882)

Ralph Waldo Emerson, the leading spokesman for Transcendentalism, was a philosopher, a poet and an essayist. He distinguished himself as a writer of Americanism because he creatively and unconventionally defined some basic parameters of the American individual, and because his social and literary liaisons helped decisively the formation of American culture and letters.

Emerson's major works can be categorized into 3 groups: his early essays and lectures including *Nature* (1836), *The American Scholar* (1837), and *Divinity School Address* (1838), his essay collections including *Essays*, *First Series* (1841) and *Essays*, *Second Series* (1844), and his later essays, lectures and his poems including *Woman* (1855) and *Thoreau* (1862).

(2) Henry David Thoreau (1817–1862)

Henry David Thoreau was born in Concord, Massachusetts. When Emerson moved to Concord, Thoreau was only seventeen. Their association led Thoreau to the Transcendental Club and to a lifelong friendship. Thoreau adopted a kind of nonparticipation attitude towards government. He insisted that the price paid for material progress is too high and therefore simplification is the remedy for the problems in modern civilization.

Today Thoreau is primarily remembered by two of his works: *Walden* (1854) and the essay *Civil Disobedience* (1849). They were written as a result of two of his most extreme acts: that he went to live in a hut in the woods by the Walden Pond, and that he once refused to pay tax to protest against the Mexican War and was imprisoned for it. Thoreau's writings can be easily recognized for their sense of wit, humor and irony. However, the most important part of Thoreau's style is the mark of Transcendentalism: the style as the thinking in imagery.

(3) Nathaniel Hawthorne (1804–1864)

Nathaniel Hawthorne was born in Salem, Massachusetts. Salem, with its Puritan heritage and its history of witchcraft, was the symbolic locale for Hawthorne's creative imagination. The guilty stains of human nature are a theme in Hawthorne's writings.

Hawthorne is the author of four remarkable novels: *The Scarlet Letter* (1850), *The House of the Seven Gables* (1851), *The Blithedale Romance* (1852), and *The Marble Faun* (1860). The other novels are *Twice Told Tales* (1837), *Moses from an Old Manse* (1843). His short stories like *Young Goodman Brown*, *The Minister's Black Veil*, and *Dr. Rappacini's Daughter* are also worth reading.

The Scarlet Letter was believed to be the first great American novel which is focused on the adulterous love between a Puritan minister and a married woman in his congregation. But adultery is not the main focus as the novel is not really a love story. The novel's focus is on the complex moral implications of the affair. Indeed, when the novel begins and unfolds, it is the consequence of the adultery and the respective struggles of the two lovers that get us involved.

Hawthorne's interest is mainly in the complexity of the human heart in contradiction. Therefore, there in his writing is a consistent concern with the psychological currents beneath the conscious. The internal conflict in Hawthorne's characters is often moral in nature and should be read in the Puritan context.

Hawthorne's style is elevated in diction and restrained in rhetoric, thus graceful and polished. His truth is conveyed mainly through allegory and symbol.

(4) Herman Melville (1819–1891)

Herman Melville is one of the greatest fiction writers in American literature. He was born in New York City and grew up a displaced person in a world of alienating and harsh reality. He took various occupations: a store clerk, a bank messenger, a country schoolteacher, a sailor on a merchant ship and a whaler ship. Such varied experiences are reflected in the different aspects of his writing. Melville's male central characters are the classic wanderers who struggle against odds and are initiated into some harsh rite of passage, and the world in Melville's fiction mirrors the world he saw—defined by the rough seas and the ubiquity of evil.

Melville is best known for his fiction *Moby Dick.* It tells the strange story of the possessed and implacable Captain, Ahab, risking his life, those of his crew and his ship on the rough seas in search of a monstrous white whale. The quest ended in catastrophe. Everybody died except Ishmael who survived to tell the story. The fiction is full of symbols. The ship is the microcosmic representation of the multicultural, cosmopolitan society of the US. The goal of this ship is to discover in Moby Dick, the white whale, the ultimate force governing the cosmos. Moby Dick, the symbol of nature, is ubiquitous, creative and destructive, all too powerful and inextinguishable. The human society as symbolized by the whaler cannot be compared to the vastness of the whole ocean which is his realm, his kingdom.

Melville also wrote a number of short stories, among which the novella *Billy Budd* (1924), and the short stories *Bartleby the Scrivener* (1853) and *Benito Cereno* (1855) rank the best.

(5) Edgar Ellen Poe (1809–1849)

Edgar Ellen Poe is a critic, poet and short story writer, and is important in all three aspects. Born the son of an American actor and English actress, he was orphaned at the age of two and adopted to a tobacco merchant. At the age of 27 he married his cousin whom he loved dearly but lost to tuberculosis, and he died at the age of 40. Though he lived a short life, he is remembered for his literary imagination in his poems and fictions.

Edgar Ellen Poe

In poetry, Poe is a master of moods. He conveys a mood through rhymes, rhythms, onomatopoeia, and subtle suggestiveness. The death of a beautiful woman seems to be a repeated theme of his poems. *The Raven* (1845) captures the mourning of the narrator for the loss of his beloved; *Annabel Lee* (1849) is another poem about the loss of a beautiful woman; *Ulalume* (1847) serves as another example, written as Poe's mourning for the death of his wife, and *To Helen* (1831) expresses Poe's grief at the death of Mrs Jane Standard.

Poe, together with Hawthorne, modernized American short stories. Poe's stories are not just Gothic tales but they show, through carefully crafted symbols, complex characters in deep psychological states. *The Fall of the House of Usher* is narrated by someone who is likely to be dreaming since he tries to shake off what must have been a dream. The narrator in *The Cask of Amontillado* has committed a murder and is confessing the crime to someone he trusts, after 50 years. A narrator who is a dreamer or criminal immediately complicates the truth being told. This ability to manipulate narrative point of view was quite new in Poe's time.

Poe is also recognized as father of detective stories whose short story *A Purloined Letter* is as gripping as any mystery.

(6) Walt Whitman (1819–1892)

Walt Whitman

Walt Whitman is claimed as one of the few truly great American men of letters and the greatest democratic poet. He devised the poetic style of free verse[3] in his *Leaves of Grass* (1855), a masterpiece to whose influence contemporay American poetry, whatever school or form, bears witness.

Born in 1819 into a humble Quaker family, Whitman did not have too much of a formal education but primarily taught himself by reading and writing and by learning from life. All of Whitman's poems are in *Leaves of Grass*, which consists of various themes. There we can find a poet who is a fervent advocate for equality and democracy, a poet celebrating the people in villages and cities of America, a poet in love with a nature embodying the over-soul, and a poet who expressed the pleasures of sex and the sensuality of the body. *Song of Myself* (1855) is the longest and one of the best of Whitman's poems. *When Lilac*

Last in the Dooryard Bloom'd (1865) and *O Captain! My Captain* (1865) are concerned with President Abraham Lincoln's tragic death and the subsequent nation-wide mourning.

Whitman is also known for his prose works *Democratic Vistas* (1871), in which he examines the urgent problems confronting democracy and suggests that a great national literature should be the educative agency for democracy.

(7) Emily Dickinson (1830–1886)

Emily Dickinson is one of the most innovative poets of the 19th-century American literature. Actually, she is such a unique poet that it is difficult to put her in any single tradition. She wrote nearly two thousand poems, but fewer than 20 got published in her time. Her greatest achievement in poetry is her diamond-hard language—she often writes in aphoristically, compressing a great deal of meaning into a very small number of words.

Born in Amherst, Massachusetts, Dickinson lived the life of a recluse there all her life. She was in frail health most of her life and died in 1886. Her poems are mostly based on her life experience, exploring themes of joys and sorrows. To be more specific, nature (kind and cruel), love (suffering and frustration), and death (desire for death, moment of death, and death and immortality) are the most frequently portrayed topics in her poems.

The style of Dickinson's poems is unique in that her poems are short, often with two stanzas, that her poems are always without a title, that the poems are written in a way of severe economy of expressions, and that capital letters and dashes are employed to show emphasis.

Most readers are familiar with Dickinson's poems such as *I'm Nobody! Who Are You?*, *Because I Could not Stop for Death*, and *I Heard a Fly Buzz—When I Died.*

6.3 American Realism (1865–1914)

6.3.1 The Rise of Realism

The Civil War (1861–1865) and the financial crisis after 1800 made the US lose its innocence and enter into its adolescence. And like an adolescent, the country experienced restlessness and moments of violence. A new literature, that of realism, emerged for this age.

Realism is a mode of writing that gives the impression of recording or reflecting faithfully an actual way of life. It reacts against Romanticism's emphasis on intuition, imagination, an innocent sense of wonder, idealism, faith in nature, and general optimistic belief in the goodness of things, but advocates a truthful description of life in an objective way. Realists claim that they seek truth that is verifiable by experience and has practical consequences. Local color and regional writings constituted the early phase of realism. Naturalism is another variation of realism in that it emphasizes a biological or socioeconomic determinism.

6.3.2 Representative Writers of Realism

(1) Mark Twain (1835–1910)

Mark Twain (pen name of Samuel Langhorne Clemens) is a writer of great importance in American literature, and he was one of the pioneers in stories that captured the "local color" of the West.

Mark Twain

Twain was born in Florida, but the family soon moved to the very small town of Hannibal, Missouri, which was to become the setting for many of his novels. At the age of 12 his father died and he started working as an apprentice. That his boyhood was so short was perhaps why he valued it so much in his novels like *The Adventures of Tom Sawyer* (1875) and *The Adventures of Huckleberry Finn* (1876).

The Adventures of Huckleberry Finn is believed to be Twain's masterpiece. The plotline of the novel follows a run-away motif. Huck runs from his depraved father while at the same time Jim, a slave, escapes from being sold down the river. The two meet and raft south on the Mississippi River. They get involved with thieves on a wrecked riverboat, witness the murder of a harmless drunkard, encounter feuding planet families, and are dragged into the schemes of two fugitive con-men. Besides portraying a vivid picture of life along the Mississippi and revealing the symbolic theme of a united race in search of freedom and identity, *The Adventures of Huckleberry Finn* has become a milestone in the history of American literature. Ernest Hemingway once remarked: "All modern literature comes from one book by Mark Twain called *Huckleberry Finn*."

Generally speaking, Twain's writings can be categorized into three groups. The first type may be termed the "personalized fiction" which refers to works that fictionalize people and events that Mark Twain were familiar with, including *The Adventures of Tom Sawyer*, *The Adventures of Huckleberry Finn*, *The Gilded Age: A Tale of Today* (1873), etc. The second type may be called "travel fiction" and these include *The Innocents Abroad* (1869), *Roughing It* (1873), and *Life on the Mississippi* (1883). The third type may be named "historical romances" which show Mark Twain's familiarity with the romance tradition and his ability to subvert its conventionalized implications. These include *The Prince and Pauper* (1882), *A Connecticut Yankee in King Arthur's Court* (1889), and *Personal Recollections of Joan of Arc by the Sieur Louis Conte* (1896). Then fourthly, there are the short stories and those "tall tales" suggesting Mark Twain's connection with the frontier spirit and his fondness of local color. Two of the best known ones are *The Celebrated Jumping Frog of Calaveras County* (1865) and *The Man That Corrupted Hadleyburg* (1900).

Mark Twain is also well-known for his sense of humor and his employment of dialect as a means to achieve the local color in his writing.

(2) Theodore Dreiser (1871–1945)

Dreiser, a poet, playwright, philosopher and fiction writer, is always recognized as a naturalist. His novels, *Sister Carrie* (1900) and *An American Tragedy* (1925) are well known to readers in China.

Dreiser's fiction is built with realistic observations in chronological sequences, with details selected and arranged to suggest causation and motivation. A major theme of his is that men and women will, according to their place in society, talent and temperament, seek to achieve the fulfillment of such desires as sexual gratification, power and materialism. That is, the forces arranged against an individual are so strong that he or she can either yield to them or be destroyed by them. A case in point is *Sister Carrie* which tells how Carrie, a beautiful girl from the Middle West achieved what she had desired in Chicago by all means.

(3) Jack London (1876–1916)

Jack London, a popular writer among Chinese readers, was one of America's most talented and most prolific writers: He is the author of 49 volumes of fiction, plays and essays. His major works are *Martin Eden*, *The Call of the Wild*, and *White Fang*.

London's narratives are mostly based on his personal experience, and his writing is chronological and simple, using the common speech. He used the romantic fiction to preach the radicalism of his day—a combination of evolutionist theory and the vision of a classless society.

There is a general determinist overtone in his themes: Men and women are more evolved animals whose behavior is determined by laws of nature. For the purpose of survival, humans can act like beasts. These naturalist themes came from Jack London's reading of Darwin, Marx, Herbert Spencer[4] and Friedrich Nietzsche[5].

Such is the spirit of dog Buck in London's masterpiece *The Call of the*

Wild (1903). Buck is taken to the Alaskan Klondike where, in the wilderness, he must retrieve ancient instincts in order to survive. Buck answers and becomes the call of the wild. Through his fights he comes to be the head of a pack of wolves, howling with his head up at the arctic moon.

6.4 Modern Period (1914–1945)

6.4.1 General Introduction

During the period between 1914 and 1945, there occurred two world wars. The US experienced the economic boom in the 1920s and the Great Depression in the 1930s, and Sigmund Freud's psychological theory became popular. All these factors produced great influences upon American literature.

Literature in this period is characterized by stylistic innovations and literary experimentation, which are the features of Modernism. Modernism is a complex and diverse international movement in all the creative arts, which emerged at the end of the 19th century and provided the greatest creative renaissance of the 20th century. As the tradition of the new, Modernism is well-known for its conscious rejection of established rules, traditions and conventions. It strives to reflect the social and political changes, the dangers and anxieties, and the rapid economic growth in technological and psychological knowledge in the 20th century, and it provides new ways of looking at man's position in the universe.

The most discussed stylistic features of modern literature are as follows:

The uses of narrative points of view become a very sophisticated art form, and the first person point of view is used more often. Multi-perspectives are adopted to interpret reality. Gender, race, class begin to be accepted as registers allowing the expression of marginalized perspectives. Fragmentation and open-endedness become new structuring principles as a resistance to totalized views of reality. Interests in the psychological depths of characters are inspired by Freudian psychoanalysis. Irony and ambiguity are favored rhetorical modes, which reflect a general disillusionment in the social, economic and spiritual values of the Western world. And there is a broad dependence on the image in modern poetry.

Imagism poets with Ezra Pound as the representative, the Lost Generation novelists F. Scott Fitzgerald and Earnest Hemingway, and Southern literature representative William Falkner are remarkable literary figures in this period.

6.4.2 Imagism Poet—Ezra Pound (1885–1972)

As American poet, Ezra Pound did not spend much of his life in the States. He settled in London where he became a leading figure of the Imagist Movement.

Imagist Movement was a literary movement popular in the first decade of the 20th century. Led by Ezra Pound first and then by Amy Lowell, a small but influential group of American and British poets rejected most 19th-century poetry as cloudy verbiage, and aimed in stead at a new clarity and exactness in the short lyric poem. Influenced by the Japanese haiku and partly by ancient Greek lyrics, the imagists cultivated concision and directness, building their short poems around single images.

Ezra Pound was well-known for his anthology of poetry under the title *Des Imagists* (1914) which launched the Imagist Movement in England and in America, *Hugh Selwyn Mauberley* (1920) which later influenced T. S. Eilot's *The Waste Land*, and *In a Station of the Metro* (1913) which has become a classic poem of Imagism.

Pound exerted tremendous influence on Modernism, particularly on modern verse, but his pro-Nazi attitude during World War Ⅱ made him a controversial figure.

6.4.3 The Lost Generation Novelists

The Lost Generation is a term used to describe a group of American intellectuals, poets, artists and novelists who fled to France in the post World War Ⅱ years to reject the values of American materialism and to seek the Bohemian lifestyle in Paris. These young survived the war physically but were afterwards spiritually and morally adrift. F. Scott Fitzgerald and Earnest Hemingway are recognized as the spokesmen of the Lost Generation.

(1) F. Scott Fitzgerald (1896–1940)

To literary historians, Fitzgerald is the novelist who best captured the fashion, the wealth, the changing sexual habits, the charm, the deceit, and confusion in the social life of the 1920s. What his works revealed is the deeply invested dreams, the illusions and the social vulgarities of his generation, which is still pertinent to American culture today.

F. Scott Fitzgerald was born in a middle class neighborhood in St. Paul, Minnesota in 1896. In his early twenties he met Zelda, and fell in love with her. Fitzgerald's courtship of Zelda left a noticeable mark not only on his life but also on his writing. In 1919 he went to New York City, determined to make a fortune and win

Zelda. Amazingly, he succeeded, and published his first novel *This Side of Paradise* (1920) which became an immediate best-seller. After Scott and Zelda married, they lived an extravagant life, spending a lot more than the money Fitzgerald made. In 1924, the Fitzgeralds moved to Europe to live more cheaply. During this time Fitzgerald published his best-known and most successful novel, *The Great Gatsby* (1925), and another book of short stories, *All the Sad Young Men* (1926).

The Great Gatsby tells the story of a self-made young man whose dream of success, personified in a rich and beautiful young woman named Daisy, turns out to be a fantasy in every sense: Daisy belongs to a corrupt society, Gatsby corrupts himself in the quest for her, and above all, the rich have no intention of sharing their privileges. The novel is narrated from the point of view of an onlooker who is both moved and repelled by the tale he tells. The structure of *The Great Gatsby* is compact, the style dazzling; and its images of automobiles, parties, and garbage heaps seem to capture the contradictions of a consumer society. The novel became an instant classic and remains so to this day.

(2) Earnest Hemingway (1899–1961)

Earnest Hemingway, novelist and short story writer, was one of the most celebrated and influential writers of the 20th century. At the time of his death, he was probably the famous writer in the world. In 1954 he was awarded the Nobel Prize for his mastery of art of narration.

Earnest Hemingway

Earnest Hemingway was born and raised in Oak Park, Illinois, and his family often spent summers at their cottage in northern Michigan, where many of Hemingway's stories are set. After high school, Hemingway worked as a journalist for the *Kansas City Star*. The experience taught him the basic of a clear and plain style, for which his writing are well-known.

Hemingway became an international celebrity after the publication of his first important novel, *The Sun Also Rises* in 1926. *The Sun Also Rises* depicts Jake's efforts to live according to a self-conscious code dignity, of "grace under pressure", in the midst of a circle of self-seeking American and English expatriates in Paris. In 1927 Hemingway brought out his second collection of stories, *Men Without Women*. Adapting journalistic techniques in telegraphic prose that minimized narrator commentary and depended heavily on uncontextualized dialogue, these stories developed a modern, speeded-up, streamlined style that has been endlessly imitated. His next famous novel, *A Farewell to Arms*, appeared in 1929, which described a romance between an American army officer and a British nurse. In 1940 his novel about Spanish Civil War *For Whom the Bell Tolls* came out, and 1952 witnessed the publication of his masterpiece *The Old Man and the Sea*, which won him the Pulitzer Prize in 1953 and the Nobel Prize in 1954. Subject increasingly to depression and an incapacitating paranoia, he was hospitalized several times before killing himself in 1961.

The Old Man and the Sea narrates a story about an old Cuban fisherman, Santiago, who was determined to catch one big fish, only to find that the big fish was eaten and became a skeleton when he was ashore. The message of the novel may be best conveyed in the following sentences taken from the book: "Man is not made for defeat. A man can be destroyed, but not defeated."

Hemingway was renowned for his unique writing style which is direct, terse, and often monotonous. His language is characterized by features including economy of expression, short sentences and short paragraphs, and deliberate avoidance of adjectives and adverbs.

6.4.4 Southern Literature Representative William Faulkner (1897–1962)

William Faulkner, American novelist and short story writer, is one of the Nobel Prize winners. He writes about America's south and employs the literary technique of the stream of consciousness and multiple narrators.

A recognized writer of southern literature, William Faulkner is well-known for his creation of a Yoknapatawpha community modeled on his own county in Mississippi. It is in this community that he put his characters. The theme of his writings focus on conflict: the conflicts of different generations, of social classes, of races, and of men. His philosophy is that the brotherhood of man would triumph.

Faulkner is the author of a number of novels and many short stories. Due to the employment of the stream of consciousness technique and multiple narrators in some of his writings, he is difficult to read. His two best-known novels are *The Sound and the Fury* (1929) and *As I Lay Dying* (1930).

The Sound and the Fury centers around the Compson family, an aristocratic family that is past its prosperity. Their decline is seen, first of all, in how the family is divided into the camp of Mr Compson and the camp of Mrs Compson. The result is confusion and despair for the children. The novel is divided into four sections, each related through the mind of a different character.

As I Lay Dying is a comedy with a profoundly tragic center. The novel is a book typical of his style. It is a story of a family told by almost every family member. The reader is presented with the inner selves of these people, and multiple points of view are involved.

William Faulkner was also popular among the readers for his novellas and short stories such as *Light in August* (1932), *A Rose for Emily* (1930), *Barn Burning* (1939), etc.

6.4.5 New England Poet Robert Frost (1874–1963)

Robert Frost is the most popular modern poet. Towards the end of his life, he received more literary awards, government recognitions and institutional honors than any other poet of the 20th century.

Robert Frost was born in San Francisco in a teacher's family. He spent his childhood in the west, but when he was 11, his family moved back to New England. He had his early education from his mother, and in 1897, he came to Harvard for two years as a special student. In 1899 his grandfather bought him a farm in Derry, New Hampshire and he lived and worked on the farm, while writing.

Frost achieved literary recognition in England when he published his first collection of poetry *A Boy's Will* in 1913. Ezra Pound, whom he met in England, helped him publish his second volume *North of Boston* (1914) which contains some of Frost's most stunning poems, including *Mending Wall*, *Home Burial* and *Apple-Picking*. Then he became known also in the US. He came back in 1917 and took a teaching position at Amherst College.

Frost's poetry addresses familiar subjects, uses an accessible language, and shows, on the surface, a simplicity of thought. But his poetry accommodates irony and ambiguity in such a way that we eventually realize that beneath the surface simplicity is a profound understanding of life. The contemplations on life in some of Frost's poems assure him a permanent status in the temple of poetry. *The Road Not Taken* (1915) depicts a choice made that "made all the difference", but the mood of the poem really lingers on the choice not made, on the road not taken. *Stopping by the Woods on a Snowy Evening* (1923) is about a weary old journeyer stopping by the woods to contemplate over death on "the darkest evening of the year".

Frost is a traditional and innovative poet. He is a traditionalist in his preferences in form, and he is innovative because he brings a distinctive voice to the familiar form. The amazing fact of Frost's poetry is the voice he has created: It has a shrewd, grainy vernacular tone with a stoic moral wisdom to it. This voice remains steady in the many volumes of lyrics, dramatic monologues, political poems and verse plays published during his lifetime.

6.4.6 Playwright Eugene O'Neill (1888–1953)

Eugene O'Neill, America's first major playwright, was the first to explore serious themes in the theater and to experiment with theatrical conventions. He was born in a Broadway hotel room in New York's theatre district in an actor's family, and grew up in the world of theatre.

O'Neil was America's first dramatist of world stature. In the course of a long and prolific career, O'Neill won four Pulitzer Prizes (1920, 1922, 1928, 1957), gained international recognition, and in 1936 won the Nobel Prize.

O'Neill's plays show a profound understanding of human existence, with a wide-ranging themes that include the need for a sustaining illusion, the felt need to justify one's existence, the desire to ally oneself with some larger purpose, the destructive consequences of abusing alcohol and drugs, the persistence of racial memories, the Oedipal triangle, the eternally tragic predicament of humanity.

O'Neill's major works include *Beyond the Horizon* (1920), *The Emperor Jones* (1920), *Anna Christie* (1922), *The Hairy Ape* (1922), *Desire under the Elms* (1924) and *The Iceman Cometh* (1946).

Notes

[1] American Revolution (1775–1783), also known as the American Revolutionary War, was fought between Great Britain and the thirteen colonies, and its result was a formation of a new nation—the United States of America.

[2] The Middle Ages (476–1453) a period in Western European history that followed the disintegration of the West Roman Empire in the 4th and 5th centuries and lasted into the 15th century (i. e. into the period of the Renaissance). The ideas and institutions of Western civilization derive largely from the turbulent events of the Early Middle Ages and the rebirth of culture in the later years.

[3] A kind of poetry that doesn't conform to any regular meters; the length of its lines is irregular, as its use of rhyme—if any. As the most widely practiced verse form in English now, it established itself in the late 19th and early 20th centuries with Walt Whitman.

[4] Herbert Spencer (1820–1903) is a British Social Darwinist who proposed that human society and biological organization shared the same functions.

[5] Friedrich Nietzsche (1844–1900) is a German philosopher of the late 19th century who challenged the foundations of Christianity and traditional morality. He was

interested in the enhancement of individual and cultural health, and believed in life, creativity, power, and the realities of the world we live in, rather than those situated in a world beyond. Central to his philosophy is the idea of "life-affirmation", which involves an honest questioning of all doctrines that drain life's expansive energies, however socially prevalent those views might be.

Exercises

I. Fill in the following blanks with proper words or expressions.

1. American literature may be the ________ national literature in the world. Its real history, if calculated from the end of the American Revolution, is only over ________ years. Yet within a short period, American literature grew rapidly, began to receive ________, and has exerted great influence upon ________.
2. Many factors have contributed to the transition of the American nationhood to the status of independence and federation, and the shaping of American literature in its true sense. Namely, they are ________, ________, and ________.
3. Washington Irving was the ________ to achieve international recognition, who, accordingly, was known as ________. Two of Irving's best known stories are *Rip Van Winkle* and ________.
4. Herman Melville is one of the greatest ________ in American literature whose varied experiences are reflected in the different aspects of his writing. Melville's ________ are the classic wanderers who struggle against odds and are initiated into some harsh rite of passage, and the world in Melville's fiction mirrors the world he saw—defined by the rough seas and ________.
5. In poetry, Edgar Allen Poe is a ________. He conveys a mood through rhymes, rhythms, onomatopoeia, and ________. ________ seems to be a repeated theme of his poems.
6. The style of Dickinson's poems is unique in that her poems are short, often with ________, that her poems are always without ________, that the poems are written in a way of severe economy of expressions, and that capital letters and ________ are employed to show emphasis.
7. *The Great Gatsby* tells the story of a ________ young man whose dream of success, personified in a rich and beautiful young woman named Daisy, turns out to be ________ in every sense: Daisy belongs to a corrupt society, Gatsby corrupts himself in the quest for her, and above all, the rich have no intention of sharing their privileges.
8. Hemingway was renowned for his unique writing style which is direct, ________, and

often monotonous. His language is characterized by features including ________, short sentences and short paragraphs, and deliberate avoidance of ________.

9. A recognized writer of southern literature, William Faulkner is well-known for his creation of a ________ community modeled on his own county in Mississippi. It is in this community that he put his characters. The theme of his writings focus on ________, and his philosophy is that ________ would triumph.

10. Eugene O'Neill, America's ________, was the first to explore serious themes in the theater and to experiment with ________. In the course of a long and prolific career, O'Neill won ________ Pulitzer Prizes, gained international recognition, and in 1936 won the Nobel Prize.

Ⅱ. Explain the following terms.

1. Transcendentalism
2. Realism
3. the Lost Generation
4. Imagist Movement

Ⅲ. Discuss the following questions.

1. As far as the literary significance of *The Adventures of Huckleberry Finn* is concerned, Ernest Hemingway once remarked: "All modern literature comes from one book by Mark Twain called *Huckleberry Finn.*" Please make a brief comment on Hemingway's remark.
2. What do you think makes *The Old Man and the Sea* the most remarkable fiction of Hemingway?

Chapter Seven

Education

Education in the US is provided mainly by government, with control and funding coming from three levels: federal, state, and local. School attendance is mandatory and nearly universal at the elementary and high school levels. At these levels, school curricula, funding, teaching, and other policies are set through locally elected school boards with jurisdiction over school districts. School districts are usually separate from other local jurisdictions, with independent officials and budgets. Educational standards and standardized testing decisions are usually made by state governments.

7.1 School Grades

In the US the first year of compulsory schooling begins with children at the age of five or six. Children are then placed in year groups known as grades, beginning with first grade and culminating in twelfth grade. The US uses ordinal numbers for naming grades, unlike Canada and Australia where cardinal numbers are preferred. Thus, when asked what grade they are in, typical American children are more likely to say "first grade" rather than "Grade 1".

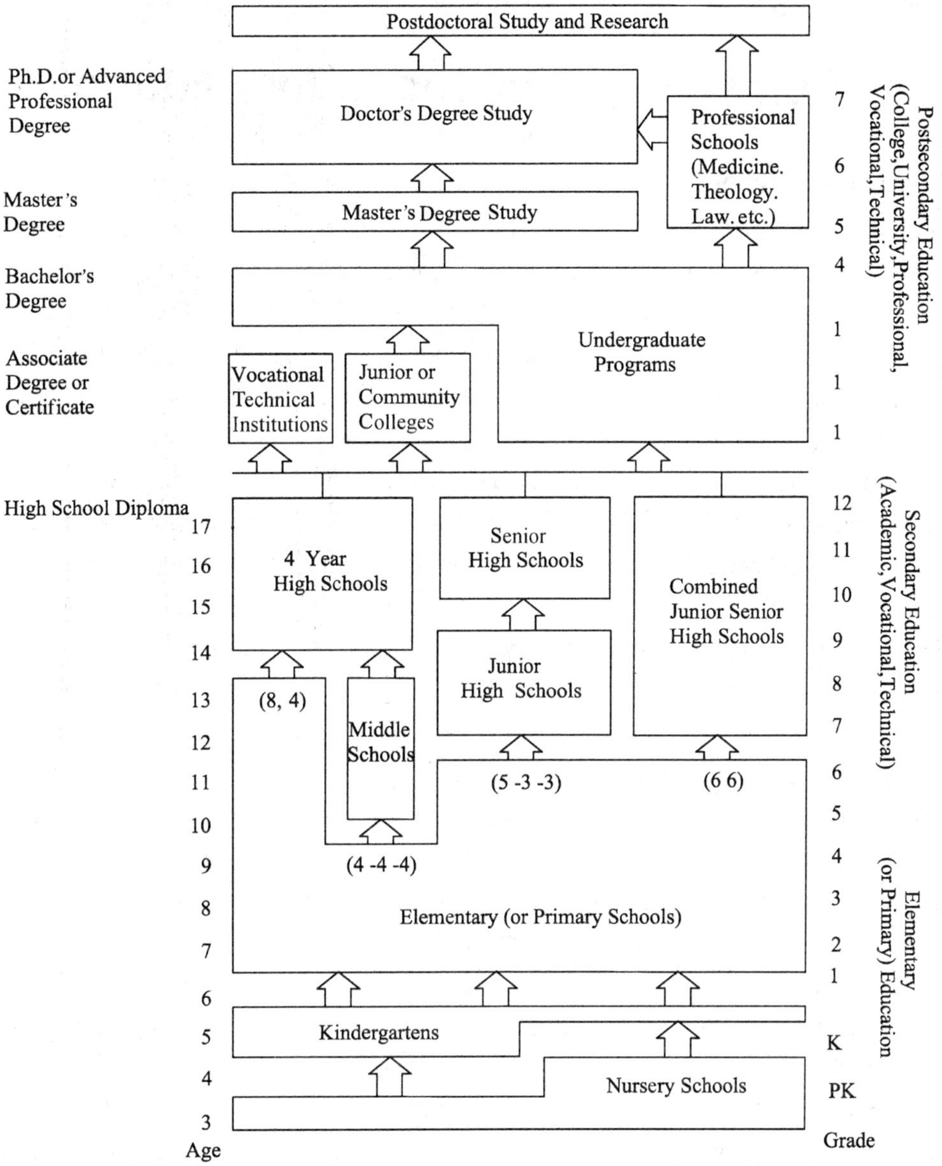

7.1.1 Preschool

The federal government funds the Head Start preschool program for children of low-income families, but most families are on their own with regard to finding a preschool or childcare. Head Start is a program of the US Department of Health and Human Services that focuses on assisting children from low-income families. Created in 1965, Head Start is the longest-running program for stopping the cycle of poverty in the US. It provides comprehensive education, health, nutrition, and parent involvement services to low-income children and their families.

7.1.2 Elementary and Secondary Education

Elementary School

Elementary school, also known as grade school or grammar school, is a school of kindergarten through fifth grade, where basic subjects are taught. Elementary school provides a common daily routine for all students except the most disadvantaged. Students do not choose a course structure and often remain in one or two classrooms throughout the school day, with the exceptions of physical education, music, or art classes.

Typically, the curriculum within public elementary education is determined by individual school districts. The school district selects curriculum guides and textbooks that are reflective of a state's learning standards and benchmarks for a given grade level. Learning standards are the goals by which states and school districts must meet adequate yearly progress (AYP) as mandated by No Child Left Behind (NCLB). This description of school governance is simplistic at best, however, school systems vary widely not only in the way curricular decisions are made but in how teaching and learning takes place. Some states and/or school districts impose more top-down mandates than others. In many schools, teachers play a significant role in curriculum design and there are few top-down mandates. Curricular decisions within private schools are made differently from in public schools and in most cases without consideration for NCLB.

The No Child Left Behind Act of 2001, often abbreviated in print as NCLB and shortened in pronunciation to "nickelbee", is a controversial US federal law (Act of Congress) that reauthorized a number of federal programs aiming to improve the performance of US primary and secondary schools by increasing the standards of accountability for states, school districts, and schools, as well as providing parents more flexibility in choosing which schools their children will attend. NCLB is the latest federal legislation which enacts the theories of standards-based education reform, formerly known as outcome-based education, which is based on the belief that setting high expectations and establishing measurable goals can improve individual outcomes in education. The Act requires states to develop assessments in basic skills to be given to all students in certain grades, if those states are to receive federal funding for schools.

The effectiveness and desirability of NCLB's measures are hotly debated. A primary criticism asserts that NCLB could reduce effective instruction and student learning because it may cause states to lower achievement goals and motivate teachers to "teach to the test". A primary supportive claim asserts that systematic testing provides data that sheds light on which schools are not teaching basic skills effectively, so that interventions can be made to improve outcomes for all students while reducing the achievement gap for disadvantaged and disabled students.

Public elementary school teachers typically instruct between twenty and thirty students of diverse learning needs. A typical classroom will include children with identified special needs as listed in Individuals with Disabilities Act to those that are cognitively, athletically or artistically gifted. At times an individual school district identifies areas of need within the curriculum. Teachers and advisory administrators form committees to develop supplemental materials to support learning for diverse learners and identify enrichment for textbooks. Many school districts post information about the curriculum and supplemental materials on websites for public access. Teachers receive a book to give to the students for each subject and brief overviews of what they are expected to teach. In general, a student learns basic arithmetic and sometimes rudimentary algebra in mathematics, English proficiency, and fundamentals of other subjects. Learning standards are identified for all areas of curriculum by individual states, including those for math, social studies, science, physical development, the fine arts as well as reading. While the concept of state learning standards has been around for some time, NCLB has mandated standards exist at the state level.

Elementary school teachers are trained with emphases on human cognitive and psychological development and the principles of curriculum development and instruction earning either a Bachelor's or master's degree in early childhood and elementary education. The teaching of social studies and science are often underdeveloped in some elementary school programs and some attribute this to the fact that elementary school teachers are trained as generalists. However, teachers attribute this to the priority placed on developing reading, writing and math proficiency in the elementary grades and the amount of time needed to do so. Reading, writing and math proficiency greatly affect performance in social studies, science and other content areas. Certification standards for teachers are determined by individual states, with individual colleges and universities determining the rigor of the college education provided for future teachers.

Junior and Senior High School

Junior high school is any school intermediate between elementary school and senior high school. It usually includes Grades Seven and Eight, and sometimes Six or Nine. In some locations, junior high school includes Grade Nine only, allowing students to adjust to a high school environment. Middle school is often used instead of junior high school when demographic factors increase the number of younger students. At this time, students are given more independence as choosing their own classes. Starting in ninth grade, grades become part of a student's official transcript. Future employers or colleges may want to see steady improvement in grades and a good attendance record on the official transcript. Therefore, students are encouraged to take much more responsibility for their education.

Senior high school is a school attended after junior high school. High school is often used instead of senior high school and distinguished from junior high school.

7.2 Basic Curricular Structure

Generally, at the high school level, students take a broad variety of classes without special emphasis in any particular subject. Curricula vary widely in quality and rigidity; for example, some states consider 70 (on a 100-point scale) to be a passing grade, while others consider it to be as low as 60 or as high as 75.

The following are the typical minimum course sequences that one must take in order to obtain a high school diploma; they are not indicative of the necessary minimum courses or course rigor required for attending college in the US:

Science (usually three years minimum, including biology, chemistry, physics)

Mathematics (usually three years minimum, including algebra, geometry, algebra Ⅱ, and/or precalculus/trigonometry)

English (four years)

Social science (various history, government, and economics courses, always including American history)

Physical education (at least one year)

Many states require a "health" course in which students learn about anatomy, nutrition, first aid, sexuality, and birth control. Anti-drug use programs are also usually part of health courses. Foreign languages and some form of art education are also a mandatory part of the curriculum in some schools.

7.2.1 Electives

Many high schools offer a wide variety of elective courses, although the availability of such courses depends upon each particular school's financial resources and desired curriculum emphases.

Common types of electives include:

Visual arts (drawing, sculpture, painting, photography, film)

Performing arts (drama, band, chorus, orchestra, dance)

Technology education (woodworking, metalworking, automobile repair, robotics)

Computers (word processing, programming, graphic design)

Athletics (cross-country, football, baseball, basketball, track and field, swimming, tennis, gymnastics, water polo, soccer, wrestling, cheerleading)

Publishing (journalism/student newspaper, yearbook/annual, literary magazine)

Foreign languages (French, German, and Spanish are common; Chinese, Latin, Greek and Japanese are less common)

7.2.2 Grading Scale

In schools in the US children are continuously assessed throughout the school year by their teachers, and report cards are issued to parents at varying intervals. Generally the scores for individual assignments and tests are recorded for each student in a grade book, along with the maximum number of points for each assignment. At any time, the total number of points for a student when divided by the total number of possible points produces a percent grade which can be translated to a letter grade. Letter grades are often used on report cards at the end of a marking period, although the current grade may be available at other times (particularly when an electronic grade book connected to an online service is in use). Although grading scales usually differ from school to school, the grade scale which seems to be most common is as follows. The grading is based on a scale of 0 - 100 or a percentile.

Grade Scale

A			B			C			D			E, U or F
+		-	+		-	+		-	+		-	
100-97	96-93	92-90	89-87	86-83	82-80	79-77	76-73	72-70	69-67	66-63	62-60	Below 60 Percent

7.2.3 Standardized Testing

Under the No Child Left Behind Act, all American states must test students in public schools statewide to ensure that they are achieving the desired level of minimum education; students being educated at home or in private schools are not included. The Act also requires that students and schools show "adequate yearly progress". This means they must show some improvement each year.

This research based on testing allows elementary school teachers to have ongoing access to students' progress. Teachers using this system can identify strengths and weaknesses of individual student and remediate where necessary. When a student fails to make adequate yearly progress, No Child Left Behind mandates remediation through summer school and/or tutoring available to a given student.

During high school, students (usually in eleventh grade) may take one or more standardized tests depending on their postsecondary education preferences and their local graduation requirements. In theory, these tests evaluate the overall level of knowledge and learning aptitude of the students. The SAT and ACT are the most common standardized tests that students take when applying to college. A student may take the SAT, ACT, or both depending upon the college the student plans to apply to for admission. Most competitive schools also require two or three SAT subject tests, which are shorter exams that focus strictly on a particular subject matter.

7.2.4 Extracurricular Activities

A major characteristic of American schools is the high priority given to sports, clubs and activities by the community, the parents, the schools and the students themselves. Extracurricular activities are educational activities not falling within the scope of the regular curriculum but under the supervision of the school. These activities can extend to large amounts of time outside the normal school day; home-schooled students, however, are not normally allowed to participate. Students' participation in sports programs, drill teams, bands, and spirit groups can amount to hours of practices and performances. Most states have organizations which develop rules for competition between groups. The idea of having sports teams associated with high schools is relatively unique to the US in comparison with other countries.

In addition to sports, numerous non-athletic extracurricular activities are available in American schools, both public and private. Activities include musical groups, marching bands, student government, school newspapers, science fairs, debate teams, and clubs focused on an academic area or cultural interests.

7.3 College and University

Postsecondary education in the US is known as college or university and commonly consists of four years of study at an institution of higher learning. Like high school, the four undergraduate grades are commonly called freshman, sophomore, junior, and senior years. Students traditionally apply to receive admission into college, with varying difficulties of entrance. Schools differ in their competitiveness and reputation; generally, the most prestigious schools are private, rather than public. Admissions criteria involve the rigor and grades earned in high school courses taken, the students' GPA, class ranking, and standardized test scores (such as the SAT or the ACT tests). Most colleges also consider more subjective factors such as a commitment to extracurricular activities, a personal essay, and an interview. While numerical factors rarely ever are absolute required values, each college usually has a rough threshold below which admission is unlikely.

Once admitted, students engage in undergraduate study, which consists of satisfying university and class requirements to achieve a Bachelor's degree in a field of concentration known as a major. The most common method consists of four years of study leading to a Bachelor of Arts (B. A.), a Bachelor of Science (B. S.), or sometimes another Bachelor's degree such as Bachelor of Fine Arts (B. F. A.), Bachelor of Social Work (B. S. W.), Bachelor of Engineering (B. Eng.) or Bachelor of Philosophy (B. Phil.). Five-Year Professional Architecture programs offer the Bachelor of Architecture Degree (B. Arch.)

Unlike in the British model, degrees in law and medicine are not offered at the undergraduate level and are completed as graduate study after earning a Bachelor's degree. Neither field specifies or prefers any undergraduate major, though medicine has set prerequisite courses that must be taken before enrollment.

Some students choose to attend a community college for two years prior to further study at another college or university. In most states, community colleges are operated either by a division of the state university or by local special districts subject to guidance from a state agency. Community colleges may award Associate of Arts (AA) or Associate of Science (AS) degree after two years. Those seeking to continue their education may transfer to a four-year college or university. Some community colleges have automatic enrollment agreements with a local four-year college, where the community college provides the first two years of study and the university provides the remaining years of study, sometimes all on one campus. The community college awards the Associate's degree, and the university awards the Bachelor's and master's degrees.

Graduate study, conducted after obtaining an initial degree and sometimes after several years of professional work, leads to a more advanced degree such as a master's degree, which could be a Master of Arts (MA), Master of Science (MS), Master of Business Administration (MBA), or other less common master's degrees such as Master of Education (MEd), and Master of Fine Arts (MFA). After additional years of study and sometimes in conjunction with the completion of a master's degree, students may earn a Doctor of Philosophy (Ph. D.) or other doctoral degree, such as Doctor of Arts, Doctor of Education, Doctor of Theology, Doctor of Medicine, Doctor of Pharmacy, Doctor of Physical Therapy, or Doctor of Jurisprudence. Some programs, such as medicine, have formal apprenticeship procedures post graduation like residency and internship which must be completed after graduation and before one is considered to be fully trained. Other professional programs like law and business have no formal apprenticeship requirements after graduation (although law school graduates must take the bar exam in order to legally practice law in nearly all states).

Entrance into graduate programs usually depends upon a student's undergraduate academic performance or professional experience as well as their score on a standardized entrance exam like the Graduate Record Examination (GRE), the Medical College Admissions Test (MCAT), or the Law School Admissions Test (LSAT). Many graduate and law schools do not require experience after earning a Bachelor's degree to enter their programs; however, business school candidates are usually required to gain a few years of professional work experience before applying. Only 8.9 percent of students ever receive postgraduate degrees, and most, after obtaining their Bachelor's degree, proceed directly into the workforce.

American college and university faculty, staff, alumni, students, and applicants monitor rankings is produced by magazines such as *US News*, *World Report*, and *Academic Ranking of World Universities*, test preparation services such as The Princeton Review or another university itself such as the Top American Research Universities by the University of Florida's The Center. These rankings are based on factors like brand recognition, selectivity in admissions, generosity of alumni donors, and volume of faculty research. Fifty-five US universities are listed in the top 200 in the world in the THES-QS World University Rankings.

In the popular mind, approximately twenty-five institutions compose "the top tier" of American higher learning. However, this "ladder" is not absolute. Most would cite the eight universities that compose the Ivy League and a small number of elite, private research universities, e. g. (alphabetical order) Caltech, Duke, Johns Hopkins, MIT, Northwestern, Stanford, University of Chicago, Washington University in St. Louis, etc. A small percentage of students who apply for these schools gain admission. Many Americans would also recognize the so-called "Little Ivies" as a handful of liberal arts colleges known for their high-quality instruction. These include (alphabetical order) Amherst, Swarthmore, Williams, Wesleyan, etc. This group would likely also include the all-female institutions such as Smith and Wellesley that were former members of the "Seven Sisters".

Exercises

I. Fill in the following blanks with proper words or expressions.

1. In the US the first year of compulsory schooling begins with children at the age of ______.
2. The federal government funds the ______ preschool program for children of low-income families.
3. ______, also known as grade school or grammar school, is a school of kindergarten through fifth grade, where basic subjects are taught.
4. Public elementary school teachers typically instruct between ______ students of diverse learning needs.
5. Elementary school teachers are trained with emphases on ______ development and the principles of curriculum development and instruction.
6. Many states require a ______ course in which students learn about anatomy, nutrition, first aid, sexuality, and birth control.
7. Many high schools offer a wide variety of ______ courses, although the availability of such courses depends upon each particular school's financial resources and desired curriculum emphases.
8. A major characteristic of American schools is the high priority given to ______, clubs and activities by the community, the parents, the schools and the students themselves.
9. Like high school, the four undergraduate grades are commonly called freshman, ______, junior, and ______ years.
10. Some students choose to attend a ______ for two years prior to further study at another college or university.

II. Explain the following terms.

1. No Child Left Behind Act
2. elective courses
3. extracurricular activities
4. the Ivy League

III. Discuss the following questions.

1. How much importance does America attach to its elementary school education?
2. Which American university would you willingly attend? Why?

Chapter Eight

Foreign Policy

This chapter specially make a study of American foreign policy, which is an access of getting to know better about the US. The foreign policy and its making definitely reflect the political attitudes and philosophical beliefs. The US always takes a heritage of making her foreign policy with top priority of considering the national interests. What are the US interests in the world? An illustrative list might include: security of US territory and citizens; prosperity of the nation and freedom of the people as well as controlling access to US territory against illegal drugs and immigrants; preventing the emergence of a hostile superpower; reducing existing inventories of weapons of mass destruction and lesser arms; preventing the spread or use of weapons of mass destruction and so on.

8.1 The American Heritage in Decision of Foreign Policy

It is essential to have an analysis of the American heritage in decision of foreign policy, through which we can have a better understanding of the historical experiences and philosophical beliefs that the objectives of American foreign policy are forged in different periods of history.

8.1.1 Isolationism

American foreign policy, traditionally, was supported by geographic isolation. Away from the Old World, the Americans laid the foundations of a new nation. To the new immigrants, the old world of Europe was full of turmoil, hopelessness, and bigotry. They wanted to bury it forever, with one objective in mind: to find a new birth, as it were, in a far-off continent.

This type of thought had deep psychological effects on the American outlook of life. They had escaped the political intrigues and conflicts witnessed on the continent of Europe; therefore, they were determined to divorce all the links with Europe. On the New World Americans diverted all their energies, thoughts, and ambitions inward. The idea of progress settled deep in American thought and they blended this concept with pragmatism. Isolationism thus derived as much from the dominant concern of the American society with domestic affairs as it did from a deliberate rejection of foreign entanglements. The achievement of virtually every goal associated with the American Dream demanded that internal interests receive primary attention. This fact prompted one of the nation's leading modern historians, Charles A. Beard, to prefer the term "continentalism" rather than isolationism, to characterize the nation's historic orientation in foreign policy.

Charles A. Beard

Isolationism, therefore, was not merely the desire to avoid foreign entanglement. It was a much deeper phenomenon, which reflected above all a habit of mind, a cluster of national attitudes, a feeling of spiritual separation from other countries, especially Europe, with roots penetrating deeply into the nation's heritage and experience. Isolationism reflected the American cultural experience and its philosophy, which may be called more generally "the American way of life". Later, the Monroe Doctrines was proclaimed and Americans adopted isolationism as a philosophy of national character. The isolationist philosophy, the theory of progress, mounting success, and strong national feelings created a sense of pride and superiority in the American mind. Here was a people blessed by the Almighty. They were the chosen people, entrusted with a mission to lead the world. They were to provide a model and guidance; they had the torch of enlightenment. Dignity, faith, honor, prosperity, and enlightenment were bestowed on them by the will of God and the American mission was to reform the world, to remodel it into their pattern. The salvation of the world was to adopt "the American way of life".

8.1.2 The American Mission

The sense of mission was also the outcome of the search by Americans for a precise definition of their national purpose and the development of an American ideology. After all, this was a young country full of nationalistic enthusiasm and it was felt that the development of a conviction of national purpose was a historical necessity. In the first place, it provided a basis for continuity for a new nation which had no developed historic past. Second, it established a concept in which the American could define the meaning of his life and his institutions, and set goals for his purpose and destination.

This conviction of mission also provided grounds to incorporate religion into the new American ideology. This combination supported the basic American concept of liberty and freedom in all spheres of life. The success of the new nation made it conscious of its unique position as a republic in a world of monarchies. The Americans were well prepared and even anxious to proclaim their political and social concepts to the rest of the world. The doctrine of an American mission had an indirect connection with the US foreign policy. Scientific and technological breakthroughs that Americans made provided new inputs to the American sense of pride and confidence and enhanced its prestige abroad.

8.1.3 The Moral Explanations for International Interventions

Americans began to search for some moral principles and justification for their increasingly interventionist conduct of international affairs. Psychologically, it was impossible for them to perceive a role without "good" aims and ideals. Politically, the stage had already been reached in which America was involved in international affairs simply because of the reality of its increasing power politics base and expanding economic system. Subsequently, the net effect Theodore Roosevelt's interventionist and aggressive diplomacy around the world was the maintenance of a strong US position in Latin America and its monitoring of the continuance of the precarious balance of power among the nations in the Far East and Europe. But Americans maintained that all such foreign policies were conducted in the cause of peace and democracy.

The rapid changes in the international environment, however, presented a paradox. Along with the pursuit of peace and democracy, for example, went peripheral involvement in war an power politics and the paradox of a growing peace movement in the midst of mounting appropriations for armaments and battleships.

For virtually the first time in its history, except in war, the US began to take very seriously the establishment of a strong military force.

But the moral rhetoric of American foreign policy continued to be the underlying basis of its aims. Exercising its new-found powers, America moved toward world leadership, intervening in the cause of peace and democracy and urging the view that peace must be enforced, if necessary—through what was certainly the ultimate paradox—by war.

8.2 The Foreign Policy in and out of the World War Time

The American foreign policy in and out of the world war time can surely take a thoughtful reflection of the American's characteristics in dealing with the world affairs.

8.2.1 The Foreign Policy in World War Ⅰ

The foreign policy of the US was characterized by neutrality in World War Ⅰ. World War Ⅰ broke out in June 1914 as the result of fierce struggle between two imperialist power groups for colonies, markets and spheres of influence. When the war began in Europe, which is far away from the US and its territory, most Americans felt that their country had no vital interests in the war; therefore, they showed little concern about the war fairs in the beginning. And in August, 1914, two months later, President Wilson issued an official statement proclaiming American neutral stand. He said that the US "must be neutral in fact as well as in name" and "we must be impartial in thought as well as in action".

The US, however, changed her neutral stand, and turned to the side of the Allies consisting of Britain, France, Russia and Italy because of ethnic ties, cultural tradition, social background and economic connections. The public of the US, generally speaking, was in favour of the allies, and, what is more, Britain controlled the wartime news that frequently went into the US. In the first period of the war, Britain and France could either buy arms and war materials, or get loans from American banks and financial institutions, while Germany also could get something that it wanted from the US. As the old saying goes that the US burned the candle at its two ends. As the war lasted, Britain controlled waters of Atlantic, which was the nearer passage to Europe, the war fields. When Britain blocked American ships sailing towards Germany, the US only protested for that. The British blockage infuriated Germany, and German used submarines to cut British sea routes and sink American ships. This aggravated the US government, and soon the US threatened to go to war against Germany. In the end, when Germany refused to give up its submarine warfare, and even tried to get Mexico into the war against the US, promising Mexico the return of lost territory of Texas, New Mexico and Arizona. At that time Britain and France were exhausted by the war, and might be defeated by Germany. For fear of losing the business interests and bringing the threat to the security of the US, American government declared war on Germany on April 16, 1917.

The war ended on November 11, 1918 when the armistice was signed and fighting stopped. The Peace Conference, i. e. the Paris Conference began on January 18, 1919. In the conference, the Big Four, that is, the US together with Britain, France and Italy, dominated the division of colonies of Germany, Austro-Hungary and the Ottoman Empire (now Turky). Through this conference, the US grabbed as much as it wanted, President Wilson took the great advantage of this opportunity to advance American interests as well as its hegenomy position.

8.2.2 The Foreign Policy in World War II

World War II resulted from the struggle between the great powers for controlling of the world and Military expansion of the countries of Nazi Germany, Fascist Italy and Militarist Japan. This struggle was worsened by the world economic crisis. World War II broke out through the continual incidents caused by the Axis powers: in July 1937, Japanese invaded China; in September, 1939, Germany blitzed upon Poland, then in June attacked on Russia; and in December, 1941, Japanese destroyed the American Pacific fleet in the Pearl Harbour. Till then the war spread all over the world and involved all the great powers in the world.

Isolationism, the core of American foreign policy in the early 1930s, kept the US out of the fighting that was going on in Europe and Asia. The US Congress was very active in passing three neutrality acts which were all signed into law by President Roosevelt. These neutrality laws all focused on one point of preventing the US from being involved in the wars. Because of these laws, the spirit of the Axis powers in invading the other countries was greatly encouraged, for they knew no matter what they had done, the Americans would do nothing but watch on the other side of the oceans. As the German Nazi arms trampled on the vast lands of Europe frenziedly, the situation of the battle fields became worse, especially when France was occupied and the Soviet Union was exhausted confronting the well-equipped German arms, and only Britain arms was spread alone in fighting against Nazi Germany, the US seemed unrest for the ominous situation, which would be unfavorable for the interests of the US itself. So the US suddenly changed its stand of neutrality and tried to support Britain. In order not to run the risk of offending the tough isolationists in Congress, President Roosevelt put forward a compromising program as the Lend-Lease program to aid Britain.

Lend-Lease program allowed the US to provide Allied nations with defense supplies without actually going to war with the Axis powers. The US gave Lend-Lease aid to Great Britain, the USSR, China, and over 30 other nations. Lend-Lease program showed the US partly-veiled about its behavior and attitude to the war; however, the Pearl Harbour Incident smashed the partly-veiled attitude of the US, and the US had to declare war on Nazi Germany.

The involvement of the US in the war basically changed its neutrality as well as linkage together with Britain and the USSR. The foreign policy of the wartime was adjusted out of two reasons: One is to defeat Nazi Germany, and the other is to establish a postwar political structure in accordance with American interests and prevent the Soviet Union from over-expansion. Thus, the leaders of the three powers met together three times discussing the war affairs. In September, 1945, the World War II ended with the clear clash of interests between the two countries.

8.2.3 The Foreign Policy in Post-World War II

The post-World War II era is usually called the Cold War period, during which no large scale battle fighting existed but the political struggles were fierce between the sides of the capitalist and the socialist. The origins of the Cold War resulted from the separate concepts of the two superpowers, the US and the Soviet Union. When World War II ended in 1945, on the one side the US government intended to take the opportunity to establish its leadership in the world and open the world market to American goods and capital; meanwhile, it tried to break down the Soviet Union's sphere of influence in Eastern Europe; on the other side the Soviet Union, out of its own security concern and fear of capitalist encirclement, was determined to keep its hold on the Eastern European countries and defend its sphere of influence at all cost. The relationship between the two big powers became more and more intense. George Kennan, a high-ranking official in the American embassy to Moscow, on February 22, 1946, sent a long telegram to the State Department, analyzing Soviet Union's intention and putting forward suggestion, which emphasized the US policy should be "a long-term, patient but firm and vigilant containment of Russian expansive tendencies". Later, the containment policy was put in force and it also became the official policy towards the Soviet Union until 1989.

The open declaration of the containment policy was issued and implemented by President Truman. On March 12, 1949, President Truman made a speech to the joint session of Congress, for Greece and Turkey at the risk of falling into the hands of the Soviet Union. He formally stated his proclamation of containing the Communism centered by the Soviet Union, in his speech containing "it must be the policy of the US to support free peoples who are resisting attempted subjugation by armed minorities or by outside pressures." That is to say, the US government would aid and support any country which was fighting against Communism.

The US government in the Cold War also intervened in Asia. The US government, at the end of WW Ⅱ in 1945, helped shipping Kuomintang (KMT) troops to coastal cities right after Japanese surrender and ordered Japanese troops to hand over the arms only to KMT troops. When armed clashes broke out between Communist-led troops and KMT troops, President Truman sent Marshall to China to mediate the two Chinese Parties. Unfortunately, the mediating work failed. Jiang Kaishek, the leader of KMT decided to use military means to deal with the Communist Party, and planned to wipe it out within three months with the support of the US goverment. In June, 1946, the Chinese Civil War broke out, and lasted till 1949. On October 1, 1949, New China declared its foundation of People's Republic of China to the world.

As soon as New China was founded, the Korean War broke out in June, 1950, and the Truman Administration sent its troops to South Korea by the name of the Union States to fight North Korean troops, and meanwhile sent the 7th Fleet to protect Taiwan from being liberated by PLA. The North Korean troops were badly beaten by American and South Korean troops, and the war fire was spreading quickly to Yalu River, the border of China. In order to prevent the war fire spreading into her own territory, Chinese government sent the volunteers crossing the Yalu River in October, 1950, and fought side by side with the North Koreans for about three years until an armistice was signed on July 27, 1953.

The enlargement policy of the US involved itself in the war in Vietnam from 1950 to 1975, which lasted 25 years, maybe the longest war it has ever fought in 20th century. Almost at the same time of sending the troops to the Korean war, Truman sent another troops to Vietnam to help French arms recontrolling, for the Vietminh was a great threat to French governing in Vietnam. French arms withdrawed from Vietnam according to the Geneva Conference in 1954, and the US replaced French and became the main force in Vietman to support the South Vietnam puppet government in its suppression of revoluntionary forces led by Ho Chi Minh, the great leader of the Democratic Republic of Vietnam (North Vietnam).

The Vietnam war was typical of the enlargement policy of the US government presented in the fear of lossing Vietnam to the Communist. The war was fought with American money, weapon and soldiers, and by 1969, 543,400 American troops were fighting in Vietnam and about 60,000 American soldiers lost their lives in this war.

This caused the Anti-war Movement in the US, and under the pressure, President Johnson could not realize his second run for the presidency. When Richard Nixon came into office as the 37th president of the US, he ended the war in 1975.

The Cold War Era winded up in 1985 with the Soviet Union's collapse. With its collapse, the US also took a new start in its foreign policy ,which was dominated by the idea of the adaption or change.

8.3 Three Dimensions of the US Foreign Policy

In the new post-Cold War era, the US found itself confronted with new challenges and circumstances, which made the American policymakers direct attention to a more diverse set of complicated situations. They began to think about adjusting the former policy, at the beginning of the 1990s, the Department of State has officially committed itself to "building democracy; promoting and maintaining peace; promoting economic growth and sustainable development; addressing global problems; and providing humanitarian assistance". Based on the new agenda, the three dimensions of the foreign policy was forged and implemented soon.

8.3.1 The Diplomatic Dimension

Over the course of American history, diplomacy has been a key national power resource and a means of ensuring numerous foreign policy successes, including wartime alliances, peace settlements, trade pacts, and arms control treaties. Not only will diplomacy continue its salience in the new era, it will likely play an even greater role. Instead of the post-Cold War world divided by political ideology and military alliances, the US now faces an international environment in which the globalization of the world economy has accompanied the spread of democratic political systems and market economies. Globalization in turn demands that maintenance of America's preeminent position within the international system depends on co-opting, rather than provoking, the major states that have the potential to frustrate the exercise of the US hegemony. Thus the US will be compelled to rely on its soft power, its ability to persuade and to set the agenda in diplomatic negotiations, not on its coercive power as measured by its military resources, if it is to promote and protect its interests effectively.

Diplomacy will also be critical in responding to a host of transnational challenges and nontraditional foreign affairs concerns, including terrorism, drug trafficking, global migration, and environmental degradation. These problems cannot be remedied by unilateral action; all require international cooperation for which diplomacy is essential. Relatedly, diplomacy will be crucial in fostering and maintaining the collective action necessary to address future regional and ethnic conflicts. Diplomats will also be called on to assist the US companies wishing to expand their trade opportunities. Although the trade orientation is partially a product of the Clinton administration's foreign policy and the State Department's new focus in the post-Cold War world, it is also tied to the fact that diplomacy allows the US to tackle new challenges in a relatively affordable and flexible manner.

8.3.2 The Military Dimension

A preference for military force and a penchant for overt and covert intervention in the affairs of others have been hallmarks of American foreign policy since World War Ⅱ, and especially since NSC-68[1] was issued. The ability of the US to pursue its goals through such means has depended on policymakers' capacity to draw on a broad array of economic, intelligence, and military strategic and tactical assets. Public diplomacy abroad (and sometimes at home) and foreign economic and military aid and sales are exemplary. Militarily, nuclear weapons have figured prominently among the nation's assets, as the US historically depended heavily on the deterrent threat of nuclear weapons to preserve its own physical security and that of its allies against a potential Soviet Union military attack. Conventional weapons contributed to the US posture of "extended deterrence", as in Europe where the US committed itself to defend its North Atlantic Treaty Organization (NATO) allies from the Warsaw Pact[2] attack at whatever level it might occur.

Conventional military forces also provided the means with which to seek influence over political events in other countries. By dispatching an aircraft carrier from one theater to another, conducting military exercises near the border of an adversary, sending military aircraft over its capital city at supersonic speeds, or engaging in other shows of force, the US repeatedly used its vast military might to shape political outcomes abroad without resorting to the actual use of force. But on seven conspicuous occasions, overt military force was used: in Korea (1950–1953), Lebanon (1958), Vietnam(1962–1973), the Dominican Republic (1965), Grenada (1983), Panama (1989), and most recently, Iraq and Kuwait (1991). A common characteristic of these interventionist episodes is that all occurred in the Global South. Except for Panama and the Iraq-Kuwaiti conflict, a second characteristic is that all were motivated by fear of Communism and Soviet Union's expansionism.

Clearly the reasons for the symbolic or actual use of American military force will be different in the new era. Before the fall of the Soviet Union, there were 18 active army divisions, 15 aircraft carrier groups, 540 ships, and 24 active Air Force fighter wings. As the Cold War faded, the Bush administration altered the strategy marginally, to a two-war doctrine[3] which anticipated that the US should be prepared to fight concurrently two major regional wars, presumably in the Middle East and Asia. The underlying logic was to deter any potential adversary from initiating a conflict while the US was engaged in another major war. At the beginning of the Clinton administration, there were indications that this strategy would be revised to reflect the new president's planned defense cuts. One proposal, for instance, embraced a "win-hold-win strategy", where the US would seek to win a major regional war, hold the line in another (largely with air power), and then fight the second war to win.

The changing nature of America's security environment and defense policy extends to the use of nuclear weapons. In November 1997, President Clinton issued a directive designed to update the nation's nuclear policy for the first time since 1981. Reflecting positive developments in US-Russian relations and the administration's earlier Quadrennial Defense Review (QDR)[4], the revised guidelines sought to relate the nation's formidable nuclear capabilities to the security challenges the US faced in the post-Cold War era. In certain respects, the revised nuclear posture incorporated the views expressed in the Project on Eliminating Weapons of Mass Destruction, chaired by General Andrew J. Goodpaster. The Goodpaster committee expressed clear agreement with the Clinton administration's policy about the continuing importance of both a survivable nuclear deterrent and the appropriate of a smaller strategic arsenal. Such a forcesize would be consistent with the levels proposed for a third Strategic Arms Reduction Treaty (START)[5] with Russia. Even as the threat of nuclear war recedes with that, chemical and biological weapons of mass destruction are a growing concern, especially since weapons the weak can use against the strong become comparatively easy.

Today the conventional wisdom is that the US military will undergo such a transformation in the next century where continued advances in weapon, computer, and information technology will afford it "increased stealth, mobility, and dispersion, all under the shield of information superiority". The Department of Defense has been particularly receptive to this perspective because it views the Revolution in Military Affairs (RMA)[6] concept as a way to cope with fewer resources and reduce the number of lives lost in future wars. Metz believes these goals are attainable but warns the vigor with which the US is now pursuing the RMA may not be prudent in the long term. Instead, it "may generate unintended political and diplomatic side effects and lead to a more dangerous world ..., by provoking a symmetric responses and arms races" on the part of America's enemies.

8.3.3 The Economic Dimension

When the US emerged powerfully from World War Ⅱ, it was the world's unrivaled hegemony; little seemed beyond its reach. The German and Japanese's challenges to the existing global order had been turned back as both were decisively beaten in war, and even America's victorious allies in Western Europe and the Eurasian landmass lay exhausted and in ruins. In the years immediately following the war, the US achieved a level of economic and military power unparalleled in history. In 1947 it accounted for 50 percent of the combined gross world product. It was also the world's preeminent manufacturing center and leading exporter, and its monopoly of the atomic bomb gave it military superiority. Thus the US did indeed seem poised on the threshold of an American century.

Today, a little more than a decade after many observers were predicting the nation's decline, it appears the US is at the dawn of another American century. The US military superiority contributes to this emerging reality. Surging domestic productivity, declining unemployment, and expanding exports have enabled the US to dim other major industrialized states. Against this background, the economic challenge the US faces at the dawn of the millennium is whether it can sustain its economic robustness into the future. Noteworthy in this respect is that while the US economy is preeminent in the world, its share of gross world product has declined steadily since World War Ⅱ, dropping by more than half, from 50 percent to about 22 percent, between the late 1940s and the late 1980s. Furthermore, the World Bank projects a further decline in the next century, to 17 percent by 2020.

As globalization transforms international economics, such a strategy is prudent because "the US competitiveness is improving, and the economy increasingly relies on exports to sustain growth and create good jobs". Peter Morici[7] stresses that "an effective US policy for opening foreign markets does not require unequivocal reliance on multilateral institutions" like the World Trade Organization. Instead, other methods such as regional pacts, bilateral agreements, and transatlantic cooperation may be more appropriate as long as they produce results consistent with the central WTO goal of fostering market-responsive trade. In fact, Morici contends that forging a stronger economic relationship with Europe is particularly critical, because it would offer broader markets to firms in both continents and create benefits for nations in Latin America, Asia, and Africa. It would also place significant additional pressure on Japan to open its markets.

Advocates of managed trade and other forms of neomercantilism[8] often cite, as justifications for their policy prescriptions, the fact that the income of American wage earners (measured in constant dollars) has generally remained stagnant for more than two decades. At the same time, the differences between the nation's richest and poorest citizens has widened markedly. To many Americans, the causes underlying these disturbing facts are found in the world political economy. In particular, the rapid globalization of the world economy coupled with the perception that the US trade partners engage in neomercantitist practices. Many Americans think that they have been victimized by an international economic system in which capital and production are highly mobile, but labor is not.

Paul Robin Krugman[9], a prominent trade theorist, criticizes this prescription in his work: "A Dangerous Obsession". Rather, evidence concerning a decline in American living standards after 1973 indicates the US income growth is related overwhelmingly to domestic productivity. Thus while it may be interesting to compare states as though they were engaged in a zero-sum struggle over international market shares, such a view is neither an accurate description of reality nor a useful guide for action. For American policymakers, Krugman warns, "thinking and speaking in terms of competitiveness poses three real dangers. First, it could result in the wasteful spending of government money supposedly to enhance the US competitiveness. Second, it could lead to protectionism and trade wars. Finally, and most important, it would result in bad public policy on a spectrum of important issues." Krugman's fear of declination of the US was becoming a hard and provoking fact that, in 2008, the financial crisis took the evil start in the US on account of its non-performing loans and overdraft cosuming habits as well as its deficient monitoring and managing financial system.

Notes

[1] NSC-68 (National Security Council Report 68) was a 58-page formerly-classified report issued by the US National Security Council on April 14, 1950, during the presidency of Harry S. Truman. Written during the formative stage of the Cold War, it has become one of the most significant historical documents of the Cold War. NSC-68 would shape the US foreign policy in the Cold War for the next 20 years and has subsequently been labeled its "blueprint".

[2] The Warsaw Pact (1955–1991) is the informal name for the mutual defense Treaty of Friendship, Cooperation and Mutual Assistance subscribed by eight Communist states in Eastern Europe. It was established at the USSR's initiative and realised on May 14, 1955, in Warsaw, Poland. In the Communist Bloc, the

treaty was the military analogue of the Council for Mutual Economic Assistance, the Communist (East) European economic community. The Warsaw Treaty was the Soviet Bloc's military response to West Germany's October 1954 integration to NATO Pact through the Paris Pacts of 1954.

[3] The Bush administration argued against the military strategy that US troops should be able to win two major wars in different regions at the same time. The doctrine was not necessary and had outlived its usefulness in a post-Cold War era, it said. But as President Bush inches toward a new confrontation with Iraq while continuing the American-led anti-terror war, it's conceivable that the US could end up doing just that—fighting two wars simultaneously, although hardly in the same way.

[4] It is a study carried by the US Department of Defense that analyzes strategic objectives and potential military threats. The congressionally mandated Quadrennial Defense Review (QDR) directs to undertake a wide-ranging review of strategy, programs, and resources. Specifically, the QDR is expected to illustrate a national defense strategy consistent with the most recent National Security Strategy by defining force structure, modernization plans, and a budget plan allowing the military to successfully execute the full range of missions within that strategy.

[5] It is a bilateral treaty between the US and the Soviet Union on the Reduction and Limitation of Strategic Offensive Arms. The treaty was signed on July 31, 1991 and entered into force on December 5, 1994. START negotiated the largest and most complex arms control treaty in history, and its final implementation in late 2001 resulted in the removal of about 80 percent of all strategic nuclear weapons then in existence.

[6] It is a theory about the future of warfare, often connected to technological and organizational recommendations for change in the US military and others. Especially tied to modern information, communications, and space technology, RMA is often linked to current discussions under the label of transformation and total systems integration in the US military. The original theorizing was done by the Soviet Armed Forces in the 1970s and 1980s. The US initially became interested in it through Andrew Marshall, the head of the Office of Net Assessment, a Department of Defense think tank. It slowly gained credence within official military circles, and other nations began exploring similar shifts in organization and technology.

[7] Peter Morici is a Professor of International Business at the University of Maryland. Prior to joining the University, he served as Director of Economics at the US International Trade Commission. He directed the agency's professional

economists working on ITC investigations and provided international economic policy advice to the House Ways and Means and Senate Finance Committees, US Trade Representative, Council of Economic Advisors, and other government agencies.

[8] It is a term used to describe a policy regime which encourages exports, discourages imports, controls capital movement and centralizes currency decisions in the hands of a central government. The objective of neomercantilist policies is to increase the level of foreign reserves held by the government, allowing more effective monetary policy and fiscal policy.

[9] Paul Robin Krugman, born on February 28, 1953, is an American economist, columnist and author. He is Professor of Economics and International Affairs at the Woodrow Wilson School of Public and International Affairs, Princeton University, Centenary Professor at the London School of Economics. In 2008, Krugman won the Nobel Memorial Prize in Economics for his contributions to New Trade Theory and New Economic Geography. He was voted sixth in *Prospect Magazine's* 2005 global poll of the world's top 100 intellectuals.

Exercises

I. Fill in the following blanks with proper words or expressions.

1. The US will be compelled to rely on its soft power, its ability to persuade and to set the agenda in ________________.
2. ________________ will also be critical in responding to a host of transnational challenges and nontraditional foreign affairs concerns.
3. The diplomacy allows the US to tackle new challenges in a relatively ________________ manner.
4. Militarily, ________________ have figured prominently among the nation's assets.
5. ________________ also provided the means with which to seek influence over political events in other countries.
6. As the ________________ faded, the Bush administration altered the strategy marginally, to a two-war doctrine.
7. The changing nature of ________________ environment and defense policy extends to the use of nuclear weapons.
8. The US achieved a level of economic and military power ____________.
9. As ________________ international economics, such a strategy is prudent because the US competitiveness is improving.
10. ________________ warns, thinking and speaking in terms of competitiveness poses

three real dangers.

Ⅱ. Explain the following terms.

1. NSC-68
2. win-hold-win strategy
3. Strategic Arms Reduction Treaty
4. neomercantitist

Ⅲ. Discuss the following questions.

1. What is the main content of the new diplomacy of the US?
2. How does the US adjust its military policy according to the new era of the world?

Chapter Nine

Religion

The US is a religious country, and the influence of the God on the American people can be seen everywhere. Because of the complexity of the nationality of the American people and their right to choose their own church to worship, there are as many as over 333,000 local church groups, and more than 250 religious sects throughout the country. That is because the country is largely composed of immigrants, and those overseas workers came to the US with different religions.

Between 1950 and 1970, church membership in the US increased by almost 55%. Today, about nine out of ten of the American people are members of a temple or a church.

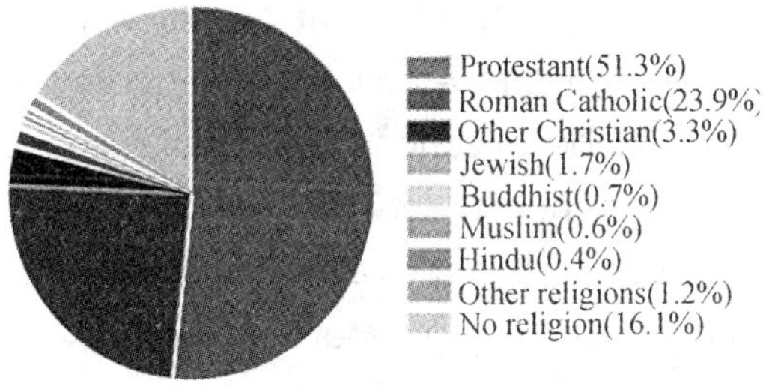

Religious groups in the US (2007)

In general, Christianity and Judaism have the greatest influence on nation. The largest religion in the US is Christianity, practiced by the majority of the population (78% in 2007). Protestantism, a branch of the Christianity, processes 51.3% of the population and those people label themselves as Protestants, so as to be distinguished from Roman Catholics, another branch of Christianity, which make up about 24% of the population. The proportion of the population for those who worship the Judaism is 1.7%. It is a small ratio, but the Judaism does have great effect on

American's life. Jewish organizations exist in about 200 towns in the US, and the Jewish people publish more than 200 newspapers and magazines.

According to the principle of "separation of church and state", the government of the US gives no direct subsidies to any faiths, but exempts them from paying taxes on income and property.

9.1 Protestants

Protestantism is a religion of all non-Catholic Western Christians. The term "Protestant" was originally applied to followers of Luther, who protested at the Diet of Spires[1] against the decree that prohibited all further religious reforms. The chief Protestant tenet is that the Bible is the only one rule of faith and practice. Therefore, the decrees of the Pope or other authorities of the Church are not correct or obligatory. Justification by faith, individual responsibility, and the right to believe and worship according to one's conscience are cardinal points in the system.

Puritans, members of a faction of Protestantism, arrived in Massachusetts by Mayflower in 1620. They came to America to pursue their religious freedom. In the belief of "Chosen People"[2], these Puritans attempted to establish new religion and political order to form a holy republic of Puritans revealing the God's will. Puritans did achieve some success in their primitive aims, but with the arrival of other immigrants, their influence was weakened gradually.

From the 1730s to the 1830s, two "Great Awakening"[3] Movements broke out throughout the continent of the North America. The division amongst ministers over the Awakening has tended to be described as a battle between "Old Lights" and "New Lights". Old Lights opposed the revivals in favor of traditional Christian religion, whereas New Lights saw the revivals as proof of a new outpouring of God's grace. After the two "Great Awakening" Movements, the Christianity expanded its influence to every part of the US, and it even became a weapon for founders of the nation. In the American Revolution, many priests took the advantage of the Bible to justify the war and made great contribution to the victory of the independence of the country. However, with the relationship between the South and the North worsening, the conflicts in the Christianity intensified. After the American Civil War, society regained its peace, but some factions of the Christianity separated, such as the Baptist Churches.

The Baptists are the largest Protestant group. The Baptist Churches were divided into two sects during the American Civil War, and until now, the Southern

Baptist Convention still exists. Baptist churches are generally regarded as being Protestant and many are Evangelical. A diverse group from their beginning, Baptists differ today—and they did from their beginning—in what they believe, how they worship, their attitudes toward other Christians, and their understanding of what is important in Christian discipleship. Most Baptists cherish the values held by the Puritan Movement in Britain and Holland in the 17th century. They believe, the descendants of the disciples cannot be baptized until they hold the Christian faith; God establishes not only the church, but also the government, and He entrusts to them different missions; the government is supposed to keep the justice while the church is to preach the Gospel; the government and the church should go in an independent way. Baptists number over 110 million worldwide in more than 220,000 congregations and are considered the largest world communion of Protestants. In the US, Baptists distribute mostly in the southern areas. In the states of Mississippi, Alabama and Georgia, Baptists take up more than 50% of the local residents. And the number of Baptists in Texas, North Carolina, Georgia and California account for one third of the total Baptists' population in the US.

Next to Baptists, the largest group of Protestants are the Methodists. Methodism is a movement of Christianity represented by a number of organizations, claiming a total of approximately seventy million adherents worldwide. The history of Methodism in the US began in the year 1766 when Philip Embury, a local preacher, delivered his first sermon in his own house at New York. Only four persons were present at the first sermon, but the number soon increased, especially after the arrival of Captain Thomas Webb, another local preacher. The latter displayed a stirring zeal, and in 1768 the first Methodist chapel in America was dedicated.

More recent studies show that the overall percentage of Americans identifying themselves as Christians is sliding. Around half of American adults leave the faith tradition of their upbringing to either switch allegiances or abandon religious affiliation altogether.

9.2 Catholics

The word "Catholic" is derived from a Greek adjective, meaning "universal". The term "Catholic Church" typically refers to the Roman Catholic Church: in full communion with the Bishop of Rome, made up of the Latin Rite and the 22 Eastern Catholic Churches.

Among Christianity, Protestants take up the largest proportion, but meanwhile, there are various factions separated from each other, and among them, only a few own more than 100,000 members. However, Catholics in the US can be regarded as a whole, because they follow the same doctrines and there are few factions within the Catholicism. As a single faction of religion, Catholicism is blessed with the largest population.

Geographically, Catholics in the east account for 38% of all the total Catholics' population of the US, followed by the Mid-west region, owning 25%. One obvious feature of the distribution of Catholics is that, they live mainly in the metropolitans. Nowadays, 40% of the Catholics live in the city, which outnumbers the percentage of other factions of churches. With more than 62,000,000 members, the Roman Catholic Church enjoys its irreplaceable status. The Church's leadership body in the US is the US Conference of Catholic Bishops[4], made up of the hierarchy of bishops and archbishops of the US and the US Virgin Islands, although each bishop is independent in his own diocese, answerable only to the Pope.

Catholicism arrived in what is now Continental US during the earliest days of European colonization of America. In 1492 and onward, the Spanish Catholic missionaries followed closely on the heels of Columbus. However, Catholicism did not have an easy way in the American continent, even though it came earlier than Protestantism. In the colony established by the Englishmen, it was Protestantism that took the dominance. In the early 13 colonies governed by Britain, only the Catholic Church in Maryland which was established in 1634 got the approval of the government. The First Amendment of the US Constitution in 1789 brought protection to all the religion, including Catholicism. And thus, Catholics got rights equal to other church-goers, which helped strengthen the numbers in this religion. With about 70 million registered residents professing the faith in 2008, the US has the fourth largest Catholic population in the world after Brazil, Mexico, and the Philippines, respectively.

In the 20th century, the Catholic Church undertook great changes with the development of the American society. The Second Vatican Council, summoned up by Pope John XXIII in 1962, was the catalyst for the internal reform. With an impact on the global church, this council promulgated and published 16 documents. This is a concrete response of the Catholic Church in the face of social change and challenges. And the Catholic Church in the US, holding the fruit of the council, took reforms in many aspects in the church, and thus the Catholic Church took on a new look. The new changes not only appeared in the organizational structure, leadership system, readjustment of the administrative matters in the Church, but also in the concepts of the Catholics. First, the religious ideas became more on-limits. In the past, the Pope's thoughts had a decisive impact on the Catholics, but nowadays, three quarters of the Catholics in the US declare that their views on many issues depend on their own conscience instead of the Pope's guidance. Second, Catholics became more tolerant of social morality. For example, the problems of abortion, homosexuality, premarital sex, unmarried cohabitation have long been focuses in American society, and the official attitude of the Pope and the Roman Catholic Church was against them. But with the influence of the reformation, more and more American Catholics became tolerant of these behaviors. According to the Gallup poll in 1991, 57% of the American Catholics were in favor of avoiding pregnancy with drugs; 75% held that women's abortion was legal in some special cases; 67% believed homosexuals could also be good Catholics; 58% didn't consider premarital sex to be wrong. Third, American Catholics paid close attention to social justice. They would be tolerant of social morality, but they still had great desire in social justice, which could be seen in the rights of women and the minority descendants. Many Catholics hoped that discrimination towards women and minority descendants could be eliminated.

Roman Catholic Church has struggled for a long time in the US, and it is still confronted with many new challenges nowadays. But it still exerts its influence on all fields of the American life.

9.3 The Orthodox Church

The term "Orthodox" is translated from the Greek to mean "correctly believing" or "correctly glorifying". The Orthodox Church, also officially called the Orthodox Catholic Church and commonly referred to in English-speaking countries as the Eastern Orthodox Church, is the world's second largest Christian communion, estimated to number 300 million. Orthodox Christians believe in the Trinity. The Holy Trinity is three, distinct, divine persons, without overlap or modality among them, who share one divine essence—uncreated, immaterial and eternal. They believe the Father is the cause or origin of the Godhead, from whom the Son is begotten eternally and also from whom the Holy Spirit proceeds eternally. The Orthodox Church is composed of several self-governing church bodies, each geographically and nationally distinct but theologically unified. In general, men and women dress respectfully, typically wearing their "Sunday best" to enter the church.

The Orthodox Church, Protestantism and Roman Catholicism are the top three branches of Christianity. The history of the Orthodox Church in the US can date back to the 18th century. In 1794, eight missionaries began their propaganda work in

Alaska. And the first American Orthodox Church was built in New Orleans in 1864, which was a Greek Orthodox Church, for most of the members in the church were immigrants from Greece. In 1867 and 1870, Orthodox Churches were built respectively in San Francisco and New York City. With the coming of Russia's October Revolution in 1917, blocks of Eastern Orthodox Christians immigrated to the US. And in 1959, when Alaska became a part of the US, the Eastern Orthodox Christians in this state strengthened the American Orthodox Church greatly in number. Now, there are about 20 organizations of Orthodox Church, with 5,000,000 members. There are also many dioceses in the US. The Orthodox Church in America Diocese of Washington and New York (OCA) is one of them. It existed from 2005 to July 1, 2009 when the Diocese of Washington and the Diocese of New York-New Jersey were reestablished as separate dioceses. Its territory included parishes, monasteries, and missions located in five states in the northeastern US (as well as Washington, D. C., southern Delaware, Maryland, New Jersey, New York, and Virginia. The diocesan chancery is located in Syosset, New York).

9.4 Judaism

Judaism is a set of beliefs and practices originating in the Hebrew Bible, also known as the Tanakh[5]. Jews consider Judaism to be the expression of the relationship God developed with the Children of Israel-originally a group of around a dozen tribes claiming descent from the Biblical patriarch forefather and later the Jewish people.

Traditionally, Jews recite prayers three times daily, with a fourth prayer added on Shabbat[6] and holidays. In addition to prayer services, observant traditional Jews recite prayers and benedictions throughout the day when performing various acts. Prayers are recited upon waking up in the morning, before eating or drinking different foods, after eating a meal, and so on. American Jews are more likely to be atheist or agnostic than most Americans, especially so compared with Protestants or Catholics. A 2003 poll found that while 79% of Americans believe in God, only 48% of American Jews do, compared with 79% and 90% for Catholics and Protestants respectively. While 66% of Americans said they were "absolutely certain" of God's existence, 24% of American Jews said the same. And though 9% of Americans believe there is no God (8% Catholic and 4% Protestant), 19% of American Jews believe God does not exist.

Jews have been present in the US as early as the 17th century, if not earlier, though they were small in numbers. Large scale Jewish immigration did not commence until the 19th century, and most of them primarily becoming merchants and shop-owners. There were approximately 250,000 Jews in the US by 1880, many of whom being the educated. After World War Ⅱ Jewish families joined the new trend of suburbanization. There, Jews became increasingly assimilated as rising intermarriage rates. At the same time, new centers of Jewish communities formed, as Jewish school enrollment more than doubled between the end of World War Ⅱ and the mid-1950s. More recent waves of Jewish immigration from Cuba, Venezuela, Iran, North Africa, Russia, and other regions have largely joined the mainstream American Jewish community and assimilated as well. And in the recent decades, Jews played important roles in the American life. By the 1990s, five Jews had been judges of the Supreme Court in the US. In the 101st Congress, there were 8% of the senators being Jews. That was a percentage much higher than the Jews' proportion in the total population in the US, which was only 2%.

9.5 Religion and Politics

Religion exerts great influence on the American politics. On one hand, the US is a nation established on the basis of religion; on the other hand, it has enforced strictly the policy of separation of the church from the state. The early immigrants to this continent were primitively on the purpose of pursuing religious freedom, and they set up their religious system. However, when the American Constitution was made, it stated clearly that the Congress could not make any laws to support the church or to limit the religious freedom.

The early immigrants mainly came from Europe, and most of them were the victims of the religious reformation. They left their homes and settled in what is called the US now, hoping to hold their religious faith. In the colonial period, disciple believers established a religious system supported by law and government. Almost in all the colonies, there were official churches. In the state of Massachusetts, the church was not only a place for religious activities, but also a spot for the government affairs. In the field of education, for example, churches played a very important role. Most teachers in the colonial period were priests and missionaries. And most schools, including elementary schools, middle schools and universities, were founded by the churches.

There are numbers of religious factions in the US, but none can dominate the politics. The First Amendment of the US Constitution in 1789 stated: "Congress shall make no law respecting an establishment of religion, or prohibiting the free exercise there of ... "The concept of separation is commonly credited to the combination of the two clauses: the establishment clause, generally interpreted as preventing the government from establishing a national religion, providing tax money in support of religion, or otherwise favoring any single religion or religion generally; and the free exercise clause, ensuring that private religious practices are not restricted by the government. The effect of prohibiting direct connections between religious and governmental institutions while protecting private religious freedom and autonomy has been termed the "separation of church and state". Keeping the religious faith out of the Congress could help different factions to guarantee their freedom. That is to say, all the religions are equal before the law, and none has the privilege to fleece others.

However, the policy cannot separate the religion from politics thoroughly. Although the separation of church and state is grounded firmly in the constitution of the US, this does not mean that there is no religious dimension in the political society of the US. Most of the Americans are members of one church, and their faith and ideas would be brought into their political decisions and perspectives unconsciously. Clergymen would not be holy enough to care only the religious business. And church-goers and many religious organizations still have great impact on the American politics. In 1905, President Theodore Roosevelt attempted to give reform on the currency. He wanted to remove the motto "In God We Trust" and issue the new monetary currency in November, 1907. When the news was released, objections throughout the country were aroused. Confronted with the church-goers' dissatisfaction, the Congress passed a bill to maintain the motto on the currency. Theodore Roosevelt had no choice but to sign the bill. From the event, the power of religion was seen clearly. However, religion also does good to politics. In such a religious country, religion can be more persuasive and appealing than any political speech. From the establishment of the country, the US was blessed with many disciples as its founders, such as George Washington, Thomas Jefferson, Benjamin Franklin and Abraham Lincoln. They were all masters of religion, and they took the advantage of religion to form the morality basis and got the social coherence. The Americans would be crazy when they believe that a certain decision or requirement is the God's will.

Notes

[1] It refers to a series of conferences held in Spires from 1526 to 1529.

[2] It refers to various groups and individuals who considered themselves chosen by

God for some purpose such as to act as God's agent on Earth. This status may be viewed as a self-imposed higher standard to fulfill God's expectation. Specifically, in the Hebrew Bible, called the *Old Testament* by Christians, the phrase Chosen People refers to the Hebrews/Israelites.

[3] The Great Awakenings were periods of rapid and dramatic religious revival in Anglo-American religious history, generally recognized as beginning in the 1730s. The first Great Awakening in the continent of the North America lasted for about half a century from the 1730s. And the second Great Awakening came in the 1790s, and ended in the 1830s. Many people also take the reawakening Evangelical faith in the 1890s as the third Great Awakening, but anyhow, its impact cannot rival the former two.

[4] Founded in 1966, it is the official leadership body of the Roman Catholic Church in the US.

[5] It is a name used in Judaism for the Hebrew Bible.

[6] Shabbat is the seventh day of the Jewish week. It is a day for relaxation, rest and studying the verses of Judaism. People are not allowed to work on this day. Shabbat is observed from sundown on Friday until the appearance of three stars in the sky on Saturday night. The exact time, therefore, differs from week to week and from place to place, depending on the time of sunset at each location.

Exercises

I. Fill in the following blanks with proper words or expressions.

1. Catholics, Baptists and __________ are all Christians.
2. The Second Vatican Council was summoned up by __________ in 1962.
3. __________, Protestantism and Roman Catholicism are the top three branches of Christianity.
4. Traditionally, Jews recite prayers __________ times daily.
5. The most important policy about religion in The First Amendment of the US Constitution in 1789 is "__________".
6. Puritans came to America by Mayflower in 1620 to __________.
7. __________ wanted to remove the motto "In God We Trust" from the currency in 1907, but church-goers protested strongly.
8. In the colonial era, the church in the state of Massachusetts was not only a place for religious activities, but also a spot for __________.
9. Within Christianity, the faction of __________ holds the largest population.

10. The history of the Orthodox Church in the US can date back to ________.

Ⅱ. Explain the following terms.

1. Chosen People
2. Great Awakening
3. Orthodox Church
4. Tanakh
5. Shabbat

Ⅲ. Discuss the following questions.

1. What's the relationship between religion and politics in the US?
2. What happened to the Catholic Church after its reformation in the US?

Chapter Ten

News Media

The news media refer to the means through which current news is transmitted to the public. In the US, its news media include print news media (newspapers, magazines), broadcast news media (radio stations, television stations, television networks), news agencies, and Internet-based news media (World Wide Web pages, weblogs). After many years of development, the US news media have become indispensable to the American people and the operation of the country. It has influenced and penetrated into American households over the years, and changed the way they perceive the world around them. It has played key roles in changing the political picture in the US. Besides, the expansion of the US influence in the world has led to growing attention to the US news media.

10.1 Different Forms of News Media

10.1.1 Print News Media

Newspaper

The earliest form of news media in the US was the newspapers published in its colonial period. The first newspaper in Britian's North American colonies was Benjamin Harris' *Publick Occurrences Both Foreign and Domestick* published in Boston, Massachusetts, on september 25, 1690. Unfortunately, it was suppressed after the first issue under a 1662 Massachusetts law that forbade printing without a license.

America's first continuously-published newspaper is *The Boston News-Letter* published on April 24, 1704. John Campbell, a bookseller and postmaster of Boston, was its first editor. The paper originally appeared on a single page, printed on both sides and issued weekly. Its early publications copied the British press, reported foreign news and listed ship arrivals, deaths, sermons, political appointments, fires, accidents and the like. This newspaper was heavily subsidized by the British government, with a limited circulation.

The first truly independent American newspaper was *New England Courant*, founded in Boston in 1721 by James Franklin, Benjamin Franklin's elder brother. Unlike the politically neutral colonial newspapers at that time, *New England Courant* was the first paper to attempt to give voice to political debate. It participated in several controversies and was suppressed in 1727. Besides political bravery, this newspaper also made a number of innovations. It was the first American newspaper to use literary content and humorous essays. It was also the most expensive newspaper of that time, at 4 pence a copy.

Of the 30-plus newspapers in colonial America before the American Revolution, about one third supported British rule and two thirds were patriotic. Historians say the criticisms of the latter helped lead to the American Revolution.

At the time of the American Revolution, 89 newspapers were published in 35 cities in the 13 colonies. Most of them were anti-royalist, chiefly because of opposition to the Stamp Act taxing newsprint. They were committed to challenging, even overthrowing, governmental authorities. They aroused and supported the often discouraged and indifferent public spirit. They played an important role in the war by awakening a consciousness of a common purpose, interest and destiny among the separated colonies and unifying them.

Newspapers flourished in the early years of the new republic, but turned partisan and became party organs. The Federalists and the Republicans had their newspapers, and these papers promoted and disseminated their different viewpoints and directed much abuse toward their political opponents. The "party press" dominated American journalism until the end of the 19th century, and its influence persisted for a long time thereafter.

Most newspapers in the early 19th century cost 6 cents and were distributed through subscriptions. However, this changed during the 1830s, when technology and publicity popularized "penny papers". The penny press was most famous for its low price, a penny per paper. The first successful penny paper in the US was Benjamin Day's *New York Sun* in 1833. It had the following motto at the top of every front page:

"*The object of this paper is to lay before the public, at a price within the means of every one, all the news of the day, and at the same time offer an advantageous medium for advertisements.*"

The second half of the 19th century witnessed tremendous growth in newspapers in the US. There were 3,000 newspapers in 1860, 4,500 in 1870 and 7,000 in 1880.

The Civil War during this period had a profound effect on American journalism. Large newspapers hired war correspondents to cover the battlefields. These reporters used the new telegraph and expanding railways to move news reports faster to their newspapers. The cost of sending telegraph messages helped create a new concise or "tight" style of writing which became a standard for journalism throughout the next century.

In 1878 Joseph Pulitzer created *The Post-Dispatch*, and remade American journalism in the last twenty years of the 19th century. Part of his policy reads as follows: *The Post and Dispatch* will serve no party but the people; be no organ of Republicanism but the organ of truth; will follow no causes but its conclusions; will not support the Administration but criticize it; will oppose all frauds and shams wherever and whatever they are; will advocate principles and ideas rather than prejudices and partisanship.

In 1883, Pulitzer purchased *New York World* and shifted its focus to human-interest stories, scandal, and sensationalism. In the hands of Pulitzer the new journalism was much more than merely sensational and yellow journalism was the inevitable consequence.

The years since the era of yellow journalism's sensationalism had seen an end to the massive growth in newspapers. The number of newspapers in the US began to decline dramatically in the first half of the 20th century. There were once 20 daily newspapers in New York City, by 1940 there were eight. Moreover, increasing numbers of the newspapers that survived were owned not by local citizens but by large national newspaper chains.

The first large newspaper chain in the US was assembled by E. W. Scripps. In 1914, the Scripps-McRae League was publishing 23 newspapers. By 1929, Scripps-Howard, the new name of the chain, owned 25 newspapers. William Randolph Hearst assembled a similar chain and by the end of 1922, in addition to twenty daily and eleven Sunday newspapers, Hearst owned two wire services, six magazines and a newsreel company. Such media conglomerates grew even larger as the century progressed.

In the second half of the 20th century competition from radio and television stations, cable networks, magazines and new computer information services has also led to the decline in newspaper readership, the number and the circulation of

American newspapers. For example, in 1950, there were 1,772 daily papers (about 70 percent of them were evening papers) while in 2000, there were 1,480 daily papers (about half of them were evening papers.)

Newspapers have been struggling to fight back. The look of American newspapers changed after *USA Today* arrived in 1982. It imitated the short stories featured on television newscasts, made heavy use of color in pictures, maps and graphics, and included things like opinion polls. Its new design succeeded and influenced many other papers.

However, newspaper industry profits are shrinking. Newspapers are looking for new ways to reinvent themselves and looking to redesign themselves for an increasingly online world.

With the introduction of the Internet, virtually all printed newspapers have online editions. One American newspaper, *Seattle Post-Intelligencer*, after 149 years of publishing, went online only in March, 2009. various attempts have been made to establish local, regional or national online-only newspapers to do original reporting instead of commentary or summaries of reporting from other publications.

The US does not have a national paper per se although *USA Today* has tried to establish itself as a national paper because it has been widely derided by the academic world as the "McPaper" and is not subscribed to by most libraries. However, some newspapers like *The New York Times* and *The Wall Street Journal* are sold in most American cities. In addition, all major metropolitan areas have their own local newspapers.

According to the Audit Bureau of Circulation, the top ten newspapers in the US by daily circulation for the 6th month period ending September 30, 2009 are the following: *The Wall Street Journal*, *USA Today*, *The New York Times*, *Los Angeles Times*, *The Washington Post*, *Daily News*, *New York Post*, *Chicago Tribune*, *Houston Chronical*, *The Philadelphia Inquire/ Philadephia Daily News.*

THE WALL STREET JOURNAL.
What's News—
Mars, Buffett Team Up in Wrigley Bid
Rise of Nationalism Frays Global Ties
Continental Rejects Merger Overtures
Cash Before Chemo: Hospitals Get Tough
What's Ahead—

USA TODAY
YOUR HEALTH
IS THERE A DOCTOR IN THE HOUSE?
Can Public Plan Keep Private Policy Costs in Line?
Medicine Gets a Face-lift
Downright Special Artists
Inside
Complete contents on page 2

The New York Times

The Wall Street Journal was founded in 1889 by Charles Dow, Edward Jones and Charles Bergstresser, and became a division of Rupert Murdoch's News Corporation in 2007. It is published by Dow Jones & Company in New York City with Asian and European editions. This paper primarily covers US and international business and financial news and issues. Its website is WSJ. com.

USA Today, a daily general-interest newspaper, was founded in 1982 with the goal of providing a national newspaper in the US. It is the most widely circulated print newspaper in America. With plenty colorful graphics and very brief stories, *USA Today* breaks the typical newspaper layout and is famous for its national polls on public sentiment. Its website is USAToday. com.

Los Angeles Times
Lab backlog dooms 200 assault cases
Patients pay more, get less – if they're lucky

The Washington Post
Va. GOP makes timely changes

The New York Times, founded in 1851 and published in New York City, is the largest metropolitan newspaper in the US. Known for its general reporting and international coverage, the paper is frequently relied on as the official and authoritative reference for modern events. Its website is nytimes. com.

***Los Angeles Times* (*LA Times*)**, a morning daily newspaper established in 1881, is published in Los Angeles, California and distributed throughout the Western US. It is the second largest metropolitan newspaper in the US. Its website is latimes. com.

The Washington Post, founded in 1877, is one of the leading daily American newspapers. Located in the nation's capital, the paper is known for its reporting on the workings of the White House, Congress, and other aspects of the American government. In the early 1970s *The Post's* unrelenting reporting of the Watergate Scandal greatly contributed to the resignation of American President Richard Nixon. Its website is washingtonpost. com.

Newsmagazine

American magazine journalism began in 1741 with Benjamin Franklin's *General Magazine and Historical Chronicle for All the British Plantations in America* and Andrew Bradford's *American Magazine*. Before the American Revolution only about 15 periodicals, with an average life of 10 months, were published in the colonies. After the war magazines appeared in large numbers. The period from 1830 to 1850 saw the rise of nationally circulated monthlies. With the outbreak of the American Civil War, magazines played an increasingly journalistic role, and shaped public opinion. During the Civil War, *Harper's Weekly* furthered magazine journalism by sending reporters, and artists and photographers to battlefields for firsthand coverage. From the late 19th to the mid-20th century, magazines became the dominant mass medium in the US. Some magazines of the early 20th century provided a real service to society. For example, *McClure's*, founded by S. S. McClure in 1894, exposed oil monopolies, railroad injustices, political corruption and life insurance fraud, starting a new reporting style called muckraking investigative journalism. Despite the rise of competing media since the mid-20th century, the US has a large magazine industry with hundreds of magazines serving almost every interest. For example, more than 17,000 consumer magazines were published in the US in 2000.

According to *US Industrial Outlook* (1991), American magazines are classified into three groups: consumer magazines (65%), business publications(34%), farm magazines(1%). Consumer magazines include all those publications found on the newsstand and consist of general interest publications and special interest publications. Their contents attempt to appeal to the general public or to large groups in society that share common interests.

Newsmagazines qualify as general interest publications. They concentrate primarily on news and current events, and their material is presented in an easily read style that explains a news story in a way any reader can understand.

The first weekly newsmagazine in the US is *Time*. Currently, the major American newsmagazines include the following: *Newsweek*, *Time*, *US News & World Report*, *the Nation*, *National Review*, *The New Republic*, *the Weekly Standard*.

Time is a weekly newsmagazine created in 1923 and has become the most influential newsmagazines in the US. It is targeted at busy Americans who cannot keep abreast of the news in the daily newspaper. In addition to the American circulation, *Time* has editions published in Canada, Europe, Asia, and the Pacific, but at the end of 2008, *Time* discontinued publication of its Canadian edition. The newsmagazine's format of short articles arranged in subject "department" has become the standard for general newsmagazines. *Time*'s most famous feature throughout its history has been the annual "Person of the Year" (formerly "Man of the Year") cover story, in which it recognizes the individual or group of individuals who have had the biggest effect on the year's news. Despite the title, the recipient is not necessarily individuals or even human beings.

Time's first cover (March 3, 1923)

Newsweek, May 24, 2009

U. S. News & World Report Cover

Time became part of Time Warner in 1989 when Warner Communications and Time Inc. merged in 2000 and has been part of AOL Time Warner since 2000. Its website is time. com.

Newsweek, founded in 1993, is the second largest weekly newsmagazine in America. It is published in four English language editions and 12 global editions in the language of the circulation region, and distributed throughout the US and internationally. This newsmagazine has a strong reputation for accurate, brisk, and vivid reporting and presents news in terse summary form, organized by departments.

In May, 2009, because of profit loss, the magazine's owner the Washington Post Company overhauled the magazine, refocusing its content and using higher-quality paper, to target a smaller and more "elite audience" and to identify itself as a "thought leader". Its website is newsweek. com.

U. S. News & World Report is one of the three leading American weekly newsmagazines. *United States News* was founded in 1933 by David Lawrence, who started *World Report* in 1945. The two magazines were merged into *U. S. News & World Report* in 1948. In 1984 the magazine was bought by real-estate developer Mortimer B. Zuckerman. *U. S. News & World Report* focuses on national and international news, business, science, education and health, but avoids sports, entertainment and celebrity news. It is particularly well-known for its ranking system and annual reports on American colleges, graduate schools and hospitals.

In June 2008, the magazine switched its publication frequency from weekly to biweekly, and it is now published monthly. Its website "usnews. com" was launched in 1995 and provides access to all articles from the print edition.

Besides the traditional print newsmagazines, television and radio newsmagazines have also been developed in the US. They generally go more in-depth into stories than regular newscasts, trying to give the viewer and listener an understanding of the context surrounding important events, rather than just the facts. Some radio newsmagazines in the US are: *All Things Considered*, *Morning Edition*, *Weekend Edition*, *The World*. Examples of American television newsmagazines are: 60 *Minutes*, 48 *Hours*, *Primetime*, and *Dateline NBC*.

10.1.2 Broadcast News Media

Newscast refers to radio or television summary of news events read by a newscaster or produced with a combination of reading and audio tape for radio or a combination of reading and film or video tape for television.

Radio

The radio newscast started in the US in the 1920s with infrequent readings of headlines and front-page stories from the late editions of newspapers. It reached its golden age in the 1930s when millions of American homes were equipped with radio and public interest in news grew significantly with the events that led to World War Ⅱ. However, the growth of radio newscast in the 1940s was soon interrupted with the advent of the television newscast as a televised version of the radio form.

The US has 1,460 public radio stations, 4,793 AM and 5,662 FM commercial radio stations. Satellite radio is growing in popularity, but is only available by subscription now. At most news/talk radio stations, newscasts run from :00 –:06 minutes after the top of each hour. Some stations produce the entire six minutes on their own. Others begin with a network newscast, which covers national and world news, followed by a 2- or 3-minute local newscast.

Corporate logo of Clear Channel

Clear Channel Communications, a diversified media conglomerate company founded in 1972 and headquartered in Texas, is the largest radio station group owner in the US, both by number of stations and by revenue. Besides domestic radio stations, Clear Channel Communications operates broadcasting properties in foreign countries like New Zealand and Australia. The company also specializes in concert promotion and hosting, and outdoor advertising.

NPR logo

National Public Radio (**NPR**) is a private publicly funded non-profit radio network created in America in 1970 to provide news and cultural programming to the country's noncommercial and educational radio stations. It features the daily news broadcasts, *Morning Edition* and the afternoon *All Things Considered*. In a Harris poll conducted in 2005, NPR was voted the most trusted news source in the US.

Voice of America logo

Voice of America (**VOA**) is funded entirely by the US government and may only broadcast outside the US. As the official external radio and television broadcasting service of the US federal government, VOA was established in 1942 to produce and broadcast radio programs in English and foreign languages to other countries so as to promote a positive view of the US. Its daily broadcasts include news reports, editorials, and discussions of US political and cultural events. Its website is www.voanews.com.

Television

It is estimated that 99% of American homes have a television set, and most households have more than one. There are three basic types of television in the US: broadcast (freely available to anyone with a TV in the broadcast area), cable television, and satellite television (both of which require subscriptions to receive).

The first-ever news broadcast on television was hosted by Lowell Thomas in 1930 and the first regularly scheduled television news was broadcast in 1940. Television newscast began entering American homes in the 1940s and has evolved over many years. It has gone from a simple 10- to 15-minute format in the evenings, to a variety of programs and channels.

The US television news programming can be categorized into three groups: local news, produced by local broadcast television stations; network news, produced by the news divisions of some radio and television networks like ABC, CBS, and NBC; cable news, produced by cable television stations. Today, most television news operations will publish the text of the stories broadcast during their newscasts on their websites. Some of them even post videos of the stories on their websites, too.

Today, local, regional and national news programming is available to American viewers in many different ways, any time of the day. The major providers of television news include the following: ABC, CBS News, CNN, Fox News Channel, MSNBC, NBC News.

ABC logo　　ABC News headquarters in New York City

American Broadcasting Company (**ABC**), created in 1943 from the former NBC blue radio network, is an American radio and television network. It is owned by The Walt Disney Company and is part of Disney-ABC Television Group. As one of the major broadcasting networks, ABC had a tremendous impact on American culture in the 20th century. ABC News is a news organizing and broadcasting division of ABC. It offers the following programs: America This Morning, Good Morning America, Good Morning America Weekend Edition, This Week with George Stephanopoulos, ABC World News with Charles Gibson, ABC World News Saturday & Sunday, 20/20, Primetime, i-CAUGHT, Nightline, ABC World News Now. ABC News' website is ABCnews. com.

CBS logo　　CBS News current logo　　CBS News secondary logo

CBS Broadcasting, Inc. (**CBS**) is one of the largest radio and television networks in the US. CBS started out as a radio network, called Columbia Broadcasting System. According to Nielsen[1] ratings, CBS ended up as the top-rated network for the 2008 –2009 season. CBS News is the news division of CBS. It offers the following shows: Morning News, The Early Show, The Saturday Early Show, CBS News Sunday Morning, Face the Nation with Bob Schieffer, CBS Evening News with Katie Couric, CBS Evening News with Thalia Assuras, CBS Evening News with Russ Mitchell, 60 Minutes, 48 Hours Mystery, Up to the Minute. CBS News' website is www. cbsnews. com.

CBS News also runs CBS Radio News, a branch that produces newscasts and features to radio stations. The radio network is the oldest unit of CBS and traced its roots to the company's founding in 1927. CBS is now the only broadcast television network with its original radio link.

CNN logo

The CNN Center in Atlanta

CNN breaking the news about the September 11, 2001 attacks

Cable News Network (**CNN**) is a major US cable television network founded in 1980 by Ted Turner. It was the first all-news television network in the US and the first network to present 24-hour live news broadcasts, using satellites to transmit reports from news bureaus around the world. It rates as America's number one cable news source. In terms of regular viewers, according to Nielsen Ratings, CNN is America's number two cable news network and has the most unique viewers. Its website is CNN. com.

FNC logo

FNC's newsroom

Fox News Channel (**FNC**), commonly referred to as ***Fox*** or ***Fox News***, is a US cable and satellite news channel created by Australian-American media mogul Rupert Murdoch in 1996. It is available to more than 100 million households in the US and to viewers internationally. The Channel is rated as the cable news network with the largest number of regular viewers in America. Its website is Foxnews. com.

MSNBC logo

The current MSNBC studio in New York City

MSNBC, started in 1996, is a cable news channel based in the US and available in both the US and Canada. Its name is a combination of "Microsoft" and "NBC". Some news programs provided by MSNBC are First Look, Way Too Early with Willie Geist, Morning Joe and MSNBC Live. Its website is msnbc. msn. com.

NBC News logo

1959–1972 NBC News logo

NBC News is the news division of American television network NBC. It is the top-rated broadcast news division and has been for a decade. It offers the following programs: Early Today, Today, Weekend Today, Meet the Press with Tim Russert, NBC Nightly News with Brian Williams, NBC Nightly News with Lester Holt, Dateline NBC. Its website is NBCnews. com.

PBS logo

Public Broadcasting Service (**PBS**), founded in 1969, is a non-profit public broadcasting television service with over 300 member public TV stations in the US. PBS provides its member stations with quality programming in cultural, educational, and scientific areas, in children's care, and in news and public affairs. These programs are produced by its members and independent producers worldwide. Unlike the commercial television broadcast model of American networks such as ABC, CBS, FOX, and NBC, in which affiliates give up portions of their local advertising airtime in exchange for network programming, PBS member stations pay substantial fees for the shows acquired and distributed by the national organization. PBS is mainly funded by viewers' contributions, state governments, and grants from businesses and private foundations; the US government, through the Corporation for Public Broadcasting, supplies about 15% for its operation.

10.1.3 News Agency

A news agency (news service, newswire, press agency, press association, wire service) refers to an organization that gathers, writes, and distributes news to newspapers, periodicals, radio and television broadcasters, government agencies, and other users. It does not publish news itself but supplies news to subscribers.

In the US, as early as the 1820s, a news agency called the Association of Morning Newspapers was formed in New York City to gather incoming reports from Europe. Some major US news agencies are the Associated Press, United Press

International, and CNN.

Associated Press logo

Current AP headquarters in New York City

Associated Press (**AP**) is a cooperative news agency, the oldest and largest in the US and the largest in the world. It was formed when the five major New York City papers that organized to receive Mexican War news in 1846 agreed to form a Harbor News Association and share the expense of gathering news from vessels arriving in New York harbor. In 1892 the modern Associated Press was founded under the law of Illinois. Several years later it moved to New York. The AP's member newspapers, radio and television stations in the US both contribute stories to the AP and use material written by its staff journalists. Many newspapers and broadcasters outside the US are AP subscribers, paying a fee to use AP material without being contributing members of the cooperative.

The collapse of AP's traditional rival, United Press International, has left AP as the only nationally oriented news service based in the US.

United Press International building in Washington, D.C.

United Press International (**UPI**) is a US news agency. It can trace its beginnings back to 1907 when the United Press Associations (UP) began service. In 1958 International News Service (INS) was merged with UP, forming United Press International (UPI). The new UPI had 6,000 employees and 5,000 subscribers, 1,000 of them newspapers. Once a mainstay in the press world and one of the three biggest news agencies, along with the Associated Press and Reuters, UPI was hurt by changes in the modern news business, especially the closing of many of America's afternoon newspapers, resulting in its customer base shrinking. In 2000, UPI was purchased by News World Communications, a media company owned by Unification Church. In recent years it has faced difficult financial times, and currently it has only five reporters in its Washington, D. C. headquarters, with several dozen stringers filing regular reports from key regions of the world and more than a dozen editors stationed in various cities in the US and elsewhere. UPI files its news stories in English, Spanish and Arabic. Its website is upi. com.

CNN WIRE

CNN launched a wire service in 2008, posing a threat to the Associated Press by offering at a lower cost similar breaking news to what the AP offers. In September 2009 the CNN Wire Store (www. cnnwirestore. com) was launched, allowing publishers to browse through CNN wire articles and download individual CNN wire stories for US $199 per story for a single use through a credit card transaction.

10.1.4 Internet-Based News Media

A news site is a website with the primary purpose of reporting news. There are two main types of news site: general news and subject-specific news. Subject-specific news sites offer rich in-depth reporting of specialized topic areas. The first set of news sites emerged when traditional news providers moved their content online. An early leader was *The News & Observer* in Raleigh, North Carolina, US. This newspaper launched its companion site NandO. net in 1994. Now many print newspapers and magazines in the US also have online versions. Many news organizations based in other media also distribute news online. Examples are *USA Today*, *The New York Times*, MSNBC. com, and CNN.

Some news sites contribute no original content of their own other than reader comments and often do not even have editorial oversight. They are called news aggregator websites where the website owner collects headlines either manually or automatically. Examples of this sort of website are the Drudge Report and Google News.

According to the State of the News Media 2009 by the Pew Research Center's[2] Project for Excellence in Journalism (PEJ)[3], the number of Americans who began to rely on the Web as a regular or even their main news source appeared to jump in 2008. About 37% of Americans regularly go online for news. For national and international news, the Web surpass all other media except for the television as a destination. The data from Hitwise, Inc[4]. show that the top ten news sites in 2008 were Yahoo News (news. yahoo. com), CNN. com (www. cnn. com), MSNBC. com (www. msnbc. com), GoogleNews (news. google. com), Drudge Report (www. drudgereport. com), The New York Times (www. nytimes. com), Fox News (www. foxnews. com), USA Today (www. usatoday. com), BBC News (news. bbc. co. uk), and The Washington Post (www. washingtonpost. com).

YAHOO! NEWS

Yahoo! News is an Internet-based news aggregator provided by Yahoo!. It features Top Stories, US National, World, Business, Entertainment, Science, Health, Weather, Most Popular, News Photos, Op/Ed, and Local news. Its news articles come from the following news services: Associated Press (AP), Reuters, Agence France-Presse (AFP), *Christian Science Monitor*, NPR, *USA Today*, CNN. com, CBC News, Seven News, BBC News, and others. In April 2009, Yahoo! News ranked second among global news sites in US users, after msnbc. com and ahead of CNN, according to Nielsen/NetRatings.

CNN. com, started on August 30, 1995, is the news website of Cable News Network. The site attracted growing interest over its first decade and is now one of the most popular news websites in the world. In April 2009, CNN. com ranked third place among online global news sites in unique users in the US, after MSNBC. com and Yahoo! News, according to Nielsen/NetRatings.

MSNBC.com turns 10 in 2006

MSNBC. com, launched in 1996, is the news website for the NBC News family. It covers national and international news of general interest, using original and wire service reporting, as well as videos from the network's television division, and partners including *The New York Times*, *Newsweek* and *The Washington Post*. The website contains business and health news, sports and entertainment coverage. As of May 2009, MSNBC. com had ranked first in US unique users among global news sites for 12 months in a row.

Google news

Google News, started in April 2002, is a news aggregator provided by Google Inc. It uses its own software to determine which stories to show from the online news sources it watches. Different versions of the aggregator are available for more than 20 regions in different languages. Currently, service in the following languages is offered: English, German, French, Spanish, Italian, Portuguese, Chinese (traditional and simplified characters), Japanese, Korean, Dutch, Arabic, Hebrew, Norwegian and Swedish. The service covers news articles appearing within the past 30 days on various news websites. For the English language, it covers about 4,500 sites. Its front page provides roughly the first 200 characters of the article selected.

DRUDGE REPORT

Drudge Report, originated in 1994, is a US-based news aggregation website run by Matt Drudge. It consists mainly of links to stories from the US and international mainstream media about politics, entertainment, and current events. The site also offers links to many popular columnists. Occasionally Drudge writes news stories himself. According to Nielsen NetRatings, Drudge Report had 3.4 million unique visitors in February, 2009.

The New York Times (nytimes.com), launched in 1994, is the online edition of the newspaper's news and commentary. It has been ranked one of the top websites and the number one newspaper site.

Fox News (foxnews.com), introduced in December, 1995, is the news website of Fox News Channel. It offers worldwide news coverage, analysis, show profiles, broadcast schedules, team biographies, and email news alerts, including video clips from the network's television division, audio clips from Fox News Radio, in addition to columns from the network's assorted television, radio, and online personalities.

USA Today (USAToday.com), launched in 1995, is the official website of the daily newspaper *USA Today*. This news and information website is updated 24 hours per day, seven days per week. Its interactive features, information graphics and multi-media functions including audio, video and live webcasts attracts more than 30 million monthly readers to experience comprehensive, convenient news and information.

The Washington Post (washingtonpost.com), established in 1996, is the official website of the daily newspaper *The Washington Post*. In addition to content from *The Washington Post* newspaper, this website has its own newsroom, editors, and contributors. It is a leading source for news and video on politics, national and federal government, foreign policy, business, green issues, science and local issues. It also offers award-winning opinion writing, entertainment information and restaurant reviews and local coverage.

10.2 Features of News Media

10.2.1 Private Ownership

Unlike news media throughout most of the world where they are owned directly or indirectly by the government, the US news media are privately owned and operated, with the exception of one domestic broadcasting network. They are possessed either by large conglomerates such as Walt Disney Company, News Corporation, Viacom and Time Warner, by small chains or in a situation that becomes increasingly rare, by individuals or families. For example, CNN, the first network to provide 24-hour television news coverage and the first all-news television network in the US, is owned by its parent company Time Warner. *The New York Times*, the largest metropolitan newspaper in the US, is owned by the New York Times Company, in which descendants of Adolph Ochs[5], principally the Sulzberger family[6], maintain a dominant role.

The public service broadcasting is very limited in the US and the role of the government-funded media is small. As a matter of fact, there is no federal state-owned broadcasting authority. The Public Broadcasting Service (PBS), partly funded by the Corporation for Public Broadcasting, the steward of the federal government's investment in public broadcasting, may be seen as a public-funded alternative to the commercial stations. Even so, it is funded more by viewers' contributions, state governments, grants from businesses, and private foundations than by the federal government. According to the Associated Press, some 15 percent of public broadcasting's funding comes from the federal government. And PBS is responsible for a relatively small portion of the US media output.

10.2.2 Profit-Orientation

The American news media are essentially profit-making enterprises and they depend for their existence on advertising revenue.

Commercial broadcasting is the dominant type of broadcasting in the US. Revenue for commercial radio and television stations and networks comes from the sale of advertising time. The rates paid by advertisers depend on the popularity or ratings of a program, a station or network. Competition for ratings in commercial broadcasting leads entertainment values to influence much of the commercial news media and a reliance on ratings leads commercial broadcasters to give the public what they want, not what they need to know. Although cable news revenues come from two sources: advertising and subscriber fees, advertising is viewed as having greater potential than subscriptions for long-term growth. Some of the best known US commercial broadcasters are ABC, CBS, FOX, and NBC television networks and the radio giant Clear Channel Communications. According to the Pew Project for Excellence in Journalism, ABC news had revenues closer to \$700 million, including close to \$200 for World News, about \$400 for Good Morning America, and the rest from its magazine programs such as Nightline.

The main source of newspaper income is advertising, in the form of classified and inserted advertising circulars. On average, a newspaper generates 80% of its revenue from advertising and 20% from sales. To attract more advertisers and charge more for the service, publishers of commercial newspapers strive for higher circulation so as to make advertising in their newspaper more effective. But some publishers might sacrifice higher circulation numbers in favor of a readership with a higher income. In the US, the beginning of the 21st century witnessed large media corporations taking possession of a greater number of newspapers, including all of the largest ones. The growing need for profit growth natural to corporations may have a negative impact on the overall quality of journalism.

Changes in the US newsmagazines indicate the influence on news media by the profit-orientation of the US corporate media. The Pew Project for Excellence in Journalism (2009) found that for the eight news magazines examined, ad pages were down 16% and ad dollars fell by nearly 19% in 2008. In order to get more advertising income, *Newsweek* announced it would double its subscription rates, focusing on a core of affluent, highly educated readers. The magazine hopes that with a smaller, more dedicated audience it will attract more luxury goods advertisers and get higher rates for ads. Therefore, the news media's dependence on advertising revenue promotes a bias to please the advertisers and drives news, commentary public affairs toward supporting industry and mercantilism.

10.2.3 Significant Independence

Compared with news media in many other countries, the US news media enjoy relatively more independence. The First Amendment to the US Constitution prohibits the Congress from infringing on the freedom of speech and the freedom of the press. Freedom of the media has been assumed by many to be a necessity to any democratic society and the media is called "the Fourth Estate", or the fourth branch of government (an addition to the legislative, the executive and the judiciary branches), an important force in the democratic system of checks and balances. The media's function is to act as a guardian of the public interest and as a watchdog on the activities of government.

Besides, the private ownership of the US news media somehow frees them from acting as a mouthpiece of or being directly controlled by the government or any political party. Their relative independence even enables them to oversee the government. However, their private ownership may lead to media bias.

10.3 New Trends

10.3.1 Diversity and Audience Preference

People in the US today have diverse forms of news media available to them, thanks to the rapid development of science and technology in the past few decades, especially progress in computer technology. They can get news on the air, in print or online. Besides the traditional news media (newspapers, magazines, radio stations, television stations, news agencies), new forms have been emerging: television networks, webpages, news-oriented weblogs, podcasts, mobile devices, social networks like Twitter and Facebook, etc.

The emerging forms of news media offer Americans more choices of news sources, but they adversely affect some traditional forms of news media due to a growing "on demand" news culture. Audiences today prefer those forms that can deliver them news when they want it rather than at appointed times. As a result, the Internet and cable have increasing audiences while newspapers in print and weekly newsmagazines see audiences shrink in recent years. For example, a survey in 2008 found that less than a quarter of American adults said they read a magazine of some kind the day before the survey. Some newspaper companies have sought bankruptcy protection. To rewrite the sad story, different measures have been taken by newspaper people: going online, cutting cost, publishing monthly instead of weekly.

10.3.2 Concentration

There have been a lot of mergers and buyouts of media and entertainment companies since the 1980s. Mainstream media have since become more concentrated in terms of ownership. In 1984, about fifty companies owned or operated thousands of media in North America, including daily newspapers, magazines, radio and television stations and book publishers. In the first decade of the 21st century, only a handful of corporate conglomerates (for example, Disney, CBS Corporation, News Corporation, Time Warner, and General Electric) own the majority of mass media outlets in the US. CBS Corporation has holdings in radio (e. g. CBS Radio Network), radio stations (CBS Radio), Internet (e. g. CBS Interactive), publishing (e. g. The Free Press), television networks (e. g. CBS), television production and distribution (e. g. CBS Studios), television stations (a total of 28 stations).

The concentration of media ownership has led to growing concern that this trend will increase media bias, and reduce the diversity of information provided and the accountability of information providers to the public. Some critics believe that the ultimate consequence of media ownership consolidation is a poorly-informed public because they have reduced media options and they are offered biased information, information beneficial to media owners and advertisers.

Notes

[1] It is the company that creates the Nielsen Ratings (a rating system used to gauge television viewing habits in the US).

[2] It is an American think tank organization based in Washington, D. C. that provides information on issues, attitudes and trends shaping the US and the world. The Center and its projects receive funding from the Pew Charitable Trusts.

[3] It is a US non-partisan, non-profit research organization of the Pew Research Center. It uses empirical methods to evaluate and study the performance of the press.

[4] As the leading global online competitive intelligence service provider, Hitwise Inc. has over 200 staff and is headquartered in New York.

[5] An American newspaper publisher and former owner of *The New York Times*.

[6] Owners of the New York Times Company.

Exercises

I. Fill in the following blanks with proper words or expressions.

1. The earliest form of news media in the US was the ________ published in its colonial

period.

2. The first American newspaper to use literary content and humorous essays was ________.
3. During the 1830s, the ________ was most noted for its extremely low price of only one cent per paper, making the news available to more than just upper class citizens.
4. The newspaper ________, started in 1982, imitates the short stories featured on television newscasts, makes heavy use of color in pictures, maps and graphics, and includes things like opinion polls, thus changing look of American newspapers.
5. In the early 1970s the unrelenting reporting of the Watergate scandal by the newspaper ________ greatly contributed to the resignation of American President Richard Nixon.
6. *Time*'s most famous feature throughout its history has been the annual "________" (formerly "Man of the Year") cover story, in which it recognizes the individual or group of individuals who have had the biggest effect on the year's news.
7. The newsmagazine ________ is particularly well-known for its ranking system and annual reports on American colleges, graduate schools and hospitals.
8. ________ is the largest radio station group owner in the US, both by number of stations and by revenue.
9. When ________ was introduced in 1980, it was the first all-news television network in the US and the first network to present 24-hour live news broadcasts, using satellites to transmit reports from news bureaus around the world.
10. The American news media are essentially profit-making enterprises and they depend for their existence on ________.

Ⅱ. Explain the following terms.

1. yellow journalism
2. muckracking investigative journalism
3. AP
4. Voice of America
5. the Fourth Estate

Ⅲ. Discuss the following questions.

1. What roles can news media play?
2. What causes news media bias?

Bibliography

Cook, Samantha, Tim Perry, Greg Ward. *USA: the Rough Guide.* London: Rough Guides Ltd, 7th edition, 2004.

Corbett, M. *Politics and Religion in the United States.* New York: Garland Pub, 1999.

Cressy, David. *Bonfires and Bells: National Memory and the Protestant Calendar in Elizabethan and Stuart England.* Berkeley: University of California Press, 1989.

Kosmin, B. A. & Lachman S. P. *One Nation under God.* Crown Trade Paperbacks. New York: Harmony Books, 1993.

Litwicki, Ellen M. *America's Public Holidays*, 1865–1920. Washington, D. C.: Smithsonian Institute Press, 2000.

Mead, F. S. *Handbook of Denominations in the United States.* Nashville, TN: Abingdon Press, 2001.

Queen, E. L. *Encyclopedia of American Religious History.* New York: Facts on File, 2008.

Santino, Jack. *All around the Year: Holidays and Celebrations in American Life.* Urbana: University of Illinois Press, 1994.

Santino, Jack: *New Old-Fashioned Ways: Holidays and Popular Culture.* Knoxville: University of Tennessee Press, 1996.

Shurden, W. *Turning Points in Baptist History.* Macon, GA: The Center for Baptist Studies, Mercer University, 2001.

Walker, J. Brent. *Church-state Matters: Fighting for Religious Liberty in our Nation's Capital.* Macon, GA: Mercer University Press, 2008.

Britannica Encyclopedia. http://www.britannica.com

Economy of the United States. http://en.wikipedia.org/wiki/Economy_of_the_United_States

Encyclopedia. http://encyclopedia.thefreedictionary.com
Mobile Encyclopedia. http://wapedia.mobi/en/
The New World Encyclopedia. http://www.newworldencyclopedia.org/
The State of the Media 2009. http://www.stateofthemedia.org/2009/index.htm
Wikipedia. http://www.wikipedia.org/
http://www.sonofthesouth.net/revolutionary-war/explorers/discovering-america-columbus.htm

埃德温·埃默里等著，展江译.(2009). 美国新闻史:大众传播媒介解释史(第九版). 北京：中国人民大学出版社.
蔡帼芬.(2004). 国际传播与媒体研究. 北京：中国传媒大学出版社.
蔡永良，董剑桥.(2008). 英语国家社会与文化. 苏州：苏州大学出版社.
董小川.(2002). 20世纪美国宗教与政治. 北京:人民出版社.
范悦.(2006). 美国历史概况. 北京:对外经济贸易大学出版社.
雷雨田.(1994). 上帝与美国人:基督教与美国社会. 上海:上海人民出版社.
刘继南等.(2002). 国际传播与国家形象——国际关系的新视野. 北京：北京广播学院出版社.
刘澎.(2001). 当代美国宗教. 北京:科学文献出版社.
梅仁毅.(2002). 美国文化读本. 北京:外语教学与研究出版社.
王波.(1998). 当代美国社会热点聚焦. 合肥:安徽大学出版社.
王恩铭.(2003). 美国文化与社会. 上海:上海外语教育出版社.
温洪瑞,李学珍.(2008). 英美概况. 济南:山东大学出版社.
谢福之.(2007). 英语国家概况. 北京:外语教学与研究出版社.
许鲁之.(2009). 新编英美概况. 青岛：中国海洋大学出版社.
于可.(1993). 当代基督新教. 北京:东方出版社.
余志远.(2000). 英语国家概况. 北京:外语教学与研究出版社.
袁明.(2003). 美国文化与社会十五讲. 北京：北京大学出版社.
张奎武.(1994). 英美概况. 长春：吉林科学技术出版社.
周静琼.(2003). 当代美国概况. 上海:上海外语教育出版社.
朱永涛.(1998). 英语国家社会与文化入门(下册). 北京:高等教育出版社.